Paint Shop Pro 7 & Animation Shop 3

Reference Guide

the power to create®

Jasc Software, Inc. • 7905 Fuller Road • Eden Prairie, MN 55344

Welcome

On behalf of all of us at Jasc Software, I am pleased to introduce you to the newest star in the Jasc family - Paint Shop Pro, Version 7. It's a milestone for our popular image editor, and for our company, too, because the year 2000 marks the ten-year anniversary of both Paint Shop Pro and Jasc Software.

It's been quite a decade. From a small Midwestern shareware company, we've grown to an international software provider with over 125 employees worldwide. Of course, it's all thanks to you, our users. Your feedback and support have helped Paint Shop Pro grow up to be the world's favorite image editor.

With Version 7, Paint Shop Pro has some new surprises in store. We've added an array of new, automatic tools that make it easy to enhance and restore photos, such as red eye corrector, instant scratch and crease repair, and automatic color balance and adjustment filters. In addition, we've added more drawing and illustration tools, more Web graphics optimization tools, and more animation power in Animation Shop, still included free. Whatever you're into - digital photography, scanning and sharing family photos, creating business graphics, or designing Web graphics and animations - Paint Shop Pro 7 will inspire you to new heights of creativity.

From the whole Jasc Software team, I want to say thank you for choosing Paint Shop Pro. We're happy to welcome you to the Jasc family - and to the amazing world of Paint Shop Pro 7.

Kris Tufto
President and Chief Executive Officer
Jasc Software, Inc.

Table of Contents

Paint Shop Pro Contents

Table of Contents

Table of Contents

Table of Contents

Animation Shop Contents

Table of Contents

Table of Contents

Appendixes

Introduction

Welcome to Paint Shop Pro

Jasc® Paint Shop Pro™ 7 is a powerful graphics application that can be used for anything from creating simple images to complex, multi-layered graphics. It is friendly enough for the casual user who wants to enhance family photographs, yet powerful enough for advanced users working professionally. Paint Shop Pro combines raster-based and vector-based graphics technology into one application, providing you with a wide range of painting, drawing, and image editing capabilities.

By using Paint Shop Pro along with the companion program, Animation Shop, you can create graphics and animations for a Website, presentations for business meetings, or multimedia publications. You can import animations into Paint Shop Pro for editing and return them to Animation Shop with the click of your mouse.

WELCOME to Paint Shop Pro 7.

The Paint Shop Pro Interface

The following screen capture shows the Paint Shop Pro main program window with an open image and with the main palettes and windows displayed. This screen capture is for presentation purposes only. Your screen will not look like this one unless you display all the palettes and windows and arrange them as shown below.

These windows and palettes are the tools you will use most often as you work with Paint Shop Pro. This manual provides a detailed explanation of their functions as well as descriptions of the dialog boxes contained in the program.

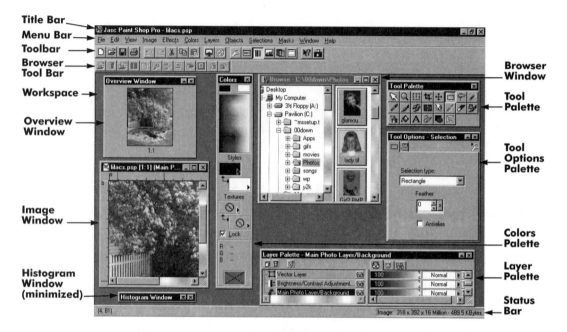

The items shown above are categorized as follows:

- Bars — Title Bar, Menu Bar, Main Toolbar, Browser Toolbar, Multiple Image Printing Toolbar (not shown), and the Status Bar

- Workspace — working area of the main program window

- Windows — Image Window, Overview Window, Histogram Window, Browse Window, and Multiple Image Printing Window (not shown)

- Palettes — Tool Palette, Tool Options Palette, Color Palette, and Layer Palette

There are preference settings you can use to change the appearance of several features within Paint Shop Pro. For complete information about preferences, please refer to Chapter 20, "Setting Preferences" in the Paint Shop Pro section of this manual.

The Animation Shop Interface

The following screen capture shows the Animation Shop main window with an open animation and a window running the open animation. Familiarize yourself with each of these items to gain a better feel for the application. Chapters 21 through 30 in this manual describe how these features are used to help you create and manipulate animations.

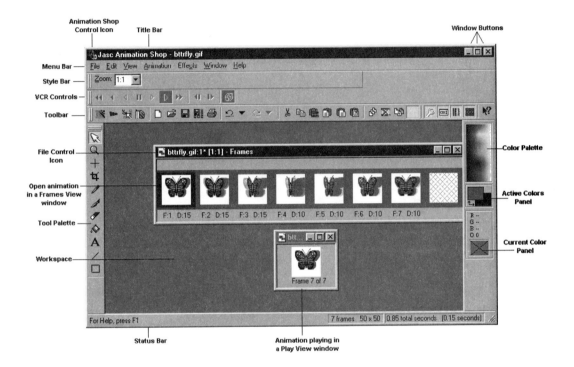

There are several preference settings you can use to change the appearance of these features. For complete information about setting preferences, please refer to Chapter 29, "Preferences and File Associations" in the Animation Shop section of this manual.

About This Manual

Intended Use

This manual is a complement to the *Getting Started Guide* and the Help files. The chapters are presented in a manner intended to help you learn about Paint Shop Pro and Animation Shop as quickly as possible.

NOTE: *The manuals and the Help files assume you are familiar with Microsoft Windows-based operating systems. If you need help using Windows, you can access Windows Help from the Start menu by choosing the Help option.*

Typographical Conventions

This manual uses the following typographical conventions:

* Menu items you are instructed to choose appear in sans serif typeface with the greater than (>) symbol separating each menu level. For example, if you are instructed to choose the Open command in the File menu, it appears as File > Open. If you are instructed to choose the General Program Preferences command from the Preferences submenu in the File menu, it appears as File > Preferences > General Program Preferences.

* Keys you are instructed to press appear within angled brackets. When you need to press keys in sequence, they are connected by a plus (+) sign. For example, you can choose the Open command in the File menu by holding the <Ctrl> key while pressing <O>. The sequence appears as <Ctrl> + <O>.

Creating and Opening Images

Paint Shop Pro provides several ways to create and open images. You can:

• Create a new image from "scratch" with only a background,

• Duplicate an open image,

• Copy an image from another application, or

• Import an image from another source. Other sources include, but are not limited to, scanners, digital cameras, and screen captures.

You can also access and open existing images using several methods. In addition, you can use the program to work with images in many different format types and open and save both raster and vector images. This chapter discusses image formats and describes how to create, import, and open image files in Paint Shop Pro.

Understanding File Formats

When you save a file, it is saved in a file format. The format is the coding that defines how the information in the file is organized. The filename is assigned a three letter extension that represents the file format. For example, in Paint Shop Pro, when you save a file with the *.psp extension, it is saved in the Paint Shop Pro format.

One benefit of using Paint Shop Pro is that you can open, work with, and save files of many different formats. You don't have to own several applications because you can do all your work in Paint Shop Pro. Please refer to the Help file for a list of all the formats this program supports.

Understanding Bitmap and Vector Images

Another benefit of using Paint Shop Pro is that the supported file formats include both raster and vector formats. This means you can open and work with almost any type of graphic (image) file in Paint Shop Pro.

Computer graphics can be divided into two basic types: raster (also referred to as bitmap) and vector. While Paint Shop Pro creates raster images, you can create and edit vector objects within a raster image. This features gives you enhanced drawing capabilities.

Raster (bitmap) and vector images differ in the way they define objects:

- Bitmap images are composed of individual elements, called pixels, arranged in an imaginary grid. If you increase the magnification level of a bitmap image, you can see how the pixels become square areas of color. Each pixel has a bit depth (also called color depth) that determines how many colors it, and therefore the image, can display. In a 1-bit image, each pixel can only display one of 2 colors; in a 24-bit image, each pixel can display one of 16.7 million colors.

  An object in a raster image is defined by the pixels that display it. For example, a line is represented by every pixel along it.

- Vector images and objects are not defined by pixels. Vector images contain commands that include information about where and how to draw an object, such as the position on the page, and the characteristics of the object. For example, a line is usually represented by a starting point, an ending point, and information about thickness, pattern, and color. In Paint Shop Pro, you use vector layers to create and edit vector objects.

Determining Dimension and Color Characteristics

Before you create a new image, think about how you will use it. This will help you determine what size, resolution, and color depth to use.

Size Refers to the physical dimensions of an image. In Paint Shop Pro, you can create images by size using inches and centimeters and by resolution using pixels. If you are creating an image that will be printed and you know the size you need, you may find it easier to use inches or centimeters rather than pixels. By starting with the final image dimensions, you can produce an image that will fit the page. If you later need to change the dimensions of the image, you can do so using the Image > Resize command. For images that will be displayed digitally (on a monitor), use pixels.

Resolution In bitmap images, the size of the pixels determines the resolution of the image. Resolution is the number of pixels per inch (ppi) or centimeter. A bitmap image is created at a specific resolution. You select the resolution based on how you will use the image. Set the resolution of an image for a web page at 72 ppi (pixels per inch). If you will be printing to a high-quality printer, set the image resolution to between one-half and one-quarter of the actual printer resolution. For example, for a laser printer at 300 to 600 dots per inch (dpi), create your image at 72 to 150 pixels per inch (ppi). Keep in mind that too low a resolution will cause pixelation, or large pixels that produce coarse output, while too high a resolution add to image's memory requirements without producing an increase in its quality.

Background Color Refers to the background, or "canvas" color. You can set the color for the background of an image as white, black, red, green, blue, the current Color palette foreground or background color, or transparent.

Color Depth Images created with a color depth of 24-bits (16 million colors) look the best because they contain the most colors. However, not all media can display 16 million colors. For example, GIF images, a popular format for the Web, can only contain up to 256 colors (8-bit depth). Even if your final image will contain fewer than 16 million colors, you probably want to create it at a 24-bit depth in the Paint Shop Pro format. Then, if you decide to apply effects that require 16 million colors, you will not have to increase the color depth. When you have finished working on the image, you can reduce its color depth and save it in another format.

Creating Images

You can create a new image by using the New Image dialog box, by duplicating an open image, by pasting an image from Animation Shop, or by pasting a selection or image from the Windows clipboard. This section describes each of these methods.

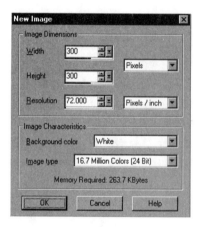 Creating a New Image

When creating a Paint Shop Pro image, you select its dimensions, resolution, and other character-istics in the New Image dialog box.

To open this dialog box, do one of the following:

- Choose File > New,

- Press <Ctrl> + <N>, or

- Click the New Image button ( ) on the toolbar.

To use the New Image dialog box:

1. Enter a width and height for the image. You can config-ure the size in inches, centimeters, or pixels. As you change the units of measurement, the width and height automatically update.

2. Enter a resolution for the image. This is the number of pixels per inch or pixels per centimeter. The Resolution box automatically displays the resolution you have set on the Rulers and Units tab of the Paint Shop Pro Prefer-ences dialog box. To change the resolution for the image, type another value. You can configure the resolution in pixels/inch or pixels/centimeters. For more information about preferences, please refer to Chapter 20, "Setting Preferences."

3. Select a background color, which is the color of the "canvas" on which you create an image. The background color can be the current foreground or background color (displayed on the Color palette), white, black, red, green, blue, or transparent. (Transparent is available only for greyscale and 24-bit images.)

4. Select the bits per pixel from the Image type box. Increasing the bit depth increases the num-ber of colors an image can display. It also increases the memory required to store and edit an image. A 24-bit image can display over 16 million colors, while a 1-bit image can display only two colors. In Paint Shop Pro, many of the editing commands are available only for greyscale or 24-bit images. For more information about color and bit depth, please refer to Chapter 5, "Working with Color."

5. Look at the minimum memory requirement of the image that appears below the Image type box. For optimum performance, your system should have at least 2-3 times this amount in RAM. Decreasing either the bits per pixel or the dimensions of the image will reduce the minimum memory requirement.

6. Click the OK button to close dialog box. The new image file appears in the workspace.

Duplicating an Image

You can copy (duplicate) an image that is already open in Paint Shop Pro and save it as a new image.

To copy an open image file:

1. Select the file by clicking its Title bar.

2. Choose Window > Duplicate or press <Shift> + <D>. A new window containing the image opens in the workspace.

NOTE: *You can also copy a single-layer image by choosing* Selections > Select All *and then choosing* Edit > Copy. *This copies the image to the clipboard. Next, choose* Edit > Paste > As New Image *to create the new image.*

Pasting from Animation Shop

You can copy an animation from Animation Shop and paste it into Paint Shop Pro as a new image. If the animation has more than one frame, a separate image is created for each frame.

To paste an animation:

1. In Animation Shop, copy the animation to the Windows clipboard using the commands on the Edit menu.

2. In Paint Shop Pro, choose Edit > Paste > AS Animation as Multiple Images. A new image opens for each frame in the animation.

Pasting from the Clipboard

You can create a new image from almost any data you place on the clipboard from Paint Shop Pro and other applications. Use an Edit menu command (Cut, Copy, or Copy Merged) to copy a selection, layer, or image to the clipboard. Then choose Edit > Paste > As New Image to paste the clipboard contents as a new image.

NOTE: *Depending on your preference settings, a format-specific dialog box may appear requesting additional information. For example, if the file format is WMF, the Meta Picture Import dialog box may appear for you to choose header information and vector information. For more information about preferences, please refer to Chapter 20, "Setting Preferences."*

Importing Images

You can create a new image by importing an animation from Animation Shop, by importing an image from a TWAIN-compliant device, such as a scanner or digital camera, or by using the screen capture feature.

Importing from Animation Shop

You can export an image from Animation Shop into Paint Shop Pro. This method is different from copying and pasting, and it automatically creates a new image in Paint Shop Pro. For more information, please refer to Chapter 30, "Interacting with Paint Shop Pro" in the Animation Shop section of this manual.

Importing from a TWAIN-Compliant Device

Paint Shop Pro supports TWAIN-compliant image devices, such as scanners and digital cameras. When Paint Shop Pro starts, it checks your computer to see if the software for a TWAIN device is installed. If it is installed, the File > Import > Twain menu commands are made available. If it is not installed, the menu commands are unavailable (greyed out).

Selecting the TWAIN-Compliant Device

To select a TWAIN-compliant device for acquiring images:

1. Choose File > Import > TWAIN > Select Source. The Select Source dialog box opens. The Sources window lists the TWAIN-compliant devices connected to your computer.

2. Click the name of the device.

3. Click the Select button to close the dialog box.

Acquiring an Image

After you have selected a TWAIN-compliant device, use these steps to access the software that controls the device. For example, if your TWAIN-compliant device is a scanner, access that software that controls your scanner. Then scan the image using the scanner's software.

To access the device's software and acquire an image:

1. Choose File > Import > TWAIN > Acquire to start the device's software.

2. Use the device's software to set the image acquisition options. For help using the device's software, consult its manual or on-line help. When the device and its software finish processing the image, the image is sent to Paint Shop Pro, and the device's software remains open. You can continue to scan images or close the software. In either case, return to Paint Shop Pro to see your new image.

3. In Paint Shop Pro, if an image contains unwanted areas, cropping it should be your first step. This reduces the memory needed to edit the image and eliminates extra areas of color, allowing you to make better color corrections. After cropping the image, you can rotate it to correct alignment problems, and then make any necessary color corrections.

Loading Digital Camera Images

You can use Paint Shop Pro to access and manage your images while they are in the digital camera, and you can load the images directly into Paint Shop Pro. Before connecting the digital camera to your computer, run the Jasc Digital Camera Installer, which contains drivers for many brands of digital cameras.

To run the installer:

1. Click the Windows Start button to open the Start menu.

2. Choose Programs > Jasc Software > Utilities > Jasc Digital Camera Support. The Digital Camera Installer opens.

3. Follow the on-screen prompts to the page containing the list of digital cameras. By default, no drivers are installed. The box to the left of every camera name displays an "X" to indicate that it has <u>not</u> been selected.

4. Click a camera name to select the driver for it. The "X" changes to an icon to indicate that the camera has been selected. As you click a selection, the installer displays the models supported by that driver. Note that a camera name may be listed more than once if it uses the same set of driver families as another camera.

5. Press the Next button to complete the installation.

NOTE: *Due to the hardware requirements of certain cameras, it may be necessary to install additional Windows networking support. A message will prompt you to indicate this.*

After you have run the installer, connect the camera to your computer, configure the camera settings, and access the digital camera images.

Configuring the Camera Settings

Remember to connect your camera to the computer before configuring your settings.

To configure the settings:

1. After you have connected the camera to the computer, choose File > Import > Digital Camera > Configure to open the Digital Camera Configuration dialog box.

2. In the Camera Type box, select your camera.

3. If you know which port on your computer you have connected to your camera, select it from the Communication Port list. If you do not know the port, or you are using a USB connection, leave the setting to Auto Detect.

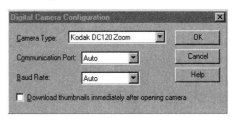

4. If you know the appropriate baud rate setting, select it from the Baud Rate list. If you do not know the setting, leave the selection at Auto Detect. Paint Shop Pro will check the computer and camera and set the fastest possible connection.

5. To download thumbnails of the images as soon as the camera connects to the computer, select the Download thumbnails immediately after opening camera check box. While this increases the time it takes to connect to the camera, it allows the preview in the Digital Camera dialog box to display a thumbnail of the image when you select it.

Accessing the Digital Camera Images

After you have configured the camera connection, access your images from the camera.

To access the images:

1. Choose File > Import > Digital Camera > Access to open the Digital Camera dialog box. A message stating that it is connecting to the camera and getting the thumbnails (if you selected that option). If necessary, press the Abort button to cancel the operation.

NOTE: *If your camera does not include a feature that is displayed in the Digital Camera dialog box, its option is unavailable (greyed-out).*

2. The top part of the dialog box displays the camera type, the image resolution, and the number of pictures taken and remaining.

3. Use the "Multiple Exposure Operations" panel to apply commands to all the pictures in the camera:

- Click Delete All to delete all the images in the camera.

- If you chose not to download thumbnails when you configured the settings, click Get Previews to download them now. When no previews have been downloaded, an "X" appears in the preview window.

- Click Save All to Disk to save all the images to the hard disk without first opening them.

- Click Open All in PSP to open all the images in the Paint Shop Pro workspace.

4. Use the "Single Exposure Operations" panel to view and work with individual images:

- Click the left and right arrows below the preview box to scroll through the images. Each picture's exposure number, time and date of creation, and preview appear. (The preview appears only if you downloaded the thumbnails.)

- If you want to take a picture and see it immediately, position the camera, click Take Picture, and then click Get Preview.

- If you chose not to download the thumbnails and now want to see a preview of the selected image, click Get Preview.

- Click Delete to delete the image from the camera.

- Click Open in PSP to open the image in the Paint Shop Pro workspace.

- Click Save to Disk to save the image on your hard disk without opening it.

5. After you have finished, click OK to close the dialog box.

6. In Paint Shop Pro, if an image contains unwanted areas, cropping it should be your first step. This reduces the memory needed to edit the image and eliminates extra areas of color, allowing you to make better color corrections. After cropping the image, you can rotate it to correct alignment problems, and then make any necessary color corrections.

Making Screen Captures

The Screen Capture function takes a picture of all or part of the screen and opens it in Paint Shop Pro. These pictures, called screen captures, can be of an area you outline, of the entire screen, of an active window, of the contents of an active window, or of the controls of an application, such as a toolbar.

The Screen Capture function can also be used with any application that supports Object Linking and Embedding (OLE). After you select your preferences, you can make screen captures while working in another application (program) without opening Paint Shop Pro.

Setting the Screen Capture Options

To use the Screen Capture function, first select the type and method of capture in the Capture Setup dialog box. You can then make a capture immediately or activate it later as needed.

To select the Screen Capture function options:

1. Choose File > Import > Screen Capture > Setup. The Capture Setup dialog box opens.

2. In the "Capture" panel, select one of the capture methods:

- Area allows you to determine the size and contents while making the capture.

- Full screen captures the entire monitor screen.

- Client area captures the contents of the active window.

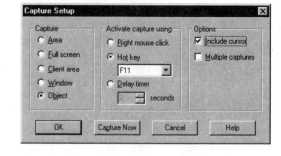

- Window captures the current active window.

- Object captures a feature or group of features.

3. In the "Activate Capture Using" panel, select a method for activating the screen capture function. If you will not be making a screen capture directly from this dialog box, select the Right mouse click or Hot key option. You use this action to make the capture after you have started the procedure. If you are starting a capture from the dialog box, select a delay timer value. This indicates how many seconds after you click the Capture Now button Paint Shop Pro waits until it makes the capture. (You have up to a minute.)

4. In the "Options" panel, select the "Include cursor" check box if you want the cursor to appear in screen captures when it is within the capture area. This option is not available for area captures.

5. In the "Options" panel, select the "Multiple captures" check box to make more than one capture at a time. When you activate the screen capture function, Paint Shop Pro minimizes. Selecting this option prevents Paint Shop Pro from being restored until you click its button on the taskbar. When the check box is not selected, Paint Shop Pro automatically reopens after a screen capture.

6. You can activate the screen capture function from this dialog box or close the dialog box without activating the function.

- To apply the options you have selected without activating the screen capture function, choose OK.

- To make a screen capture immediately, click Capture Now. Paint Shop Pro starts the capture function after the period of delay you selected in the Delay timer box.

Making a Screen Capture

After you have selected the options, you can make a Screen Capture at any time. The initial steps are the same for all the capture methods.

To activate the Screen Capture function:

1. If Paint Shop Pro is not running, start it now.

2. Choose File > Import > Screen Capture > Start, click the Start Capture button ( ) on the toolbar, or press <Shift> + <C>. Paint Shop Pro minimizes and its button appears on the Windows taskbar.

3. Open or display the image, window, or feature to be captured on the screen.

You are now ready to capture the image. The steps you use depends on the type of screen capture you selected in the Capture Setup dialog box. The steps are described next.

Making an Area Capture

To make an Area capture:

1. If you have chosen the Area method, right-click or press the Hot key you selected during the setup. The cursor changes to cross-hairs and becomes the Area Capture tool.

2. Move the cursor to where you want to create a corner of the screen capture.

3. Left-click. This action starts the actual screen capture.

4. Move the mouse to create a rectangular outline of the capture area. The rectangle displays its dimensions in pixels as you create it.

5. When the appropriate area is within the rectangle, left-click the mouse to end the screen capture.

6. If you did not select the Multiple Captures option during the setup, Paint Shop Pro automatically opens with the screen capture in the workspace.

7. If you selected the Multiple Captures option, continue making captures by using the right mouse button or Hot key to select the starting point and then using the left mouse button to create the capture area.

8. Activate Paint Shop Pro after you have finished. The screen capture is displayed as an image in the workspace.

Making an Object Capture

To make an Object capture:

1. If you have chosen the Object method, right-click or press the Hot key you selected during the setup.

2. Move the cursor over the object you want to capture. A black border appears around the area that will be captured.

3. Click the mouse to make the screen capture.

4. If you did not select the Multiple Captures option during the setup, Paint Shop Pro automatically opens. The screen capture is displayed as an image in the workspace.

5. If you selected the Multiple Captures option, continue making captures by using the right mouse button or Hot key to select objects and left-clicking to capture them.

6. Activate Paint Shop Pro after you have finished. The screen capture is displayed as an image in the workspace.

Making a Full Screen, Client Area, or Window Capture

To make a Full Screen, Client Area, or Window Capture:

1. If you have chosen the Full Screen, Client Area, or Window method, right-click or press the Hot key you selected during the setup. Paint Shop Pro makes the screen capture.

2. If you did not select the Multiple Screen Captures option during the setup, Paint Shop Pro automatically opens. The screen capture is displayed as an image in the workspace.

3. If you selected the Multiple Screen Captures option, continue making captures using the right mouse button or Hot key.

4. Activate Paint Shop Pro after you have finished. The screen capture is displayed as an image in the workspace.

Using the Screen Capture Feature within Another Program

In applications (programs) that support Object Linking and Embedding (OLE), you can use the Screen Capture function without opening Paint Shop Pro.

In most programs that support the OLE function, you insert the screenshot by choosing a menu command with a name similar to "Import Object" or "Insert Object." To see if your program supports OLE screen captures and what commands activate it, search the application's help file for OLE support.

When you choose an object insert command, Paint Shop Pro Screen Capture appears in the list of object types. Select it, and the Capture Setup dialog box opens. Set the options, click OK, and create the screen capture. It is automatically inserted in the program.

NOTE: *Due to Windows and OLE constraints, you cannot cancel the OLE Screen Capture Options dialog box after it is activated.*

Opening Images

You can open an existing image using the Paint Shop Pro file open dialog box, using standard Windows features, using the Browser, or by loading a saved Workspace. You can also use the drag-and-drop technique or the Recently Used File List on the File menu.

Using the Open Dialog Box

To use the Open dialog box to open an image:

1. Choose File > Open, or press <Ctrl> + <O>, or click the Open button ( ) on the toolbar to display the Open dialog box.

2. Use the following methods to find a file:

   - By default, Paint Shop Pro lists files for all file formats. Limit the files displayed by selecting a specific file type in the File Type box.

   - Use the Look in box and the Up One Level button to navigate to the folder containing the image you want to open.

   - Alternatively, click the Browse button to use the Browser to find and open a file. This closes the Open dialog box and opens the Browser. The Browser displays the same folder as the Open dialog box and shows thumbnails of the images within it. Within the Browser, double-click a file to open it.

3. Once you have found the file to open, click the file name to select it. When you select an image file, the "Image Information/Preview" panel of the Open dialog box displays the image file's dimensions in pixels and bits per pixel. If the "Show Preview" check box is selected, the Preview box displays a small version of the image.

4. With an image file selected, you can see more information about the image file by clicking the Details button. This opens the Details list box. This box contains information on the file format, location, compression method, memory requirements, and creation date. After viewing the information, click the OK button to close the Image Details list box and return to the Open dialog box.

5. To open the selected image file, click the Open button. The Open dialog box closes, and the image opens in an Image window in the Paint Shop Pro workspace.

NOTE: *Depending on your preference settings, a format-specific dialog box may appear requesting additional information when you open an image. This applies to Photo-CD, PostScript, RAW, or WMF files. For more information about preferences, please refer to Chapter 20, "Setting Preferences."*

NOTE: *If you try to open a file Paint Shop Pro doesn't support, a message appears stating that the file format is not supported.*

Using Standard Windows Features

You can open an image using any of the following Windows features:

- Windows Explorer
- My Computer
- Start > Run menu command
- Start > Documents List command

For more information, please use the Windows online Help file. Access the Help file by clicking the Windows Start button and then choosing Help from the Start Menu.

Using the Paint Shop Pro Browser

The Paint Shop Pro Browser is a visual method for locating files and previewing the images within. For a complete description of the Browser, please refer to Chapter 3, "Using the Browser."

To use the Browser to open an image file:

1. Choose File > Browse, press <Ctrl> + <B>, or click the Browse button on the Open dialog box (after choosing File > Open). The Browser opens.

2. On the left side of the window, scroll to locate the folder containing the image file you want to open.

3. Click the folder. Thumbnails (small previews) of the images in the folder appear on the right side of the window.

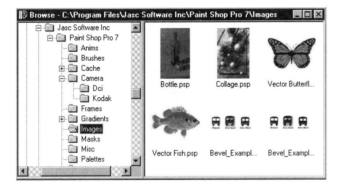

4. To view more information about an image file, do one of the following:

   - Place the cursor over the thumbnail without clicking. The Tool Tip displays information about the image.

   - Right-click the thumbnail, and choose Information from the context menu.

   - Click the thumbnail, and choose ImageFile > Information.

5. To open an image file, do one of the following:

   - Drag a thumbnail into the Paint Shop Pro workspace. You can open several images at one time by dragging them into the workspace. The number of images you can open is limited only by the memory in the computer.

   - Right-click a thumbnail and choose Open from the context menu.

   - Double-click a thumbnail. To select more than one image, press <Ctrl> while clicking each image, and then double-click the final image.

Using the Load Workspace Feature

Paint Shop Pro lets you save the layout of an entire workspace in its own file. Then, when you load the workspace, you open the file. Your saved workspace includes any images that were open and the position and visibility status of the toolbars and palettes. For more information about the Workspace feature, please refer to Chapter 4, "Managing Images."

NOTE: *The workspace file does not actually contain the image files, but it keeps a link to the image files so they open when you load the workspace.*

To open an image linked to a workspace:

1. Choose File > Workspace > Load, or press <Shift> + <Alt> + <L> to display the Open Workspace dialog box.

2. By default, Paint Shop Pro lists only files with the workspace format, *.wsp. Use the Look in box and the Up One Level button to navigate to the folder containing the workspace you want to open. Double-click a folder to open it.

3. When you find the workspace file to open, double-click the file to open it, or click the file once and then click the Open button.

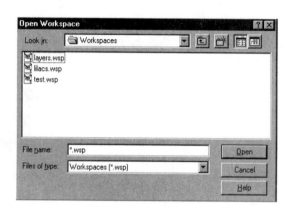

Using Drag-and-Drop

You can open image files by dragging them from the Paint Shop Pro Browser, Windows My Computer, Windows Explorer, or any application that supports Drag-and-Drop. While "dragging" an image, you can "drop" it on any of the following:

- Paint Shop Pro's workspace,
- Paint Shop Pro's executable file (labeled PSP.EXE), or
- A shortcut to Paint Shop Pro's executable file.

Using the Most-Recently Used File List

The image files that you have opened recently appear on the File menu above the Exit command. The number of files listed in the menu is controlled by the Recent File Listing option. This option is located on the Miscellaneous tab of the General Program Preferences dialog box. To open one of these files, choose its name from the File menu.

NOTE: *If you have just installed Paint Shop Pro and not opened or created any images, the list will be empty.*

Using the Browser

The Browser is a special feature of Paint Shop Pro and Animation Shop that lets you look at thumbnail views of images in the folders on your computer system. It is similar to the Windows Explorer in that it is a visual method for finding and previewing files. The Paint Shop Pro Browser displays thumbnails for all the images in formats Paint Shop Pro supports; the Animation Shop Browser displays thumbnails for all the images Animation Shop supports.

You can use the Browser to view, open, and manage your files. This chapter describes how to use the basic Browser functions and how to use the thumbnails to find, view, manage, and open your image files.

Using the Basic Browser Functions

This section describes how to use the following basic functions of the Browser window: Opening the Browser, Using the Browser Toolbar, Navigating with the Browser, Viewing the Thumbnails, Using the Context Sensitive Menus, Fitting the Browser Window to Thumbnails, Opening Images, and Closing the Browser.

Opening the Browser

To open the Browser, do one of the following:

- Choose File > Browse,

- Press <Ctrl> + <B>,

- Choose File > Open from the menu bar, and then click the Browse button (　Browse　) on the Open dialog box, or

- From Animation Shop, click the Browse button (📁) on the main toolbar.

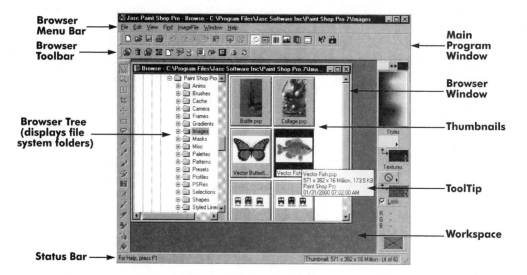

The Browser opens in a separate window within the main Paint Shop Pro window or the Animation Shop window. The left side of the Browser window shows the file system folders in your computer. The Browser opens to the folder last browsed in the application. The right side of the Browser window displays thumbnails (preview buttons) of the images within the folder that is open. With the thumbnails displayed, you can see what your images look like without actually opening them. You can use the thumbnails to select, open, and manage your image files. Once you have opened your images, you can leave the Browser window open in the workspace while you edit your images.

When the Browser window is the active window, the main menu bar changes to display the Browser menus: File, Edit, View, Find, ImageFile, Window, and Help. Some of these menus have the same commands as the Paint Shop Pro menu bar or the Animation Shop menu bar; others are specific to the Browser. For example, the Browser File menu contains the Browse New Folder, Select, Sort, and Update Thumbnail commands that are specific to the Browser and the remaining commands are the same as the Paint Shop Pro File menu options.

From the Browser menus, you can use the File commands to sort, select, preview, and print thumbnails. You can use the Find menu commands to locate specific files in the current folder, and you can use the ImageFile menu commands to manage files. You can also access many of the File menu commands by right-clicking in the background area of the right pane or by using the toolbar buttons. You can also access the ImageFile commands by right-clicking a thumbnail or by using the toolbar buttons.

The Status bar, at the bottom of the Browser window, shows information about a selected thumbnail, and shows how many files are in the selected folder.

Using the Browser Toolbar

The Browser toolbar displays buttons that correspond to frequently-used commands in the Browser menus. The toolbar is available when the following conditions are met:

- The toolbar is set to display in the Paint Shop Pro Toolbar options,
- The Browser window is opened from Paint Shop Pro, and
- The Browser window is the active window.

In Paint Shop Pro, use any of the following methods to display or hide the Browser toolbar:

- Choose View > ToolBars and select or clear the "Browser Toolbar" check box,
- Right-click any palette and choose Toolbars from the menu, then select or clear the "Browser Toolbar" check box, or
- Right-click any palette and choose Browser Toolbar from the menu.

NOTE: *You can set the toolbar preferences to Hide Disabled Toolbars so that whenever a toolbar or palette is not active, it is hidden. If you select the "Hide disabled toolbars" check box in the Toolbars dialog box, the Browser toolbar appears whenever you open the Browser and disappears when you close the Browser.*

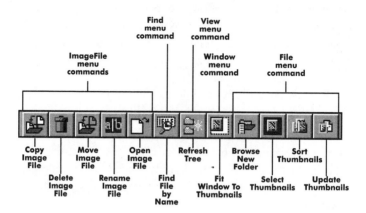

When the toolbar is displayed, it appears at the top of the main program window. You can undock it and move it anywhere on the screen, or dock it to any edge of the workspace. You can customize the toolbar by adding and removing buttons. For information about customizing the toolbar, please refer to Chapter 20, "Setting Preferences."

The Browser toolbar buttons are shown above. These buttons have ToolTips that show their names. To display a name, place the cursor over a button without clicking. To activate a button's command, click the button. If a command is unavailable, its button is shaded.

Navigating with the Browser

Navigate through the folders using the left side (pane) of the Browser window. When you click a folder, thumbnails of the images Paint Shop Pro supports appear in the right side (pane) of the window.

To select a new folder to browse, do one of the following:

- Click the folder in the left side of the Browser window,

- Choose File > Browse New Folder to open the Browse for Folder navigation box, or

- Click the Browse New Folder button ( ) on the toolbar.

Use the Browse New Folder navigation box to select the new folder. For a description of the navigation box, please refer to "Using the Browse New Folder Navigation Box" on page 28.

Viewing the Thumbnails

A thumbnail is a small preview button for an image that lets you identify and manage an image without opening it. When you navigate to folders using the Paint Shop Pro Browser, thumbnails of all images that can be opened by the program appear in the Browser's right pane.

You can select one or more thumbnails and open them, rename or delete them, and copy or move them to another folder. When you select a thumbnail, it appears pressed in and the area around the image changes colors.

You can change the size of the thumbnails, the background color for selected thumbnails, and other Browser features on the Browser tab of the General Program Preferences dialog box. For more information, please refer to Chapter 20, "Setting Preferences."

For each thumbnail, you can view either a ToolTip that contains file information or the File Information dialog box that contains file information.

To view a ToolTip:

Position the cursor over a thumbnail. The ToolTip displays the file's name and size, the image dimensions and color depth, and the date the file was last modified.

To view the File Information dialog box:

- Click the thumbnail, and choose ImageFile > Information,

- Right-click the thumbnail, and choose Information from the menu, or

- Press <Shift> + <I>.

The File Information box opens. It lists the file format, compression method, size, bit depth, and other information about the image.

Using the Context-Sensitive Menus

The Browser has two context-sensitive menus that display many of the commands for editing and managing thumbnails. The menus are available in the right pane of the window.

Right-clicking an individual thumbnail selects that thumbnail and opens a thumbnail context menu that contains the commands from the ImageFile menu. If you right-click to open the menu when more than one thumbnail is selected, the Rename and Information commands are unavailable. To keep the selected thumbnails from being deselected when you open the context menu, press the <Ctrl> or <Shift> key while right-clicking.

Right-clicking the background area of the right pane opens a general context menu that contains commands for working with the Browser in general. If a thumbnail is selected, pressing the <Ctrl> or <Shift> key while right-clicking away from the thumbnails does not open this menu. It opens the thumbnail context menu.

Fitting the Browser Window to Thumbnails

To resize the Browser window to fit the number of rows and columns of thumbnails currently visible, choose Window > Fit to Thumbnails, or click the Fit Window to Thumbnails button (▨) on the Browser toolbar. The Browser aligns to the nearest column of thumbnails. If there are too many thumbnails to fit within the window, a scrollbar appears along its edge. This works only when the Browser window is not maximized.

Opening Images

Open one or more images using any of the following methods:

- Select one or more thumbnails and click the Open Image File button (▢) on the Browser toolbar.

- Select one or more thumbnails and choose ImageFile > Open.

- Select one or more thumbnails, and then right-click any thumbnail and choose Open from the menu.

- Drag the thumbnails into the workspace. The number of images you can open is limited only by the memory of the computer.

- Double-click a thumbnail. To select more than one image, press <Ctrl> while clicking each thumbnail, and then <Ctrl> while double-clicking the final one.

NOTE: *Depending on your preference settings, when you open an image, a format-specific dialog box may appear requesting additional information. This applies to Photo-CD, PostScript, RAW, or WMF files. For more information about preferences, please refer to Chapter 20, "Setting Preferences."*

Closing the Browser

To close the Browser, do any of the following:

- Click the Browser window Close button (▨),

- Click the Browser window to activate it, and then choose File > Close,

- Double-click the Browser window control icon (▤),

- Single-click the Browser window control icon (▤) and choose Close, or

- Press <Ctrl> + <F4>.

Updating the Browser Tree and Thumbnails

Updating the Browser Tree

The Browser tree is the folder list that appears in the left pane of the Browser window. Updating the tree refreshes the view of the folders in the tree.

To update the Browser tree:

- Click the Refresh Tree button (🔲)on the Browser toolbar,
- Choose View > Refresh Tree, or
- Press <Ctrl> + <F5>.

Updating the Thumbnails of a Folder

Understanding the Cache File

When you first open a folder, the Browser searches the folder for images supported by Paint Shop Pro. It then creates a thumbnail for each supported image, stores the thumbnails in a special cache file, and displays them in the Browser. The Browser saves the cache file directly in the selected folder. The cache file is named pspbrwse.jbf. Every folder that you have opened in the Browser will have the cache file in it. The thumbnails load more quickly when the Browser stores a cache file because, rather than generating new thumbnails each time the folder is opened, the Browser displays the thumbnails from the cache file.

Each time you open a folder, the Browser reads the thumbnails from the folder's stored cache file and displays the thumbnails. Depending on your preference settings, the Browser may also search the folder for new or changed files and automatically update the thumbnails and the cache file each time you open a folder. To set the preference for automatically updating the files, use the Browser tab of the General Program Preferences dialog box. Select the "Automatically update the thumbnails" check box. For more information, please refer to chapter 20, "Setting Preferences."

Updating the Thumbnails

You can set your preferences to update automatically file changes made in a folder, or you can manually update a folder. Updating the thumbnails does the following:

- Refreshes the thumbnail images to reflect any changes to the files,
- Removes thumbnails of files that have been deleted, and
- Adds thumbnails of files that have been added to the selected folder.

To update manually the thumbnails for the current folder:

- Click the Update Thumbnails button (🔲) on the Browser toolbar,
- Choose File > Update Thumbnails, or
- Press <F5>.

Using the Browse New Folder Navigation Box

The Browse for Folder Navigation Box opens from several locations in the applications.

To use the Browser New Folder navigation box:

1. Use one of the following methods to open the navigation box:

   - Click the Browse New Folder button (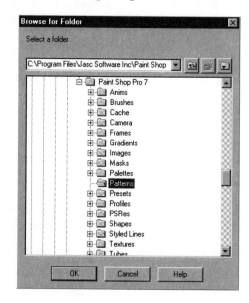) on the Browser toolbar.

   - Choose ImageFile > Copy To, or click the Copy Image File button ( ) on the Browser toolbar.

   - Choose ImageFile > Move To, or click the Move Image File button ( ) on the Browser toolbar.

   - Choose File > Preferences > File Locations. Then click the appropriate preference tab and click a Browse button (Browse). (This applies to all the File Location preference tabs except the Web Browsers tab.)

   - Choose File > Batch Conversion and click the Browse button (Browse) to display the Browse for Folder dialog box. This lets you choose a folder for placing converted files.

2. Navigate to the folder you want to select by scrolling through the tree, choosing a recent folder from the drop-down box or typing a path in the Select a folder text box. Use the Locate button ( ) at the right to display and select the folder you typed.

3. Click the folder to select it. The folder opens.

4. To create a new folder below the selected folder, click the Create New Folder button ( ).

5. To select the Paint Shop Pro folders, My Documents, or a temporary folder, click the Special Folder button ( ). You can add folders to this menu by selecting them in the tree and choosing the Add Current command.

6. Click the OK button to close the dialog box and copy, move, or perform the command.

Selecting Thumbnails

To select files, you can click the thumbnails in the right pane of the Browser window. You can select a single thumbnail, a sequential group of thumbnails, or a non-sequential group of thumbnails.

The Browser uses the Windows Explorer concept for selecting thumbnails. There are selected thumbnails, a current thumbnail, and an anchor thumbnail. Click a thumbnail to select it. Selected thumbnails change color and appear pressed in. When you select more than one thumbnail, the current thumbnail is the active one. The area around its filename is reversed.

Selecting a Single Thumbnail

Select a single thumbnail in a folder by clicking it.

Selecting Sequential Thumbnails

To select sequential thumbnails:

1. Click the first thumbnail in the sequence that you want to select.

2. Press and hold the <Shift> key.

3. Do either of the following:

   - Click the last thumbnail in the sequence.

   - Use the Up <↑>, Down <↓>, Left <←>, and Right <→> Arrow keys to move to the last thumbnail in the sequence.

Selecting and Deselecting Non-Sequential Thumbnails

To select and deselect non-sequential thumbnails:

1. Press and hold the <Ctrl> key.

2. Do either of the following:

   - Click the thumbnails you want to select. Clicking once selects a thumbnail; clicking again deselects it.

   - Use the Arrow keys to move to the thumbnails you want to select, and press the Space key to select each. Pressing the Space key once selects a thumbnail; pressing the Space key again deselects it.

Inverting Selected Thumbnails

To invert the selected thumbnails of a folder, choose Edit > Invert Selection. All previously selected thumbnails are deselected, and all previously unselected thumbnails are selected.

Selecting All Thumbnails

To select all thumbnails, choose Edit > Select All, press <Ctrl> + <A>, or use the following sequence: select any thumbnail and press <Ctrl> + <Home > followed by <Shift> + <End>. The Browser highlights every thumbnail.

Deselecting All Thumbnails

To deselect all thumbnails, choose Edit > Select None or press <Ctrl> + <D>.

Selecting Thumbnails by File Characteristics

Use the Select dialog box to select thumbnails that have specific file or image attributes, such as name, file extension, size, width, height, bits per pixel, and date.

To use the Select dialog box:

1. Open the dialog box by clicking the Select Thumbnails button (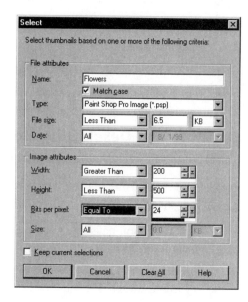)on the Browser toolbar, or by choosing File > Select.

2. In the Name box, type the names of the files to select. You can use the standard wildcard symbols of substituting a question mark (?) for one letter and an asterisk (*) for several.

3. Select the "Match case" check box to limit the selection to filenames matching the case of the letters you type.

4. In the Type drop-down box, select a file format. All formats listed in the Open dialog box are included.

5. Use the File size boxes to select files by size. Choose between files greater than, less than or equal to the specified size. You can then type a floating-point number in the middle box and choose bytes, KB, or MB from the last box. These boxes use the following rules for the floating-point number:

   - For bytes, ignore numbers after the decimal.

   - For kilobytes, use the first digit after the decimal.

   - For megabytes, use the first two digits after the decimal.

6. In the Date drop-down box, select the date the files was last saved. You can type a date or use the date picker control calendar.

7. In the Width, Height, and Bits per pixel (color depth) drop down boxes, select if you want to search for images Equal To, Greater Than, or Less Than specific dimensions and/or color depth. Enter the values to use in the boxes next to them.

8. In the Size boxes, enter the size of the memory required to open the image. These boxes operate in the same way as the File size boxes described in step 5.

9. Select the "Keep current selections" check box to add the selected files to those already selected.

10. Click the Clear All button to reset the dialog box to its default values.

11. Click the OK button to close the dialog box and select the files matching the attributes you entered.

Sorting Thumbnails in a Folder

You can arrange the thumbnails so that they appear in ascending or descending order according to file and image characteristics.

NOTE: *Sorting thumbnails is a one-time operation. The thumbnails will not remain sorted if you add new images or change the properties of the existing files. New images are always added to the end of the list.*

To sort the thumbnails in a folder:

1. Click the Sort Thumbnails button(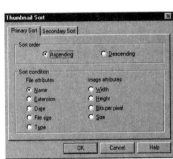) on the Browser toolbar, or choose File > Sort. The Thumbnail Sort dialog box opens. There are two criteria tabs, the Primary Sort and the Secondary Sort.

2. In the "Sort order" panel of the Primary Sort tab, select to sort the images by ascending or descending order.

3. In the "Sort condition" panel, select either a file attribute or an image attribute. You cannot select both.

4. Click the Secondary Sort tab to bring it to the front.

5. Do one of the following:

   • Repeat the process used to select the primary criteria.

   • Click the No sort option. When this option is chosen, no secondary sort criteria are used. The file and image attributes options are not available.

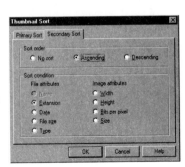

6. Click the OK button. The Browser sorts the thumbnails according to the order and criteria you selected.

Dragging-and-Dropping Thumbnails

The Browser supports full drag-and-drop behavior similar to the Windows Explorer. Thumbnails can be dragged to several locations, described below.

To A NEW POSITION WITHIN THE DISPLAYED THUMBNAILS To move a thumbnail to a new position in the same folder, drag and drop the thumbnail to the new position.

To OTHER FOLDERS IN THE LEFT PANE If the destination folder is on the same drive as the original folder: To move the thumbnail, drag and drop it in the new folder. To copy the thumbnail, press <Ctrl> while dragging the thumbnail to the new folder.

If the destination folder is on a different drive than the original folder: To copy the thumbnail, drag and drop it in the new folder. To move the thumbnail, press <Shift> while dragging the thumbnail to the new folder.

To OTHER APPLICATIONS THAT SUPPORT OLE FUNCTIONS To paste an image into a program that supports meta files, DIBs, and BMPs, such as Microsoft Word, press <Alt> and drag the thumbnail to the document. If the image has more than one layer, they are merged.

To A BUTTON ON THE WINDOWS TASKBAR To copy and paste an image into a minimized application, drag the thumbnail to the application's button on the Windows task bar. Do not release the mouse button. The application restores for you to place the thumbnail and then release the mouse button. For example, if you have opened the Browser from Paint Shop Pro and you want to paste the image in Animation Shop, you can drag the thumbnail to the Animation Shop button on the taskbar. Wait a few seconds, and Animation Shop restores. You can then drop the thumbnail on an image or on the workspace.

To THE WORKSPACE OF THE ANIMATION SHOP MAIN PROGRAM WINDOW To open an image in Animation Shop, drag and drop the thumbnail to a blank area on the workspace. To combine several images into a single animation, press <Shift> while dragging the thumbnails.

To AN OPEN ANIMATION IN THE ANIMATION SHOP MAIN PROGRAM WINDOW To add an image or animation to an open animation, drag and drop the animation's thumbnail to an open animation. To place the image between frames, release the cursor between those frames.

TO THE WORKSPACE OF THE PAINT SHOP PRO MAIN PROGRAM WINDOW To open an image file in Paint Shop Pro, drag and drop the image's thumbnail to a blank area on the workspace.

TO AN OPEN IMAGE IN THE PAINT SHOP PRO MAIN PROGRAM WINDOW This feature performs different functions depending on the type of image being copied. Basically, when you drag and drop a thumbnail to an open image, the thumbnail's image is added as a new layer.

You can drag and drop a thumbnail for a mask file into a file as a mask. This is an easy way to add a saved mask to an image. Mask files are created using the Masks > Save to Disk command. They have a file extension of *.msk. (You can create a mask by saving an 8-bit greyscale Windows bitmap with a *.msk extension.)

To drag and drop a multi-layered image to an open image, please refer to "Copying an Image's Layers into Another Image" below.

Copying an Image's Layers into Another Image

You can use the Browser to copy the layers of an image into an open image in Paint Shop Pro. This copies all three layer types: raster, vector, and adjustment.

To copy layers:

1. Open the image that will receive the new layers. The image must be a 24-bit color or a grey scale image.

2. In the Layer palette, click the layer above which you want to copy the new layers.

3. Open the Browser and navigate to the folder containing the thumbnail of the image you want to copy.

4. Drag the thumbnail from the Browser to the open image.

5. Release the mouse button. The layers are added to the open image.

NOTE: *When first added, the layers are grouped and move together. To ungroup them so that they can be moved separately, click the Group button on the Layer palette.*

Finding Files by Name

If you have a folder containing several image files, you can use the Find function of the Browser to search the folder and select thumbnails by name.

To locate and select files:

1. To open the Find dialog box, do any of the following:

- Click the Find File by Name button (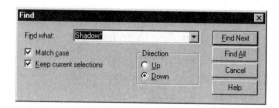) on the Browser toolbar,

- Choose Find > File Name,

- Right-click the background of the right pane and choose Find Name, or

- Press <Alt> + <F3>.

2. Type all or part of the file's name into the Find What text box. The Browser will highlight the first file it finds that matches the search string. You can search using the wildcard symbol (*). For example, to find all files in the BMP format, type *.bmp.

3. If you want the search to be case-sensitive, select the "Match case" check box. In a case-sensitive search, the Browser highlights only those files with the same case as the search text. For example, in a case-sensitive search for "Shadow," it does _not_ highlight files that contain "shadow," or "SHADOW," or any other combination of cases.

4. If you have already selected specific files and want to add the ones you find to the group, select the "Keep current selections" check box.

5. In the "Direction" panel, choose Up to have Paint Shop Pro search from the current thumbnail toward the first in the list. Choose Down to search from the current thumbnail toward the end of the list. If no thumbnail matches, it will loop back when it reaches the end.

6. Click the Find Next button to search for the closest file containing the text that you entered. Click the Find All button to find all files containing the text.

7. If the Browser finds a thumbnail with matching text, it highlights the thumbnail. To keep searching, choose Find > Repeat Find or press <F3>.

8. If the Browser doesn't find any matching text, a message appears stating that there is no match. Click the OK button to close it.

Using the Browser to Manage Files

Copying a File Using the Browser

To copy one or more files to a different folder using the Browser:

1. Open the folder containing the image or images you want to copy.

2. Select the thumbnail of one or more files.

3. Do one of the following:

    *   Click the Copy Image File button (📋) on the Browser toolbar,

    *   Choose ImageFile > Copy To,

    *   Right-click the thumbnail and choose Copy To from the menu, or

    *   Press <Ctrl> + <Y>.

4. The Browse for Folder navigation box opens.

5. Navigate to and select the folder in which you want to place the copy. For specific steps, please refer to "Using the Browse New Folder Navigation Box" on page 28.

6. Click the OK button to close the navigation box and copy the image file to the selected folder.

Moving a File Using the Browser

To move files using the Browser:

1. Open the folder containing the image or images you want to move.

2. Select the thumbnail of one or more files.

3. Do one of the following:

    *   Click the Move Image File button (📋) on the Browser toolbar,

    *   Choose ImageFile > Move,

    *   Right-click the thumbnail and choose Move To from the menu, or

    *   Press <Ctrl> + <M>.

4. The Browse for Folder navigation box opens.

5. Navigate to and highlight the new folder. For specific steps, please refer to "Using the Browse New Folder Navigation Box" on page 28.

6. Click the OK button to close the navigation box and move the file or files to the selected folder.

Renaming a File Using the Browser

To rename a file using the Browser:

1. Open the folder containing the image you want to rename.

2. Select the file's thumbnail.

3. Do one of the following:

   - Click the Rename Image File button (⟦ab⟧) on the Browser toolbar,

   - Choose ImageFile > Rename,

   - Right-click the thumbnail and choose Rename from the menu,

   - Press <Ctrl> + <R>, or

   - Press F2.

4. The Rename File dialog box opens.

5. Type the new name. The file name can be up to 255 characters long, including the path and file extension. The Browser does not automatically add the extension. If you want the file name to include an extension, add it to the name.

6. Click the OK button to rename the file and close the dialog box.

Deleting a File Using the Browser

To delete files using the Browser:

1. Open the folder containing the image or images you want to delete.

2. Select the thumbnail of one or more files.

3. Do one of the following:

   - Click the Delete Image File button (⟦🗑⟧) on the Browser toolbar,

   - Choose ImageFile > Delete,

   - Right-click the thumbnail and choose Delete from the menu, or

   - Press <Ctrl> + <Delete>.

4. A confirmation message appears. Click the Yes button to delete the selected file or files.

Printing Thumbnails

You can print the thumbnails of a folder using the Browser. Please refer to Chapter 19, "Printing Images and Thumbnails," for information about using the Browser to print thumbnails.

Managing Images

Features of an Image Window

When you open an image file or create a new image, Paint Shop Pro places it in an image window.
You can have more than one window open and can move between open windows. The image you
are currently working on is the active image; its window is the active image window. This chapter
provides basic steps for working with image windows.

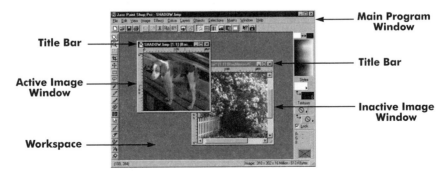

PAINT SHOP PRO   37

Understanding the Title Bar

When an image window is not maximized, it has a title bar at the top of the window. By looking at the title bar, you can see information about the image.

Control Icon   Windows Buttons

NOTE: *When an active image window is maximized, the image window title bar blends with the main program window's title bar and menu bar. The image window's control icon and Windows buttons appear at each end of the main program menu bar, and the title and image information appears in the main program window's title bar along with the application name.*

In addition to the Control icon and standard Window controls, a Paint Shop Pro image title bar contains the following items: title, file format, magnification level, and current layer. It may also display a modifier flag.

TITLE AND FORMAT The name of the file and its format appear on the title bar next to the control icon. The image identified on the title bar appears in the image window.

WATERMARK FLAG (not shown) A copyright symbol before the file name indicates the image has an embedded watermark.

MODIFIER FLAG An "*" (asterisk) after the file name indicates the image has been modified since it was last saved.

MAGNIFICATION LEVEL (ZOOM RATIO) The numbers in brackets indicate the image's current magnification level.

CURRENT (ACTIVE) LAYER The name of the layer that is current (active) appears after the Zoom Ratio.

NOTE: *Double-clicking the window title area of the title bar is the same as clicking the Windows Maximize or Restore buttons on the title bar.*

Using Rulers, Grids, and Guides

Paint Shop Pro provides rulers, grids, and guides to help you align your artwork and arrange image elements symmetrically.

Using the Rulers

You can display or hide the rulers for the image windows. When displayed, the rulers appear along the top and left sides of the image. As you work in the image, a thin line appears on each ruler to show the cursor's position.

Rulers Hidden

You can set the rulers to display inches, centimeters, or pixels. You can also set them to display black numbers on a white background or to use your default Windows colors. Use the General Program Preferences on the Rulers and Units tab to change the settings. For more information about preferences, please refer to Chapter 20, "Setting Preferences."

To display or hide the rulers:

- Choose View > Rulers, or

- Press <Ctrl> + <Alt> + <R>.

Rulers Displayed

Using the Grid

You can display or hide the grids for the image windows. When you display the grids, they appear in all open image windows. You can set the preferences for the grid spacing at inches, centimeters, or pixels. You can also set the horizontal and vertical spacing and the line color for all future grids. Use the General Program Preferences on the Rulers and Units tab to change the settings. For more information, please refer to Chapter 20, "Setting Preferences."

To display or hide the grids:

- Choose View > Grids, or

- Press <Ctrl> + <Alt> + <G>.

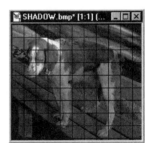

Grid Displayed

After you display the grid, you can change and save the color, units, and spacing separately for each image window. If you saved an image as a Paint Shop Pro 7 file, when you close and open it again, the grid appears as you saved it. To save a grid, right-click the image window title bar and choose Change Grid and Guide Properties from the context menu or click the Arrow tool (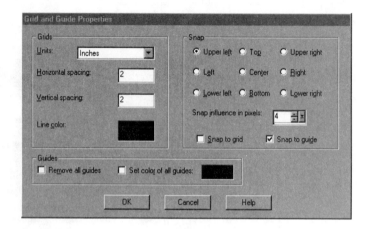) on the Tool palette, right-click the image, and choose Change Grid and Guide Properties from the context menu.

In the Grid panel of the Grid and Guide Properties dialog box:

1. Change the measurement used for the grid by choosing Pixels, Inches, or Centimeters from the Units drop-down box.

2. Change the size of the grid by typing new values in the Horizontal spacing and Vertical spacing boxes.

3. Select a new color by left-clicking the Line color box to open the Color dialog box or right-clicking to open the Recent Colors dialog box.

Using the Guides

You can hide or show the guides for the image windows. Depending on your General Program Preference settings on the Rulers and Units tab, you can set the default color for the guides. For more information about preferences, refer to Chapter 20, "Setting Preferences."

NOTE: *Before displaying the guides, make sure the rulers are displayed. Refer to "To display or hide the rulers:" on page 39.*

To display or hide the guides:

- Choose View > Guides.

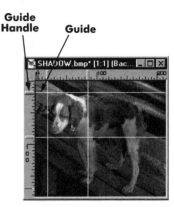

Guide Handle **Guide**

After you have set the guides to display, create individual guides by clicking the ruler and dragging the guide to the desired position. Click the ruler at the top of the image and drag to create horizontal guides; click the ruler along the left side and grad to create vertical guides. To move a guide, click the guide handle on the ruler and drag. To delete a guide, drag its handle off the image window. You can draw guides to extend beyond the edges of image canvas. This lets you align objects before placing them in the image.

NOTE: *After creating the guides, you can hide the rulers and leave the guides displayed. When you do this, choose View > Change Grid and Guide Properties to make changes to the guides.*

You can change the color or position and delete individual guides using the Guide Properties dialog box.

To display the Guide Properties dialog box:

- Right-click the guide handle on the ruler, or

- Double-click the guide handle on the ruler.

In the dialog box, do any of the following:

GUIDE COLOR Left-click the box to open the Color dialog box; right-click to open the Recent Colors dialog box. Choose a new color.

GUIDE POSITION Enter a new position, in pixels.

DELETE GUIDE CHECK BOX Select to delete the guide.

NOTE: *You can delete all guides or change the color of them using the Grid and Guide Properties dialog box. To open the dialog box, double-click the ruler or choose View > Change Grid and Guide Properties. Also, please refer to the screen capture on the previous page.*

Using the Grid and Guide Snap To Features

When you have the grids and/or guides displayed, you can use the Snap to features to automatically align your paint strokes and objects with the grid lines or the guides. The snap points represent the handles on the bounding boxes around objects.

NOTE: *Before using the Snap features, make sure the grids and/or guides are displayed.*

To use these features:

- To turn the Grid Snap feature on or off choose View > Snap To Grid or select the Snap to grid check box in the Grid and Guide Properties dialog box.

- To turn the Guide Snap feature on or off and choose View > Snap To Guides or select the Snap to guides check box in the Grid and Guide Properties dialog box.

When the grids and/or guides are on, you can set an alignment point for objects, and you can change the default snap influence. The snap influence value determines how close (in pixels) your cursor or object must be to a grid line or guide before it is automatically aligned along it.

NOTE: *If you have both the Snap To Grid and Snap to Guide features turned on and you place an object within the snap influence of both a grid line and a guide, the object snaps to the guide.*

To set the Snap To Alignment point:

Select a snap to alignment point in the Grid and Guide Properties dialog box, which you open by choosing View > Grid and Guide Properties or by double-clicking the ruler.

Your selection determines which point (handle) of an object automatically snaps to a grid line or guide when you move the object into the snap influence area. Your choices are Upper Left, Upper Right, Lower Left, Lower Right, Left, Right, Top, Bottom, and Center. The object shown here is snapped to the object's center point.

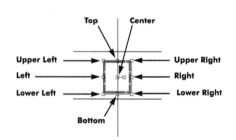

The snap to setting applies to objects you create or paste that have a bounding box around them, such as selections and vector objects. With text, it applies when you move a text object or creation, but does not apply when you create text.

To change the Snap Influence:

To change the snap influence, open the Grid and Guide Properties dialog box by choosing View >Change Grid and Guide Properties, or double-clicking the ruler. In the Snap influence in pixels control of the Snap panel, enter the number of pixels an object must be to the grid or guide before it is automatically aligned to it.

Using the Overview Window

With an image active in the workspace, you can optionally display the Overview window. The Overview window contains a thumbnail view of the active image so you can see the entire image if you zoom in on a specific area. When the image window shows only a part of the image, the Overview window indicates the displayed area with a small rectangle. By left-clicking and dragging this rectangle, you can move other areas of the original image into view in the Image window.

To display or hide the Overview window:

- Click the Toggle Overview Window button ▣ on the tool bar,

- Choose View > ToolBars and select or clear the "Overview Window" check box,

- Right-click any palette and choose Toolbars from the menu, then select or clear the "Overview Window" check box,

- Right-click any palette and choose Overview Window from the menu, or

- Press <V>.

NOTE: *You can also set the tool bar and palette preferences to Hide Disabled Toolbars. Then, whenever the window is not active, it will be hidden from view. Select View > Toolbars and then select or clear the "Hide disabled toolbars" check box.*

The Overview window title bar contains the Palette Roll-up button (if enabled in the Preference settings) and the standard Close button. The current zoom ratio of the image is displayed below the image overview.

Please note the following items about the Overview Window:

- The image in the Overview Window updates after you complete an action.

- Transparent areas of an image are displayed as white.

- Because the overview uses system resources to update as you change the image, Paint Shop Pro may operate slower than normal when the Overview Window is open.

Viewing Image Information

The Current Image Information dialog box displays information about images open in Paint Shop Pro. It always contains at least two tabs: the Image Information tab and the Creator Information tab. If the image contains a digital watermark, the Watermark Information tab also appears. When an image is in the PSP format, you can add comments such as a title, the artist's name, and copyright information in the Creator Information tab.

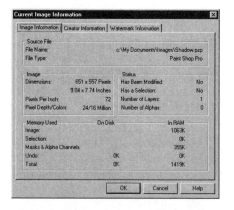

To open the Current Image Information dialog box, choose Image > Image Information, or press <Shift> + <I>.

Image Information Tab This tab contains the file name and format, its dimensions and bit depth, selection, layer, and channel information, and a breakdown of the memory used.

Creator Information Tab Unlike most file formats, the PSP format lets you save information about the image. You can type a title, the creator's name, copyright information, and any comments in this tab. Click OK to close the dialog box. This information is not saved until you save the image.

Watermark Information Tab This tab displays the Creator ID, the year of copyright, and image attributes. If your computer is connected to the Web, you can view information about the image's creator at the Digimarc Web site. To open the Browser and go to the appropriate page, click the Web Lookup button. For information on embedding a watermark in your image.

Working with Image Windows

You can drag a window around the workspace, resize, minimize, and open it as needed. You can have more than one window open while you work. A list of images that are open is displayed at the bottom of the Window menu. A check mark to the left of a name indicates the active image. To make a different image active, chose it from the list. The check mark appears next to the name you have chosen.

Resizing Windows

You can click a window's title bar and drag the window to almost any location on your screen. You can also resize a window by clicking any size or corner of the image and dragging it in or out. When you click a side or corner of the window, a double-headed arrow appears to indicate you can resize the window.

Arranging Windows

You can have more than one window open while you work. When you have several images open, you can arrange their windows in the workspace using the following Window menu commands:

- Cascade, which stacks the windows and aligns them from the upper left to the lower right of the workspace,

- Tile Horizontally, which aligns the windows in rows, and

- Tile Vertically, which aligns the windows in columns.

Changing Zoom Levels of an Image

As you edit an image, there are times when you may want to see some areas of the image close up, and times when you may want to see the entire image. You can do this by varying the zoom level. For example, zoom in to see the individual pixels for detail work and back out to adjust the color balance.

The zoom level is the magnification level of an image. The normal viewing level is the actual size of one-to-one (1:1). At three-to-one (3:1), the image is three times the normal size; at one-to-five (1:5), it is one-fifth the normal size. The magnification of an image always appears next to the title on an image's title bar.

Using the View Menu Zoom Commands

The following commands on the View menu change the magnification of an image:

- Zoom In by 1 increases the zoom factor by 1.
- Zoom In by 5 increases the zoom factor by 5.
- Zoom Out by 1 decreases the zoom factor by 1.
- Zoom Out by 5 decreases the zoom factor by 5.
- Normal View immediately returns the image to the standard magnification of 1:1.

For example, if you choose View > Zoom in by 1 two times, the image will be displayed at three times its original size. If you then choose View > Zoom in by 5, the magnification will be eight times the original.

Using the Zoom Tool

To activate the Zoom tool, click the Zoom tool button on the Tool palette. Use the left and right mouse buttons to increase and decrease the magnification level.

- To zoom in, left-click the image. The magnification increases by one level each time you click the image, and the image centers where the Zoom tool was clicked.
- You can also zoom in by left-clicking and dragging your mouse to create a rectangle around the area you want to magnify.
- To zoom out, right-click the image. The magnification decreases by one level with each click.

To return to the standard view, click the Normal Viewing button on the toolbar or press <Ctrl> + <Alt> + <N>.

Using the Numeric Keypad

Press <+> on the numeric keypad to increase the magnification by one level.

Press <-> on the numeric keypad to decrease the magnification by one level.

Using the Tool Options Palette

When the Arrow, Zoom, Mover, Dropper, and Text tools are active, the Zoom indicator on the Tool Options palette displays the current zoom level. You can change magnification by selecting a new zoom level from the drop-down box.

Using a Mouse Wheel

If your mouse has a wheel, you can use it to change the magnification level of your image. Roll the wheel away from you to zoom in. Roll it toward you to zoom out. The zoom centers around the mouse.

Moving the Image in Its Window

When you increase the magnification level of the image for detail work, you may find that the entire image no longer in its window. If you are not working on the entire image, it might be more convenient to keep the image at this higher zoom level but not increase the window's size. When you want to move to a different part of the image, you can use the Overview window, the Arrow tool, the Cursor keys, or the scrollbar.

Using The Arrow Tool

To use the Arrow tool:

1. Click the Arrow button on the Tool palette.

2. Move the cursor over the image.

3. Press and hold down the left mouse button. The cursor changes into a hand.

4. Drag the image until the area you want is visible.

5. Release the mouse button.

Using The Cursor Keys

To use the Cursor keys:

- Press <Page Up>, <Page Down>, <↑>, and <↓> to scroll vertically.

- Press <Home>, <End>, <←>, and <→> to scroll horizontally.

Using the Scrollbars

When an image is too large to fit entirely within the image window, scrollbars appear at the right side and/or bottom of the image window.

To use a scrollbar, drag the slider bar, click the arrow buttons, or click between the slider bar and an arrow button.

Fitting the Window to the Image

When you change the magnification of an image, Paint Shop Pro can enlarge or reduce the image window automatically to the new size. Select this option on the Viewing tab of the General Program Preferences.

If you have not selected this preferences, you can resize the window to fit the image by choosing Window > Fit to Image or by pressing <Ctrl> + <W>.

Opening a New Window

When you want multiple views of an image you can use the Overview window, which is described earlier in the chapter, or open new windows. These new windows are NOT new images—they are new views of the image and are linked. Any changes you make to the image in one window also makes changes to the images in the other windows. However, because the zoom factor is independent, you can use different zoom levels in each image window.

To open a new view of an image, choose Window > New Window or press <Shift> + <W>. When more than one window is open, you can close any window, including the original. The image stays open as long as at least one window is open.

Using Full Screen Edit

In Full Screen Edit, Paint Shop Pro expands the workspace to cover the screen. This gives you the largest possible space for displaying your image. The palettes are visible, but the menus are hidden. To access the menus, click at the top edge of the screen.

- To activate the Full Screen Edit, choose View > Full Screen Edit, or press <Shift> + <A>.

- Press <Shift> + <A> to return the workspace to its previous size.

Saving Image Files

Paint Shop Pro has a native *.psp format that supports layers, alpha channels, and other features you use to create images. You will find it convenient to save an image in this format while you are working on it and then convert it to a different format after you have finished.

Using Autosave

You can use the Autosave feature to save your files automatically at specified intervals. This can prevent you from losing your work if your computer shuts down unexpectedly. For more information, please refer to Chapter 20, "Setting Preferences."

Compressing a File

An image file in the *.psp format can be saved without compression, or it can be compressed to save space. Both compression methods Paint Shop Pro uses are lossless; that is, they reduce the file size without losing any image information. Saving a file without compressing it is the quicker method, but it requires more hard disk space.

Paint Shop Pro uses two compression methods:

- Run length encoding (RLE), which is fast and compresses most multi-layered images to about 75% of their original sizes. It works well with images that contain large areas of the same color.

- LZ77 compression, which is slower than RLE, but can compress an image to a smaller size than RLE. It works well with photo-realistic images.

▣ Saving a New Image File

The first time you save an image, Paint Shop Pro automatically opens the Save As dialog box, where you select a location, name, and format for the image. After this, Paint Shop Pro saves changes to the original image without opening the dialog box. You can also use this dialog box to save an image using a different file format or name by choosing File > Save As.

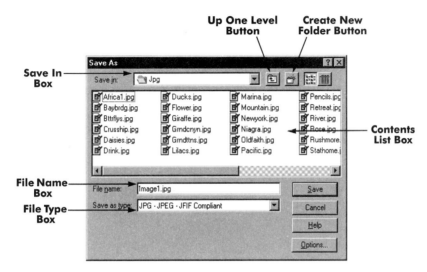

To save a new Paint Shop Pro image:

1. Choose File > Save, press <Ctrl> + <S>, or click the Save button (▣) on the toolbar. The Save As dialog box opens.

2. Use the Save In drop-down box to navigate to the folder in which you want to save the image file. If necessary, use the Up One Level button to help navigate and the Create New Folder button to create a new folder.

3. In the File Name box, type a name for the file.

4. To save the file in a new format, select the format from the Save As Type list.

5. If the file format has save options, click the Options button to open the Save Options dialog box. Select new settings, if appropriate. If you are unsure of the settings, use the default values. Click OK to return to the Save As dialog box.

6. Click Save to close the dialog box and save the file.

You can have Paint Shop Pro display the last used file type when opening this dialog box. Select this option in the Dialogs and Palettes Preferences tab of the General Program Preferences dialog box.

■ Saving an Image File in its Original Format

When you save an image and then edit it, the title bar displays a Modified tag (an asterisk) after the file's name to indicate the file has been modified. This tag disappears each time you save the file; it reappears when you again edit the image.

To save changes to an image, do one of the following:

- Choose File > Save,

- Press <Ctrl> + <S>, or

- Click the Save button on the toolbar.

To save the image using a different name or file format, choose File > Save As.

■ Saving an Image in a New File Format

If you want to save a file in another format, use the Save As command.

To save a file:

1. Choose File > Save As or press <F12>. The Save As dialog box opens.

2. Navigate to and open the folder in which you want to save the image file.

3. To rename the image file, type a new name in the File name box.

4. Open the Save as type box, and scroll to select a new format.

5. If the new format has save options, the Options button is accessible. If there are no options, it is greyed out. To select the options, click the Options button to open the Save Options dialog box. Select the options, and click OK to close the selection box.

6. Click Save to save the image file and close the dialog box.

■ Saving a Copy of an Image

When you save an image using the Save Copy As command, you are copying the original file, not saving it. Use this command to save a version of a file without affecting the original. The dialog box contains all the same features as the Save As dialog box. Paint Shop Pro saves the copy to the same directory and in the same format that was last used with the Save Copy As command (not the Save As command).

Note that using the Save Copy As command:

- Does not affect the modifier tag. It does not disappear from the title bar.

- Does not change the file name. The copy is titled *"Image Name."*

To save a copy of an image:

1. Choose the File > Save Copy As or press <Ctrl> + <F12>. The Save Copy As dialog box opens.

2. Use the Save In drop-down box to Navigate to a new folder if you want to save the copy in a different folder. If necessary, use the Up One Level button to help navigate, or the Create New Folder button to create a new folder.

3. In the File Name box, type a name for the file.

4. To save the file in a different format, select the format from the Save As Type drop-down list.

5. If the file format has save options, click the Options button to open the Save Options dialog box. Select new settings, if appropriate. If you are unsure of the settings, use the default values. Click OK to return to the Save As dialog box.

6. Click Save to close the dialog box and save a copy of the file.

To save copies of several images in a new file format, use the Batch Conversion feature, which is described at the end of this chapter.

Closing Images

Closing the Active Image

- To close an image, choose File > Close or click the Windows Close button (❎).

If you have made changes to the image since you last saved it, you are prompted to save the changes.

Closing All Open Images

- To close all the open image files in the Paint Shop Pro workspace, choose Window > Close All.

You are prompted to save any files with changes unless you have cleared the "Warn on unsaved files during Windows Close All" check box on the Warnings tab of the General Program Preferences.

Deleting Images

Deleting a Newly Created Image

To delete an image you have created but not yet saved, close it and click the No button when prompted to save changes.

Deleting a Previously Saved Image

After you have saved an image, you can delete it. To delete a saved image while it is open in the workspace, choose File > Delete or press <Ctrl> + <Del>.

Deleting an Image Using the Browser

You can delete files while you are using the Paint Shop Pro Browser. Click the Image's thumbnail and choose ImageFile > Delete or right-click the thumbnail and choose Delete from the context menu. When prompted to confirm the deletion, click Yes. If the image is open when you delete it, it remains open in the workspace and is deleted when you close it.

Saving and Loading Workspaces

Paint Shop Pro has a feature that lets you save the settings in your workspace and then reload them later. When you save a workspace, Paint Shop Pro saves information about the images, toolbar and palette locations, and ruler and grid settings.

Saving a Workspace

When you save a workspace, the information is saved in a file with a *.wsp extension. You name and create this file. The following information is stored in a workspace file:

- Open image names, screen locations, zoom levels, and scrollbar locations,

- Ruler, grid, and guide information for each open image,

- Toolbar display settings, locations, and button appearance settings, and

- Palette display settings, locations, and appearance settings.

To save the current workspace:

1. Choose File > Workspace > Save, or press <Shift> + <Alt> + <S>.

2. In the Save Workspace dialog box, navigate to the folder in which you want to save the workspace.

3. In the File name text box, type a name for the workspace. Paint Shop Pro adds the .wsp extension.

4. Click the Save button.

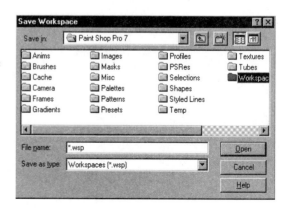

If your workspace contains any newly created images that you have not yet saved, Paint Shop Pro displays the Save As dialog box, where you can assign a name and location for saving the new images. If you press Cancel, the image is not saved as part of the workspace.

If the workspace contains any images that have been modified, Paint Shop Pro saves them before saving the workspace information. If an image cannot be saved in its current format because of the modification, a message appears describing the format limitation. Press the OK button to modify the image and save it in its current format, or press the Cancel button to display the Save As dialog box, where you can change the file format. If you cancel the dialog box rather than saving the altered image, Paint Shop Pro saves the original, unmodified image with the workspace.

NOTE: *The image filename and location rather than the actual file is saved. If you move or delete a file saved with a workspace, it will be missing when you next load the workspace.*

Loading a Saved Workspace

After you save a workspace, you can reload the saved workspace file.

To load a workspace:

1. Choose File > Workspace > Load, or press <Shift> + <Alt> + <L>.

2. In the Open Workspace dialog box, navigate to and select the filename of the workspace you want to load. Workspace files have a *.wsp extension.

3. Click the Open button. Paint Shop Pro displays the workspace images and settings.

If you have moved or deleted any image files from this workspace, the workspace opens without them. If you had two windows open for the same image when you saved the workspace, they both open again. If an image from the workspace is already open, Paint Shop Pro either displays a message or applies the workspace settings to the open image.

If you have used a workspace recently, you can load it by choosing it from the list of recent workspaces, which is located at the bottom of the File > Workspace menu.

Deleting a Saved Workspace

You can delete workspaces you have saved.

To delete a saved workspace:

1. Choose File > Workspace > Delete, or press <Shift> + <Alt> + <D>.

2. In the Delete Workspace dialog box, navigate to and select the filename of the workspace you want to delete. Workspace files have a *.wsp extension.

3. Click the Delete button. Paint Shop Pro deletes the file.

Using the Batch Conversion Utility

If you need to convert several files into a single file format, you can process them as a group using the Batch Conversion utility. Paint Shop Pro makes copies of original files, called source files. It converts the copies, and then saves them in the output folder you select. The original images are not converted.

To make batch conversions:

1. Open the Batch Conversion dialog box by choosing File > Batch Conversion.

2. Use the Look In drop-down box to navigate to the folder containing the source (original) files.

3. From the Output Settings Type drop-down list, select a new file format for the images. If a format has save options, the Options button is accessible. Click it to open the Save Option dialog box. Select the format options and click the OK button to return to the Batch Conversion dialog box.

4. To select the output (destination) folder for the new files, type a path or click the Browse button. When the Browse for Folder navigation box opens, find and click the folder in which you want to save the converted files, and then click the OK button to return to the Batch Conversion dialog box. If you do not select an output folder, Paint Shop Pro saves the converted files in the same folder as the source files.

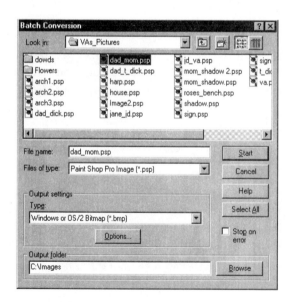

5. To stop the conversion if Paint Shop Pro encounters an error during the process, select the "Stop on error" check box. If you don't select it, the program processes all the images without stopping. The error messages appear in a Batch Conversion Status dialog box.

6. Select the files to convert using one of the following methods:

- To convert specific image files, press <Shift> while selecting contiguous files or <Ctrl> while selecting non-contiguous files.

- To convert files of a specific format, type filename wildcards (using *) in the File Name text box and then select the format from the Files of Type drop-down box. Paint Shop Pro will look for filename wildcards first. If it finds none, it will select files by file type.

- To convert all the files displayed, click the Select All button. Note that clicking the Select All button starts the conversion process.

7. If you did not click the Select All button, click the Start button to start the conversion.

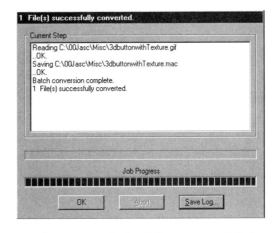

The Batch Conversion Status dialog box opens, and the batch conversion starts. The Current Step pane displays each filename and whether it is converted, while the Job Progress bar indicates the conversion progress. To stop the conversion, click the Abort button.

During the conversion, Paint Shop Pro might open other dialog boxes requesting more information if you have selected Meta, PostScript, Photo-CD, or RAW files.

After the files have been converted, either click the OK button to exit the dialog box, or click the Save Log button to save the progress messages to a text file. Clicking the Save Log button opens the Save As dialog box. Type a name for the file and click Save. Paint Shop Pro saves the information with a *.log file extension.

Working with Color

Most of us remember some time in our life when we worked with mixing colors. It may have been mixing paint, food colors, or something else. We learned that mixing the primary colors of red, yellow, and blue produced other colors. Mixing two colors produced the secondary colors of orange, green, and purple, and mixing three colors produced many intermediate colors in a rainbow of colors. All the colors make up the color wheel.

When colors are put on paper, the colors we see are the result of light being absorbed and reflected by the paint or ink. When colors are displayed on a computer monitor, the colors we see are the result of light being emitted on the screen. Because of this, working with color on a computer is different from painting on canvas or paper. Even the primary colors are different.

This chapter explains the difference between the colors used for display on your monitor and for printing, and it describes color combination methods, pixel color depth, and color selection.

Understanding Color

The Color Wheel

Although shown in black and white, the illustration here shows the color wheel used for computer images.

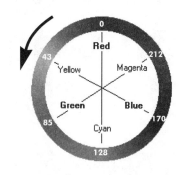

The primary colors (hues) are red, green, and blue. Mixing red and green makes yellow, mixing green and blue produces cyan, and mixing blue and red produces magenta. This color wheel works the same as the other color wheel; that is, mixing two primary colors produces the secondary colors, and mixing three primary colors produces many intermediate colors in a rainbow of colors.

Emitted Light versus Reflected Light

Three main components of color are hue, saturation (also called intensity or chroma), and lightness (also called brightness, luminance, or value). This section describes hues, and later sections describe saturation and lightness. In addition to the hue, saturation and lightness also influence the colors we see.

Hue distinguishes the various colors, such as green and blue. Our eyes interpret color hues based on wavelengths (rays) of light. The light can come from natural sunlight or artificial light, and the length of each ray of light determines the hue we see. Combining all the hues of emitted light produces pure white.

As wavelengths of light hit paper or objects, the result is different. The paper absorbs some of the hues and reflects different hues to our eyes than those we see directly from emitted light. The hues reflected from paper are not as pure and may contain a certain amount of white. Combining all the hues on paper produces grey to black.

The color system resulting from emitted light is called Additive because mixed hues are produced by adding light rays, and all the hues added together produce white. The color system resulting from reflective light on paper is called Subtractive because mixed hues are produced by absorbing (subtracting) light rays, and all the hues subtracted produce white. (Therefore, the opposite is true: the Additive system subtracts hues to produce black; the Subtractive system adds hues to produce black.)

Understanding Color Definition Methods

Paint Shop Pro uses four methods, RGB, HSL, and CMYK for defining colors in your images. It can also convert your RGB colors into their HTML equivalent for use on Web pages. Each of the methods uses a different combination of the three color elements: hues, saturation, and lightness. The RGB, and HSL methods are used to create colored images. The CMYK method is generally used to prepare images for printing.

RGB Method

The RGB (Red/Green/Blue) method, one of the Additive Color methods, is used on computer monitors. It has three primary colors—red, green, and blue—that it creates by emitting light. All the colors on your screen are produced by combining these three colors in various proportions.

To measure the color produced by combining red, green, and blue, each of the three colors is assigned a value from 0 to 255. The value 0 means none of the primary color is present, the value 255 means the color is added "at full strength." For example, pure red is produced by combining a red value of 255, a green value of 0, and a blue value of 0. Yellow is a combination of a red value of 255, a green value of 255, and a blue value of 0. Combining all three primary colors at values of 255 produces white; combining all three at values of 0 produces black.

HSL Method

The HSL (Hue/Saturation/Lightness) method, another Additive Color method, is also used on monitors. Rather than combining primary colors to produce other colors, the HSL method combines hue, saturation, and lightness. This method is based on how we actually perceive color. As with the RGB method, the three HSL components are assigned a value from 0 to 255 when they are combined to produce a color. The components are described below.

Hue, which is the *length* of a light ray, defines the various colors, such as red, yellow, and blue. Each hue is assigned a value based on its position on the color wheel. In the Paint Shop Pro Color wheel, the hues are arranged around the wheel and assigned values in a counter-clockwise direction. At the top is red at 0. Moving counter-clockwise, yellow is at 43, green is at 85, cyan is at 128, blue is at 170, and magenta is at 212.

Saturation is the *quality* of light or level of grey in the color. When the saturation level is low, the color is very grey; when the saturation level is high, the color has little grey and is vivid. The values assigned to the saturation component are 0 to 255; with 0 meaning the color is entirely grey and is desaturated, and 255 meaning the color has no grey and is fully saturated. With a value of 255 (100% saturation), a color is considered pure.

NOTE: *You can desaturate an image by choosing the Grey Scale command in the Colors menu. In Paint Shop Pro, a greyscale image refers to a particular type of image— one that contains 256 levels of grey.*

Lightness is perceived amount or intensity of light in the color. When the light is low, a color is dim; and when the light is bright, a color is bright. The values assigned to the lightness component are 0 to 255; with 0 meaning total darkness or black, and 255 meaning total lightness or white. At 50% lightness (127 on the scale), a color is considered pure. For example, in pure red, the saturation is 255 (100%) and the lightness is 128 (50%); in pure blue, which has a hue of 170, saturation is 255 and lightness is 128.

Notice the lightness for white is 255, and for black is 0. As long as the lightness is 0 or 255, changing the hue or saturation does not change the color. This means that this method belongs to the Additive color system. Also notice that if you change the lightness to any other value, changing the saturation produces a different intensity of color (red in this case), and changing the hue produces an entirely different color.

CMYK Method

The CMYK (Cyan/Magenta/Yellow/Black) method, one of the Subtractive Color methods, is based on light being absorbed and reflected by paint and ink. This method is often used in printing. The primary colors, cyan, magenta, and yellow, are combined in various proportions to produce the other colors. When all three are combined, they produce black. Because impurities in ink make it difficult to produce a true black, a fourth color, black (the K), is added when printing.

Although you cannot create images in Paint Shop Pro using the CMYK method, you can "split" your images into CMYK channels. Splitting the image creates a new greyscale file for each primary color. For more information about splitting images to CMYK channels, please refer to the next section.

You can also set an image to print CMYK separations. This prints a separate page prints for each primary color. For more information about printing CMYK separations, please refer to Chapter 19, "Printing Images and Thumbnails."

HTML Code

The HTML (Hypertext Markup Language) code for referring to color is based on the computer language used to display images on web pages. The HTML conversion in Paint Shop Pro converts the RGB values of a color to six-digit hexadecimal numbers that can be read by web browsers.

The six-digit numbers are actually three sets of two-digit numbers that use a base 16 numbering system. The first two digits in the HTML code represent the red value, the second two represent the green value, and the last two represent the blue value. For example, RGB pure red has a red value of 255, a green value of 0, and a blue value of 0 hexadecimal. In HTML, this is written as FF0000.

Understanding Color Channels

An image file stores its color information in channels, or planes of color. The information contained in the channels depends on the color definition method (RGB, HSL, or CMYK) used for the image. An RGB image has three channels, one for each of the three primary colors; an HSL image has three channels, and a CMYK image has four channels.

To split an active image, choose Colors > Split Channel, and then RGB, HSL, or CMYK. This creates a new image for each color channel; the original image is not affected. Each new image is a greyscale file that is named after its channel. For example, an HSL image is split into three separate greyscale images with the names "Hue," "Saturation," and "Lightness."

You can edit the greyscale images and use them to create interesting effects or masks. After editing the greyscale images, you can combine them again by choosing Colors > Combine Channel, and then RGB, HSL, or CMYK.

NOTE: *Color channels are not the same thing as alpha channels. Color channels are separate image files that you create for each color in an image. Alpha channels are "storage areas" within a file that you use for saving special information, such as selection or mask information. For more information saving selections and masks to alpha channels, please refer to Chapter 10, "Working with Selections" and Chapter 14, "Working with Masks."*

Understanding Color Depth

Color depth, often called bit depth, refers to the number of colors each pixel (and its image) can display. As the bit depth increases, the number of colors an image can display increases. A 1-bit image can display 2 colors, black and white; an 8-bit image can display 256 colors (2 to the 8th); a 16-bit image can display 65,536 colors (2 to the 16th); a 24-bit image can display 16.7 million colors (2 to the 24th). The term greyscale is used to indicate an 8-bit image that contains black, white, and 254 shades of grey. A black and white image of any other bit depth is not a greyscale image.

Some commands in Paint Shop Pro are available only for certain color depths. For example, the Effects commands, many color adjustments, and some painting tools in Paint Shop Pro can only be used with 24-bit and greyscale images. If your image is of a lower color depth, you need to increase the color depth to 24-bits to make the commands available. Then, after you have finished editing it, you can decrease it back to its original depth.

Viewing Color Depth of an Image

The color depth (bit depth) of the image is not the same as the actual number of colors it contains. The color depth tells you the maximum number of colors the image is capable of containing, not how many are actually in it.

To view the color depth of the image choose Image > Image Information. The Current Image Information dialog box opens. In the "Image" panel, look at the Pixel Depth/Colors line. If you are using the painting tools, the Pixel Depth should be at least 8-bit and the colors should be at least 256. Click the OK button to close the box.

Viewing Number of Colors in a Layer

To view the actual number of colors a layer contains, choose Colors > Count Colors Used. In an image with one layer, this displays the total number of colors in the image. If the image contains more than one layer, this displays the number of colors in the current layer.

Viewing Color Depth of a Monitor

If you display a saved image at one color depth on a monitor with a lower color depth, the image is limited to the color depth of the monitor. The additional colors in the image cannot be viewed. This can produce color distortion and degradation of the image's appearance. However, it does not affect the actual image, only how it looks on that monitor. When you view it on a monitor with the appropriate color depth, you can see all the colors.

To view color depth of the monitor choose Help > About Paint Shop Pro. The splash screen appears. Click the System Info button to open the System Information list box. Scroll to the Video Driver Information section, where the color depth is listed.

NOTE: *If you need to adjust your monitor settings, please use the Windows online Help.*

Increasing the Color Depth of an Image

Increasing the color depth of an image increases the number of colors it can display. Images in Paint Shop Pro can display from 2 to 16 million colors.

NOTE: *If you are increasing several images to a specific color depth, you may find it convenient to add the color depth's button to the toolbar. For more information about customizing the toolbar, please refer to Chapter 20, "Setting Preferences."*

Increasing an Image to 16 Colors (4-bit)

To increase the color depth of an image to 16 colors (4-bit):

- Choose Colors > Increase Color Depth > 16 Colors (4 bit), or

- Press <Shift> + <Ctrl> + <8>.

Increasing an Image to 256 Colors (8-bit)

NOTE: *A colored 256 Color (8-bit) image is not the same as a greyscale 256 color (8-bit) image. The steps below apply to colored images only. For more information about greyscale images, please refer to "Creating a Greyscale Image" on page 69.*

To increase the color depth of an image to 256 colors (8-bit):

• Choose Colors > Increase Color Depth > 256 Colors (8 bit), or

• Press <Shift> + <Ctrl> + <9>.

Increasing an Image to 16 Million Colors (24-bit)

Many of the Paint Shop Pro commands are not available unless an image is a 24-bit image (can display 16 million colors). Therefore, you may need to increase the color depth of some images before you can apply some of the commands. After you increase the color depth, the previously unavailable commands are made available. For example, an image's color depth must be 24-bit in order to apply the Effects > Artistic Effects commands.

Because all colors are available in a 24-bit image, increasing the color depth to 24-bit automatically loads either the Jasc or Windows Color dialog box to the image, depending on your preference settings. Before you increase the color depth of an image that has its own palette, you may want to save the palette. For example, if you are adding an effect or editing an image with a specific palette and need to keep those exact colors, save the palette before increasing the color depth. After editing the image, reload the image's original palette. For more information about image palettes, please refer to "Working with Image Palettes" on page 69.

To increase the color depth of an image to 16 million colors (24-bit):

• Choose Colors > Increase Color Depth > 16 Million Colors (24 bit), or

• Press <Shift> + <Ctrl> + <0>.

Decreasing the Color Depth of an Image

Decreasing the color depth of an image decreases the number of colors it can display. This makes several features and commands unavailable. For example, images other than greyscale and 24-bit color cannot contain multiple raster layers or adjustment layers.

Although images of any color depth can contain multiple vector layers, when you decrease an image's color depth, you must first merge (flatten) all the layers. If you do not, Paint Shop Pro displays a message asking to flatten the image. After you decrease the color depth, you can add the vector layers again or add new vector layers. However, each time you decrease the color depth, you must first flatten the image.

When you decrease an image's color depth, a dialog box appears asking you to choose a reduction method and a palette generation option. These methods, which determine how Paint Shop Pro compensates for missing colors, are described next.

Choosing a Color Reduction Method

The final color depth of the image determines which color reduction methods are available. When you decrease an image to 8, 24, or X-bits per pixel, you can choose either the Nearest Color or Error Diffusion method. When decreasing colors to 1 or 2-bits per pixel, you can also choose the Ordered Dither method.

Nearest Color Method   Use this method to eliminate dithering and produce a high contrast image. Paint Shop Pro replaces the original color of a pixel with the color in the newly generated palette that is closest to its RGB value.

Error Diffusion Method   With this method, Paint Shop Pro replaces the original color of a pixel with the most similar color in the palette, but it spreads discrepancy between the original and new color to the surrounding pixels. After it replaces a color, it adds the "error," or discrepancy to the next pixel, before selecting the most similar color. This process is repeated for every pixel in the image.

Ordered Dither Method   Use this method to give the image the appearance of containing more colors than it contains. Paint Shop Pro adjusts adjacent pixels so that two colors give the illusion of a third color, and it intermingles pixels to produce patterns based on a known palette. Images may appear to be composed of cross-hatches and dots, and may have distinct patterns of light and dark areas.

Choosing a Color Palette Generation Option

Because images that have bit depths lower than 24-bits have color palettes, these images are referred to as "paletted images." An image's color palette contains the colors it can display. A 24-bit image is not restricted to a palette because it can display every color in the spectrum.

You can edit an image palette and save it as a file that you can use with other images. You can also decrease the color depth of an active image by loading a saved palette. For more information about using image palettes, please refer to "Working with Image Palettes" on page 69.

When you decrease the color depth to create a paletted image, Paint Shop Pro generates a new palette based on options you choose. Two options, Optimized Median Cut and Optimized Octree, use different methods to create a custom palette for your image. The Windows option creates a standard windows 16-color palette. The Standard/Web-safe option produce images that display correctly in Web browsers.

Optimized Median Cut Method This method is accurate only to 5 bits per channel. Even if your image contains fewer colors than the palette that is generated, this method may not represent each color exactly. It measures each color by frequency in the image and ranks it accordingly. It uses the Heckbert median cut algorithm.

Optimized Octree Method This method is accurate to 8-bits per channel, but it is not as good at weighting color importance as the previous method. If your image contains fewer colors than the palette that is generated, every color in the image is represented. Paint Shop Pro generates this palette more quickly than the Optimized Median Cut palette.

Standard/Web-safe Palette Use this method to create images for the Web that can be viewed without color distortion on most monitors. The palette is a generic palette that contains a balanced number of colors.

Decreasing an Image to 2 Colors

Paint Shop Pro always uses black and white when decreasing an image to two colors.

To decrease an image to 2 colors (1-bit):

1. Choose Colors > Decrease Color Depth > 2 Colors (1-bit), or press <Shift> + <Ctrl> + <1> to open the Decrease Color Depth - 2 Colors dialog box.

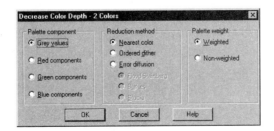

2. In the "Palette Component" panel, choose the color channel to use for the final image. Choose the Red, Green, or Blue option to use those channels. Choose the Grey values option to use the lightness values of the image. This produces the best results in most cases. However, if an image consists mostly of a single color, selecting that color may produce the best result.

3. In the "Reduction Method" panel, select a color reduction method. For descriptions, please refer to "Choosing a Color Reduction Method" on page 64.

   NOTE: *With the Error Diffusion method, you must also select the Floyd-Steinberg, Burkes, or Stucki option. These are three algorithms used to determine the dithering pattern. For descriptions, click the Help button.*

4. In the "Palette weight" panel, choose whether to use a weighted palette. Weighting the palette sets the image's current colors closer to black and white before decreasing them. This results in less dithering, which produces sharper edges. A non-weighted palette produces more dithering and softer edges.

5. Click the OK button to close the dialog box and decrease the colors in the image.

Decreasing an Image to 16 Colors

NOTE: *To use the "Boost marked colors by" option, make a selection of an area that contains the colors you want to emphasize before performing these steps.*

To decrease an image to 16 colors (4-bit):

1. Choose Colors > Decrease Color Depth > 16 Colors (4-bit), or press <Shift> + <Ctrl> + <2> to open the Decrease Color Depth - 16 Colors dialog box.

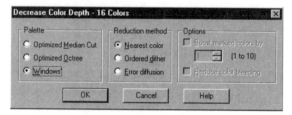

2. In the "Palette" panel, select a palette option. For descriptions, please refer to "Choosing a Color Palette Generation Option" on page 65.

3. In the "Reduction Method" panel, choose a color reduction method. For descriptions, please refer to "Choosing a Color Reduction Method" on page 64.

   NOTE: *The Ordered dither option is available only for the Windows palette.*

4. In the "Options" panel, select the "Boost marked colors by" check box and enter a value to emphasize the importance of specific colors. (An area containing the colors must already be selected.) This option makes the colors "more important" by a factor of the value you enter. The selected colors will stand out from the rest of the image.

5. If you chose the Optimized Median Cut or the Optimized Octree palette and then the Error Diffusion reduction method, you may want to select the "Reduce color bleeding" check box in the "Options" panel. This makes the left-to-right "bleed effect" of colors less noticeable.

6. Click the OK button to close the dialog box and decrease the colors in the image.

Decreasing an Image to 256 Colors

NOTE: *To use the "Boost marked colors by" option, make a selection of an area that contains the colors you want to emphasize before performing these steps.*

To decrease the color depth of an image to 256 (8-bit):

1. Choose Colors > Decrease Color Depth > 256 Colors (8-bit), or press <Shift> + <Ctrl> + <3>to open the Decrease Color Depth - 256 Colors dialog box.

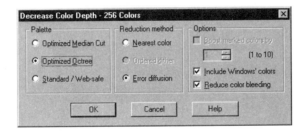

2. In the "Palette" panel, select a palette option. For descriptions, please refer to "Choosing a Color Palette Generation Option" on page 65.

3. In the "Reduction Method" panel, choose a color reduction method. For descriptions, please refer to "Choosing a Color Reduction Method" on page 64.

   NOTE: *The Ordered dither option is available only if you have chosen to use the Standard/Web-safe palette.*

4. In the "Options" panel, select the "Boost marked colors by" check box and enter a value to emphasize the importance of specific colors. (An area containing the colors must already be selected.) This option makes the colors "more important" by a factor of the value you enter. The selected colors will stand out from the rest of the image.

5. If you chose the Optimized Median Cut or the Optimized Octree palette, select the "Include Windows colors" check box if you want the 16 standard Windows colors to be included in the palette.

6. If you selected the Error Diffusion option for color reduction, you may want to select the "Reduce color bleeding" check box in the "Options" panel. This makes the left-to-right "bleed effect" of colors less noticeable.

7. Click the OK button to close the dialog box and decrease the colors in the image.

Decreasing an Image to 32K or 64K Colors

Paint Shop Pro treats a 32K or 64K color image as a 24-bit color image. This means that any operation performed after the conversion may result in an image that is no longer 32K or 64K colors.

NOTE: *The steps are combined for decreasing to 32K and 64K colors because the Decrease Color Depth dialog boxes are identical.*

To decrease the color depth of an image to 32K or 64K (24-bit depth):

1. Choose Colors > Decrease Color Depth, and then either 32K Colors or 64K Colors (24-bit), or press <Shift> + <Ctrl> + <4> to decrease to 32K colors, or press <Shift> + <Ctrl> + <5> to decrease to 64K colors. The Decrease Color Depth dialog box opens.

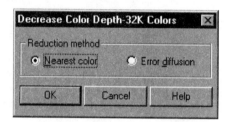

2. Select either the Nearest color or Error diffusion option. For descriptions, please refer to "Choosing a Color Reduction Method" on page 64.

3. Click the OK button to close the dialog box and decrease the colors in the image.

Decreasing an Image to X (2-256) Colors

NOTE: *To use the "Boost marked colors by" option, make a selection of an area that contains the colors you want to emphasize before performing these steps.*

To decrease the color depth of an image to any value between 2 and 256:

1. Choose Colors > Decrease Color Depth > X Colors (4/8-bit), or press <Shift> + <Ctrl> + <6>. The Decrease Color Depth - X Colors dialog box opens.

2. In the "Palette" panel, enter the number of colors for the new palette. You can choose any number from 2 to 256.

3. Choose whether to load the Optimized Median Cut or the Standard/Web-safe palette. For descriptions, please refer to "Choosing a Color Palette Generation Option" on page 65.

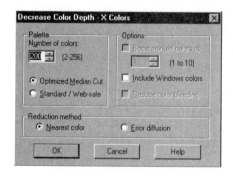

4. In the "Reduction Method" panel, select either Nearest Color or Error Diffusion. For descriptions, please refer to "Choosing a Color Reduction Method" on page 64.

5. In the "Options" panel, select the "Boost marked colors by" check box and enter a value to emphasize the importance of specific colors. (An area containing the colors must already be selected.) This option makes the colors "more important" by a factor of the value you enter. The selected colors will stand out from the rest of the image.

6. To include the standard Windows colors in the palette, select the "Include Windows colors" check box.

7. If you selected the Error Diffusion option for color reduction, you may want to select the "Reduce color bleeding" check box in the "Options" panel. This makes the left-to-right "bleed effect" of colors less noticeable.

8. Click the OK button to close the dialog box and decrease the colors in the image.

Creating a Greyscale Image

A greyscale image is an 8-bit image with a palette containing white, black, and 254 shades of grey. Because it can contain only 256 shades, converting an image with a higher color depth into a greyscale image automatically decreases it to an 8-bit image.

The Greyscale command removes the colors from an image and replaces each color with a grey matching its luminance value. The effect is similar to a black-and-white photograph.

To convert an image to greyscale choose Colors > Greyscale.

Working with Image Palettes

An image palette is a collection of the colors in an image with 16 to 256 colors, and it is similar to a painter's palette of paints. It displays the colors for painting and drawing in the image. You can edit this palette, save it in a file separate from the image, and load it into other images.

To view the palette of an image containing fewer than 256 colors, click the Recent Background or Foreground Colors boxes on the Color palette; if you have a solid color set in one of the Styles boxes, you can click that Style box.

NOTE: *For more information about the Recent Colors or Styles boxes, please refer to Chapter 9, "Using the Color Palette."*

Paint Shop Pro contains several preset image palettes, which are located in the Palettes folder of the Paint Shop Pro 7 program folder. If you create and save palettes, you'll probably find it convenient to save them in the same folder.

Editing an Image Palette

NOTE: *While you can change any color in the palette, you cannot increase the number of colors.*

To edit an image palette:

1. Choose Colors > Edit Palette, or press <Shift> + <P> to open the Edit Palette dialog box.

2. In the Sort Order drop-down box, select a method for sorting the colors. Use whichever one you find most convenient; sorting the palette merely changes the arrangement of the colors:

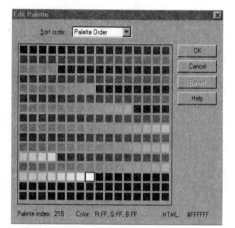

   - Palette Order, which arranges the colors in rows by palette numbers, from 0 on the left of the top row to 255 on the right of the bottom,

   - By Luminance, which arranges the colors by their level of lightness. Lighter colors are at the top; darker colors are at the bottom, or

   - By Hue, which arranges the colors according to their location on the color wheel.

3. To replace a color, double-click it. The Color dialog box opens. Make your selection, and then click the OK to button return to the Edit Palette dialog box.

4. To return the palette to its original colors without closing the dialog box, click the Revert button.

5. To save the edited palette and close the dialog box, click the OK button.

Saving an Image Palette

To save an image palette:

1. Choose Colors > Save Palette to open the Save Palette As dialog box.

2. Navigate to the folder where you want to save the palette. You'll probably find it most convenient to save it in the Palettes folder of the Paint Shop Pro program folder. This folder contains the palettes that are loaded when you install the program.

3. Type a name for the palette in the File Name text box. Paint Shop Pro automatically adds the file extension to the saved file.

4. Select a palette format from the File Type box. The default is the Jasc format. To use the palette with an application other than Paint Shop Pro, save it in the Microsoft format.

5. Click the Save button to close the dialog box and save the palette.

Loading an Image Palette

You can load palettes into images with 16 or more colors. When necessary, the color depth of the image decreases to match the palette.

To load a palette to an image:

1. Choose Colors > Load Palette or press <Shift> + <O> to open the Load Palette dialog box.

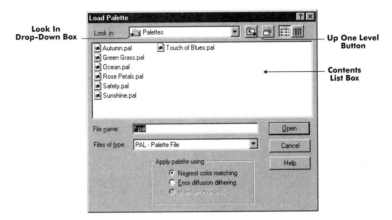

2. Navigate to and open the folder where you saved the palette.

3. Highlight the palette.

4. In the "Apply palette using" panel, choose one of the three methods for loading the palette:

- Nearest Color Matching - Changes each color in the image to the color in the palette that is the closest match.

- Error Diffusion Dithering - Attempts to maintain the image's appearance by dithering colors that are not in the palette.

- Maintain Indexes - Assigns each color in the palette a sequential index number, does the same for the colors in the image, and then changes each color in the image to the like-numbered color in the palette.

5. Click the Open button to load the palette.

Using the Jasc Safety Palette

An easy way to convert an image to a Web-safe palette is to load the Jasc Safety palette. Choose Colors > Load Palette. In the Load Palette dialog box, open the Safety.pal file. Paint Shop Pro automatically decreases the image to an 8-bit depth.

Making a Color Transparent

Paint Shop Pro lets you assign a transparent value to one color in an image's palette. This can be the background color or any color from the image. This is useful when working with certain file formats, such as .gif and .png. To set a transparent color, your image must be single-layered and paletted (that is, the image must have a color depth of less than 24 bits). If it isn't, a message appears asking you to decrease the color depth and / or merge the layers of the image. If you need to, please refer to "Decreasing the Color Depth of an Image" on page 64. Note that the transparent color remains visible in your image until you hide the it by choosing the View Palette Transparency command, as described below.

NOTE: *Paint Shop Pro also has a transparent .gif optimizer that makes it easy to create transparent .gif files. Please refer to Chapter 18, "Using the Web Features."*

Setting a Transparent Color

To set a transparent color:

1. Choose Colors > Set Palette Transparency or press <Shift> + <Ctrl> + <V>. The Set Palette Transparency dialog box opens.

2. Select the appropriate option:

   • To undo the transparency of a color, select "No Transparency."

   • To assign the background color, select "Set the transparency value to the current background color."

   • To assign a color by palette number, enter the number in the palette entry box. The color appears in the color box.

   • To select a color from the image, move the cursor over the image. It becomes the Dropper tool. Click the image to select a color. The third option is chosen, the palette entry box fills in, and the color box displays the color.

3. To temporarily view the transparency, click the Proof button.

4. Click the OK button to close the dialog box and make the selected color transparent.

Displaying or Hiding a Transparent Color

To display or hide a transparent color:

• Choose Colors > View Palette Transparency, or

• Press <Shift> + <V>.

Selecting Active Colors

The colors you use while painting and drawing are called the active colors. An image has two active colors—the foreground and background colors.

When you paint or draw in an image, you select a tool from the Tool palette, set the tool options on the Tool Options palette, and choose your foreground and background styles and textures on the Color palette. The available styles are solid colors, gradient, pattern, or no style. When you set a style to solid colors, you then select a color for the foreground / stroke or the background / fill.

The active colors are displayed in the Styles boxes on the "Active Styles" panel of the Color palette. The upper box contains the foreground / stroke color. The lower box contains the background / fill color. You can reverse the position of these two colors by clicking the color switcher (the double-headed arrow connecting the two colors).

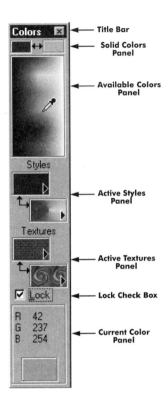

NOTE: *This section introduces the features for selecting active colors. For details about using these features, please refer to the "Setting the Styles" and "Using the Solid Color Style" sections in Chapter 9, "Using the Color Palette."*

You can select active solid colors from:

- The "Solid Colors" panel of the Color palette,

- The "Available Colors" panel of the Color palette,

- The Jasc or Windows Color dialog box,

- The Select Color From Palette dialog box,

- The Recent Colors dialog box, and

- The image (using the Dropper tool).

NOTE: *For details about using these features, please refer to the "Setting the Styles" and "Using the Solid Color Style" sections in Chapter 9, "Using the Color Palette."*

COLOR DIALOG BOX If the active image has a color depth of 24-bits, when you left-click inside any Color box in Paint Shop Pro, the Color dialog box appears. The Color dialog box displays either the Jasc color palette (color picker) or the Windows color palette (color picker), depending on your preference settings. The Jasc color palette is shown below.

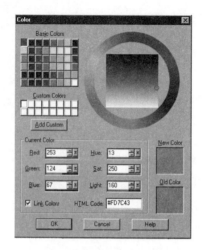

SELECT COLOR FROM PALETTE DIALOG BOX If your active image has a color depth lower than 24-bits (is paletted), when you left-click inside any Color box in Paint Shop Pro, the Select Color From Palette dialog box appears. The Select Color From Palette Dialog Box is similar to the Edit Palette dialog box shown on page 70.

RECENT COLORS DIALOG BOX When you right-click inside any Color box, the Recent Colors dialog box appears. If the color depth of an image is lower than 24-bits, some colors may be unavailable and are signified by a circle with a line through it.

Improving Photographs

When you import photographs, frames from videos, and other images into Paint Shop Pro, they may contain defects, such as odd colors, bad lighting, scratches, or people with red eyes. Paint Shop Pro has many automatic photo enhancement features that help you correct these defects. The program also has tools for making manual corrections and adding effects to create artistic looking images. No matter what your final goal is, your first step should be to clean up and improve your images so you are working with clear, detailed, well-adjusted images.

This chapter describes the photo enhancement features. The first section describes why and when you should use the features. The remaining sections explain how to use specific features. To make manual color corrections, please refer to Chapter 7, "Making Color Adjustments" and Chapter 16, "Using Adjustment Layers." To add artistic effects, please refer to Chapter 17, "Adding Effects." In addition, reading Chapter 5, "Working with Color," will help you understand the color components you will be adjusting.

Understanding the Photo Enhancement Features

This section will help you understand the photo enhancement features and when to use them. Read through this section to determine which features you can use to correct your images.

NOTE: *Before using the enhancement features, you may want to use the* Monitor Gamma *command on the* Preferences *menu to adjust your computer monitor. For details, please refer to "Adjusting Your Monitor Gamma" on page 81.*

The photo enhancement commands are on the Effects menu. They include all the commands on the Blur, Sharpen, Edge, and Noise menus, and all the commands on the Enhance Photo menu, shown below. The photo enhancement features can be categorized and used as follows:

- **Features for making general adjustments to all images:** These features correct colors, contrast, and saturation. Use them first to make initial corrections to your images. They include: Automatic Color Balance, Manual Color Correction, Fade Correction, Automatic Contrast Enhancement, Histogram Adjustment (which is on the Colors menu not the Effects menu), and Automatic Saturation Enhancement.

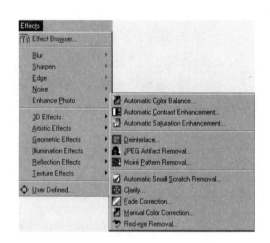

- **Features for correcting defects caused by the image source (video, scanner, etc.):** Use these features after you have made the general adjustments. They include: Deinterlace, JPEG Artifact Removal, and Moiré Pattern Removal.

- **Features for correcting image defects:**
  Use these features after you have made general adjustments and corrected source defects. They include: Automatic Small Scratch Removal, Red-eye Removal, Noise, and Blur. These features also include the Scratch Remover and Retouch tools on the Tool palette.

- **Features for making overall, final adjustments for clarity:** Use these features last. They include: Clarify, Sharpen, and Edge.

NOTE: *This section provides suggestions, you may want to experiment with all the features to see what other methods work for your images.*

Understanding the General Adjustment Features

Deciding What to Adjust

The general adjustments to color balance, contrast, and saturation are the first adjustments you should make to all your images.

NOTE: *If you refer to Chapter 5, "Working with Color," you will see that these adjustments are actually adjustments to the basic components of color: hue, saturation, and lightness (HSL). Adjusting color changes the hue component, adjusting contrast changes the lightness component, and adjusting saturation changes the saturation component, though the filters do not actually operate in the HSL color space.*

Use the following guidelines for making the general adjustments:

- Use the Histogram to determine which adjustments to make. For details, refer to "Using the Histogram" on page 81.

- For greyscale images, adjust only the contrast, since there is no color.

- For colored images, if you need to make all three adjustments, adjust the color balance first and then the contrast. An exception is when an image is extremely dark or light and the color information is not clearly visible. In this case, first adjust the contrast, then make the color adjustments, and then perhaps adjust the contrast again. In either case, after adjusting the color balance and / or contrast, adjust the saturation.

Adjusting the Color Balance

Paint Shop Pro contains several features you can use to adjust color balance. When you adjust color balance, you remove any evident color imbalance to achieve a realistic looking image. For example, grasses should be natural and not too yellow or blue; a clear, cloudless sky should be blue rather than green or purple. To adjust the color balance, use the Automatic Color Balance feature. If you want finer control or have an exceptionally difficult image to adjust, you may prefer using the Manual Color Correction feature. If you have faded photographs or are in a hurry to make corrections, use the Fade Correction feature.

Please refer to the following sections:

- "Using Automatic Color Balance" on page 84.

- "Using Manual Color Correction" on page 85.

- "Using Fade Correction" on page 88.

NOTE: *Other features available for adjusting colors are located on the* Colors > Adjust *menu. These features include* Channel Mixer, Color Balance, Red/Green/Blue, and Hue/Saturation/Lightness. *The* Channel Mixer, Color Balance, and Hue/Saturation/ Lightness *features can alternatively be added as adjustment layers using the* Layers > New Adjustment Layer *menu. For more information, please refer to Chapter 7, "Making Color Adjustments" and Chapter 16, "Using Adjustment Layers."*

Adjusting the Contrast

When you adjust contrast, you correct the overall impression of an image's brightness. The darkest and lightest areas should have a proper brightness, and details in both areas should be clearly visible. Also, they should be properly balanced with respect to the intermediate brightness areas (the midtones). To adjust the contrast, use the Automatic Contrast Enhancement feature. For more control and flexibility, use the Histogram Adjustment features (on the Colors menu). This feature can also be used for special effects.

Please refer to the following sections:

- "Using Automatic Contrast Enhancement" on page 89.
- "Equalizing the Histogram" on page 90
- "Stretching the Histogram" on page 91
- "Adjusting the Histogram" on page 91.

NOTE: *Other features available in Paint Shop Pro for adjusting contrast are located on the Colors > Adjust menu. These features include Brightness/Contrast, Highlight/Midtone/ Shadow, Levels, Gamma Correction, and Curves. The Brightness/Contrast, Levels, and Curves features can alternatively be added as adjustment layers using the Layers > New Adjustment Layer menu. For more information, please refer to Chapter 7, "Making Color Adjustments" and Chapter 16, "Using Adjustment Layers."*

Adjusting the Saturation

When you adjust saturation, you optimize the vividness of the colors in your image. An image should be colorful, but not gaudy or unnatural. To adjust the saturation, use the Automatic Saturation Enhancement feature.

Please refer to the following section:

- "Using Automatic Saturation Enhancement" on page 94.

NOTE: *Another feature available in Paint Shop Pro for adjusting saturation is Hue/ Saturation/Luminance, located on the Colors > Adjust menu. This feature can alternatively be added as an adjustment layer using the Layers > New Adjustment Layer menu. For more information, please refer to Chapter 7, "Making Color Adjustments" and Chapter 16, "Using Adjustment Layers."*

Understanding the Image Source Correction Features

After making the general adjustments, look for and correct any image source defects that are visible. Image source defects are caused by the method used to capture photographs and images.

- Images captured from video may show visible scan lines. Use the Deinterlace feature to correct these defects. Please refer to "Using Deinterlace for Video Images" on page 95.

- Images that have undergone heavy JPEG compression may have visible "artifact" defects, such as blockiness. Use the JPEG Artifact Removal feature to correct these defects. Please refer to "Using JPEG Artifact Removal" on page 96.

- Images scanned from printed copy may show a moiré pattern or color banding. Use the Moiré Pattern Removal feature to correct these defects. Please refer to "Using Moiré Pattern Removal for Scanned Images" on page 97.

Understanding the Defect Correction Features

After making general adjustments and image source corrections, look for and correct image-specific defects, such as "noise," dust, scratches, or flash effects. The first defect to look for and correct is "noise." After that, correct larger defects, such as scratches and red-eye.

Correcting "Noise"

"Noise" occurs when an image has very small defects that are scattered everywhere in the image. Noise is easiest to see in smooth areas of an image, such as a wall or the sky. If noise is present, you may see a grainy appearance, a local variation in color, a random dot-like effect, or even a dithered look.

Because many noise correction techniques treat all of an image's pixels the same way whether they are noise or image details, correcting noise is a compromise between noise reduction and loss of image detail. The best feature to use depends on the image's content and your personal taste. To correct noise defects, first try the Edge-Preserving Smoothing and Texture-Preserving Smoothing features on the Noise menu. These features attempt to distinguish noise from image detail and correct only the noise. Other commands you can use include the following: for grainy-looking noise, use the Blur features: Soften, Soften More, Average, Blur, Blur More, and Gaussian Blur; for dot-like noise, use the Noise features: Despeckle, Median Cut, Median, and Salt And Pepper Filter. You can also use the Retouch tool on the Tool palette to correct certain defects.

Please refer to the following sections:

- "Using the Noise Features" on page 98.
- "Using the Blur Features" on page 101.
- "Using the Retouch Tool" on page 104.

Correcting Scratches and Small Defects

For images that contain large defects caused by scratches and tears, use the Scratch Remover tool on the Tool palette. You can also use this tool to remove unwanted objects from an image. For images that contain small line-like scratches a few pixels wide, use the Automatic Small Scratch Removal feature. If the small defects are light, roughly circular dots of a few pixels on a dark background, and/or similar dark dots on a light background, try using the Salt And Pepper Filter feature in the Noise menu. The Median and Despeckle filters can also be effective on this type of defect. In addition, you can use the Retouch tool on the Tool palette to correct specific defects.

Please refer to the following sections:

- "Using the Noise Features" on page 98.
- "Using the Scratch Remover Tool" on page 103.
- "Using Automatic Small Scratch Removal" on page 105.
- "Using the Retouch Tool" on page 104.

Correcting Red Eyes

When you use a flash while taking photographs, the eyes of people and animals in the picture may have a "red-eye" defect (though often animal eyes are not actually red). To remove this defect, use the Red-eye Removal feature.

Please refer to the following section:

- "Using Red-Eye Removal" on page 106.

Understanding the Final Adjustment Features

The last step in photo correction is enhancing an image to give it a crisp, detailed look. When sharpening an image, a level of sharpening that is good for one area of the image can lead to defects in another. For this reason, first use the Clarify feature, which reveals image detail in a more subtle way and is less prone to creating new defects. Instead, you can sharpen the image using the Sharpen, Sharpen More, and Unsharp Mask features in the Sharpen submenu or the Edge Enhance and Edge Enhance More features in the Edge submenu to make final adjustments. These features make the edges of objects in the image more pronounced.

Please refer to the following sections:

- "Using Clarify" on page 110.
- "Using the Sharpen Features" on page 110.
- "Using the Edge Features" on page 112

Adjusting Your Monitor Gamma

Monitor gamma is a preference setting that lets you adjust the colors displayed by your monitor. If you are producing images for printing, adjust the monitor gamma or enable color management (Windows 98 users) before correcting the images. This ensures that the on-screen and printed images match as closely as possible, and that the colors are consistent from image to image. If you are producing images for the Web, do not adjust the monitor gamma or enable color management. Because most computer users don't adjust their monitor gamma, the color correction resulting from your adjusted monitor will appear distorted on their unadjusted ones. For help with color management or monitor gamma adjustment, please refer to Chapter 20, "Setting Preferences."

NOTE: *Monitor Gamma is NOT the same as the* Colors > Adjust > Gamma Correction *command. The former adjusts the monitor; the latter adjusts the contrast of an image. For information about gamma correction in an image, please refer to Chapter 7, "Making Color Adjustments."*

Using the Histogram

The Histogram displays a graph of the distribution of red, green, blue, greyscale, hue, saturation, and lightness values in an image. Use the Histogram to analyze photographs and images before making adjustments to them.

NOTE: *Paint Shop Pro may operate slowly with the Histogram window open because it uses system resources to update as you change the image.*

Using the Histogram to Analyze an Image

To analyze an image using the Histogram, display the Histogram window.

Use any of the following methods to display or hide the Histogram window:

- Click the Toggle Histogram Window button (⬚) on the tool bar,
- Choose View > ToolBars and select or clear the "Histogram Window" check box,
- Right-click any palette and choose Toolbars from the menu, and then select or clear the "Histogram Window" check box,
- Right-click any palette and choose Histogram Window from the menu, or
- Press <H>.

The Histogram displays selected information about the color components in your open image. Use the check boxes below the graph to select the components to include. The graph displays a line for each selected item. The right side of the Histogram window shows statistics about a single point or a selected range within a color channel. Select a color channel from the Display Channel box, and then click or drag your mouse over the graph to select a specific point or a range. The statistics change as you make a selection.

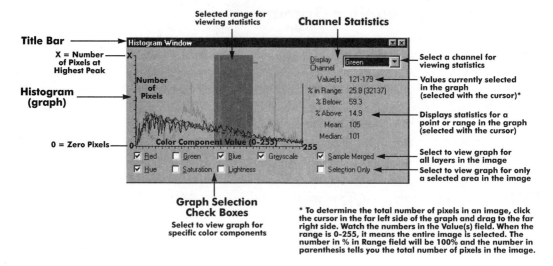

The graph's horizontal axis indicates color component values from 0 to 255 as follows:

- Greyscale values are the levels of grey; 0 is black and 255 is white. You can think of these as representing the brightness or luminosity of an image. The distribution of grey values determines the contrast of an image and this is the easiest type of histogram to understand.

- Colors in a color image are formed by the combination of Red, Green and Blue channels. A channel value of 0 indicates the color is not present and 255 indicates it is at full strength. You can think of this as adding from 0 to 255 drops of each of the colors red, green and blue at any given pixel.

- Colors can be represented as hue, saturation and lightness instead of as channels. Hue is the actual color and is the number assigned to a specific hue on the color wheel; for example Red is 0, Yellow is 43, Green is 85, Cyan is 128, Blue is 170, and Magenta is 212. Saturation is the level of grey added to the hue; 0 is very grey and unsaturated, and 255 is very little grey and saturated. Lightness is the brightness of the hue; 0 is black, 127 is a mid grey, and 255 is white. Lightness has information similar to that in the greyscale.

To learn more about color components and the meaning of their values (0 to 255), please refer to Chapter 5, "Working with Color."

The vertical axis indicates the number of pixels at each 0 to 255 value as follows:

The vertical axis values range from 0 to X, with X representing the number of pixels in the highest peak in the graph. The value of X depends on the size of the image and on the quantity or quantities being displayed. Its exact value is not important. What is important is the relative amount of low values to high values. For example, if an image contained a dark box surrounded by a narrow light border, the greyscale histogram would show a large peak in the range 0 to about 127 and a small peak in the range 128 to 255. If the border were made larger and the box smaller, the light peak would grow at the expense of the dark. If the image were darkened, the dark peak would then grow at the expense of the light peak. The shape of the greyscale histogram depends, therefore, both on the image content and on the image contrast. Similarly, an image with a histogram that displays a big saturation peak on the left side is unsaturated, but the image is strongly saturated if the peak of the histogram is on the right side. Whether this is appropriate depends on the image content--for instance, pale desaturated skin versus a bright red fire engine. You can use your understanding of the image content along with the shape and statistics of the histogram to decide how best to adjust the image.

Examine the graph to determine whether your image has enough detail to be corrected successfully, and, if it does, where it needs correcting. If your image contains more than one layer, the graph displays information on the current (active) layer. To view the information of all layers combined, select the "Sample Merged" check box. To limit the information displayed to a selection, select the "Selection Only" check box.

Use the following guidelines for understanding the histogram:

- If a line spikes, there are many pixels at that level.
- If a line is close to the horizontal axis, there are few pixels at that level.
- If the graph is spread out, the image has a balanced composition and probably has enough detail to be corrected.
- If the lines are compressed into a narrow area, the image probably doesn't contain enough detail; you should try a new scan or find another picture.
- If the greyscale graph is mostly at the left side, the image is too dark; you may need to increase the image's lightness.
- If the greyscale graph is mostly at the right side, the image is too light; you may need to decrease the image's lightness.
- If the greyscale lines are not spread out enough, you may need to stretch the histogram or increase the contrast.

Improving the Colors

Use the Automatic Color Balance, Manual Color Correction, and Fade Correction features to improve the colors in your image. This section describes these features.

Using Automatic Color Balance

Different types of lighting, photographic equipment, and photo processing can cause incorrect coloring in images. Use the Automatic Color Balance feature to correct the coloring, remove any color cast, and create natural-looking colors in your image.

NOTE: *Please notice the following before you begin this adjustment:*

- *This feature works on 24-bit and greyscale images. If necessary, increase the color depth of your image to use this feature. For more information, please refer to Chapter 5, "Working with Color."*

- *This adjustment works best for correcting images with several colors rather than images with variations of one color.*

- *To limit the adjustment to a specific selection area, make the selection before beginning the adjustment.*

To use Automatic Color Balance:

1. Choose Effects > Enhance Photo > Automatic Color Balance to open the Automatic Color Balance dialog box. Notice the following about this dialog box:

   - The Jasc dialog box standard preview area appears at the top. For details, please refer to the *Getting Started Guide*.

   - Because dialog box options retain their last settings, you may want to click the Reset (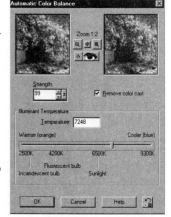) button to set all the options to their default values.

2. In the Strength box, use the numeric edit controls to set the amount of correction for your image. The best approach is to start with 30, and then adjust the control until the image looks the most natural.

3. If the image has an overall color cast (a particular color added to all the colors in the image), select the "Remove C.olor Cast" check box. This drastic step may result in some loss of image information

4. In the "Illuminance Temperature" panel, type a number in the Temperature box or click and drag the slider to adjust the lighting temperature for the image. The default setting is 6500K color temperature, which assumes the image was taken in typical daylight. Indoor lighting requires a lower temperature and sky light a higher one.

5. Click the OK button close the dialog box and apply the adjustments.

Using Manual Color Correction

Use the Manual Color Correction feature to make color changes to an image or to create a variety of unusual effects. This feature adjusts colors based on the hue, saturation and lightness (though it does not use the HSL color space). The feature lets you automatically shift the hues in an image by defining a source hue to shift from, and then selecting a target hue to shift to. In your image, all the pixels containing the source hue are shifted to the target hue. Based on this initial shift, all the remaining hues in the image also shift to appropriate hues. Please notice the following before you begin this adjustment:

- *This feature works on 24-bit colored images. If necessary, increase the color depth of your image to use this feature. For more information, please refer to Chapter 5, "Working with Color."*
- *Refer to Chapter 5, "Working with Color," for a description of the HSL color definition method.*
- *This adjustment is useful when it is particularly important to get some color, such as a skin tone or a corporate logo, exactly right. It is also effective for images with grossly incorrect colors.*
- *To limit the adjustment to a specific selection area, make the selection before beginning the adjustment.*

To use Manual Color Correction:

1. Choose Effects > Enhance Photo > Manual Color Correction to open the Manual Color Correction dialog box. Notice the preview area is slightly different from the Jasc standard preview area. Use the left preview box to make a color selection and the right preview box and the control buttons to adjust the previews.

2. Use the preview box on the left side to define the source color to shift from. Make a selection of the area that includes the source color(s). Click to select one pixel, drag to select a rectangular area, or select the "Freehand Selection" check box and then drag to outline an irregularly shaped area. To change your selection, click the Clear Selection button or click somewhere else in the preview box.

NOTE: *If you left-click to select one pixel, you may want to zoom in to be sure you select the correct color. If you are making a selection, generally, you do not have to be very accurate with your selection area, as long as it is mostly one color. The colors of the pixels in the selection are averaged to determine the source color to shift from. This "averaged color" then becomes the initial, source color that is shifted (adjusted) and all the other colors in the image are shifted accordingly.*

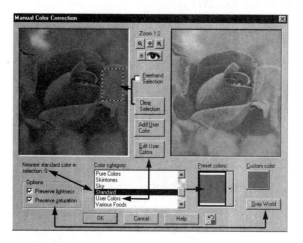

3. Use the Preset Colors drop-down box or the Custom Color box to select the target color hue that you want to shift to. Do any of the following:

- In the Color Category drop down list, select a category for which to display the preset colors. Then, click the arrow in the Preset Colors box to display the colors within the selected category. Click the color you want to use as the target color.

- Left click the Custom Color box to open the Color Picker. To use this dialog box, please refer to "Using the Color Dialog Box" in Chapter 9, "Using the Color Palette."

- Right-click the Custom Color box to open the Recent Colors dialog box. To use this dialog box, please refer to "Using the Recent Colors Dialog Box" in Chapter 9, "Using the Color Palette."

- Move the cursor over any open image. When the cursor changes to the Dropper, click to select a color.

The Color Category list includes a variety of frequently occurring colors. Particularly important ones include the following:

MEMORY COLORS These are colors that people remember particularly well and, as a result, are especially sensitive to errors in these colors. Typical examples are skin tones (Skintones category), vegetation (Foliage and Grasses categories), sky (Sky category) and foodstuffs (Beverages, Fruits, Various Foods and Vegetables categories).

STANDARD The Standard color category is a set of colors designed to let you make very small, subtle changes in hue. When you make a selection or select a specific color as the source color, the "Nearest standard color in selection" data field (below the left preview box) displays a number for the color that is the closest match to the source color. This number represents one of the preset colors in the Standard colors category. If you select a preset color that is near this color number, you can very slightly shift the hue of an image or a previously selected area in an image. If you select a preset color that is further away from this color number, you can drastically shift the hue of an image.

USER COLORS The User Colors category lets you add your own colors to the preset colors. This can be useful when you have several photos of a person taken under different conditions and you want to achieve a consistent skin tone in all the photos. It can also be useful if you have a roll of film with a color bias that you want to correct in all the photos. If a group of images or photos has something in common, you can first correct one, store an appropriate user color and then apply it to each of the images in turn.

To add a User Color, set the color in the Custom Color box and click the Add User Color button to open the Add User Colors dialog box. In the Name box, type up to 10 characters to name the color. In the Description box, optionally type up to 256 characters for a description of the color. Use the Enter key to add multiple lines. Click the Add button to add the color and close the dialog box. The color appears in the Preset Colors box for the User Colors category.

To edit a user color, select the color to edit in the Preset Colors box and click the Edit User Colors button to open the Edit User Colors dialog box. Edit the properties of the color and click the OK button to save the changes and close the dialog box. Alternatively, click the Delete button to delete the selected color or click the Cancel button to close the dialog box without saving the color changes.

Changes to the User Colors are retained when the OK button is used to exit from Manual Color Correction; if the Cancel button is used, the changes are discarded.

4. In the "Options" panel, select the "Preserve Saturation" to retain the saturation in the image. Clear the check box to adjust the saturation in the image.

NOTE: *Normally, both these check boxes should be selected so that only the hue color component changes in the image. However, you can clear either one or both of the check boxes to create a different effect. If you have already adjusted the contrast, you should select the "Preserve Lightness" check box. Similarly, if you have already adjusted the saturation, you should select both check boxes.*

5. An alternative to steps 2 through 5 is to use the Gray World button to adjust the image color. When you click this button, any selection you have made in the left preview box clears and the entire image is selected instead, the "Preserve Saturation" check box clears, "Preserve lightness" is set, and the Preset Color automatically becomes a medium grey. The source color becomes the average of all the colors in the image, which is typically grey; and the target color is set at a balanced shade of grey. This works because the colors in many outdoor scenes, when averaged over the whole image, have grey as the mean value.

NOTE: *Alternatively, you could select the whole image, pick a medium grey from the Grays color category, clear the "Preserve Saturation" check box, and see if it gives a good color balance. The Gray World button does all this in one step. Often pressing this button may be all you need to do to correct the color.*

6. After making all your adjustments, click the OK button to close the dialog box and apply the adjustments.

Using Fade Correction

With time and exposure to the elements, especially light, the dyes in a photograph can fade. Colors become less vivid, the image can acquire an undesirable color cast, and contrast can be lost. Use the Fade Correction feature to automatically restore color and contrast to a faded photographic image.

NOTE: *Please notice the following before you begin this adjustment:*

- *This feature works on 24-bit, colored images. If necessary, increase the color depth of your image to use this feature. For more information, please refer to Chapter 5, "Working with Color."*

- *If your photograph is a a faded black and white photograph, there are no colors to correct. Instead, restore the photograph with the Automatic Contrast Adjustment feature (refer to page 89).*

- *Fade Correction is designed as a quick and simple one-step adjustment of color and contrast. Better results may be obtained with the sequence of Automatic Color Adjustment, Automatic Contrast Adjustment and Automatic Saturation Adjustment.*

- *To limit the adjustment to a specific area, create a selection before beginning the adjustment.*

To use Fade Correction:

1. Choose Effects > Enhance Photo > Fade Correction to open the Fade Correction dialog box.

   Notice the following about this dialog box:

   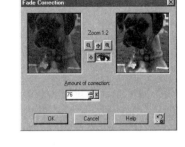

   - The Jasc dialog box standard preview area appears at the top. For details, please refer to the *Getting Started Guide*.

   - Because dialog box options retain their last settings, you may want to click the Reset ( ) button to set all the options to their default values.

2. In the "Amount of Correction" panel, type a number or click and drag the slider to select the amount of correction for your image. The best approach is to start with 45 and move the slider until the image looks the most natural. If you apply too much correction, highlight and shadow regions may lose their detail or objects in these areas may blend together.

3. Click the OK button to close the dialog box and apply the adjustments.

Improving the Contrast

Use the Automatic Contrast Enhancement and the Histogram Adjustment features to improve the contrast in an image. This section describes these features.

Using Automatic Contrast Enhancement

To look its best, an image should use the full available range of intensities, should not be too dark or too light overall, and should have the proper balance between highlights, shadows and midtones. Use the Automatic Contrast Enhancement feature to adjust your image's overall light and intensity automatically and to balance its highlights, midtones, and shadows.

NOTE: *Please notice the following before you begin this adjustment:*

- *This feature works on 24-bit and greyscale images. If necessary, increase the color depth of your image to use this feature. For more information, please refer to Chapter 5, "Working with Color."*

- *To limit the adjustment to a specific selection area, make the selection before beginning the adjustment. (By doing this, all image information is not available and the adjustment may not work correctly.)*

To use Automatic Contrast Enhancement:

1. Choose Effects > Enhance Photo > Automatic Contrast Enhancement to open the Automatic Contrast Enhancement dialog box.

Notice the following about this dialog box:

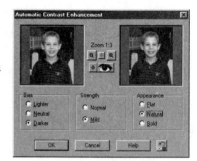

- The Jasc dialog box standard preview area appears at the top. For details, please refer to the *Getting Started Guide.*

- Because dialog box options retain their last settings, you may want to click the Reset ( ) button to set all the options to their default values.

2. In the "Strength" panel, select Normal to use the normal strength of the automatic adjustments. Select Mild to reduce the strength of the adjustments.

3. In the "Bias" panel, select Neutral to use the normal bias of the automatic adjustments. Select Lighter or Darker to change the bias of the adjustments.

4. In the "Appearance" panel, select Natural to use the normal automatic adjustments to the image's contents. Select Flat or Bold to change the effect of the adjustments.

5. Click the OK button to close the dialog box and apply the adjustments.

Equalizing the Histogram

The Equalize feature changes the shape of the histogram, which changes the image. This command distributes the lightness values of the pixels more evenly across the lightness spectrum from black to white. It makes the darkest pixel as close to black and the lightest pixel as close to white as possible. It then distributes the remaining pixels evenly between these two values. This produces a tempering, or averaging, of the image brightness. In some cases the effect may be too severe and better result is obtained when the original image is blended with the equalized version.

NOTE: *To limit the adjustment to a specific selection area, make the selection before making the adjustment.*

To equalize the Histogram:

- Choose Colors > Histogram Functions > Equalize, or press <Shift> + <E>.

Stretching the Histogram

The Stretch feature changes the shape of the histogram, which changes the image. If the histogram does not cover the entire lightness spectrum, it indicates that the image does not contain very dark or very light areas; it lacks contrast. The Stretch command stretches the graph closer to both ends so that it covers more of the spectrum. This task, along with others, can also be done with Histogram Adjustment.

NOTE: *To limit the adjustment to a specific selection area, make the selection before making the adjustment.*

To stretch the Histogram:

- Choose Colors > Histogram Functions > Stretch, or press <Shift> + <T>.

Adjusting the Histogram

Use the Histogram Adjustment feature to adjust the contrast of your image by adjusting the histogram. This brings out details in the image without losing important information.

NOTE: *Please notice the following before you begin this adjustment:*

- *This feature works on 24-bit and greyscale images. If necessary, increase the color depth of your image to use this feature. For more information, please refer to Chapter 5, "Working with Color."*

- *To limit the adjustment to a specific selection area, make the selection before beginning the adjustment.*

- *Make sure your monitor is set up correctly in terms of contrast, brightness, and gamma. Refer to "Adjusting Your Monitor Gamma" on page 81*

- *You may want to display the Histogram window. Then, if you use the Auto-Proof feature while adjusting the histogram, you can see the changes in the Histogram window.*

To adjust the Histogram:

1. Choose Colors > Histogram Functions > Histogram Adjustment to open the Histogram Adjustment dialog box. Notice the following about this dialog box:

- The Jasc dialog box standard preview area appears at the top. For details, please refer to the *Getting Started Guide.*

- The histogram appears in the center. It displays the graph for the component selected in the Edit box. The horizontal axis represents values from 0 to 255. The vertical axis represents values from 0 to X. For a complete description, please refer to page 83.

- The adjustment options appear around the histogram. Because dialog boxes retain their last settings, you may want to click the Reset (🔁) button to set all the options to their default values.

- To zoom in and out on the view of the histogram, use the Magnification buttons (▲ 1:1 ▼). The 1:1 Button resets the histogram to the original size.

2. In the Edit drop-down box, select the color component you want to adjust. The options are Luminosity, Red, Green, and Blue. If you are correcting contrast, the best approach is to start by adjusting the Luminosity, which shows values of lightness from darkest on the left (0) to lightest on the right (255).

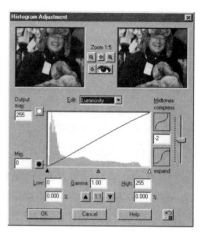

3. Look for a gap between the left edge of the histogram window and the point where the graph values start to rise. This gap shows that the darkest pixels in the image are not completely black. Click and drag the black Low value triangle slider to the point where the graph rises. As you move the triangle slider, the values in the Low value boxes below the triangle slider change. The top box displays the position of the slider as an intensity from 0 to 255; the bottom box displays the percentage of pixels that are contained between 0 and the Low value, whose contrast will be lost. As a general rule, keep the percentage below 0.1%. The position of the slider defines a "lower clip limit".

4. On the right side of the histogram window, look for a gap between the point where the graph values end and the right edge of the window. Click and drag the white High value triangle slider to the upper end of the graph values. This changes the lightest pixels in the image to white by changing the "upper clip limit." As a general rule, keep the High value percentage below 0.1%.

5. If the overall image is too dark or too light, adjust the Gamma triangle slider. If the image is too dark, drag the triangle slider to the right; if it is too light, drag the triangle slider to the left. As you move the slider, the Gamma number below it changes. (Gamma is a standard measure of change in an image's contrast and this slider balances the shadows and highlights in the image.) As you move the slider to the right and increase the Gamma, the image lightens and shadow details increase, but highlight details may be lost. As you move the slider to the left and decrease the Gamma, the image darkens and highlight details increase, but shadow details may be lost.

   NOTE: *When the majority of the graph values peaks on the left, it usually means the image needs brightening. When the majority of the graph values peaks on the right, it usually means the image needs darkening.*

6. If the graph still has peaks on the left and the right sides and contains low points in the center, or has low points on the sides with a peak in the center, you need to balance the midtones relative to shadows and highlights. Use the Midtones slider on the right side of the histogram to make this adjustment as follows:

   - If the graph has peaks on the left and right sides, the midtones should be compressed because they contain little information. Shadows and highlights should be expanded to reveal the information they contain. This often occurs in flash photographs when a subject is too close to the camera. The subject appears brightly illuminated, but the background of the photo is very dark. To compress the midtones, click and drag the Midtones slider up.

   - If the graph peaks in the center and has low values at the left (dark) and right (light) sides, the midtones should be expanded. To expand the midtones, drag the Midtones slider down.

7. If you are trying to improve the visible information in your image, your adjustments are now complete. The line on the histogram shows the changes that will be applied to the image values. To interpret the line, pick a value on the horizontal axis (along the bottom). Mentally, trace vertically upwards till you reach the curve. From that point, trace to the left until you reach the edge of the histogram window. This is what the new pixel count will be for that value in the image. (If you were to click the OK button and close the dialog box and then reopen it, this is the new number of pixels that will display in the histogram for the value on the horizontal axis). Alternatively, use the ToolTip that appears as you move the cursor over the histogram. The ToolTip displays the following information: Input is the value on the horizontal axis, Count is the number of pixels having that Input value (i.e. X); Integral is the percentage of pixels in the image with that Input value, and Output is the value on the vertical axis, which is also what the Input value would change to if you were to click the OK button to save the changes.

8. If you are improving your image, skip this step. If you are using the Histogram Adjustment feature to create artistic effects, use the Output Max and Min sliders on the left side of the histogram to make further adjustments. The Max slider has a sun icon, the Min slider has a moon icon. To darken the image's whites, click and drag the Max slider down. To lighten the image's blacks, click and drag the Min slider up.

NOTE: *You can use these sliders to create a pastel, low-contrast image that can be used as a background for a Web page or a watermark for a document.*

9. If you want to adjust a different color component, in the Edit drop-down box select the color component you want to adjust and return to step 3. Otherwise, click the OK button to close the dialog box and apply the adjustments.

NOTE: *You can create exotic variations of an image by editing its individual Red, Green or Blue components rather than working with Luminosity. Correcting an image by individually manipulating the channels is, however, rather tricky.*

Improving the Saturation

Use the Automatic Saturation Enhancement feature to improve the saturation in an image.

Using Automatic Saturation Enhancement

The saturation of a color determines its vividness. Saturated colors appear bright and brilliant, like fire-engine red. Desaturated colors appear subdued or washed-out, like pastels. Use the Automatic Saturation Enhancement feature to adjust the saturation of the colors in your image automatically.

NOTE: *Please notice the following before you begin this adjustment:*

- *This feature works on 24-bit, colored images. If necessary, increase the color depth of your image to use this feature. For more information, please refer to Chapter 5, "Working with Color."*

- *This feature has no effect on greyscale images because they have no color, but it can be used with sepia or duotone images.*

- *To limit the adjustment to a specific selection area, make the selection before beginning the adjustment. (By doing this, all image information is not available and the adjustment may not work correctly.)*

To use Automatic Saturation Enhancement:

1. Choose Effects > Enhance Photo > Automatic Saturation Enhancement to open the Automatic Saturation Enhancement dialog box.

   Notice the following about this dialog box:

   - The Jasc dialog box standard preview area is at the top. For details, please refer to the *Getting Started Guide.*

   - Because dialog box options retain their last settings, you may want to click the Reset (🔲) button to set all the options to their default values.

2. Select the "Skintones Present" check box if there are significant skin tone areas in your image; clear the check box if there are not any significant skin tone areas. This gives your image a more realistic look.

3. In the "Strength" panel, select Normal to use the normal strength of the automatic adjustments. Select Weak to reduce the strength of the adjustments. Select Strong to increase the strength of the adjustments.

4. In the "Bias" panel, select Normal to use the normal bias of the automatic adjustments. Select Less Colorful or More Colorful to change the bias of the adjustments.

5. Click the OK button to close the dialog box and apply the adjustments.

Removing Source Defects

Use the Deinterlace, JPEG Artifact Removal, and Moiré Pattern Removal Features to remove the source defects from an image.

Using Deinterlace for Video Images

Video images can contain visible scan lines caused by television signals that update every second set of scan lines in each frame. In these images, every second set of lines can be missing or can be out of alignment with other lines. Use the Deinterlace feature to eliminate missing or misaligned lines from your image and to reconstruct missing information. If the image contains any noise, it may become more visible after removing the scan lines.

NOTE: *Please notice the following before you begin this adjustment:*

- *This feature works on 24-bit and greyscale images. If necessary, increase the color depth of your image to use this feature. For more information, please refer to Chapter 5, "Working with Color."*

- *Because this feature is for use on an entire image, its command is not available if the image contains a selection.*

- *Apply this command before you resize the image. If your image has been resized, zoom in until you can see individual pixels. Determine how many pixels make up one scan line and resize the image so each scan line is only one pixel high. Apply the Deinterlace feature and then return the image to its original size.*

To use Deinterlace:

1. Choose Effects > Enhance Photo > Deinterlace to open the Deinterlace dialog box.

   Notice the dialog box has the Jasc standard preview area at the top. For details, please refer to the *Getting Started Guide*.

   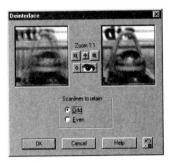

2. In the "Scanlines to retain" panel, select either Odd or Even to determine whether the odd-numbered or even-numbered scan lines are kept. (Usually it makes little difference which you select; text, however, may look better with one rather than the other.)

3. Click the OK button to close the dialog box and apply the correction.

Using JPEG Artifact Removal

JPEG images can contain artifacts caused by excessive compression. Artifacts can appear as halos or color leakage beyond edges of objects, checkerboard patterns in smooth areas, or blocky-looking areas in an image. Use the JPEG Artifact Removal feature to restore a JPEG image to its original appearance. Because JPEG compression is lossy (and so discards image information), there are limits to how well the image can be restored.

NOTE: *Please notice the following before you begin this adjustment:*

- *This feature works on 24-bit and greyscale images. If necessary, increase the color depth of your image to use this feature. For more information, please refer to Chapter 5, "Working with Color."*
- *Because this feature is for use on an entire image, its command is not available if the image contains a selection.*
- *The image does not have to be in JPEG format to use this feature.*
- *For best results, do not use this feature on a resized image.*
- *If an image has been heavily JPEG-compressed several times at several different sizes, it may be very difficult to restore.*
- *This feature does a considerable amount of processing and may take some time to work, especially with large images.*

To use JPEG Artifact Removal:

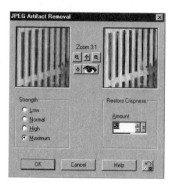

1. Choose Effects > Enhance Photo > JPEG Artifact Removal to open the Deinterlace dialog box. Notice the following about this dialog box:

   - The Jasc dialog box standard preview area is at the top. For details, please refer to the *Getting Started Guide*.

   - Because dialog box options retain their last settings, you may want to click the Reset (⬚) button to set all the options to their default values.

2. In the "Strength" panel, select Normal to use the normal strength of the automatic correction. Select Low, High, or Maximum to change the strength of the correction. To make your choice, examine all areas of the image.

3. In the "Restore Crispness" panel, use the numeric edit controls to select the amount of correction for your image. Start with 50, and then adjust the value until the image looks the most natural. This control determines how much fine-detail information the artifact remover should attempt to create. This can only be a guess since the original information is lost. Excessive crispness may appear as fine dots in the image.

4. Click the OK button to close the dialog box and apply the correction.

Using Moiré Pattern Removal for Scanned Images

Scanning printed images can produce undesirable patterns in an image. Use the Moiré Pattern Removal feature to remove these patterns, as well as patterns from photographs printed on textured paper.

NOTE: *Please notice the following before you begin this adjustment:*

- *This feature works on 24-bit and greyscale images. If necessary, increase the color depth of your image to use this feature. For more information, please refer to Chapter 5, "Working with Color."*

- *To limit the correction to a specific area, create a selection before beginning the correction.*

- *This feature does a considerable amount of processing and may take some time to work, especially with large images.*

To use Moiré Pattern Removal:

1. Choose Effects > Enhance Photo > Moiré Pattern Removal to open the Moiré Pattern Removal dialog box.

    Notice the following about this dialog box:

    - The Jasc dialog box standard preview area appears at the top. For details, please refer to the *Getting Started Guide.*

    - Because dialog box options retain their last settings, you may want to click the Reset ( ) button to set all the options to their default values.

2. Use the Zoom-In button to enlarge the previews until you can see the fine patterns clearly.

3. Drag the Fine Details slider one number at a time until the pattern just disappears. (In some cases it may be possible to smooth this pattern more severely and subsequently sharpen the image to restore detail without bringing the pattern back.)

4. Use the Zoom-Out button to reduce the image until you can see bands or color blotches clearly in the previews. Bands or blotches may be visible when the image is at natural size (1:1 zoom ratio), but may be more visible at a 1:3 ratio.

5. Drag the Remove Bands slider one number at a time until any color bands or "blobs" are less visible. They may not disappear completely, but should be reduced. This control does not work in the usual "less to more" sense; instead, it tries to match the band pattern, though you should use the lowest value possible to avoid desaturation of small objects.

6. Click the OK button to close the dialog box and apply the correction.

Removing "Noise"

Use the Noise and Blur commands on the Effects menu to remove noise from your images.

Using the Noise Features

The commands on the Noise submenu remove noise from your images. These commands include Despeckle, Edge Preserving Smooth, Median Cut, Median Filter, Salt And Pepper Filter, and Texture Preserving Smooth. This section describes these commands.

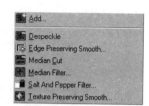

NOTE: *Please notice the following about the Noise commands:*

- *These commands work on 24-bit and greyscale images. If necessary, increase the color depth of your image to use the commands. For more information, please refer to Chapter 5, "Working with Color."*

- *For best results, use each command on a specific selection area that contains defects. To do this, create a selection before using a command.*

- *The Add command adds noise and is not a photo enhancement feature. For information about this command, please refer to Chapter 17, "Adding Effects."*

- *If the entire image contains noise, the Effects > Blur > Average command may work best. For more information, please refer to "Using the Blur Features" on page 101.*

- *When specks of noise are single-pixel specks of color, the Median command may work best.*

- *When specks of noise are larger than one pixel, or are neither very bright or very dark, the Salt And Pepper Filter command may work best.*

- *When specks of noise are very large (about 10 pixels or more in size), the Scratch Remover tool (on the Tool palette) may work best. For more information, please refer to "Using the Scratch Remover Tool" on page 103.*

- *When specks of noise are line-like and have a definite direction, like small scratches, the Effects > Photo Enhance > Automatic Small Scratch Removal feature may work best. For more information, please refer to "Using Automatic Small Scratch Removal" on page 105.*

- *Most of these commands open a dialog box. Each dialog box has the Jasc dialog box standard preview area at the top. For details, please refer to the Getting Started Guide. In addition, because dialog box options retain their last settings, when you first open a dialog box you may want to click the Reset ( ) button to set all the options to their default values.*

Using Despeckle

Use this command to remove single-pixel specks that are mostly white or black. This feature analyzes the brightness of each pixel in the image and compares each pixel to its surrounding pixels to determine if it is a speck that should be removed.

To use the Despeckle command:

NOTE: *This command applies directly to your image without displaying a dialog box.*

- Choose Effects > Noise > Despeckle.

Using Edge Preserve Smoothing

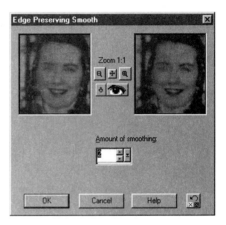

Use this command to remove noise in an image without losing edge details. This feature finds details that may be object edges and leaves these areas unchanged while smoothing the areas between the edges. For example, edges of facial features may be preserved while removing a blotchy complexion. This feature is good for minimizing film grain.

To use the Edge Preserve Smoothing command:

1. Choose Effects > Noise > Edge Preserve Smoothing to open the Edge Preserve Smoothing dialog box.

2. Use the Amount of Smoothing numeric edit controls to set the strength of the correction.

3. Click the OK button to close the dialog box and apply the correction.

Using Median Filter

Use this command to remove small, random areas of noise where the noise is distinctly different from the surrounding area. This feature adjusts the intensity of each pixel in the image to the median intensity of its surrounding pixels. With this command, you choose the number of surrounding pixels to include in determining the median intensity allowing different-sized defects to be addressed.

To use the Median Filter command:

1. Choose Effects > Noise > Median Filter to open the Median Filter dialog box.

2. Use the Filter Aperture numeric edit controls to set the number of surrounding pixels to include in calculating the median adjustment for each pixel. The median is the midpoint intensity of all the surrounding pixels. The aperture is always an odd number of pixels square. A pixel that is very different from its surrounding pixels is adjusted more than a pixel that is similar to its surrounding pixel. This correction preserves object edges, though larger values increase noise removal they may cause loss of detail.

3. Click the OK button to close the dialog box and apply the correction.

Using Salt And Pepper Filter

Use this command to remove black or white specks from an image, such as those caused by dust on a film or video. This feature compares each pixel to its surrounding pixels to determine it if it is a speck or not. If determined to be a speck, the pixel is adjusted.

NOTE: *This command works best if you create a selection of the area containing the specks before using the command.*

To use the Salt And Pepper Filter command:

1. Choose Effects > Noise > Salt And Pepper Filter to open the Salt And Pepper Filter dialog box.

2. Use the Speck Size numeric edit controls to set the minimum size, in pixels, of the largest speck that can be completely removed. This is always an odd number.

3. Use the Sensitivity to Specks numeric edit controls to set how different an area must be from its surrounding pixels to be considered a speck.

4. Select the "Include all lower speck sizes" check box to include and remove all speck sizes smaller the "Speck Size" control setting. Clear the check box to not include or adjust smaller speck sizes.

5. Select the "Aggressive action" check box to increase the strength of the correction. Clear the check box to not increase the strength.

6. Click the OK button to close the dialog box and apply the correction.

Using Texture Preserve Smoothing

Use this command to remove noise in an image without losing texture details. This feature analyzes an image's pixels to determine if they are textured areas or smooth areas. Textured areas are preserved, and smooth areas are adjusted to remove noise. For example, textures in clothing may be preserved while removing noise from another area (such as a person's face).

To use the Texture Preserve Smoothing command:

1. Choose Effects > Noise > Texture Preserve Smoothing to open the Texture Preserve Smoothing dialog box.

2. Use the Amount of Correction numeric edit controls to set the strength of the correction. At lower amounts, textured areas are preserved but little noise is removed. At higher amounts, textured areas may not be preserved, but more noise is removed.

3. Click the OK button to close the dialog box and apply the correction.

Using the Blur Features

The commands on the Blur submenu remove noise from your images. These commands include Average, Blur, Blur More, Gaussian Blur, Motion Blur, Soften, and Soften More. This section describes these commands.

NOTE: *Please notice the following about the* Blur *commands:*

- *These commands work on 24-bit and greyscale images. If necessary, increase the color depth of your image to use the commands. For more information, please refer to Chapter 5, "Working with Color."*

- *The Motion Blur command is actually a special effect. For information about this command, please refer to Chapter 17, "Adding Effects."*

- *For best results, use each command on a specific selection area that contains defects. To do this, create a selection before using a command.*

Using Average Blur

Use this command to remove noise when the entire image has noise and to remove color dithering caused by increasing the color depth of an image from paletted to 24 bit. This feature adjusts the intensity of each pixel to the average intensity of its surrounding pixels.

To use Average Blur:

1. Choose Effects > Blur > Average to open the Average dialog box. For details about the Jasc standard preview area in the dialog box, please refer to the *Getting Started Guide*.

2. Use the Filter Aperture numeric edit controls to set the number of surrounding pixels to average when calculating the adjustment for each pixel. Aperture is always an odd number of pixels square. Larger values increase noise removal but may cause loss of detail.

3. Click the OK button to close the dialog box and apply the correction.

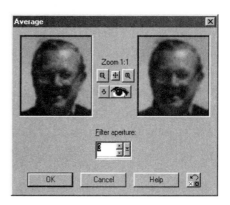

Using Blur and Blur More

Use the Blur command to remove noise by applying smooth transitions and decreasing the contrast in your image. Use the Blur More command to apply the Blur command with more intensity. In addition, use either command to reduce graininess in your image.

NOTE: *These commands apply directly to your image without displaying a dialog box.*

To use Blur or Blur More:

• Choose Effects > Blur > Blur or Effects > Blur > Blur More.

Using Gaussian Blur

Use the Gaussian Blur command when you want more control over the Blur effect. This command blends a specific number of pixels incrementally, following a bell-shaped curve. The blurring is dense in the center and feathers at the edges.

To use Gaussian Blur:

1. Choose Effects > Blur > Gaussian Blur to open the Gaussian Blur dialog box. The Jasc standard preview area is at the top of the dialog box. For details, please refer to the *Getting Started Guide.*

2. Use the Radius numeric edit controls to set the width of the area to blur.

3. Click the OK button to close the dialog box and apply the correction.

Using Soften and Soften More

Use the Soften command to remove noise by applying a uniform blur to your image. Use the Soften More command to apply the Soften command with more intensity. In addition, use either command to reduce graininess in your image.

NOTE: *These commands apply directly to your image without displaying a dialog box.*

To use Soften or Soften More:

• Choose Effects > Blur > Soften or Effects > Blur > Soften More.

Removing Scratches, Red-Eye, and Other Defects

Use the Scratch Removal tool, the Retouch tool, the Automatic Small Scratch Removal feature, and the Red-eye Removal feature to remove scratches, red eyes, and other defects from your images.

Using the Scratch Remover Tool

Use the Scratch Remover tool () to remove scratches, cracks, and other unwanted objects from your images.

NOTE: *Please notice the following about the Scratch Remover tool:*

- *This tool works on the background layer of any 24-bit color or 8-bit greyscale, non-transparent image. If necessary, increase the color depth of your image to use the tool. For more information, please refer to Chapter 5, "Working with Color."*

- *For best results, use the Scratch Remover tool to remove scratches from a relatively smooth background. When removing scratches from a textured area, you may prefer to use the Clone tool ( ) to cover the scratches. For more information about the Clone tool, please refer to Chapter 8, "Using the Painting Tools."*

- *To limit the correction to a specific area in the image, create a selection before using the Scratch Remover tool. The tool appears to work outside of the selection area, but the correction is actually limited to the selected area.*

To use the Scratch Remover tool:

1. Activate the Scratch Remover tool by clicking its button ( ) on the Tool palette, or by choosing it from the Tool Selection menu ( ) of the Tool Options palette.

2. If necessary, make the Tool Options palette visible by clicking its toolbar icon ( ) or by pressing the <O> on your keyboard.

3. On the first tab of the Tool Options palette, use the Width numeric edit controls to set the width of the tool.

4. Click one of the Selection Boxes buttons to choose the shape of the tool:

- Use the flat-end option to correct scratches that are in an open area or are perpendicular to any object edges in the image.

- Use the pointed-end option to correct scratches that are at an angle to any object edges in the image. This lets you place the tool closer to an object's edge without including the edge in the correction.

5. Move your cursor over the image to the point where you want to start removing the scratch.

6. Click and hold the left mouse button and begin to drag the cursor to the opposite end of the scratch. A bounding box appears around the area of the scratch. There are two versions of this box as follows:

   • If you set the Width on the Tool Options palette to 10 or fewer pixels, the bounding box is single-edged. Position this box so it entirely encloses the scratch, but the sides do not touch the scratch.

   • If you set the Width on the Tool Options palette to more than 10 pixels, the bounding box is double-edged. Position this box so the inside edges enclose, but do not touch, the scratch, and so the double-edges enclose a good area of the image.

7. Continue dragging the cursor to the point where you want to stop removing the scratch. Do not release the mouse button until the bounding box properly encloses the scratch. While holding the mouse button down, you can do any of the following to change the size and position of the bounding box:

   • Press the Left Arrow key to move the starting point to the left by 1 pixel.

   • Press the Right Arrow key to move the starting point to the right by 1 pixel.

   • Press the Up Arrow key to move the starting point up by 1 pixel.

   • Press the Down Arrow key to move the starting point down by 1 pixel.

   • Press the Page Up key to increase the width of the box by 1 pixel.

   • Press the Page Down key to decrease the width of the box by 1 pixel.

   NOTE: *Using these accelerator keys is the fastest way to match the tool to the object being removed.*

8. When you have properly enclosed the scratch, release the mouse button. The scratch disappears.

NOTE: *If necessary, use the Undo button (⟳) to reverse the correction.*

Using the Retouch Tool

Use the Retouch tool (🖌) on the Tool palette to lighten, emboss, change the saturation, and make other retouches to your image. For specific steps, please refer to "Using the Retouch Tool" in Chapter 8, "Using the Painting Tools."

Using Automatic Small Scratch Removal

Use the Automatic Small Scratch Removal feature to remove small scratches and noise automatically from your image. This feature finds and eliminates small, line-like defects that are either lighter than or darker than the surrounding area.

NOTE: *Please notice the following before you use this feature:*

- *This feature works on 24-bit, colored images. If necessary, increase the color depth of your image to use this feature. For more information, please refer to Chapter 5, "Working with Color."*

- *This feature may work best if you create a selection of the area containing the scratch(es) before using the feature.*

To use Automatic Small Scratch Removal:

1. Choose Effects > Enhance Photo > Automatic Small Scratch Removal to open the Automatic Small Scratch Removal dialog box.

   Notice the following about this dialog box:

   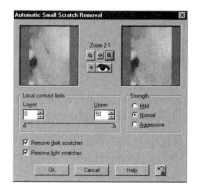

   - The Jasc dialog box standard preview area appears at the top. For details, please refer to the *Getting Started Guide.*

   - Because dialog box options retain their last settings, you may want to click the Reset (　) button to set all the options to their default values.

2. Select the "Remove dark scratches" check box if you want to automatically remove scratches that are darker than their background. Clear the check box to not automatically remove these scratches.

3. Select the "Remove dark scratches" check box if you want to automatically remove scratches that are darker than their background. Clear the check box to not automatically remove these scratches.

NOTE: *You must select one of the check boxes for the scratch removal to work. However, both can be selected simultaneously.*

4. In the "Local contrast limits" panel, type a number, use the arrow controls, or use the sliders to set the upper and lower contrast limits where they achieve the best results. First set these to the top and bottom of the range. If the scratches persist, the Automatic Small Scratch Remover will not remove them. Slide the lower limit up to the value just below the point at which the scratches reappear. Similarly lower the upper limit to the value just above the point at which the scratches reappear. This optimizes the removal of scratches while minimizing loss of image detail.

5. In the "Strength" panel, select Normal to use the normal strength of the automatic scratch removal. Select Mild to reduce the strength of the scratch removal, or select Aggressive to increase the strength of the scratch removal. Look at all areas of your image to make sure important details are not lost.

6. Click the OK button to close the dialog box and apply the correction.

Using Red-Eye Removal

Use the Red-eye Removal feature to remove the red-eye effect from photographs of humans and animals automatically or manually. You select the area within an eye and then customize the automatic correction. Because the default settings can automatically correct a wide range of red-eye effects, you may only need to click the eye. You can also use this feature to enhance or change a person or animal's eye color.

NOTE: *Please notice the following before you use this feature:*

- *This feature works on 24-bit colored images. If necessary, increase the color depth of your image to use this feature. For more information, please refer to Chapter 5, "Working with Color."*
- *Because this feature is for use on an entire image, its command is not available if the image contains a selection.*

To use Red-Eye Removal:

1. Choose Effects > Enhance Photo > Red Eye Removal to open the Red Eye Removal dialog box.

    Notice the following about this dialog box:

    - The preview area is slightly different from the Jasc dialog box standard preview area. Use the left preview box to select the eye area, and use the right preview box and the control buttons to adjust the previews.

    - Because dialog box options retain their last settings, click the Reset (⟲) button to set all the options to their default settings.

        NOTE: *You can also press <Shift> while clicking the Reset button to return the settings to where they were when you first opened the dialog box.*

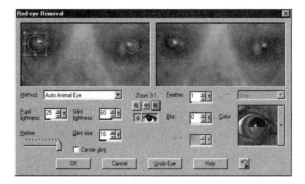

2. In the Method box, select a method for making the correction:

AUTO HUMAN EYE: This method automatically selects the correction area and makes the appropriate corrections to a human eye. You can then customize the automatic corrections. If you are correcting human eyes, try this method first.

AUTO ANIMAL EYE: This method automatically selects the correction area and makes the appropriate corrections to an animal eye. You can then customize the automatic corrections. If you are correcting animal eyes, try this method first.

FREEHAND PUPIL OUTLINE: This method lets you manually select the correction area using a Freehand selection tool. Use this method for difficult situations, like a partially obscured eye. You can use this on human and animal eyes.

POINT-TO-POINT PUPIL OUTLINE: This method lets you manually select the correction area using a Point-to-Point Selection tool. Use this method for difficult situations, like a partially obscured eye. You can use this on human and animal eyes.

3. If necessary, use the Zoom controls to get a closer view of the eye(s) in the previews.

4. In the left preview box, select the first eye to correct as follows:

   • If you are using the Auto Human Eye or the Auto Animal Eye method, click anywhere inside the "red" area of the eye. This automatically selects the eye, displays a control box around the eye area, and displays the correction in the right preview box. (Alternatively, you can click and drag from the center of the red-eye area to the outside edge of the area.)

   • If you are using the Freehand Pupil Outline method, left-click and hold the mouse button anywhere on the edge of the red-eye area. Drag the cursor to outline the area to correct. When you reach the beginning point, release the mouse button. This displays a control box around the selected eye area, and displays the correction in the right preview box.

- If you are using the Point-to-Point Pupil Outline method, left-click anywhere on the edge of the red-eye area. Move the cursor a few pixels around the edge of the area and click again. Continue moving the cursor and clicking until the area is outlined. (You can right-click to reverse a click.) When you reach the beginning point, double-click to create the selection. This displays a control box around the selected eye area and displays the correction in the right preview box.

NOTE: *You can right click in the left preview box or click the Undo Eye button to remove a selection and start over.*

5. Make sure the selection is positioned and sized properly over the red-eye area. To resize the selection, click and drag any of the control handles on the control box, or press <Alt> + <Page Up> to increase the size or <Alt> + <Page Down> to decrease the size. To move the selection, drag it to the new location or press <Alt> + any Arrow key. If you are using the Auto Animal Eye method, you can drag the center rotation handle to rotate the selection. Note that with the Auto Animal Eye method the selection can be reshaped to an ellipse by pulling on its edges.

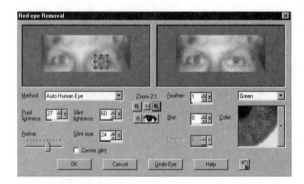

6. If you are correcting a human eye, look at the corrected eye in the right preview box and determine if you need to add an iris area around the pupil. If the iris is visible or you are correcting an animal eye, skip this step. (An animal eye usually does not show an iris). Use the controls to add an iris to the corrected eye as follows:

IRIS SIZE: Use the numeric edit controls to set the size of the iris.

HUE: Click the down arrow and choose the correct hue.

COLOR: Click inside the control box to display thumbnails of the color variations. Click the thumbnail for the correct color variation.

7. Determine if the pupil should be lighter or darker, and, if necessary, do the following:

PUPIL LIGHTNESS: Use the numeric edit controls to adjust the pupil lightness. Lower values darken the pupil; higher values lighten it.

8. Examine the glint in the eye. It should add a natural, lively look to the eye; its absence makes the eye look "dead." If necessary, use the controls to adjust the glint as follows:

   GLINT SIZE: Use the numeric edit controls to set the size of the glint.

   GLINT LIGHTNESS: Use the numeric edit controls to adjust the lightness of the glint. Lower values darken the glint; higher values lighten it.

   CENTER GLINT: Select the check box to move the glint to the center of the pupil. Clear the check box to leave the position of the glint unchanged.

9. Look at the eye in the left preview box. If part of the eye is obscured in the original image, adjust the corrected eye to look the same. For example, if the eyelid is covering part of the eye in the original, you should make it look that way in the corrected eye. If necessary, use the following control:

   REFINE: Click and drag the slider to the left one unit at a time until the visible area of the corrected eye looks similar to the eye in the original image. If the eye does not correct properly, you may need to click the Undo Eye button and correct the eye using the Freehand Pupil Outline or the Point-to-Point Pupil Outline method.

10. Look at the corrected eye in the right preview and make sure it blends with the rest of the image. If necessary, use the controls to adjust the corrected eye as follows:

    FEATHER: Use the numeric edit controls to adjust the edges of the corrected eye. Small values make the edges more pronounced; larger values make them less pronounced.

    BLUR: Use the numeric edit controls to blend the eye with the surrounding pixels when the photo has a grainy appearance. Increase the setting one unit at a time until the eye blends naturally with the rest of the image.

11. The eye should now be completely corrected. If you need to correct another eye, repeat these steps. As you correct the next eye, the controls retain their settings from the first correction, making it much easier to correct the second eye. When you select the next eye, the previously-corrected eye still has a circle around it. You can click this circle to go back and make further corrections to the eye.

12. When you are finished making the corrections, click the OK button to close the dialog box and apply the corrections.

Clarifying and Sharpening Images

Use the Clarify, Sharpen, and Edge features to clarify and sharpen your images.

Using Clarify

Use the Clarify feature to add a sense of depth and clarity to an image by adjusting the intensity distribution in the image. This feature can give your image a crisp, focused look so that objects stand out. It can also correct some defects caused by fog, haze, or a slight lack of focus.

NOTE: *Please notice the following before you begin this adjustment:*

- *This feature works on 24-bit and greyscale images. If necessary, increase the color depth of your image to use this feature. For more information, please refer to Chapter 5, "Working with Color."*

- *Because this feature is for use on an entire image, its command is not available if the image contains a selection.*

- *This feature does a considerable amount of processing and may take some time to work, especially with large images.*

To use Clarify:

1. Choose Effects > Enhance Photo > Clarify to open the Clarify dialog box.

   Notice the following about this dialog box:

   - The Jasc dialog box standard preview area appears at the top. For details, please refer to the *Getting Started Guide.*

   - Because dialog box options retain their last settings, you may want to click the Reset (![reset icon]) button to set all the options to their default values.

2. Drag the Strength of Effect slider or type a value in the box to the amount of adjustment.

3. Click the OK button to close the dialog box and apply the adjustment.

Using the Sharpen Features

The commands on the Sharpen submenu sharpen your images by increasing the contrast in them. These commands, which are described in this section, include Sharpen, Sharpen More, and Unsharp Mask.

NOTE: *Please notice the following about the Sharpen commands:*

- *These commands work on 24-bit and greyscale images. If necessary, increase the color depth of your image to use the commands. For more information, please refer to Chapter 5, "Working with Color."*

- *To limit a command to a specific area, create a selection before using the command.*

Using Sharpen and Sharpen More

Use the Sharpen command to automatically sharpen your image by increasing the contrast between adjacent pixels where there are significant color contrasts, usually at the edges of objects. Use the Sharpen More command to apply the Sharpen command with more intensity. Both commands lighten the light pixels and darken the dark pixels in your image.

NOTE: *These commands apply directly to your image without displaying a dialog box.*

To use Sharpen or Sharpen More:

- Choose Effects > Sharpen > Sharpen, or Effects > Sharpen > Sharpen More.

Using Unsharp Mask

Use the Unsharp Mask command to sharpen the mid to high contrast edges in your image without enhancing any noise in the image. This command locates adjacent pixels that have a difference in lightness values that you specify, and it increases their contrast by an amount that your specify.

NOTE: *While this command is similar to the* Sharpen *and* Sharpen More *commands, you have more control with this command and can choose the settings.*

To use Unsharp Mask:

1. Choose Effects > Sharpen > Unsharp Mask to open the Unsharp Mask dialog box.

   Notice the following about this dialog box:

   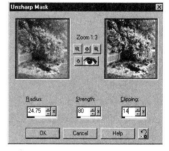

   - The Jasc dialog box standard preview area appears at the top. For details, please refer to the *Getting Started Guide*.

   - Because dialog box options retain their last settings, you may want to click the Reset (⬚) button to set all the options to their default values.

2. Use the Radius numeric edit controls to specify the number of pixels to adjust around each edge. 0.5 to 2 usually works best. Use lower ranges for on-screen images, higher ranges for high resolution printed images.

3. Use the Strength numeric edit controls to specify the amount of contrast by which you want to increase the pixels in your image. It is better to start with a low number and then increase the setting gradually.

4. Use the Clipping numeric edit controls to specify the difference in lightness values that adjacent pixels must have before they are sharpened.

5. Click the OK button to close the dialog box and apply the correction.

Using the Edge Features

Use the commands on the Effect submenu to clarify your image and to accentuate the areas of contrast and edges in your image. The Edge commands include the following:

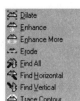

DILATE enhances the light areas in the image.

ENHANCE increases the contrast along the edges in the image.

ENHANCE MORE applies a stronger contrast to the edges in the image.

ERODE enhances the dark areas of the image.

FIND ALL enhances the contrasts between light and dark in the image by darkening the image and then highlighting the edges.

FIND HORIZONTAL enhances the horizontal edges in the image using the method of the Find All command.

FIND VERTICAL enhances the vertical edges in the image using the method of the Find All command.

TRACE CONTOUR traces a series of single-pixel lines around areas of contrast and turns the rest of the pixels white.

NOTE: *Please notice the following about the Edge commands:*

- *These commands work on 24-bit and greyscale images. If necessary, increase the color depth of your image to use the commands. For more information, please refer to Chapter 5, "Working with Color."*

- *To limit a command to a specific area, create a selection before using the command.*

- *All the Edge commands apply directly to your image without displaying a dialog box.*

To use an Edge command:

- Choose Effects > Edge, and choose the command you want to use.

Making Color Adjustments

As you work with your images in Paint Shop Pro, you may want to make manual corrections or adjustments to the colors. Paint Shop Pro has many features that can help you do this. You can adjust your images directly, or you can add adjustments as layers to your images. In addition, Paint Shop Pro has features that let you add special effects to your images or automatically enhance photographs.

This chapter describes the color adjustment features. If you want add color adjustments as layers, please refer to Chapter 16, "Using Adjustment Layers." If you want to add artistic effects to your images, please refer to Chapter 17, "Adding Effects." To enhance your photographs and other images, please refer to Chapter 6, "Improving Photographs." In addition, reading Chapter 5, "Working with Color" should help you understand the color components you will be adjusting.

▥ Using the Histogram Features

The Histogram displays a graph of the distribution of red, green, blue, greyscale, hue, saturation, and lightness values in an image. You can use the Histogram to analyze your images before making adjustments to them. In addition, the histogram features, located on the Colors > Histogram Adjustment menu, let you use the histogram to make adjustments to your images. These include: Equalize, Histogram Adjustment, and Stretch.

For details, about these features, please refer to "Using the Histogram" in Chapter 6, "Improving Photographs."

Using the Dialog Boxes

As you use the color adjustment dialog boxes, you'll notice that the sliders remain in the final position when you close the boxes. This lets you correct multiple images with the same problem without having to adjust the settings each time. You'll also notice each dialog box has two preview windows and zoom buttons, a Proof button (👁), an Auto Proof button (⬇), and a Reset button (🔁). For information about these features, please refer to the *Getting Started Guide*. Because the dialog boxes retain their last settings, you might want to click the Reset (🔁) button to set all the options to their default values before you begin an adjustment.

Adjusting Colors

Paint Shop Pro provides several commands for adjusting your images and photographs. Use them to make color corrections, improve the results of faulty lighting, and create special effects. For example, perhaps your image has a yellowish cast. Use the Hue/Saturation/Lightness function to remove it. Perhaps the shadowed areas are too dark. Use the Highlight/Midtone/Shadow function to bring out the detail.

NOTE: *Before using the color correction features, you might want to adjust your computer monitor or enable Windows Color Management. For details, please refer to "Adjusting Your Monitor Gamma" in Chapter 6, "Improving Photographs."*

▥ Adjusting the Brightness and Contrast

The Brightness command lightens or darkens the entire image or selection. It is often used to lighten pictures that are too dark after scanning.

The Contrast command changes the amount of shading between areas. You can use it to sharpen or blur an image, to make colors appear more saturated, and make specific areas stand out.

NOTE: *To limit the Brightness/Contrast effect to a selection, the image must be a greyscale or 24-bit color image. To use the effect on a selection, create the selection before choosing the command.*

To adjust the Brightness and Contrast:

1. Open the Brightness/Contrast dialog box in one of the following ways:

   - Choose Colors > Adjust > Brightness/Contrast.

   - Press <Shift> + <B>.

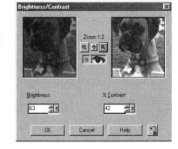

2. To brighten the image, move the Brightness slider to the right or type a positive number in the box. To darken the image, move a slider to the left or type a negative number in the box. The number you enter is added to or subtracted from the Brightness values (0-255) of all the pixels.

3. To increase the contrast, move the Contrast slider to the right or type a positive number in the box. To decrease the contrast, move a slider to the left or type a negative number in the box.

4. Click the OK button to close the dialog box and apply the settings.

Adjusting the Color Channels

Use this adjustment to increase or decrease a color channel by a percentage of itself and the other two channels.

To adjust the color channels:

1. Choose Colors > Adjust > Channel Mixer to open the Channel Mixer dialog box.

NOTE: *To create a greyscale image, select the "Monochrome" check box. This automatically sets the Output channel to black. You can then use the sliders to set the percentage of each channel to use for the greyscale value of the final image.*

2. Select a color channel to edit from the Output Channel drop-down box.

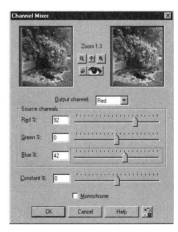

3. Use the Red, Green, and Blue sliders to change the current percentage of that color in the channel you are editing. For example, if you select the Red channel in the Output channel drop-down box and then set the Red slider to 50, you reduce the amount of red in the image to 50% of its original amount.

4. Use the Constant numeric box and slider to brighten or darken the image across each channel. The default of 0 is the original setting. To brighten the channel, move the slider to the right or type a positive number in the box. To darken the channel, move the slider to the left or type a negative number in the box.

5. Click the OK button to close the dialog box and apply the settings.

▲ Adjusting the Color Balance

Use the color balance adjustment to shift the balance of a color and its opposite on the color wheel. There are three pairs: cyan and red, magenta and green, and yellow and blue. Increasing the amount of one decreases the amount of its opposite. You can adjust the balance in each of the three tonal ranges.

To adjust the Color Balance:

1. Choose Colors > Adjust > Color Balance to open the Color Balance dialog box.

2. In the "Tonal Balance" panel, select which lightness level, or tonal range, of colors to adjust. Adjust each one individually.

   - The Shadows option controls the colors at the dark end of the lightness scale;

   - The Midtones option controls the colors in the middle range;

   - The Highlight option controls the colors at the bright end of the scale.

3. Select or clear the "Preserve luminosity" check box to retain or change the luminosity.

4. In the "Color balance" panel, drag the sliders or type values in the boxes to set the color balance. Increasing the proportion of one color decreases the proportion of its opposite. The Color Levels boxes display the balance as you drag the sliders. The box on the left displays the Cyan/Red balance. The middle box displays the Magenta/Green balance. The box at the right displays the Yellow/Blue balance. The original color balance of the image is represented by values of 0 in the boxes and the sliders at the middle of the bars.

5. Click the OK button to close the dialog box and apply the settings.

Adjusting the Curves

Use the curves adjustment to adjust your image's brightness values. You can change any brightness value on the 0-255 scale.

To adjust the curves:

1. Choose Colors > Adjust > Curves to open the Curves dialog box.

2. Select a color channel to edit from the Channel drop-down box. You can edit the three RGB channels together or individually. If you change channels, the values on the graph update and display the new settings.

3. Use the points on the graph to adjust the relationship between the input and output levels. At the lower left of the chart, both values are 0 (black). At the upper right, both values are 255 (white).

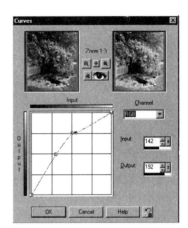

   - To add a point to the graph, move the cursor over line. When the cursor changes to an arrowhead and displays "+add," click the line. Drag this point or enter values in the number box to move the line. The input value displays the original setting for the point. As you drag the point, the output value changes. You can add up to 16 points to the curve. You can also slide a point along the line to substitute values.

   - To remove a point, drag it off the top or bottom edge of the graph.

4. Click the OK button to close the dialog box and apply the settings.

Adjusting the Image Gamma

Use the Gamma Correction command to adjust the brightness and contrast of an image along with the color balance of an image. The Gamma of an image is a measure of its contrast and brightness. By correcting the gamma, you can adjust these two elements in unison.

The gamma curve has three components – the red, green, and blue of the image. You can adjust the color balance of an image by unlinking the curves and moving them separately. For example, if an image has a red cast to it, move the Red slider to the left to reduce it.

NOTE: To limit the Gamma Correction effect to a selection, the image must be a greyscale or 24-bit color image. To use the effect on a selection, create the selection before choosing the command.

To use the Gamma Correction command:

1. Open the Gamma Correction dialog box in one of the following ways:

   • Choose Colors > Adjust > Gamma Correction.

   • Press <Shift> + <G>.

2. To adjust the red, green, and blue curves individually, clear the Link check box. By default, the sliders are linked so that they move in unison.

3. The graph to the left of the sliders shows the curves for the three colors. The left side of the graph represents the shadows of the image; the right side represents the highlights. To view the image's current settings, move the sliders to a setting of 1.00. The three curves will combine into a single straight line. This line mirrors the slider values in the Highlight/Midtone/Shadow dialog box, where the current image settings are 0% Shadow, 50% Midtone, and 100% highlight.

4. If the sliders are linked, drag any slider or type a number into any box to move the curve. Dragging to the right pushes more pixels into a higher lightness value and lightens the image. Dragging to the left darkens the image.

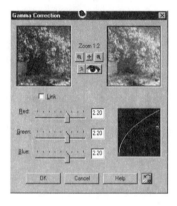

5. To change the color balance of the image, clear the Link check box and adjust the sliders individually. Drag to the right to add more of the color and to the left to remove it.

6. Click the OK button to close the dialog box and apply the settings.

NOTE: *Because this command can leave an image looking somewhat flat, you may want to increase the contrast after correcting the gamma.*

Adjusting the Highlights, Midtones, and Shadows

Use the Highlight/Midtone/Shadow function when you want to adjust the dark, middle, and light values (tonal values) of a photograph separately. You can emphasize highlights or shadows or lighten or darken an image's mid-range colors.

The Highlight slider at 100%, Midtone slider at 50%, and Shadow slider at 0% represent the image's current settings.

NOTE: *To limit the Hue/Saturation/Lightness effect to a selection, the image must be a greyscale or 24-bit color image.*
To use the effect on a selection, create the selection before choosing the command.

To adjust the Highlight, Midtone, and Shadow:

1. Open the Highlight/Midtone/Shadow dialog box, box in either of the following ways:

- Choose Colors > Adjust > Highlight/Midtone/Shadow, or

- Press <Shift> + <M>.

2. Select a method for the adjustment. To adjust each of the values individually, select "Dynamic adjustment method." To adjust them all together, select "Linear adjustment method."

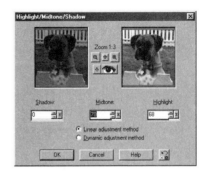

3. Use the Highlight slider to add lightness proportionally to the image. Moving the slider to the left lightens increasingly darker pixels. This moves more of the image into the highlight area.

4. Use the Midtone slider to move the middle portion of the light scale.

5. The effect of the Shadow slider is the opposite of the Highlight slider. Use it to darken increasingly lighter pixels and remove lightness proportionally.

6. Click the OK button to close the dialog box and apply the settings.

Adjusting the Hue, Saturation, and Lightness

We perceive color in terms of its hue, saturation, and lightness. Hue refers to tint, saturation to the purity of the hue, and lightness to its brightness. Altering these three characteristics changes the color we see. Use this command to shift all the colors of an image or selection and change their strength and lightness.

- The Hue function shifts all the pixels in an image around the color wheel to a different point. If you change the red pixels to green, the green pixels will turn to blue and the yellow pixels to cyan.

- Adjusting the hue is the last step in creating a duotone image.

- The Saturation function alters the amount of grey in a color. The level of grey increases as the saturation decreases.

- The Lightness function alters the intensity of light.

NOTE: *To limit the Hue/Saturation/Lightness effect to a selection, the image must be a 24-bit color image. To use the effect on a selection, create the selection before choosing the command.*

To apply the Hue/Saturation/Lightness command:

1. Open the Hue/Saturation/Lightness dialog box in either of the following ways:

   • Choose Colors > Adjust > Hue/Saturation/Lightness, or

   • Press \<Shift\> + \<H\>.

2. From the Edit drop-down box, select which color range to adjust. Choose Master to edit all the colors simultaneously. Choose a specific color range to limit the adjustment. Your choice determines the appearance of the control ring.

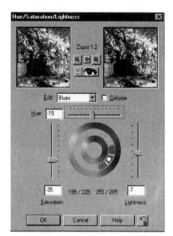

3. If you are adding color to a greyscale image, select the "Colorize" check box below the color rings. The Edit box becomes unavailable.

4. To adjust the saturation and luminance, move the sliders or type numbers in the boxes. Negative numbers decrease the saturation and luminance levels; positive numbers increase them.

5. If you are in the Master Edit mode, move the Hue slider or type a number in the box to shift every color. Negative numbers rotate the wheel to the left; positive numbers rotate it to the right. You can go half the way around the wheel by moving the slider all the way left or right. The control ring displays the new hue for each color. For example, when the slider is at 180, blue becomes yellow and green becomes magenta.

6. If you are restricting the adjustment to a color range, drag the two outer pointers on the control ring to set the range width. They mark the beginning and end of the adjustment area. You can drag them to edit as wide a range as you like. You can also drag the two inner bars. The segment between each outer pointer and inner bar shows where the adjustment is building to its full effect. The area between the two inner bars shows where the adjustment is in full effect. To move control ring, drag the white circle.

7. To choose new colors for the color range, type a number in the Hue box or drag the Hue slider. You can move from –180 to +180.

8. To change the saturation of the color range, type a number from –100 to +100 in the Saturation box or drag the Saturation slider. At –100, the colors are desaturated, or grey; at +100, they are fully saturated.

9. To change the luminance of the color range, type a number from –100 to +100 in the Luminance box or drag the Luminance slider. At –100, the colors become black; at +100, they turn white.

10. Click the OK button to close the dialog box and apply the settings.

⊞ Adjusting the Color Levels

Adjust the color levels to reset the darkest and lightest values in the image to black and white to increase the tonal range. The corresponding pixels in the other channels are also adjusted to keep the original color balance.

To adjust the color levels:

1. Choose Colors > Adjust > Levels to open the Levels dialog box.

2. Select a color channel to edit from the Channel drop-down box. You can edit the three RGB channels together or individually. If you change channels, the values on the graph update and display the new settings.

3. Drag the diamond-shaped sliders to adjust the input and outputs levels. The sliders are visual representations of the values in the boxes.

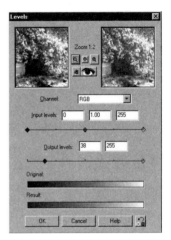

- The Input levels display the image's brightness levels. Changing the inputs levels modifies the image by darkening the darkest values and lightening the lightest values. This increases the contrast.

  The value in the left box represents where 0 begins. All values below this value become 0 (black). For example, if you enter 50 in the box, all values below 50 become 0. The box on the right represents where 255 begins. All values above it are set to 255 (white). The middle box controls the gamma curve. The range for this curve is 0 to 7.99, with 1 being in the middle. The gamma value resets the lightness of medium grey.

- The Output levels lighten the darkest pixels and darken the lightest pixels. To create a negative image effect, invert these values so that the upper value is 25 and the lower value is 200.

▣ Adjusting the Reds, Greens, and Blues

By adjusting the individual levels of red, green, or blue in an image or selection, you can change its overall color cast and correct color balance problems. To reduce the amount of color in an image, you can either increase its opposite color or reduce the amount of the adjacent colors (on the color wheel). For example, to color correct an image containing too much yellow, either increase the amount of blue or decrease the amount of red and green. You can use either this command or the Gamma Correction command to remove the color cast from an image.

NOTE: *To limit the Red/Green/Blue effect to a selection, the image must be a 24-bit color image. To use the effect on a selection, create the selection before choosing the command.*

To adjust the Red/Green/Blue values:

1. Open the Red/Green/Blue dialog box in one of the following ways:

   • Choose Colors > Adjust > Red/Green/Blue

   • Press <Shift> + <U>.

2. Move each of the red, green, and blue sliders away from center to add or remove that color proportionally. The values of the image are represented as percentages, with 0% indicating the original values.

   • Reducing the amount of blue adds a yellow cast to the image.

   • Reducing the amount of green adds a magenta cast to the image.

   • Reducing the amount of red adds a cyan cast to the image.

3. Click the OK button to close the dialog box and apply the settings.

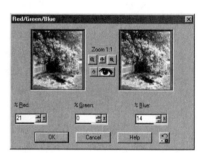

Replacing Colors

Use the Hue Map command to change individual hues (colors) in a photograph. You can replace any color with another. When painting or working with images that contain large areas of solid color, you may prefer to use the Color Replacer tool. When you want to just touch up a small area of an image, use the Retouch tool.

Using the Hue Map

NOTE: *To limit the Hue Map effect to a selection, the image must be a 24-bit color image. To use the effect on a selection, create the selection before choosing the command.*

To use the Hue Map command:

1. Open the Hue Map dialog box by choosing Colors > Adjust > Hue Map.

2. If necessary, click the Reset button to return the sliders to their default positions.

3. Move the slider of each column to shift a hue. If the image does not contain that hue, nothing happens.

4. Drag the Saturation slider to the left and right to decrease and increase the saturation of all colors in the image.

5. Drag the Lightness slider to the left and right to decrease and increase the lightness of the entire image.

6. Click the OK button to close the dialog box and apply the settings.

Using Other Methods to Replace Color

Use the Color Replacer tool ( ) when you want to replace sections of a solid color quickly or replace a color without first making a selection. You can also use the Eraser tool ( ). On a layer, the Eraser replaces a color with a transparency. On a background, it replaces a color with the foreground or background color. If you want to do simple color touch-ups, use the Retouch tool ( ). For more information about using these tools, please refer to the Chapter 8, "Using the Painting Tools."

Reducing or Removing Colors

 Adjusting the Threshold

Adjust the Threshold to create a black-and-white image.

To adjust the Threshold:

1. Choose Colors > Adjust > Threshold to open the Threshold dialog box.

2. Drag the Threshold slider or type a number in the box to adjust the brightness values in the image. All pixels in the image that have brightness values below the Threshold level become black. All pixels with brightness values at or above the level become white.

NOTE: *To see what the current brightness values are in an image, use the Histogram to analyze the image. For more information, please refer to Chapter 6, "Improving Photographs."*

Creating a Greyscale Image

A greyscale image is an 8-bit image whose palette contains 256 shades of grey. Because it can contain only 256 shades, converting an image with more colors into a greyscale image automatically reduces it to an 8-bit image.

The Greyscale command removes the colors from an image and replaces each color with a grey matching its luminance value. The effect is similar to a black-and-white photograph.

* To convert an image to greyscale, choose Colors > Greyscale or click the Greyscale button on the toolbar.

Creating a Duotone Image

Creating a greyscale image is the first step in making a duotone image.

After you have made a greyscale image, do the following to convert it into a duotone image:

1. Increase color depth to 24 bits.

2. Use the Colorize dialog box to add color and adjust saturation.

Colorizing an Image

Apply the Colorize command to replace all colors in an image or selection with a single color and saturation while leaving the lightness values unchanged. You can use it to create sepia tones (the brown seen in old photographs) and other single-color effects.

To replace individual colors, use the Hue Map dialog box or the Color Replacer tool.

To apply the Colorize command:

1. Open the Colorize dialog box by choosing Colors > Colorize or pressing <Shift> + <L>.

2. Drag the Hue slider to the left and right or type a number in the box to change the hue. Moving the slider represents moving around the color wheel. 0 is red; 43 is yellow; 85 is green; 128 is cyan; 170 is blue; 213 is magenta; 255 is back to red.

3. Drag the Saturation slider to the left or type a negative number in the box to reduce the saturation; drag it to the right or type a positive number to increase the saturation.

4. Click the OK button to close the dialog box and apply the settings.

Posterizing an Image

Apply the Posterize (pronounced with a long "o") command to reduce the number lightness levels in an image. You set a value, and the program divides the range of lightness levels (from 2 to 255) into that number of equal increments. As the number of levels decreases, it produces a flatter-looking image or selection.

When you open the dialog box, the slider displays the current number of levels of lightness in the image.

To use the Posterize command:

1. Open the Posterize dialog box by choosing Colors > Posterize or pressing <Shift> + <Z>.

2. Drag the Levels slider to the left or type a lower number in the slider box to Posterize the image. As you lower the number, you increase the effect.

3. Click the OK button to close the dialog box and apply the settings.

Original Image   Posterize Effect   Negative Image Effect   Solarize Effect

✖ Creating a Negative Image

Creating a Negative image replaces each pixel color with its opposite on the color wheel. The brightness value of the pixel changes to 255 minus the original value. Zero becomes 255, and 30 becomes 225. The new image is like a photographic negative. You can use this function to create a positive image from a scanned negative.

- To create a negative image, choose Colors > Negative Image.

⚡ Solarizing an Image

The Solarize command produces the same effect as the Negative Image command, but lets you control the threshold level. The threshold level is the lightness value above which all colors are inverted. You set the level, and all colors with a lightness value above that level are turned into their inverse (on the 255 scale).

To apply the Solarize command:

1. Open the Solarize dialog box by choosing Colors > Solarize.

2. Drag the Threshold slider or type a number into the box to set the threshold level. As the level increases, colors must be increasingly lighter to be inverted.

3. Click the OK button to close the dialog box and apply the settings.

Splitting and Combining Color Channels

Splitting Color Channels

An image stores its color information in channels. The information contained in the channels depends on the color method being used to define the image. With Paint Shop Pro, you have three choices for splitting the channels.

When you separate these channels, Paint Shop Pro creates individual greyscale images that you can edit. You can use these images to create interesting effects. For example, you can split an image into its HSL channels, apply a filter to the Lightness channel, and then recombine the channels. You can also split an image and use one of the channels to create a mask.

When you split the channels of an image, you create new images; the original image is not affected. Each new image is named after its channel. For example, an HSL image will be split into three separate images with the names "Hue," "Saturation," and "Lightness."

To split an active image, choose Colors > Split Channel, and then RGB, HSL, or CMYK.

Combining Color Channels

If you have split an image into its color channels, you can combine the channels to recreate the original image or combine other channels to create various effects. The three Channel Combining dialog boxes all operate in the same way.

To combine channels:

1. Open a Channel Combining dialog box by choosing Colors > Combine Channel > and then the RGB, HSL, or CMYK command.

2. Select the Source Images, which are the greyscale images to be combined. You can use source images that were generated by splitting the color channels of an image, or you can select other images:

   • If you generated the source images by splitting an image's channels, select the "Sync…" check box to have Paint Shop Pro use the channels from the selected image.

   • If the source images were not created by splitting an image's channels, use the drop down boxes to select a greyscale image for each channel.

3. Click the OK button. Paint Shop Pro creates an image by combining the greyscale images into color channel data.

Using the
Painting Tools

Paint Shop Pro provides several painting and drawing tools on its Tools palette. These range from standard paint brushes to photo retouching tools to the Text tool. The Paint Brush, Clone Brush, Color Replacer, Retouch, Eraser, Picture Tube, Airbrush, and Flood Fill tools have options to let you use them on raster layers. This chapter discusses the raster painting tools. The Text, Drawing, and Preset Shapes tools have options to let you use them on both raster and vector layers. For information on these tools, please refer to Chapter 12, "Using the Vector Tools."

When a vector layer is selected, the raster painting tools are unavailable, and their buttons are greyed-out. Because many of these tools operate or have the desired effect only on greyscale or 24-bit images, you may need to increase the color (bit) depth of your image before using them. For help with this, please refer to Chapter 5, "Working with Color."

Using a Painting Tool

There are four general steps for using a painting tool: activate the tool, configure the settings on the Tool Options palette, select the styles and textures on the Color palette, and apply the tool to the image.

Activating a Tool

To activate a tool using the Tool palette:

1. Display the Tool palette if it is not visible.

2. On the Tool palette, click the button of the tool you want to use.

To activate a tool using the Tool Options palette:

1. Display the Tool Options palette if it is not visible.

2. Click the Tool Selection button and choose the tool from the drop-down menu.

Configuring the Settings on the Tool Options Palette

The Tool Options palette displays the settings for the painting tools. After you activate a tool, use the Tool Options palette to configure the brush tip and options unique to each tool. Some of the tools have two tabbed pages on the Tool Options palette; others have three tabbed pages. The options that are available on the first or second tabbed pages vary for each tool. These options are described separately for each tool within this chapter.

For every tool, the last tab on the right is always the Cursor and Tablet Options tab. This tab lets you modify the cursor appearance and brush outline settings. The tab also lets you set options for a pressure sensitive tablet, as follows:

CURSORS These options let you set the type of cursor. Select the "Use precise cursor" check box to use a modified cursor in place of the standard Windows cursor. This cursor can help you select and position image elements with greater precision. Select the "Show brush outlines" check box to have the cursor show the brush shape and size when you paint.

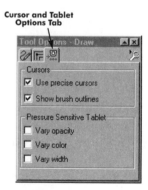

Cursor and Tablet Options Tab

PRESSURE SENSITIVE TABLET If you are using a drawing tablet, these options let you set the attributes you want to control with the pressure of the drawing pen.

Selecting Styles and Textures

The colors, gradients, or patterns you are currently using, called the styles, are displayed in the foreground/stroke and background/fill boxes on the "Active Styles" panel of the Color palette. The textures you are currently using are displayed in the foreground/stroke and background/fill boxes on the Active Textures panel of the Color palette. Many tools let you change both the styles and textures. These options are described separately for each tool.

Applying the Tool to the Image

NOTE: *To confine the paint to a specific area, create a selection before painting. You can change the brush options, style settings, and colors in between brush strokes.*

Freehand Painting

To create freehand paint strokes, use the following method:

1. If the image contains more than one layer, select the layer to paint.

2. Position the cursor where you want to start the paint stroke.

3. Press and hold down the left or right mouse button:

   - Press the left mouse button to apply the foreground/stroke style and texture.

   - Press the right mouse button to apply the background/fill style and texture.

4. Drag the mouse to apply the style and texture.

5. To end the paint stroke, release the mouse button. Each time you release the mouse button, you "lift" your brush from the canvas, ending the stroke.

Creating Straight Lines

To paint a straight line, use the following method:

1. Position the cursor where you want to begin a straight paint stroke.

2. Click the left or right mouse button:

   - Click the left mouse button to apply the foreground/stroke style and texture.

   - Click the right mouse button to apply the background/fill style and texture.

3. Press and hold the <Shift> key.

4. Position the cursor where you want to end the first brush stroke.

5. Click with the left or right mouse button to paint the foreground/stroke or background/fill style and texture.

6. Continue to add straight paint strokes by clicking with either mouse button.

7. When you have finished, release the <Shift> key.

Undoing Paint Strokes

If you make a mistake or want to redo the painting, you can remove it by choosing Undo from the Edit menu. You can undo more than one brush stroke. To undo the earlier brush strokes, choose Edit > Command History and select the brush strokes to undo. For help with the Undo/Redo settings, refer to Chapter 20 "Setting Preferences."

✏️ Working with Custom Brushes

For most of the painting tools, the first tabbed page of the Tool Options palette has a Brush Types button for setting the brush type for the tool. When you click this button, a menu appears. The menu contains a selection of brushes that replicate specific drawing instruments, including Paintbrush, Pen, Pencil, Marker, Crayon, Chalk, and Charcoal. You can also choose Custom brushes to apply paint in shapes. You can select from preset shape brush types or create your own custom brush types. This section describes how to use and create custom brush types for the tools.

Using a Custom Brush Type

Paint Shop Pro provides several custom brushes that apply paint in shapes. When you are setting the tool options for a tool on the first tab of the Tool Options palette, you can select a brush type. To select a brush type, click the Brush Types button and choose Custom from the menu that appears. From the Custom Brush dialog box, click the brush type. If you want to change the Step, click the Edit button and change the step. After selecting the brush type and changing the step, you can also change the Size, Opacity, and Build Up Brush options on the first tab of the Tool Options palette. The rest of the options are unavailable.

Creating a Custom Brush

You can create your own custom brush types. By default, they are stored in the Brushes folder of the program folder. The brush types are then available using the Custom Brush dialog box. Custom brushes can be created from selections with a width and height of up to 255 by 255 pixels.

NOTE: *To save the brush types in a folder other than the Paint Shop Pro Brushes folder, click the Edit Paths button to display the File Locations dialog box. For more information, please refer to Chapter 20, "Setting Preferences."*

To create a custom brush:

1. Make a selection of the area you want to convert into a brush type. For more information about making a selection, please refer to Chapter 10, "Working with Selections."

2. If necessary, make the Tool Options palette visible and activate a brush.

3. Click the Brush Types button to open the Custom Paintbrush menu, and choose Custom. The Custom Brush dialog box opens.

4. Click the Create button. The new brush thumbnail appears in the dialog box.

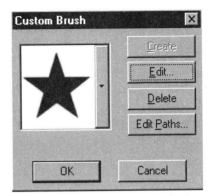

5. To set a default Step value, click the Edit button to open the Custom Brush Edit dialog box. Drag the slider or type a number in the box, and then click the OK button to close this dialog box.

6. Click the OK button to close the Custom Brush dialog box.

7. When you use the brush type for a tool, set the size, opacity, and build up brush options.

Using the Paint Brush

The Paint Brush tool simulates painting with a paint brush.

Setting the Paint Brush Options

To set the Paint Brush options:

1. Activate the Paint Brush by clicking its button on the Tool palette or in the Tool Selection menu of the Tool Options palette.

2. On the first tab of the Tool Options palette, set the brush tip options to determine how the Paint Brush applies paint. As you change the options, the preview box at the upper left of the palette displays the new tip. The options are described on the next page.

BRUSH TYPES Contains a selection of brushes with preset tips that replicate specific drawing instruments, including Paintbrush, Pen, Pencil, Marker, Crayon, Chalk, and Charcoal. You can also use Custom brushes to apply paint in shapes. You can select from preset shape brushes or create your own custom brushes. If you use a custom brush type, all options except the size, opacity, and build up brush are set automatically. For more information about using and creating custom brushes, please refer to "Working with Custom Brushes" on page 132.

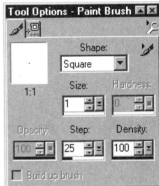

SHAPE Controls the shape of the brush tip. The choices are square, round, left slash, right slash, horizontal, and vertical. For example, if you click your image once with a square brush, the brush applies a square-shaped area of paint.

SIZE Controls the width of the brush tip in pixels. This can be from 1-255 pixels wide.

HARDNESS Controls the sharpness of the brush edges. The harder the brush, the more defined the edges of paint will be. At 100%, the paint stroke has sharply defined edges. As the hardness decreases, the brush edge softens.

OPACITY Controls how well the paint covers the image surface. Lowering the opacity is like diluting paint. At 100% opacity, the paint covers everything; at 1%, the paint is almost transparent.

STEP Controls the spacing of the discrete drops of paint, or how frequently the brush tip touches the image during a stroke. It is a percentage of the diameter of the brush tip. At 100%, a size 30 brush tip touches the surface once every 30 pixels, and the brush shape is clearly defined; at 50%, the tip touches in the middle of the previous tip. As the step decreases, the brush tip touches the surface more frequently. Its outline becomes less noticeable, and the strokes appear smoother and more dense.

DENSITY Controls the amount of paint the brush applies with each stroke. The density can be compared to the number of bristles in a brush—increasing and decreasing density adds and removes bristles. At 100%, the paint covers the surface completely. As the density decreases, the amount of paint applied with each stroke decreases. At 1%, only a few pixels of paint appear.

BUILD UP BRUSH Simulates the effect of repeated brush strokes. Each time you move the brush over the same area of the image (or layer), you apply more paint. When the option is inactive, the brush applies paint once, and repainting an area has no effect. Select the check box to activate this feature. Clear the check box to make it inactive.

3. Select the styles and textures on the Color palette.

   - For the styles, you can set the foreground/stroke and the background/fill to paint with solid colors, gradients, and pattern styles.

   - For the textures, you can set a foreground and/or a background texture.

4. Select the foreground and background colors using one of the methods described in Chapter 9, "Using the Color Palette."

Painting with the Paint Brush

To apply the paint to the image, please refer back to the general steps, "Applying the Tool to the Image" on page 131.

Using the Airbrush

The Airbrush simulates painting with an airbrush or spray can.

To use the Airbrush:

1. Activate the Airbrush by clicking its button on the Tool palette or in the Tool Selection menu of the Tool Options palette.

2. On the first tab of the Tool Options palette, set the brush tip shape and other options to determine how the Airbrush applies paint. If necessary, refer back to the descriptions on page 133.

3. Select the styles and textures using the appropriate boxes on the Color palette:

   - For the styles, you can set the foreground/stroke and the background/fill to paint with solid colors, gradients, and pattern styles.

   - For the textures, you can set a foreground and/or a background texture.

4. Select the foreground and background colors using one of the methods described in Chapter 9, "Using the Color Palette."

Painting with the Airbrush

To apply the paint to the image, please refer back to the general steps, "Applying the Tool to the Image" on page 131.

Using the Eraser

Use the Eraser to replace colors in an image with the background color or with a transparency. When you drag the Eraser across a raster layer, all the pixels in its path become transparent. When used on a background, the Eraser produces a different effect. It acts like a paintbrush, and it replaces the existing color with the current foreground or background color.

The Eraser retains the information it has removed from a layer. To restore the erased image, right-click and drag the Eraser over the transparent areas.

Setting the Eraser Options

To set the Eraser options:

1. Activate the Eraser by clicking its button on the Tool palette or in the Tool Selection menu of the Tool Options palette.

2. On the first tab of the Tool Options palette, set the brush tips and other options. If necessary, refer back to the descriptions on page 133. Note the following:

   - At 100% Hardness, the stroke has sharply defined edges. As the hardness decreases, the edge softens.

   - Lowering the Opacity reduces the eraser's strength.

   - At 100% Step, the eraser shape is clearly defined. As the step decreases, the strokes appear smoother.

   - At 100% Density, the surface is erased completely, removing all the paint. At 1%, only a few specks (pixels) of paint are erased.

   - If you select the "Build Up Brush" check box, each stroke removes more of the color. When the check box is cleared, the color is erased only on the first brush stroke. Subsequent strokes apply more of the effect.

3. Select the styles and textures on the Color palette.

   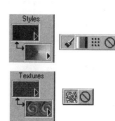

   - For the styles, you can set the foreground as stroked and the background as filled. This lets you erase with solid colors. The gradient and pattern styles are not available for the Eraser tool.

   - For the textures, you can set a foreground texture.

4. Select the foreground and background colors using one of the methods described in Chapter 9, "Using the Color Palette."

Erasing

NOTE: *To confine the Eraser to a specific area, make a selection before erasing. Right-clicking and dragging over transparent areas of the layer make those areas black. To remove the black, left-click and drag.*

Erasing with Freehand Strokes

To use the Eraser:

1. Place the cursor where you want to start erasing.

2. Click and hold the left or right mouse button:

   - Click the left mouse button to apply the background style and foreground texture.

   - Click the right mouse button to apply the foreground style and foreground texture.

3. Drag the mouse to erase.

4. Drag with the opposite mouse button to reapply the erased paint.

5. Release the mouse button to end the Eraser stroke.

Erasing with Straight Brush Strokes

To erase by creating straight line brush strokes:

1. Click where you want to begin erasing.

2. Press and hold the <Shift> key.

3. Position the cursor where you want to end the line segment.

4. Click the left or right mouse button:

   - Click the left mouse button to apply the background style and background texture.

   - Click the right mouse button to apply the foreground style and foreground texture.

5. Continue to erase in line segments by clicking with either mouse button.

6. When you have finished, release the <Shift> key.

Using the Clone Brush

Use the Clone brush to copy part of an image to another location. You can clone within a raster layer, between raster layers, or between two greyscale or 24-bit color images. For example, if a photograph has a flaw against a multi-toned or multicolored background, such as skin or cloth, you can use the Clone brush to copy the background over the flaw.

When you use the Clone brush, you work with two image areas:

- The source area, which is the area containing the data you are copying.

- The target area, which is the area you copy to. It can be within the same image or in another image of equal color depth.

NOTE: *When you clone from one image to another, make sure they are of equal color depth before you begin.*

Setting the Clone Brush Options

To set the Clone Brush Options:

1. Activate the Clone brush by clicking its button on the Tool palette or in the Tool Selection menu of the Tool Options palette.

2. On the first tab of the Tool Options palette, set the brush tip shape and other options. If necessary, refer back to the descriptions on page 133. If you select the "Build Up Brush" check box, each clone stroke applies more of the copied data. When the check box is cleared, the cloning is applied only on the first brush stroke over the area.

3. Click the second tab to bring it to the front. Set the options on the tab:

   - In the Clone Mode box, select a clone mode. The clone mode controls the position of the source area, or reference point, for cloning each time you release the mouse button and then press it again to resume cloning.

     Aligned mode - the source area moves each time you release the mouse. The source area is the reference point for the cloning. When you re-click the mouse, the brush clones the image relative to the distance from the source area.

     Non-aligned mode - the source area does <u>not</u> move when you release the mouse. Each time you release and then re-click the mouse, the starting point for cloning returns to source area.

- Select the "Sample Merged" check box to clone all visible data rather than just the data from the current layer. If the check box is not selected, only the data on the current layer when the source point was defined is cloned.

4. To add a textured effect when cloning, set the foreground texture on the Color palette.

Applying the Clone Brush

NOTE: *When you clone from one image to another, make sure they are of equal color depth before you begin. To confine the cloning to a specific area, make a selection before cloning.*

To clone part of an image:

1. To apply the tool to the images, position the cursor over the part of the image that you want to copy and set the source area by doing either of the following:

- Right-click the source area once. Your computer beeps to indicate that you have selected the source area.

- Press <Shift> and click the source area.

2. To place the cloned image on a specific layer or in a selection, select that layer or area now. Paint Shop Pro clones only within the selection.

3. Position the cursor where you want to start copying the image. This can be within the same image or in another image of the same color depth.

4. Press and hold the left mouse button. Crosshairs appear over the source area. They indicate which pixel you are copying.

5. Drag the mouse to clone from the source area to the target area.

6. Release the mouse button to end the brush stroke.

To resume copying, start over at step 4.

Remember that the location of the source area depends on the clone mode.

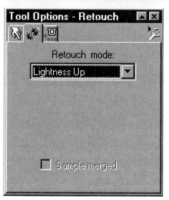 Using the Retouch Tool

Although the Retouch tool uses the same brush tips as the other brushes, you don't use it to apply paint. You use it to lighten, emboss, change the saturation, and make other retouches to your image. Some of them produce the same results as the Color Adjustment functions. The Retouch tool paints with the effect rather than applying it to an entire area.

Setting the Retouch Tool Options

To set the Retouch tool options:

1. Activate the Retouch tool by clicking its button on the Tool palette or in the Tool Selection menu of the Tool Options palette.

2. On the first tab of the Tool Options palette, set the brush tip shape and other options. If necessary, refer back to the descriptions on page 133. If you select the "Build Up Brush" check box, each stroke applies more of the effect. When the check box is cleared, the effect is applied only on the first brush stroke over the area.

3. In the Retouch mode drop down box, select a mode. The mode settings are described after these directions.

4. Click the second tab to bring it to the front.

5. Select the "Sample Merged" check box to retouch all visible data rather than just the data from the current layer. Clear the check box to retouch only the data on the current layer when the source point was defined.

6. To add a textured effect when retouching, set the foreground texture on the Color palette.

Applying the Retouch Tool

The Retouch tool is usually used on a specific area. It is generally easier if you zoom in on this area. To limit the retouching to a specific area, select the area before using the tool.

Retouching with Freehand Strokes

To retouch an image:

1. To retouch a specific layer, select the layer.

2. Click the image where you want the brush stroke to start.

3. Drag the mouse to apply the retouch effect. If necessary, increase the opacity of the tool.

4. Release the mouse button to end the brush stroke.

Retouching with Straight Strokes

To retouch using straight line brush strokes:

1. Click where you want to begin retouching.

2. Press and hold the <Shift> key.

3. Click where you want to end the first line segment.

4. You can continue applying the effect in line segments by clicking the image. After you have finished, release the <Shift> key.

Retouch Modes

Paint Shop Pro offers several Retouch modes, which are described in the following table.

Retouch Modes

Retouch Mode	Effect Produced
Lighten	Increases brightness (works on RGB values)
Darken	Decreases brightness (works on RGB values)
Soften	Smoothes edges and reduces contrasts
Sharpen	Heightens edges and accentuates contrasts
Emboss	Causes foreground to appear raised from background by suppressing color and tracing edges in black
Smudge	Spreads color from the starting point and picks up new color as it moves. The effect is similar to smearing paint.
Push	Similar to Smudge, but does not pick up any new color.
Dodge	Lightens and brings out the details in areas that are in shadow. Comes from the darkroom technique of holding back some of the light when developing film to produce lighter areas. The opposite of Burn.
Burn	Darkens areas in the image that are too light. The opposite of Dodge.
Saturation Up	Increases saturation (affects HSL value)
Saturation Down	Decreases saturation (affects HSL value)
Lightness Up	Increases lightness (affects HSL value)
Lightness Down	Decreases lightness (affects HSL value)
Hue Up	Shifts hue up (affects HSL value)
Hue Down	Shifts hue down (affects HSL value)
Saturation to Target	Applies the saturation value equal to that of the foreground color without affecting the hue or lightness
Lightness to Target	Applies the lightness value equal to that of the foreground color without affecting the saturation or hue
Hue to Target	Applies the hue of the foreground color without affecting the saturation or lightness
Color to Target	Applies the foreground color without affecting the luminance

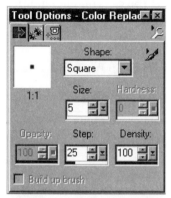 Using the Color Replacer

The Color Replacer tool uses the foreground stroke and background fill colors from the Active Styles panel of the Color palette to replace one color in an image with a new color. You can use brush strokes to replace only those areas the brush touches, or you can double-click the image to replace the color throughout. You can also set a Tolerance value on the second tab of the Tool Options palette. This lets you replace colors that are similar, but not identical, to the original.

Setting the Color Replacer Options

To set the Color Replacer options:

1. Activate the Color Replacer by clicking its button on the Tool palette or in the Tool Selection menu of the Tool Options palette.

2. Select the color you are replacing as the foreground or background color using one of the methods described in Chapter 9, "Using the Color Palette."

3. Select the color you are substituting as the other active color.

4. If you are painting with the Color Replacer, use the first tab of the Tool Options palette to configure the brush tip. If you are replacing all occurrences of a color, you only need to set the options on the second tab. If necessary, refer back to the descriptions on page 133.

5. Click the second tab to bring it to the front.

6. Set a Tolerance value to determine how closely the colors of the image must match the old color in order to be replaced. As you increase the tolerance, more colors are replaced.

Replacing a Color

Replacing All Occurrences of a Color

If you want to replace all occurrences of a color within a specific area of the image, select the area now. For making selections, please read Chapter 10, "Working with Selections."

To replace all occurrences of a color:

1. To limit the color replacement to a specific layer, select the layer.

2. Use the left or right mouse to double-click the image:

- To replace the background color with the foreground color, double-click left mouse button anywhere in the image.

- To replace the foreground color with the background color, double-click the right mouse button anywhere in the image.

Replacing Color with Freehand Strokes

You can use the Color Replacer as a brush, replacing a color only where the brush touches the image.

NOTE: *To confine the color replacement to a specific area, select the area before painting with the Color Replacer. To undo a Color Replacer stroke, immediately choose Undo from the Edit menu.*

To replace a color using brush strokes:

1. To limit the color replacement to a specific layer, select the layer.

2. Place the cursor where you want to start replacing a color.

3. Press and hold down the left or right mouse button:

- To replace the background color with the foreground color, press and hold down the left mouse button.

- To replace the foreground color with the background color, press and hold down the right mouse button.

4. Drag the mouse to replace the color where the brush touches it.

5. Release the mouse button to end a brush stroke.

Replacing Color Using Straight Brush Strokes

To replace color using straight line brush strokes:

1. Click where you want to begin replacing color.

2. Press and hold the <Shift> key.

3. Click where you want to end the first line segment.

You can continue replacing color in line segments by clicking the image. After you have finished, release the <Shift> key.

 Using the Flood Fill Tool

The Flood Fill tool fills an area with a color, pattern, or gradient. It has a number of options that control how it recognizes and replaces color.

Setting the Flood Fill Options

To set the Flood Fill tool options:

1. Activate the Flood Fill tool by clicking its button on the Tool palette or in the Tool Selection menu of the Tool Options palette.

2. On the first tab of the Tool Options palette, set the options:

- From the Blend Mode drop-down box, choose a mode other than Normal if you want the pixels of the underlying image to affect the Flood Fill colors. The same choices are used for the Layer blend modes. For an explanation of them, please refer to Chapter 11, "Working with Layers."

- In the Match Mode drop-down box, select a method for determining which pixels are covered. The modes select the pixels using the following methods:

   RGB Value - covers pixels with matching RGB values,

   Hue - covers pixels with matching hue values,

   Brightness - covers pixels with matching luminance values, and

   None - covers all pixels.

- Set a fill color Tolerance. This value determines how closely the color of a pixel must match the color of the selected pixel before it is overwritten. The Tolerance box uses a scale of 0 to 200, with 0 being no tolerance (only pixels with a perfect match are filled), and 200 being total tolerance (all pixels are filled).

- Set the Opacity for the fill. At 100% opacity, the paint covers everything; at 1%, the paint is almost transparent.

- Select the Sample Merged check box to have the Match mode select pixels from the entire image. Clear the check box to limit it to the current (active) layer.

3. Select the styles and textures on the Color palette:

- For the styles, you can set the foreground as stroked (solid color), gradient, or pattern; and the background as filled (solid color), gradient, or pattern. This lets you fill with solid colors, gradients, or patterns.

- For the textures, you can set a foreground and/or a background texture.

4. If using stroked or filled styles, or gradients, patterns, and textures, please refer to Chapter 9, "Using the Color Palette." Pattern and Gradient fills can only be applied to 24-bit color or greyscale images.

Applying a Flood Fill

NOTE: *To confine the flood fill to a specific area, select the area before applying the flood fill. To undo a flood fill, immediately choose Undo from the Edit menu.*

To apply a Flood Fill:

1. Select the layer to be covered with the fill.

2. Position the cursor on the image or selection.

3. Click the left or right mouse button:

- Click the left mouse button to apply the foreground style (color, gradient, or pattern) and the foreground texture.

- Click the right mouse button to apply the background style (color, gradient, or pattern) and the background texture.

Using the Picture Tubes

Paint Shop Pro's Picture Tube tool lets you paint with a collection of objects without having to draw them. You can add butterflies and beetles to a picnic setting, fill an aquarium with fish, or frame a picture with holly. Use one of the Picture Tubes included with the program or create your own.

By default, the Paint Shop Pro Picture Tubes are saved as .tub files in the Tubes folder of the program. If you use the Browser to view them, you can see that the objects are arranged in rows and columns. These rows are called cells.

When you paint with a Picture Tube, you can control which object appears by changing the settings in the Selection Mode box of the Picture Tube Options dialog box. This dialog box also contains a "Cell Arrangement" panel, which you use when you are painting with a Picture Tube you have created. This panel is explained in "Creating a Picture Tube" on page 147.

Setting the Picture Tube Options

To set the Picture Tube options:

1. Activate the Picture Tube tool by clicking its button on the Tool palette or in the Tool Selection menu of the Tool Options palette.

2. On the first tab of the Tool Options palette, select a Picture Tube from the Tube preview box and set the step and scale options:

3. On the first tab of the Tool Options palette, set the tool options:

   - Set the Step size. As you decrease the step size, the distance between the intervals at which the tubes appear in the image decreases.

   - Use the Scale box to set the Picture Tube size. You can reduce and enlarge it from 10% to 250% of its original size.

4. Click the second tab to bring it to the front. Set the options on the tab:

   - In the Placement Mode drop-down box, choose the Random or Continuous placement mode to control whether the Picture Tubes appear in the image at random or equal intervals.

   - In the Selection Mode drop-down box, choose how Paint Shop Pro selects the cells (images) it paints. You have a choice of 5 modes:

     Random mode randomly selects images in the tube.

     Incremental mode selects the first image in the tube and repeats it only after it has selected all the images.

     Angular mode selects images based on the direction you drag the cursor as you paint.

     Pressure mode uses pressure from a pressure sensitive pad to determine which image to select.

     Velocity mode selects images based on the speed you drag the cursor as you paint.

5. To change the Picture Tube settings, click the Options button to open the Picture Tube Options dialog box. You can apply tubes without changing the settings. Use the Picture Tube Options dialog box to change the default settings for the tool's options.

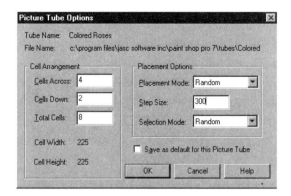

- The "Cell Arrangement" panel shows the arrangement of Picture Tube cells in the Picture Tube file. For Paint Shop Pro Picture Tubes, use the default settings.

- In the "Placement Options" panel, select Random or Continuous placement mode to control whether the Picture Tubes appear in the image at random or equal intervals.

- Type a Step size. As you decrease the step size, the distance between the intervals at which the tubes appear in the image decreases.

- Paint Shop Pro selects the cells (images) it paints based on the mode you choose from the Selection Mode list. The options are described in the Setting the Picture Tube Options section above.

- If you want these settings to become the new default settings for the tube, select the Save as default for this Picture Tube check box.

- Click the OK button to close the Picture Tube Options dialog box.

Painting with a Picture Tube

NOTE: *To confine the paint to a specific area, make a selection before painting.*

To paint with a Picture Tube:

1. If the image contains more than one layer, select the layer to paint.

2. Position the cursor where you want to begin painting.

3. Click and drag the cursor to paint the Picture Tube. If you have chosen a Selection Mode option other than Random, move the cursor accordingly.

4. To end the paint stroke, release the mouse button.

Creating a Picture Tube

To create your own Picture Tubes, you create a grid of cells and then fill each cell with an image. The cells can be any size. Remember, though, that as the size of the cells increases, the Picture Tubes require more memory to use.

Chapter 8: Using the Painting Tools

NOTE: *To save picture tubes in a folder other than the Paint Shop Pro Tubes folder, choose File > Preferences > File Locations and change the folders on the Tubes tab. For more information, please refer to Chapter 20 "Setting Preferences."*

To create a Picture Tube file:

1. Choose File > Preferences > General Program Preferences and click the Rulers and Units tab. Set the grid preferences:

   - In the "Grid" panel on the right side of the tab, type Horizontal and Vertical Spacing values in pixels. The values you enter become the length and height of the Picture Tube cell. Your images can be no larger than the cell size you select.

   - Click the OK button to close the dialog box.

2. Choose File > New. The New Image dialog box opens. Set the image options:

   - In the "Image Dimensions" panel, type values for the width and height that are multiples of the cell horizontal and vertical spacing. The number you type determines the total cells you can fill with images. For example, if the grid spacing is 100 pixels, you could create an image of 400 x 300 pixels. With an image this size, you will have 12 cells (4 across and three down).

   - Select Transparent for the Background Color.

   - Click the OK button. A new image with visible grid lines appears in the workspace.

3. If the grid is not visible, choose View > Grid to display it.

4. Create the images of the Picture Tube. Place one image in each grid square. Each square with the image becomes a Picture Tube cell.

5. To save the Picture Tube, choose File > Export > Picture Tube and set the file options:

   - In the "Cell Arrangement" panel, enter the number of image cells you created.

   - In the "Placement Options" panel, select a mode. This can be changed when you use the Picture Tube.

   - In the Step Size box, type the pixel width of one of the Picture Tube cells.

   - To use a Selection Mode other than Random, select it from the list.

   - Type a name for the Picture Tube file.

   - Click the OK button.

6. Close the image file. If you want, you can save the file.

Using the Color Palette

The Color palette contains features for using colors, gradients, patterns, and textures in your images. You use it along with the Tool palette and the Tool Options palette. You select a tool on the Tool Palette, set options for the tool on the Tool Options Palette (such as the shape, size, density, and hardness), and set the foreground and background colors, gradients, patterns, or textures on the Color palette. This chapter describes the features of the Color palette and provides instructions for selecting colors, gradients, patterns, and textures.

Understanding the Color Palette Features

This section briefly describes the features of the Color palette.

TITLE BAR Displays the palette name and the standard Close button. The title bar is visible when the palette is floating.

SOLID COLORS PANEL Displays the last solid colors used as foreground and background colors. The left box displays the foreground solid color and the right box displays the background solid color. Left-clicking a box displays the color palette. Right-clicking displays recent colors used. Clicking the Color Switcher (the double-pointed arrow) exchanges the colors.

AVAILABLE COLORS PANEL Displays either a rainbow color picker or the color palette for the active image, depending on your preference settings. Clicking this area selects solid colors for painting or drawing.

ACTIVE STYLES PANEL Displays current foreground and background styles for drawing and painting, including solid colors, gradients, and patterns. Clicking an arrow displays a menu for setting the style type. Clicking a box displays a dialog box for selecting a specific style. Clicking the Color Switcher exchanges the settings.

ACTIVE TEXTURES PANEL Displays current foreground and background textures for drawing and painting. Clicking an arrow displays a menu for turning the feature on or off. Clicking a box displays a dialog box for selecting a specific texture. Clicking the Color Switcher exchanges the settings.

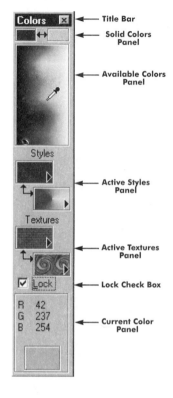

"LOCK" CHECK BOX Lets you lock the settings of the Color palette. Clearing the check box makes each tool use separate styles and textures; switching tools changes the active styles and textures. Selecting the check box makes all tools use the same colors; switching tools does not change the active styles and textures.

CURRENT COLOR PANEL displays the color values for the color under the Dropper tool when it is active.

NOTE: *Most features of the Colors Palette have a Tool Tip that displays the feature's name. Place the cursor over a feature to see the name and to have the Status bar display a tip for using it. Also, click the Help button (*▶?*) on the tool bar and then click a feature to display a description of the feature or the palette.*

Displaying and Moving the Color Palette

By default, the Color Palette is "docked" on the right side of the main program window. You can move the palette to almost any location on your screen. When you do this, the palette becomes "floating". To move the palette, left-click the background area or the title bar of the palette and drag the mouse. Alternatively, double-click any grey background area or the title bar of the palette to switch between docked or floating.

To display or hide the Color Palette:

- Click the Toggle Color Palette button (▐▐) on the tool bar,

- Choose View > ToolBars and select or clear the "Color Palette" check box,

- Right-click any palette and choose Toolbars from the menu, then select or clear the "Color Palette" check box,

- Right-click any palette and choose Color Palette from the menu, or

- Press <C>.

Locking the Color Palette Settings

When you first start to work with the Color palette styles (solid colors, gradients, and patterns) and textures, you will notice that when you switch tools the styles and textures change. This is because, by default, the tools remember their own settings; so when you switch to a different tool, the styles and textures switch to the last settings for that tool. You can work with the Color palette this way or you can lock the style and texture settings so they remain the same for every tool. Then, when you switch tools, the styles and textures do not change.

To lock and unlock the Color palette settings:

- To lock the settings, select the "Lock" check box on the Color palette.

- To unlock the settings, clear the "Lock" check box on the Color palette.

NOTE: *An exception to having the settings unlocked is that when you select the Dropper tool from the toolbar the check box is automatically locked on and the appropriate Style box automatically changes to Solid Colors.*

Setting the Styles (Colors, Gradients, and Patterns)

A style is what the painting and drawing tools apply as paint when you use them. For example, if you set a style to Pattern, the pattern is what is painted on the canvas when you use the tools. The available styles include Solid Color, Gradient, Pattern, and No Style.

Use the Styles boxes of the Color palette to set styles for the following tools: Paint Brush, Color Replacer, Retouch, Eraser, Airbrush, Flood Fill, Text, Draw, and Preset Shapes. There are two styles, foreground and background. The upper box controls the foreground style and lower box controls the background style. The way the tools apply the styles varies for each tool. To see how each tool applies the styles, please refer to "Using the Tools to Apply Styles and Textures" on page 154.

NOTE: *Gradients and patterns are available for greyscale and 24-bit color depth images. To use these features, you may need to increase your image's color depth. If your image has a lower color depth and you set a gradient or pattern, Paint Shop Pro displays a warning message. For more information about increasing color depth, please refer to Chapter 5, "Working with Color."*

Setting a Foreground or Background Style

To set a foreground or background style:

1. Left-click the arrow in the Style box to display the Styles menu.

2. Move the mouse to an icon and click to choose the style:

   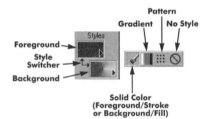

   - - Solid Color,

   - - Gradient,

   - - Pattern, or

   - - No Style.

   The style appears in the Style box.

3. After setting the style, click inside the Style box to select a specific style. For details, please refer to the following sections:

   - For the Solid Color option, please refer to "Selecting Solid Colors" on page 155.

   - For the Gradient option, please refer to "Selecting and Using Gradients" on page 164.

   - For the Pattern option, please refer to "Selecting and Creating Patterns" on page 170.

NOTE: *Choose the No Style icon when you do not want to apply any stroke or fill. To switch the foreground and background styles, click the Style Switcher arrow.*

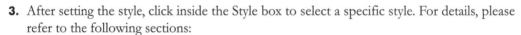

Setting the Textures

Textures, which give your images the effect of having a textured canvas or paper, are applied when you use the painting and drawing tools. For example, setting a texture as Woodgrain gives an image a wood-like effect. The textures work much like the styles, but are a separate feature so you can use textures and styles together.

Use the Textures boxes on the Color palette to set textures for the following tools: Paint Brush, Clone Brush, Retouch, Eraser, Airbrush, Flood Fill, Text, Draw, and Preset Shapes. There are two textures, foreground and background, which you can turn on or off. The upper box controls the foreground texture and lower box controls the background texture. The way the tools apply the textures varies for each tool. To see how each tool applies the textures, please refer to "Using the Tools to Apply Styles and Textures" on page 154.

NOTE: *Textures are available for greyscale and 24-bit color depth images. To use textures you may need to increase your image's color depth. For more information, please refer to Chapter 5, "Working with Color."*

Setting a Foreground or Background Texture

To set a foreground or background texture:

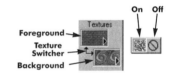

1. Left-click the arrow in the Texture box to display the Textures menu.

2. Move the mouse and click an icon to turn the feature on or off:

   - ![] - ON, use a texture, or

   - ![] - OFF, don't use a texture.

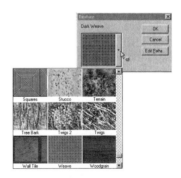

3. After setting the texture feature to ON, click inside the Texture box to display the Texture dialog box.

4. From the drop-down box, choose a texture. The box displays the textures installed with Paint Shop Pro and any you have created.

5. Click the OK button. The texture appears in the Texture box.

NOTE: *To switch the foreground and background textures, click the Texture Switcher arrow.*

Creating a New Texture

To create a new texture, save an image as a bitmap (.bmp) file. Texture files, by default, are located in a Textures folder within the Paint Shop Pro program folder. To change the default location for texture files, click the Edit Paths button. For more information, please refer to Chapter 20, "Setting Preferences."

NOTE: *Texture (.tex) files used in prior versions of Paint Shop Pro still work in this version.*

Using the Tools to Apply Styles and Textures

The way the tools apply the Color palette settings depends on the tool selected.

To paint or draw with the Color palette settings:

- For the raster tools, Paint Brush (![icon]), Airbrush (![icon]), Flood Fill (![icon]), Color Replacer (![icon]), and Retouch (![icon]), use the left mouse button to apply the foreground style and the foreground texture, and use the right mouse button to apply the background style and the background texture.

- For the Clone Brush tool (![icon]), click the area to clone with the right mouse button and use the left mouse button to clone (paint) the selected area and apply the foreground texture.

- For the Eraser tool (![icon]), use the left mouse button to apply the background style and the background texture, and use the right mouse button to apply the foreground style and the foreground texture.

- For the combination vector and raster Text tool (![icon]), use the left mouse button to select the location for the text. This applies the foreground style as the outline (stroke) and the background style as the fill. The horizontal placement of the text is where you click the mouse. The vertical placement of the text depends on the alignment of the text as set in the Text Entry dialog box. For example, if your text is centered, the center of the text object is where you click the mouse.

- For the combination vector and raster Line tool (![icon]), use the left mouse button to apply the foreground style and the foreground texture as the outline (stroke) and the background style and background texture as the fill. (To have the lines unfilled, set the backgrounds to No Style and Texture OFF.)

- For the combination vector and raster Preset Shapes tool (![icon]), use the left mouse button to select the edge for the shape and to draw from edge to edge. Use the right mouse button to select the center for the shape and to draw from the center out. Either button applies the foreground style and the foreground texture as the outline (stroke) and the background style and background texture as the fill.

You can also use <Ctrl>, <Alt>, and other keys to draw more complex lines and shapes. For more information about using the tools, please refer to Chapter 8, "Using the Painting Tools" and Chapter 12, "Using the Vector Tools."

Selecting Solid Colors

This section provides detailed steps for selecting colors. For general steps, please refer to "Setting the Styles (Colors, Gradients, and Patterns)" on page 152.

To select a solid color:

1. On the Color palette, left-click the arrow in the Style box to display the Styles menu.

2. Move the mouse to the Solid Color icon (▨) and click it to choose the style. A solid color appears in the Style box.

3. Do any of the following to select a specific color:

   • Left-click a color box in the "Solid Colors" panel to display the Color dialog box. Click a color and then click the OK button. Refer to "Using the Solid Colors Panel of the Color Palette" on page 156 for a complete description.

     NOTE: *If the active image has a color depth lower than 24-bits (that is, the image is paletted), the Select Color From Palette dialog box appears instead of the Color dialog box. In this case, refer to "Using the Select Color From Palette Dialog Box" on page 161 for a complete description.*

   • Right-click a color box in the "Solid Colors" panel to select a color from the Recent Colors dialog box. Click a color and the dialog box closes. Refer to "Using the Solid Colors Panel of the Color Palette" on page 156 for a complete description.

   • Left-click a color in the "Available Colors" panel to select a foreground color. Refer to "Using the Available Colors Panel of the Color Palette" on page 157 for a complete description.

   • Right-click a color in the "Available Colors" panel to select a background color. Refer to "Using the Available Colors Panel of the Color Palette" on page 157 for a complete description.

   • Left-click the Style box to display the Color dialog box. Click a color and then click the OK button. (See the NOTE above.) Refer to "Using the Color Dialog Box" on page 158 for a complete description.

   • Right-click the Style box to display the Recent Colors dialog box. Click a color and the dialog box closes. Refer to "Using the Recent Colors Dialog Box" on page 162 for a complete description.

   • Press <Ctrl> and move the cursor over the image to display the Dropper tool. Left-click a color in the image to select a foreground color. Right-click a color to select a background color. Refer to "Using the Dropper Tool" on page 163 for a complete description.

Using the Solid Colors Panel of the Color Palette

The "Solid Colors" panel displays your most recently selected foreground and background solid colors. The box on the left is the foreground color, the box on the right is the background color. If you have the Styles boxes set to Solid Colors, these colors also appear in the Styles boxes.

The Solid Colors boxes let you change your foreground and background solid colors without changing your styles. Then, when you set the styles to the Solid Color style, the changes appear in the Styles boxes.

NOTE: *Some dialog boxes in Paint Shop Pro have a color box option where you can select a color. If you select a color from one of these boxes, the selection is not reflected in the Solid Colors boxes.*

To use the Recent Color boxes:

* Left-click a color box to display the Color dialog box for 24-bit images or the Select Color From Palette dialog box for images with a color depth lower than 24-bits (that is, paletted images). For more information about the dialog boxes, please refer to "Using the Color Dialog Box" on page 158 and "Using the Select Color From Palette Dialog Box" on page 161.

* Right-click a color box to display the Recent Colors dialog box. For more information about the dialog box, please refer to "Using the Recent Colors Dialog Box" on page 162.

* Move your cursor over a Solid Colors box to display a ToolTip of the RGB or HSL color values. The values displayed depend on your General Preference Settings. For more information about preferences, please refer to Chapter 20, "Setting Preferences."

* Click the Color Switcher to exchange the foreground and background solid colors. If either of the Style boxes is set at Solid Colors, the exchange is also made there.

Using the Available Colors Panel of the Color Palette

The "Available Colors" panel allows you to select active solid colors. The panel displays either the Rainbow picker or an image's palette, depending on your preference settings. When the panel contains the Rainbow picker, which is a rainbow of colors, all the colors in the spectrum are displayed. Although all the colors are displayed, the number of colors (bit depth) in your image determines the number of colors actually available. For 24-bit images, all the colors are available and for lower color depth images (paletted images), fewer colors are actually available than those displayed. When your image is paletted and you select a color from the Rainbow picker, Paint Shop Pro automatically selects the color that is the closest match to the color you selected from the panel.

Use the Show Document Palette option in the Dialogs and Palettes tab of the General Program Preferences dialog box to change the setting of the "Available Colors" panel. When you choose the Show Document Palette option, the rainbow in the panel is replaced with rectangles containing the available colors. The color depth of the image determines the number of rectangles in the panel. If the image contains fewer colors than it can support, the remaining rectangles are black. For example, a 4-bit image can contain up to 16 colors. If it actually contains only 9 colors, the Available Colors panel displays 9 colored rectangles and 7 black rectangles. There are two main benefits to selecting this option:

- You can select exact colors in the paletted images, and

- When you are working with masks or adjustment layers on 24-bit images, you can alternate between greyscale colors (for masks and adjustment layers) and the 24-bit rainbow of colors.

To select an active color from the Color palette:

1. Place the cursor over the Available Colors panel. The cursor changes to the Dropper.

2. Move the cursor over the color you want to select. The color and its values appear at the bottom of the Color palette in the "Current Color" panel.

   NOTE: *The color values are RGB or HSL depending on your preference settings on the Dialogs and Palettes tab of the General Program Preferences. When no color is selected, the color box displays an "X."*

3. Click to select an active color:

   - Left-click to select the foreground color, or

   - Right-click to select the background color.

The selected color appears in the appropriate Solid Colors box above the panel. It also appears in the appropriate Styles box if you have the style set to Solid Colors.

Using the Color Dialog Box

When you left-click inside any Color box in Paint Shop Pro, either the Color dialog box or the Select Color From Palette dialog box appears. If the active image has a color depth of 24-bits, the Color dialog box appears. If the active image has a color depth lower than 24-bits (that is, the image is paletted), the Select Color From Palette dialog box appears. This section describes the Color dialog Box. For a description of the Select Color From Palette dialog box, please refer to "Using the Select Color From Palette Dialog Box" on page 161.

When the Color dialog box appears, the palette displayed within the box is either the Jasc color palette, or the Windows color palette, depending on your preference settings. The Jasc color palette (also called color picker) is the default setting. If you prefer, you can use the standard Windows color palette (color picker) by selecting the "Use standard Windows color picker" check box in the Dialogs and Palettes tab of the General Program Preferences dialog box. For more information about preferences, please refer to Chapter 20, "Setting Preferences."

Selecting Colors from the Jasc Color Palette

When the preference is set to use the Jasc color palette, it appears in the Color Dialog box when you left-click any Color box in a 24-bit image (one with 16 million colors).

SELECTING A COLOR FROM THE IMAGE To select a color from the image while the Color dialog box is open, move the dropper over the image and left-click. The selected color, its RGB and HSL values, and its HTML code appear in the Current Color panel. Click the OK button to close the Color dialog box.

SELECTING FROM THE BASIC COLORS There are forty-eight basic colors that are preset and cannot be modified. The first column displays the three primary additive and three primary subtractive colors. The last column displays six lightness levels (grey levels). In between are the additive and subtractive primaries at increasing lightness levels from left to right.

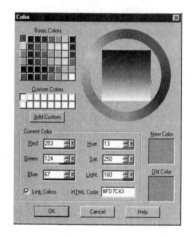

To select one of these basic colors:

1. Click the color's square in the "Basic Colors" panel. The selected color, its RGB and HSL values, and its HTML code appear in the "Current Color" panel.

2. Click the OK button. The dialog box closes and the new color appears in the Color box you originally clicked.

SELECTING A COLOR FROM THE COLOR WHEEL Selecting a color from the Color wheel is a two step process. You select a hue from the Color ring, and then adjust the hue's saturation and lightness in the Saturation/Lightness box.

Click the Color Wheel or drag the selection ring to select a hue. As the dropper moves around the wheel, the values in the "Current Color" panel update. This panel displays the RGB and HSL values, the color, and its HTML number. The HTML number appears in a text format that you can copy and paste directly into your HTML code.

Use the Saturation/Lightness box inside the Color wheel to adjust the saturation and lightness of the hue in the following way:

1. Click anywhere in the Saturation/Lightness box or drag the selection ring to change the saturation and lightness. Move from left to right to increase the saturation. Move from top to bottom to increase the lightness.

2. The selected color, its RGB and HSL values, and its HTML code (in the Current Color panel) update as you move the Dropper.

3. Click the OK button. The dialog box closes and the new color appears in the Color box you originally clicked.

SELECTING A COLOR BY COLOR COMPONENTS The "Current Color" panel displays RGB and HSL values, and the HTML code for the color in the Color box that you clicked.

To select a new color:

1. Use the numeric edit controls or type in the new values for each color component. For more information about color values, please refer to Chapter 5, "Working with Color."

    NOTE: *Use the numeric edit slider bars to set each value by sight rather than by number. Selecting the "Link Colors" check box considers all RGB or HSL components and displays actual colors on the slider bars. Clearing the check box displays only the possible values for each color component you are editing.*

2. Click the OK button. The dialog box closes and the new color appears in the Color box you originally clicked.

CREATING A CUSTOM COLOR There are 16 custom color squares you can fill with colors.

To fill an empty square or replace a Custom Color square with a new color:

1. Select a color by left-clicking the Color wheel, the Saturation/Lightness box, the Current Color box, the Old Color box, or a Basic color.

2. Click the Add Custom button, or right-click and drag the color to any Custom Color square and release the mouse button.

3. Click the OK button. The dialog box closes and the new color appears in the Color box you originally clicked.

Selecting Colors from the Windows Color Palette

When the preference is set to use the standard Windows color palette (color picker), it appears in the Color Dialog box when you left-click any Color box in a 24-bit image (one with 16 million colors).

SELECTING A BASIC COLOR There are 48 basic colors that are preset and cannot be modified.

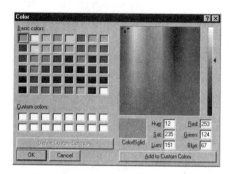

To select a basic color:

1. Click the square of the color you want in the "Basic Colors" panel. The selected color and its RGB and HSL values appear in the Current Color information area.

2. Click the OK button. The dialog box closes and the new color appears in the Color box you originally clicked.

SELECTING A FULL SPECTRUM COLOR The large Color Spectrum box modifies the current color's red, green, blue, hue and saturation values. To adjust these values, click the cursor inside the box or drag the crosshair pointer to the desired position. The controls affect the contents of the Color/Solid display box, which displays the color currently selected.

The thin Color Ribbon box modifies the current color's red, green, blue, and luminance values. To adjust these values, click the cursor inside the Color Ribbon box or drag the pointer on the right of the box up or down as desired. The Color/Solid display box changes as you move the pointer.

CREATING A CUSTOM COLOR There are 16 Custom Color squares you can fill with colors of your choice. You can fill an empty square or replace the color in a square with a new color.

To create a custom color:

1. Use the Crosshair and Pointer controls to select a color, or type the new color values in the RGB or HSL boxes.

2. Click the Add to Custom Colors button. The color appears in a Custom Color square.

3. Click the OK button. The dialog box closes and the new color appears in the Color box you originally clicked.

CHANGING A CUSTOM COLOR

To change a custom color:

1. Click the square of the color in the "Custom Colors" panel of the dialog box.

2. Use the Crosshair and Pointer controls to select a new color, or type the new color values in the RGB or HSL boxes.

3. Click the Add to Custom Colors button.

4. Click the OK button. The dialog box closes and the new color appears in the Color box you originally clicked.

Using the Select Color From Palette Dialog Box

If your active image has a color depth lower than 24-bits (is paletted), when you left-click inside any Color box in Paint Shop Pro, the Select Color From Palette dialog box appears. If the image has a color depth of 24-bits, the Color dialog box appears. For a description of the Color dialog box, please refer to "Using the Color Dialog Box" on page 158.

SELECTING A COLOR FROM THE IMAGE To select a color from the image while the Select Color From Palette dialog box is open, move the Dropper over the image and left-click. The color's square is selected on the palette. Click the OK button to close the Select Color From Palette dialog box.

SETTING A SORT ORDER In the Sort Order drop-down box, choose a method for displaying the colors. The methods are palette order, luminance (lightness), and hue (color families).

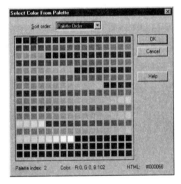

SELECTING A COLOR FROM THE PALETTE The palette displayed within the dialog box is the image's color palette. For more information about image palettes, please refer to Chapter 5, "Working with Color."

To select a color:

1. Click the square of the color you want to select. Its palette number, HSL or RGB value, and hexadecimal value appear at the bottom of the dialog box.

2. Click the OK button. The dialog box closes and the new color appears in the Color box you originally clicked.

NOTE: *You can also edit the colors of an image palette, save and reload an image palette, and set a color to transparent. For detailed steps, please refer to "Working with Image Palettes" in Chapter 5, "Working with Color."*

Using the Recent Colors Dialog Box

When you right-click inside any Color box, the Recent Colors dialog box appears. If the color depth of an image is lower than 24 bits, some colors may be unavailable and are signified by a circle with a line through it.

- The top section always displays the same ten colors or greys. For color images, they are red, green, blue, dark grey, light grey, cyan, magenta, yellow, black, and white. For greyscale images, the greys are evenly spaced from black to white.

- The middle section displays the ten colors or grey values you have used most recently (if they are not already in the top section). After you have used more than ten colors or greys, each new color replaces the earliest color selected.

- The bottom section displays the Other button. Click this button to open the Color dialog box or the Select Color From Palette dialog box. (For information about these dialog boxes, please refer to "Using the Color Dialog Box" on page 158 and "Using the Select Color From Palette Dialog Box" on page 161.)

To select a color from the Recent Colors dialog box:

Click the color that you want to select. The dialog box closes and the new color appears in the Color box you originally clicked. Alternatively, click outside the dialog box to close it without selecting a color.

Using the Dropper Tool

The Dropper tool lets you select colors directly from your active image rather than from a color palette.

NOTE: *Some dialog boxes in Paint Shop Pro have a color box option where you can select a color. If you select a color from one of these boxes, the selection is not reflected in the Solid Colors boxes.*

To make the Dropper tool active:

- Move the cursor over the "Available Colors" panel of the Color palette. The cursor changes to the Dropper tool. For details, please refer to "Using the Available Colors Panel of the Color Palette" on page 157.

- Click the Dropper tool on the Tools palette. The cursor changes to the Dropper tool. (If you select the "Use Precise Cursors" check box on the second tab of the Tool Options palette, the cursor changes to the precision cursor but still works as a Dropper tool.)

- On the Tool Options palette, click the Tool Selection button and choose the Dropper tool from the menu.

- While using a painting or drawing tool, press the <Ctrl> key. The cursor changes to the Dropper tool. Keep the <Ctrl> key pressed while selecting a color.

- While using the Jasc color palette in the Color dialog box, or while using the Select Color From Palette dialog box, the Dropper tool is active. For details, please refer to "Selecting Colors from the Jasc Color Palette" on page 158 and "Using the Select Color From Palette Dialog Box" on page 161.

- While using any dialog box containing a Color box, move the cursor over an image.

To select a color using the Dropper tool:

1. Move the cursor over the color you want to select. A ToolTip displays the color's values, and the color and its values appear at the bottom of the Color palette in the "Current Color" panel.

  NOTE: *The color values are RGB or HSL depending on your preference settings on the Dialogs and Palettes tab of the General Program Preferences. When no color is selected, the color box displays an "X."*

2. Click to select a color:

   - Left-click to select the foreground color, or

   - Right-click to select the background color.

The selected color appears in the appropriate Color box.

Selecting and Using Gradients

This section provides detailed steps for selecting gradients. For general steps, please refer to "Setting the Styles (Colors, Gradients, and Patterns)" on page 152.

NOTE: *Gradients and patterns are available for greyscale and 24-bit color depth images. You may need to increase your image's color depth to use these features. For more information about increasing color depth, please refer to Chapter 5, "Working with Color."*

Selecting a Specific Gradient

To select a specific gradient:

1. On the Color palette, left-click the arrow in the Style box to display the Styles menu.

2. Move the mouse to the Gradient icon ( ) to choose the style. A gradient appears in the Style box.

3. Left-click the Style box to display the Gradient dialog box.

4. Set the options in the Gradient dialog box:

   GRADIENT BOX Click the arrow and select a gradient. The box displays the gradients installed with Paint Shop Pro and any you have created.

   STYLE Select the style for the gradient. The options, from top to bottom, are: Linear Gradient, Rectangular Gradient, Sunburst Gradient, and Radial Gradient.

   NOTE: *After selecting a gradient and style, you can drag the control needle to change the options automatically.*

   HORIZONTAL Use the numeric edit controls or type a value for the horizontal center for the gradient, which is the point from which the gradient disperses or radiates. The distance is measured as a percentage of the fill area's width. This option applies to Rectangular, Sunburst, and Radial gradients.

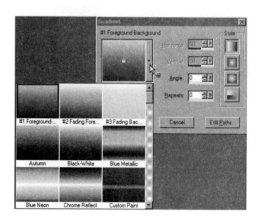

   VERTICAL Use the numeric edit controls or type a value for the vertical center for the gradient. The distance is measured as a percentage of the fill area's height. This option applies to Rectangular, Sunburst, and Radial gradients.

ANGLE Use the numeric edit controls or type a value for the angle (direction) of the gradient. The range is 0 to 360. This applies to Linear gradients.

REPEATS Use the numeric edit controls or type a value for the number of times to repeat the gradient pattern in the image. This applies to all gradient styles.

INVERT CHECK BOX To invert the colors of the gradient, select this check box.

EDIT BUTTON To edit the gradient, click the Edit button to open the Gradient Editor dialog box. For specific steps, please refer to "Editing Gradients" on page 165.

NOTE: *To save your gradients in a folder other than the Paint Shop Pro Gradients folder, click the Edit Paths button to display the File Locations dialog box. For more information, please refer to Chapter 20, "Setting Preferences."*

5. Click the OK button. The dialog box closes and the gradient appears in the Style box you originally clicked.

Editing Gradients

To open the Gradient Editor dialog box, please refer to "Selecting a Specific Gradient" on page 164 and open the Gradient dialog box. On the Gradient dialog box, click the Edit button to open the Gradient Editor dialog box. Use the Gradient Editor dialog box to create, edit, and manage multi-color gradients.

The "Types" panel of the dialog box displays the available gradients and the buttons for creating and managing them. The list contains the gradients installed by Paint Shop Pro and those you have created and imported. If you are deleting or exporting gradients, you can choose more than one by pressing the <Ctrl> key while clicking names in the list. Use the tools and settings in the area below the panel to configure or edit the gradient.

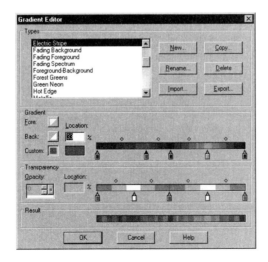

To edit a gradient, click its name in the "Types" list box and configure it using the Gradient and Transparency bars in the lower portion of the dialog box.

Use the Gradient bar to set the gradient's color placement, the color buttons and color box to set the colors, the Transparency bar to set the transparencies, and the Result bar to preview the resulting gradient.

NOTE: *Changes to gradient files do not take effect until you click the OK button on the Gradient Editor dialog box. Clicking the Cancel button reverts all gradient files to their previous states.*

Using the Gradient Bar, Color Buttons, and Color Box

The gradient bar, color buttons, and color boxes are located in the "Gradient" panel of the Gradient Editor dialog box. The bar shows the gradient. The markers below the bar indicate the points of solid color; the midpoints above it indicate where the two colors are equally blended. The color buttons and boxes on the left let you change the marker colors.

USING MARKERS AND MIDPOINTS

Every two markers have a midpoint between them.

To add a marker:

Click a spot under the Gradient bar to add a marker using the color displayed in the color box.

To move a marker or midpoint:

• Click and drag it along the bar, or

• Click it and type a value in the Location box. The scale ranges from 0% at the left end to 100% at the right. A marker can be assigned any value on the scale. A midpoint must have a value in between its two marker values.

To remove a marker:

Click and drag it away from the Gradient bar.

To activate a marker or midpoint:

Click the marker or midpoint. A black triangular point on a marker and a black midpoint diamond indicate they are active.

To deactivate a marker or midpoint:

Click the dialog box away from the editing area.

🖊 CHANGING MARKER COLORS

You can set marker colors using the foreground color, background color, or a color you select. To change a marker's color, click it and then click one of the three color buttons located to the left of the bar. The three buttons are the Foreground Color button (Fore), the Background Color button (Back), and the Custom Color button (Custom).

The color box to the right of the Custom Color button displays the current user-defined color. To change this color:

1. Click the Custom Color button.

2. Click the color box. Left-click to open the Color dialog box; right-click to open the Recent Colors dialog box.

3. Choose a new color and close the dialog box.

Another way to change a marker color is to click the marker to select it and then click a color between the gradient bar.

If the gradient contains the foreground or background color, when you next apply the gradient it uses the current foreground and background colors of the image. To create a gradient that always contains the same colors, color all the markers with user defined colors.

Using the Transparency Bar

The transparency bar is located in the "Transparency" panel of the Gradient Editor dialog box. Use the Transparency bar to alter the opacity of the gradient. The bar is white where it has a 0% opacity (it is transparent) and black where it has 100% opacity (it cover the underlying pixels completely). Add, move, and delete markers and midpoints of the Transparency bar the same way as you do the Gradient markers and midpoints.

The Transparency bar always contains at least two markers. To create a gradient with no transparency, set them both to 100% opacity. To vary the transparency along the gradient, activate a marker, type a value in the Opacity box, and then move the marker. Move the midpoint to shift the balance point between markers. When you change the opacity of a marker, its lightness varies. A darker marker indicates a point lower opacity (more transparency), and a lighter marker indicates a point higher opacity (less transparency).

When using the Transparency bar:

- To add a marker, click a spot under the Transparency bar. New markers are set to 100% opacity by default.

- To remove a marker, click and drag it away from the Transparency bar.

- To activate a marker or midpoint, click it. A black triangular point on a marker and a black midpoint diamond indicate they are active.

- To deactivate a marker or midpoint, click the dialog box away from the editing area.

- To move a marker or midpoint, drag it along the bar or click it and then type a value in the Location box. The scale ranges from 0% at the left end to 100% at the right. A marker can be assigned any value on the scale. A midpoint must have a value in between its two marker values.

- To change a marker's transparency, activate it and then change the value in the Opacity box. The marker is completely transparent at 0 and completely opaque at 100.

Creating a New Gradient

To create a new gradient file:

1. Open the Gradient Editor dialog box. For specific steps, please refer to "Editing Gradients" on page 165.

2. Click the New button. The New Gradient dialog box opens.

3. Type a unique name for the new gradient in the text box.

4. Click the OK button. If the name is a duplicate, you are asked to supply a different one. Refer to the previous steps for editing a gradient and edit the default gradient that appears in the lower portion of the Gradient Editor dialog box.

Exporting a Gradient

After creating a gradient file, you may want to export it and use it in another application.

To export a gradient file:

1. Open the Gradient Editor dialog box. For specific steps, please refer to "Editing Gradients" on page 165.

2. Choose a gradient from the Types list box.

3. Click the Export button. The Export Gradient dialog box opens.

4. Navigate to the folder to which you want to export the gradient. The default format is the .grd format, which automatically appears in the Save As Type box.

5. Type a unique name for the gradient file in the text box.

6. Click the OK button to close the dialog box and export the gradient.

Loading (Importing) a Gradient

To import a gradient file:

1. Open the Gradient Editor dialog box. For specific steps, please refer to "Editing Gradients" on page 165.

2. Click the Import Button. The Import Gradient dialog box opens.

3. Navigate to the folder containing the gradient you want to load. The default format is the .grd format, which automatically appears in the Files of Type box.

4. Click the file to highlight it.

5. Click the OK button to close the dialog box and import the gradient. It appears in the Types list box.

NOTE: *To import a Paint Shop Pro gradient in the .jgd file format, place the gradient file in the Gradients folder of the program. It is automatically added to the gradient list.*

Other Gradient Actions

You can also do any of the following actions with the Gradient Editor dialog box displayed. To open the dialog box, please refer to "Editing Gradients" on page 165.

To copy a gradient file to a new gradient:

1. Choose the source gradient from the Types list box.

2. Click the Copy button. The Copy Gradient dialog box opens.

3. Type a name for the copied gradient and click the OK button. If the name is a duplicate, you are asked to supply a different one. The new gradient appears in the Types list box.

To rename a gradient file:

1. Choose the gradient from the Types list box.

2. Click the Rename button. The Rename Gradient dialog box opens.

3. Type a new name for the gradient in the text box and click the OK button. If the name is a duplicate, you are asked to supply a different one. The new name replaces the old one in the Types list box.

To delete a gradient file:

1. Choose the gradient(s) from the Types list box.

2. Click the Delete button. The gradient(s) are removed from the list.

3. If you accidentally delete a gradient, click the Cancel button to undo the deletion. You also undo any changes you made to gradients.

4. Click the OK button to close the dialog box and delete the gradient file(s).

Selecting and Creating Patterns

This section provides detailed steps for selecting patterns. For general steps, please refer to "Setting the Styles (Colors, Gradients, and Patterns)" on page 152.

NOTE: *Patterns are currently available for only 24-bit color depth images. You may need to increase your image's color depth to use these features. For more information, please refer to Chapter 5, "Working with Color."*

Selecting a Specific Pattern

To select a specific pattern:

1. On the Color palette, left-click the arrow in the Style box to display the Styles menu.

2. Move the mouse and click the Pattern icon (▦) to choose the style. A pattern appears in the Style box.

3. Left-click the Style box to display the Pattern dialog box.

4. Set the options in the Pattern dialog box:

   PATTERN BOX Click the arrow and select a pattern. The box displays the patterns installed with Paint Shop Pro and any you have created.

   SCALE Use the numeric edit controls to change the size of the pattern. The range is from 10 to 250 percent of the pattern's actual size.

   ANGLE Type an angle for the pattern, or drag the control's needle to set the angle. The range is -0 to 359.

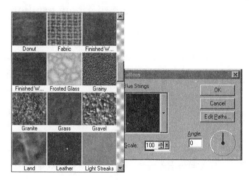

5. Click the OK button. The dialog box closes and the pattern appears in the Style box you originally clicked.

Using an Image as a Pattern

You can use an open image or a selection within an open image as a pattern. To do this, use open the image and use the "Selecting a Specific Pattern" steps above. All open images and selections you have made automatically appear in the Pattern box on the Pattern dialog box. Look for your pattern at the top of the list.

Creating a New Pattern

To create a new pattern, save an image as a bitmap (.bmp) file. Pattern files, by default, are located in a Patterns folder within the Paint Shop Pro program folder. To change the default location of pattern files, click the Edit Paths button and change your File Location preferences. For more information, please refer to Chapter 20, "Setting Preferences."

Working with Selections

What is a Selection?

When you edit an image or apply a command, you usually alter the entire image. However, you can limit the area altered by making a selection. A selection is a temporarily isolated partial area of an image that you can edit without altering the non-selected area. You can move a selection, copy it, paint it, and apply special effects to it.

A selection is identified by a border of black and white dashes called a marquee. The marquee defines the area of a selection, but is not restricted to that area. The marquee can be moved with or without the selected area it defines. When you move only the marquee, the new area within the marquee becomes the new selection. The area no longer surrounded by the marquee is deselected.

Paint Shop Pro provides three raster selection tools on its Tools palette. Some of the tools work on raster layers, and some work on vector layers and objects. This chapter describes these tools and how to alter, move, and save selections. In addition to the tools, Paint Shop Pro provides several commands in the Selections and Edit menus that you can use to create and work with selections. This chapter also describes these menu commands.

Using the Selection Tools

Understanding the Tools

You can make a selection by selecting an entire image or layer, by making a selection from a mask, by selecting a specific area or specific colors, by creating a text-shaped selection, by selecting a vector object, or by pasting the contents of the clipboard as a selection. Paint Shop Pro provides five tools for making selections:

- The Selection tool (▢), which makes a selection of a precise shape,
- The Freehand tool (♀), which makes a selection of an irregular shape,
- The Magic Wand tool (✎), which makes a selection based on a color, hue, or brightness,
- The Text tool (**A**), which can be used to make a selection of text shapes, and
- The Vector Object Selection tool (▨), which makes a selection of vector objects.

The Selection, Freehand, and Magic Wand tools have options to let you use them on both raster and vector layers. These tools are described in this chapter.

The Text tool has options to make a text-shaped selection area and to create text-shaped raster objects or vector objects. The Vector Object Selection tool is used to select and edit vector objects. For more information about these tools, please refer to Chapter 12, "Using the Vector Tools."

▨ Using the Selection Tool

The Selection tool makes a selection in a specific shape: Rectangle, Square, Rounded Rectangle, Rounded Square, Ellipse, Circle, Triangle, Pentagon, Hexagon, or Octagon.

Setting the Selection Tool Options

To set the Selection Tool options:

1. Activate the Selection tool by clicking its button on the Tool palette or in the Tool Selection menu of the Tool Options palette.

2. On the first tab of the Tool Options palette, set the shape and other options:

SELECTION TYPE Makes a selection in one of the shapes listed above.

FEATHER Feathering controls the sharpness of a selection's edges. By fading a set width (in pixels) along the edges, it produces a smooth transition between a selection and the surrounding area. The feathering value is the width of the transition area in pixels. The width can be from 0 to 200 pixels. A higher feathering value creates softer edges. Set the width to 0 to create a selection with no feathering.

Feathering is useful when pasting a selection. It helps the selection blend into the background and appear more natural. You can feather a selection before or after you create it. Feather a selection before you create it by entering a feather value on the Tool Options palette tab; feather it after by choosing the Selections > Modify > Feather from the menu. You must feather a selection before editing the data it contains.

ANTIALIAS Antialiasing is similar to feathering, but more precise. It produces a smooth-edged selection by partially filling in pixels along the edge, making them semi-transparent. If antialiasing is not applied, the edges of a selection can appear jagged. Antialiasing is useful when combining images and working with text.

NOTE: *You must select this option before making a selection; after making a selection, you cannot add it.*

Making a Selection

To make a selection:

1. Position the cursor in the image where you want the selection to originate.

2. Click and drag the cursor to make the selection.

   NOTE: *To constrain the selection proportionally, press and hold the <Shift> key while making the selection.*

3. Drag the mouse until the selection is the size you want. As the mouse moves, a line appears to indicate the border of the selection.

4. Release the mouse button. The selection border becomes a marquee.

Using the Freehand Tool

Use the Freehand tool to make selections by creating one of three types of borders: irregularly shaped borders, point to point straight borders, and borders from edges between contrasting color or light.

Setting the Freehand Tool Options

To set the Selection tool options:

1. Activate the Freehand tool by clicking its button on the Tool palette or in the Tool Selection menu of the Tool Options palette.

2. On the first tab of the Tool Options palette, set the shape and other options:

SELECTION TYPE Makes a selection in one of the three Freehand tools styles: Freehand, Point to Point, and Smart Edge.

FEATHER Feathering controls the sharpness of a selection's edges. Refer to the previous page for a complete description.

NOTE: *Be sure to feather a selection before you apply any editing changes.*

ANTIALIAS Antialiasing produces a smooth-edged selection by partially filling in pixels along the edge, making them semi-transparent.

NOTE: *You must select this option before making a selection; after making a selection, you cannot add it.*

SAMPLE MERGED (SMART EDGE TOOL) When selected, the Smart Edge tool makes the selection from all layers of the image within the selected area. When the option is not selected, the Smart Edge tool limits the selection to the active layer.

Making a Freehand Selection

To make a Freehand selection:

1. Set the Selection Type to Freehand and set the other options as described above.

2. Move the cursor over the image. The center of the crosshairs is the point.

3. Click the image at any point you want to make part of the border of the selection.

4. Drag the cursor to create an outline of the area you want to select. IMPORTANT: Do not release the mouse while creating your selection.

5. If you release the mouse, start again or modify the selection using the method described in "Adding to a Selection" on page 179.

6. When the line encloses the selection, release the mouse. The line becomes a marquee indicating the border of the selection.

Making a Point to Point Selection

Use the Point to Point selection when you want to connect straight lines.

To make a Point to Point selection:

1. Set the Selection Type to Point to Point and set the other options as described previously.

2. Click the cursor on the point in the image where you want your line to start. The center of the crosshairs is the point.

3. Move the mouse to the next point you want in the selection. As the mouse moves, a straight line connects from the starting point.

4. Click the image wherever you want to anchor the line and change its direction.

5. To delete an anchor point from the line, press <Delete> as you move to the next point.

6. When the line encloses the selected area and has connected to the starting point, either double-click or right-click the point. The line becomes a marquee to indicate that the selection is complete.

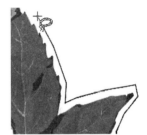

Point to Point Selection

Making a Smart Edge Selection

Use the Smart Edge selection to select the border between two areas of contrasting color or light.

To make a Smart Edge selection:

1. Set the Selection Type to Smart Edge and set the other options as described previously.

2. Move the cursor over the image. The center of the crosshairs is the point.

3. Click where you want to start the selection, and then move the mouse. As you move it, a selection box encloses the edge.

4. Click the image as needed to keep the edge inside the selection box. Each time you click, the box shrinks into a line that follows the edge.

5. When you have completed the selection, double-click or right-click the mouse. The line becomes a marquee indicating the border of the selection.

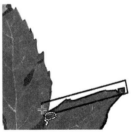

Smart Edge Selection

NOTE: *If the border crosses over itself, everything within the border is selected.*

Using the Magic Wand Tool

Unlike the other selection tools, the Magic Wand tool works by selecting content instead of defining edges. You can choose from four types of values for making selections: RGB values, hue, brightness, or all pixels.

Setting the Magic Wand Options

To set the Magic Wand tool options:

1. Activate the Magic Wand tool by clicking its button on the Tool palette or in the Tool Selection menu of the Tool Options palette.

2. On the first tab of the Tool Options palette, set the shape and other options:

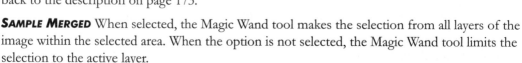

MATCH MODE Makes a selection based on one of the four values listed above. With RGB Value, it selects pixels based on the amount of Red, Green, and Blue they contain. With Hue, it selects pixels based on the position in the color wheel of the hues. With Brightness, it selects pixels based on the amount of white they contain. With All Pixels, it selects only areas containing pixels. No transparent areas are selected.

TOLERANCE Controls how similar to the selected mode the value of a pixel must be before it is selected. At low settings, the values must be close. At higher settings the tolerance is greater, so the Magic Wand chooses more pixels.

FEATHER Controls the sharpness of a selection's edges. Refer back to the description on page 173.

SAMPLE MERGED When selected, the Magic Wand tool makes the selection from all layers of the image within the selected area. When the option is not selected, the Magic Wand tool limits the selection to the active layer.

Making a Magic Wand Selection

To make a Magic Wand selection:

1. Move the cursor over the image. The center of the crosshairs is the point.

2. Click the color you want to select.

3. Release the mouse button. A marquee surrounds the selection.

Using the Text Tool to Make a Selection

The Text tool works by creating text as a selection instead of as a painted object. This section briefly describes the Text tool. For detailed information about the Text tool, please refer to Chapter 12, "Using the Vector Tools."

Setting the Text Tool Options

To set the Text tool options:

1. Activate the Text tool by clicking its button on the Tool palette or in the Tool Selection menu of the Tool Options palette.

2. On the tabs of the Tool Options palette, set the width and line style options. For information about customized line styles, please refer to Chapter 12, "Using the Vector Tools."

Making a Text Selection

To make a Text selection:

1. Position the Text cursor over the image.

2. Click where you want to start the text selection. The Text Entry dialog box opens.

3. In the Text Entry dialog box, select the text options, type the text, and make sure you choose the Selection option in the "Create As" panel. Click the OK button to create the text selection. Alternatively, you can choose the Floating option. This creates a painted Raster object that has the selection marquee around it.

4. Modify, edit, or save the selection as necessary.

Creating a Selection from a Mask

Creating a selection from a mask selects all non-masked (white) areas and omits all masked (non-white) areas.

To make a selection from a mask:

1. Create a mask using any of the methods described in Chapter 14, "Working with Masks."

2. Select the layer that contains the mask.

3. Choose Mask > Selections from the menu, or press <Shift> + <Ctrl> + <S>.

NOTE: *You can also load any mask that you have saved to an alpha channel as a selection by choosing Selections > Load from Alpha Channel.*

Selecting an Entire Image or Layer

To select an entire layer or image:

1. If the image contains more than one layer, click the Layer Name button of a layer to make it active.

2. Choose Selections > Select All, press <Ctrl> + <A>, or click the Select All button on the toolbar. A marquee appears around the layer.

Pasting a Selection

Pasting places a copy of the selection from the clipboard into an image. To paste a selection, choose the method of pasting from the Paste command of the Edit menu. There are several ways to paste a selection. For information on using these commands, please refer to the "Using the Paste Commands" section of Chapter 10, "Working with Selections."

Pasting as a New Image Creates a new image from the selection. The background color of the new image is the current background color.

Pasting as a New Layer Creates a new layer from the selection in the same or a different image. A selection must be no larger than the image into which it is pasted.

Pasting as a New Selection Pastes the selection as a floating selection above the active layer of the original or a different image.

Pasting as a Transparent Selection Pastes the selection as a floating selection above the active layer of the original or a different image. This command uses the background color for transparency and the tolerance designated in the preferences. If a color in the selection has previously been designated as transparent, areas of this color are not pasted. (See the section "Removing a Selected Color" on page 185.)

Pasting into a Selection Resizes the pasted selection to the size of the selection it is pasted into.

Pasting an AS Animation as Multiple Images Pastes a selection of frames copied from Jasc Animation Shop. Pastes each frame as a separate image.

Pasting as a New Vector Selection Pastes a vector selection as a new vector selection.

Modifying a Selection

Moving the Marquee

If you want to change the area the selection encloses, you can move the marquee. This is useful when you want to fine-tune the area inside an oval or other selection shape.

NOTE: *Before moving the marquee, you must click the Mover tool button.*
If you right-click the image with a selection tool, you remove the selection; if you click and drag within the selection, you float it and move the floating selection.

To move the marquee:

1. Click the Mover tool button on the Tool palette.

2. Right-click anywhere inside or on the marquee.

3. Drag the marquee to a new location and release the mouse button.

▣ Inverting a Selection

At times, the easiest way to select an area is to isolate the part of the image you don't want and then reverse the selection. For example, if the background is one color, select it and then invert the selection.

• To invert a selection, make your selection using one of the methods listed above. Then Choose Selections > Invert from the menu. The marquee changes so that it encloses the opposite area of the image.

Adding to a Selection

There are several ways to increase the area within a selection.

Using the Selection Tools

• To add to a selection using the Selection and Freehand tools, press and hold down the <Shift> key while outlining the area you want to add.

• To add to a selection using the Magic Wand tool, press and hold down the <Shift> key while clicking the color you want to add.

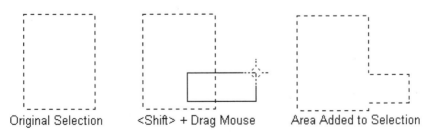

Original Selection　　　<Shift> + Drag Mouse　　　Area Added to Selection

Using the Expand Command

The Expand command enlarges the selection by a specific number of pixels while retaining its original shape. To expand a selection:

1. Choose Selections > Modify > Expand. The Expand Selection dialog box opens.

2. Select the number of pixels by which you want to expand the selection. You can select up to 100 pixels.

3. Click the OK button to close the dialog box and expand the selection.

Using the Grow Selection Command

NOTE: *The Grow command can only be applied to a 24-bit color or a greyscale image.*

The Grow Selection command expands the selection to include adjacent areas of similar color using the Magic Wand tolerance settings.

• To use the command, choose Selections > Modify > Grow Selection.

Using the Select Similar Command

NOTE: *The Select Similar command can only be applied to a 24-bit color or a greyscale image.*

The Select Similar command selects all areas in the image with the same colors as are present in the current selection using the Magic Wand tolerance settings. The areas do not have to be adjacent to the current selection.

• To use the command, choose Selections > Modify > Select Similar.

Subtracting from a Selection

Using the Selection Tools

• To subtract from a selection using the Selection and Freehand tools, press and hold down the <Ctrl> key while outlining the area you want to remove.

• To subtract an area from a selection using the Magic Wand tool, press and hold down the <Ctrl> key while clicking the area you want to remove.

Using the Contract Command

The Contract command shrinks the selection by a specific number of pixels while retaining its original shape.

To contract a selection:

1. Choose Selections > Modify > Contract. The Contract Selection dialog box opens.

2. Select the number of pixels by which you want the selection to contract. Use the spin controls or type a number. You can select up to 100 pixels.

3. Click the OK button to close the dialog box and contract the selection.

Modifying the Edges of a Selection

Matting a Selection

When you move a selection, some of the pixels surrounding the border are included, especially when the selection has been antialiased or feathered. Matting cleans up the border by removing these pixels. The matting commands can also be applied to layers.

Removing Black and White Matte

NOTE: *The Matting commands can only be applied to a floating selection and to an image that is 24-bit color or greyscale.*

When you copy (or cut) and paste an antialiased or feathered selection from a white or black to a colored background, the edge contains black and white. The Remove White Matte removes the white from the edge; the Remove Black Matte removes the black.

To remove the black or white matte:

1. If the selection is not floating, choose Selections > Float.

2. To remove the black matte, choose Selections > Matting > Remove Black Matte; to remove the white matte, choose Selections > Matting > Remove White Matte.

Applying the Defringe Command

Applying the Defringe command bleeds non-feathered pixels in the selection outward and over the "jaggies" in the feathered part of the selection. Use defringe when the background of selection is a color (not black or white).

To defringe a selection:

1. If the selection is not floating, choose Selections > Float.

2. Choose Selections > Matting > Defringe. The Defringe dialog box opens.

3. Enter the width you want to defringe by using the spin controls or typing a number.

4. Click the OK button. The dialog box closes, and Paint Shop Pro defringes the selection.

Feathering a Selection

Feathering controls the sharpness of a selection's edges. By fading along the edges, it produces a smooth transition between a selection and the surrounding area. The feathering value is the width of the transition area in pixels. A higher feathering value creates softer edges by feathering more pixels. Feathering is useful when pasting a selection. The fading helps the selection blend into the background and appear more natural. Unlike antialiasing, feathering produces a loss of detail.

NOTE: *Be sure to feather a selection before you apply any editing changes.*

To feather a selection:

1. Choose Selections > Modify > Feather. The Feather Selection dialog box opens.

2. Select the number of pixels (up to 200) by which you want to feather the selection.

3. Click the OK button to close the dialog box and feather the selection.

Hiding and Viewing the Marquee

The marquee is normally visible. However, as you work with selections, there will be times when you want to hide the marquee. For example, you may want see the results of pasting a selection or feathering a selection's edges.

NOTE: *Hiding the marquee does NOT disable the selection; it merely hides it from view.*

To hide the marquee, do one of the following:

- Choose Selections > Hide Marquee, or

- Press <Shift> + <Ctrl> + <M>.

To view the marquee again:

- Choose Selections > Hide Marquee again. The marquee reappears.

Using Selection Modes

There are two selection modes:

STANDARD A standard selection is part of an image or layer. When you move or edit a standard selection, you modify the image itself.

FLOATING A floating selection temporarily rests above the image or layer. You can move or modify it without changing the original image. The Layer palette displays a button labeled *Floating Selection* to indicate a selection is floating.

Floating a Selection

To float a selection, choose Selections > Float from the menu, or press <Ctrl> + <F>.

The following actions also create or convert a selection to floating mode:

- Selecting the Floating option when creating text,

- Pasting a selection by choosing Edit > Paste as New Selection,

- Dragging a selection using a selection tool and the <Alt> key, and

- Dragging a selection when using a selection tool.

Defloating a Selection

To change a selection from the floating to standard mode, choose Selections > Defloat from the menu, or press <Shift> + <Ctrl> + <F>. Paint Shop Pro pastes the selection's contents into the layer underneath. The selection is still active; it has been defloated, not deselected.

The following actions also create or put a selection in standard mode:

- Creating a new selection (except when the Floating option is selected), and

- Adding an area to or removing an area from a floating selection.

Editing A Selection

Moving a Selection Within Its Image

When moving a selection, you can move the original selection and leave the space empty, or you can move a copy of the selection, leaving the original. Use the same tool to move the selection as you used to create it.

Dragging the Selection

CUTTING AND DRAGGING To move a selection by cutting it from the layer and leaving a transparent area, drag the selection with the selection tool. When you drag the selection, it changes to a floating selection.

COPYING AND DRAGGING To move a copy of a selection while leaving the original intact, press <Alt> while clicking and dragging the selection with the selection tool. When you drag the selection, it changes to a floating selection.

Moving Pixel by Pixel

To move a selection one pixel at a time, press and hold the <Shift> key while pressing the keyboard arrows. <Shift> + <↑> moves the selection up, <Shift> + <↓> the selection down, <Shift> + <←> moves the selection to the left, <Shift> + <→> moves the selection to the right. When you nudge the selection, it changes to a floating selection. Cutting the selection leaves a transparent area.

To move a selection ten pixels at a time, use the same method while pressing <Shift> + <Ctrl>.

Deselecting a Selection

The Deselect command removes the marquee and border from a selection and integrates the area back into the image. If the selection is in the floating mode, Paint Shop Pro defloats it and integrates it into the underlying layer.

To deselect a selection, you can either of the following methods:

* Choose Selections > Select None,

* With a Selection tool active, right-click the image, or

* Press <Ctrl> + <D>.

Clearing a Selection

The Clear command affects a floating and standard selection differently. With a floating selection, the Clear command deletes the selection and its marquee.

• To clear a selection, you can either choose Edit > Clear or press <Del>.

With a non-floating raster selection, the command deletes the contents of the selection while leaving the area selected. On a layer, the cleared selection area becomes transparent. With a vector selection, the command deletes the selected object.

If there is no selection on a raster or vector layer, the command deletes the contents of the layer, but not the actual layer. On a background layer or an 8-bit or lower image, the cleared selection area changes to the background color.

Cutting a Selection

Cutting a selection removes it from the image or layer and places it on the clipboard. From the clipboard you can paste it into a different image or into a different area or layer of the same image. If you cut from a paletted image (256 or fewer colors) or background layer, the selected area is filled in with the background color. If you cut from a layer, the cut selection area becomes transparent.

• To cut a selection, choose Edit > Cut.

Copying a Selection

Copying a selection places a copy of a selection on the clipboard while leaving the original image intact. From here you can paste it into a different image or into a different area or layer of the same image.

• To copy a selection, choose Edit > Copy.

Using the Copy Merged Command

This command is accessible when an image has two or more layers. The Copy command copies only from the same layer as a selection. The Copy Merged command copies from all the layers, not just the active layer. It copies whatever is visible within the selection.

• To copy a selection in the merged mode, choose Edit > Copy Merged.

Using the Flip, Mirror, and Rotate Commands

You can flip mirror, and rotate selections in the same way that you flip, mirror, and rotate images. If the selection is not already floating, it is floated before the command is applied.

Using Effects

You can apply effects to selections. Please refer to Chapter 17, "Adding Effects," for help with using these functions. To apply some effects to selections, the image must be a 24-bit color or a greyscale image.

Removing a Selected Color

The Transparent Color command removes areas of a specific color from a selection. The areas become transparent. You can remove the following colors: white, black, red, green, blue, plus the foreground or the background color.

To remove areas of a specific color:

1. Make a selection.

2. If the color to be removed is not one of the five colors mentioned above, select it as the foreground or background color. For help with selecting colors, please refer to Chapter 5, "Working with Color," and Chapter 9, "Using the Color Palette."

3. Choose Selections > Modify > Transparent Color. The Remove Selected Color dialog box opens.

4. From the Transparent Color box, select the color.

5. Enter a tolerance value. The tolerance controls how closely a color must match the selected color to be removed. A high tolerance includes more colors.

6. Click the OK button. The dialog box closes and the color is removed from the selection.

Converting a Selection

Promoting to a Layer

NOTE: *To promote a selection to a layer, the image must be a 24-bit color or greyscale image.*

Both floating and standard selections can be promoted. This command copies a selection and creates a new layer from it. The selection area is retained in the new layer, and the original selection is not affected. When applied to a floating selection, the command converts the selection to a layer. The new layer appears above the original selection's layer; the selection's button on the Layer palette changes to read *Promoted Selection*.

Use this command only to promote a selection within its image. To transform a selection into a layer in a different image from a selection, use the Paste as New Layer command described in "Pasting a Selection" on page 178.

• To promote a selection to a layer, choose Selections > Promote to Layer.

Converting to a Seamless Pattern

NOTE: *To convert a selection to a seamless pattern, the image must be a 24-bit color or a greyscale image.*

You create seamless patterns from selections. These custom-made patterns can then be used from the "Active Styles" panel of the Color palette for painting, or can be used for Web page backgrounds. The patterns created are always rectangular. When you use this command, a new window is created with the seamless pattern and the original image is not affected.

- To convert a selection, choose Selections > Convert to Seamless Pattern.

When Paint Shop Pro converts a selection to a seamless pattern, it uses the area surrounding the selection to eliminate the appearance of seams. If the selection is too close the edge of the image, a message indicating this appears. If this happens, either move the marquee or make a new selection closer to the center of the image, and choose the command again.

Saving and Loading a Selection

You can save a Paint Shop Pro selection in two ways:

- As a file with the .sel extension on your hard drive, and

- As an alpha channel within the image.

When you save a selection as an .sel file on your hard disk, it saves as a separate file. When you save a selection as an alpha channel, it saves as a greyscale bitmap within the image.

A channel contains information about the color elements in an image; for example, a RGB image contains a red channel, a green channel, and a blue channel. An alpha channel is a channel that saves information on a mask or selection you create. An advantage of the .psp format is that the files hold the alpha channels within the image; .tif and .tga files can hold one alpha channel; almost all the others will not hold any.

Saving to a Disk

To save a selection to the hard disk:

1. Choose Selections > Save to Disk. The Save Selection Area dialog box opens.

2. Navigate to the folder in which you want to save your selection.

3. Type a file name for the selection in the File Name box.

4. Click the OK button. The dialog box closes, and Paint Shop Pro saves the selection as an .sel file.

Saving to the Alpha Channel

Use the alpha channel to save a selection within the image.

To save a selection to the alpha channel:

1. Choose Selections > Save To Alpha Channel to open the Save to Alpha dialog box. The image name appears in the Available Documents box and the Preview displays the selection.

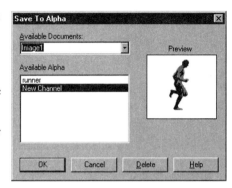

2. In the Available Alpha channels list, double-click the New Channel option.

3. When the New Channel box opens, type a name for the selection.

4. Click the OK button. The selection saves to the alpha channel and both dialog boxes close.

NOTE: *After you have saved the selection, it is still selected in the image. Choose Select None from the Selections menu to deselect it.*

Loading from a Disk

To load a selection from the hard disk or another disk connected to your computer:

1. If the image has more than one layer, make active the layer in which you want to place the selection.

2. Choose Selections > Load from Disk. The Load Selection Area dialog box opens. Selections are saved in the .sel format. This format automatically appears in the File Type box.

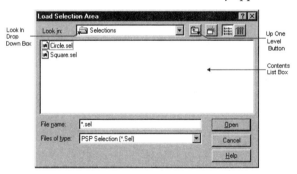

3. Navigate to the file you want to load or type its name in the File Name box.

4. If you navigated to the file in the previous step, click to highlight the file.

5. Click the Open button. The dialog box closes and the selection appears in the image.

Loading from the Alpha Channel

Both selections and masks can be saved to the alpha channel, so you can load a mask as a selection and a selection as a mask. You can load a selection from the alpha channel of the current active image or any other image open in the workspace.

To load a selection from the alpha channel:

1. If the image contains more than one layer, select the layer in which you want to place the selection.

2. Choose Selections > Load from Alpha Channel. The Load From Alpha dialog box opens. This dialog box is the same as the Save To Alpha dialog box.

3. To load a selection from the active image, leave the current image name in the Available Documents box. To load a selection from another image, highlight its file name. For an image to be listed, it must be open and have a mask or selection saved to its alpha channel.

4. In the Available Alpha Channels list, click the selection or mask you want to load. A preview of it appears to the right of the list. You can view any selection or mask by clicking its name.

5. To delete any of the saved selections, select its name and click the Delete button.

6. After you have chosen a selection, click the OK button. The dialog box closes, and the selection appears in the image.

Deleting a Selection from an Alpha Channel

Deleting a selection from the alpha channel and deleting a selection from a layer are two separate functions. Deleting a selection from the layer or image does not delete it from the alpha channel. To delete a selection from the alpha channel, use the Load From Alpha dialog box.

To delete a selection from an alpha channel:

1. Open the dialog box, by choosing either Selections > Load From Alpha Channel or Selections > Save To Alpha Channel.

2. From the Available Documents list, select the name of the image containing the selection you want to delete. For an image to be listed, it must be open and have a mask or selection saved to its alpha channel.

3. In the Available Alpha Channels list, highlight the selection. The preview displays the selection.

4. Click the Delete button.

5. At the prompt message, click the Yes button. Paint Shop Pro deletes the selection.

6. Click the OK button to close the dialog box.

Working with Layers

What is a Layer?

A layer is an individual level of an image. Think of it as a transparent sheet. In a multi-layered image, these sheets are placed in a stack, as shown on the following page. When you apply paint to a layer, it is like covering one of these sheets. Some layers are completely covered in paint; others contain unpainted areas. The areas you haven't covered remain transparent, and you can see the layer underneath. You can add and delete layers, rearrange their order, and blend their pixels in a variety of ways. Until you merge the layers, each one remains independent and can be edited without affecting the others.

A newly created Paint Shop Pro image consists of one raster layer, the background layer. This is analogous to the canvas of a painting; every image must have at least one layer. Paint Shop Pro supports up to 100 layers per image. The actual number of layers you can create may be further limited by the amount of memory in your computer.

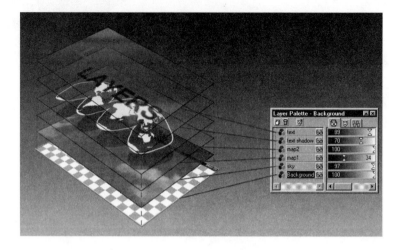

The drawing above shows the concept of layers, and the relationship of the Layer palette to the layers in the image. The layer you are editing is called the current (active) layer. When you make a layer the active layer by clicking its Layer Name button on the Layer palette, it is made visible. However, a visible current layer will be transparent if it contains no data. As you work with images containing multiple layers, make sure that the appropriate layer is the active layer. To make a layer active, either select the layer name from the list at the bottom of the Layers menu, or click the layer's button on the Layer palette. On the Layer palette, the current layer's Layer and Visibility buttons appear "pressed in."

In Paint Shop Pro, you can work on three types of layers: raster, adjustment (which is a special kind of raster layer), and vector:

- A raster layer is pixel oriented, while a vector layer is object oriented. Raster images (and layers) display objects by combining units of colored light, called pixels. If you zoom in, you can see each pixel as a small square. An "object" on a raster layer is actually a group of selected pixels. When you move an object in a raster image (or layer), you move the pixels, which affects the entire image.

- Adjustment layers, which are a form of a raster layer, contain color correction information. They are used to change the appearance of the underlying layers. For more information about Adjustment Layers, please refer to Chapter 16, "Using Adjustment Layers."

- Vector layers do not use pixels for storing image information. Instead, they store each vector object as a set of properties that describe its attributes, dimensions, and position in the image. Each time an image is opened, these properties are used as instructions for drawing the vector "objects." Because these objects are independent elements, you can move them without affecting the rest of the image.

You cannot place vector objects on raster layers or raster objects on vector layers. If you try to create a vector object on a raster layer, Paint Shop Pro automatically creates a vector layer for you. If you are working on a vector layer, Paint Shop Pro merely adds the new object to the layer.

Unlike raster layers, vector layers can be added to images of any color depth. You can add vector layers to images of color depths that are too low to support raster layers. While only greyscale and 24-bit color images can contain multiple raster layers, images of any color depth can contain multiple vector layers. When you reduce the color depth of an image, Paint Shop Pro merges both raster and vector layers. You can then create new vector layers in this image, even if it does not support raster layers.

Paint Shop Pro provides the Layer Properties dialog box, the Layer palette, and various commands in the Layers menu for working with layers. The Layer Properties dialog box shows the settings for an individual layer, and it provides access to the adjustment layer settings. The Layer palette displays each layer, its order in the layer stack, its current properties, and for a vector layer, a button for each vector object you draw. The Layers menu contains the general commands for creating, managing, and merging layers. It also lists the layers in the image.

NOTE: *An image must be a greyscale or 24-bit color image to contain more than one raster layer or an adjustment layer. To add these layers, you must increase an image's color depth.*

Using the Layer Properties Dialog Box

The Layer Properties dialog box opens automatically when you create a new layer. You can also open the dialog box to view or edit the properties of an existing layer. Use the Layer Properties dialog box to select and edit the attributes of individual layers.

The dialog box automatically opens when you create a new layer using one of the following methods:

- Click the Create Layer Name button ( ) on the Layer palette. This creates a raster layer.

- Right-click the Create Layer Name button and choose New Raster Layer, New Vector Layer, or New Adjustment Layer from the context menu. For an adjustment layer, choose a layer type.

- Right-click a Layer Name button on the Layer palette and choose New Raster Layer, New Vector Layer, or New Adjustment Layer from the context menu. For an adjustment layer, choose a layer type.

- Choose Layers > New Raster Layer, Layers > New Vector Layer, or Layers > New Adjustment Layer from the Menu bar. For an adjustment layer, choose a layer type.

Open the dialog box for an existing layer using one of the following methods:

- Click its Layer Name button on the Layer palette and choose Layers > Properties,

- Right-click its Layer Name button on the Layer palette and choose Properties from the context menu, or

- Double-click its Layer Name button on the Layer palette.

For Raster and Vector layers, the Layer Properties dialog box contains the General and Blend Ranges tabs. For Adjustment layers, the Layer Properties dialog box contains the General and Adjustment tabs.

The General tab contains the "Layer" and the "Mask" panels. The options within them can also be controlled using the Layer palette. The default names for new raster and vector layers are "Layer1," "Layer2," etc. The default name for a new adjustment layer is the type of the adjustment.

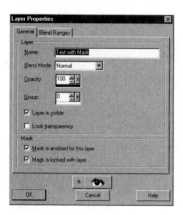 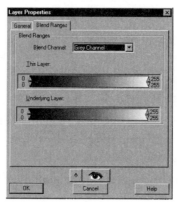 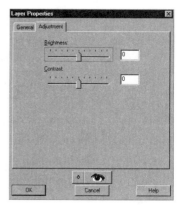

The Blend Ranges tab contains the "Blend Ranges" panel. When you change the Blend Mode using the Layer Properties dialog box or Layer palette, Paint Shop Pro applies the blend to all the pixels in the layers. Use the Blend Range controls to limit the pixels that the Blend mode affects. By setting opacity based on brightness or a channel value, you can remove colors from the current layer and make other colors show through. For more information about blend ranges, please refer to "About Layer Blend Ranges" on page 205.

The Adjustment tab contains the controls for the following adjustment layers: Brightness/Contrast, Channel Mixer, Color Balance, Curves, Hue/Saturation/Lightness, Levels, Posterize, and Threshold. The contents of the tab depend on the type of adjustment layer you choose. Because there are no options for the Invert adjustment layer, its Adjustment tab is blank. For more information about Adjustment Layers, please refer to Chapter 16, "Using Adjustment Layers."

At the bottom of the Layer Properties dialog box are the Auto Proof and Proof buttons. The Auto Proof button lets you automatically update the image as you change the tab settings. The Proof button lets you view changes before applying them. For more information about these buttons, please refer to the "Dialog Boxes" section of the "Getting to Know Paint Shop Pro" chapter in the *Getting Started Guide*.

Using the Layer Palette

The Layer palette provides quick access to many of the commands and controls in the Layers menu and Layer Properties dialog box. The palette displays into two panes. By dragging the divider, you can change their sizes. The left pane displays the layer type icons, the Layer and Object Name buttons, and the Layer Visibility buttons. It also shows if a layer is masked and if the Blend Range settings are used. The right pane displays the Appearance, Mask, and Group tabs. The tabs apply to raster, vector, and adjustment layers, but not to vector objects.

If the palette is not visible, do one of the following to display it:

- Press <L>.

- Click the Toggle Layer Palette button on the Toolbar.

- Right-click any palette or bar and choose Tool Palette from the context menu.

- Choose View > Toolbars to open the Toolbars dialog box. In the Toolbars dialog box, select the Layer Palette check box, and then click the OK button.

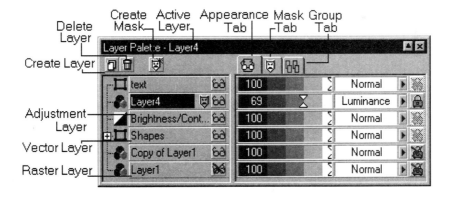

About the Layer Palette Layer Name Buttons

Each layer in an image has a Layer Name button on the Layer palette that displays the layer's name. An icon to the left of the Layer Name button indicates whether the layer is a raster layer, a vector layer, or an adjustment layer. When you add an object to a vector layer, a plus sign (+) appears next to its button. When you click the plus sign (+), it changes to a minus sign (-) and a Vector Object Name button appears below the Layer Name button. If the vector object is a text object, the text icon (**A**) appears next to the name of the object. If the vector object is a line or shape object, the vector object icon ( ) appears next to the name of the object.

Note the following button properties:

- When you click a Layer Name button to make its layer active, or current, it changes color (dark blue with the default system settings). When you click a Vector Object Name button, its text appears in bold.

- When you add a layer, a Layer Name button corresponding to the new layer appears on the palette and in the Layers menu list (at the bottom of the menu); when you delete or merge a layer, its Layer Name button disappears.

- When you right-click a Layer Name button, a context menu appears. It contains many of the same commands that you find in the Layers menu.

- When you right-click a Vector Object Name button, a context menu containing many of the editing commands opens. From the menu, choose Properties to open the Vector Properties dialog box.

- When you rest the cursor over a Layer Name button, a thumbnail image of that layer appears. When you rest it over a Vector Object Name button, a thumbnail of the object appears. Move the cursor to close the thumbnail.

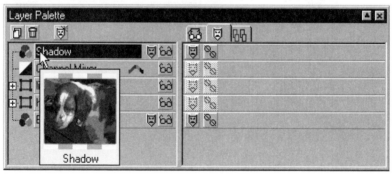

Layer Thumbnail

About the Layer Palette Tabs

There are three tabs that make up the right side of the Layer palette: Appearance, Mask, and Group. The Appearance tab (🔲) controls the opacity, blend mode, and transparency lock state of each layer. The Mask tab (🔲) controls the enable mask and link mask to layer options. The Group tab (🔲) controls the layer groups.

Layer Palette Tabs

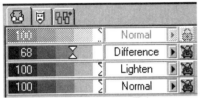

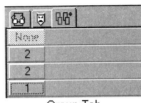

Appearance Tab · Mask Tab · Group Tab

Creating Layers

Background vs. Background Layer

A background layer is not the same as a background. When you create a new image and choose transparent as the background color, the new image contains a transparent layer floating above the checkered background. It is labeled "Layer 1." Because it is a layer and not a background, you can move it in the stack as is.

When you create a new image and choose a background color other than transparent, the image consists of a Background layer in the selected color. A Background layer, like a background, cannot be moved within the stack. However, unlike a background, a Background layer can be promoted to a "regular" layer.

To promote a Background layer, use one of the following methods:

- Right-click the Background button on the Layer palette and choose Promote to Layer from the context menu.

- Open the Layer Properties dialog box. Notice that the dialog box is actually named Promote Layer & Edit Properties. Rename the layer and close the dialog box. You can now move it.

Creating a Layer

To create a new layer in an image, do one of the following:

NOTE: *For detailed information about creating an Adjustment Layer, please refer to Chapter 16, "Using Adjustment Layers."*

- Choose Layers > New Raster Layer, Layers > New Vector Layer, or Layers > New Adjustment Layer from the main Menu bar. For an adjustment layer, choose one of the layer types. The Layer Properties dialog box opens.

- Click the Create Layer button ( ) at the upper left of the Layer palette. The Layer Properties dialog box opens with default properties for raster layers. If it is not a greyscale or 24-bit image, only a Vector layer can be created. Paint Shop Pro warns you and offers to create a vector layer. If you clear the "Show this next time" check box in the message, when you next use this method to create a layer in a paletted image (one that is not greyscale or 24-bit), Paint Shop Pro automatically creates a vector layer.

- Right-click any Layer Name button on the Layer palette and choose New Raster Layer, New Vector Layer, or New Adjustment Layer. For an adjustment layer, choose one of the layer types. The Layer Properties dialog box opens.

- Right-click the Create Layer button on the Layer palette and choose New Raster Layer, New Vector Layer, or New Adjustment Layer. For an adjustment layer, choose one of the layer types. The Layer Properties dialog box opens.

- Press <Shift> while clicking the Create Layer button on the Layer palette. Paint Shop Pro creates a new raster layer. A new button appears on the Layer palette, bypassing the Layer Properties dialog box.

NOTE: *An image must be a greyscale or 24-bit color image to contain an adjustment layer or more than one raster layer. To add these layers, increase an image's color depth.*

Duplicating a Layer

There are four ways to duplicate a layer:

- Click its Layer Name button on the Layer palette, and then choose Layers > Duplicate from the Menu bar.

- Right-click its Layer Name button, and then choose Duplicate from the context menu.

- Drag its Layer Name button to the Create Layer button at the upper left of the Layer palette.

- Click its Layer Name button, choose Edit > Copy from the Menu bar to copy the layer, and then choose Edit > Paste > As New Layer.

The duplicated layer is placed in the image above the original layer, and its Layer Name button appears on the Layer palette above the Layer Name button of the original layer.

Creating a Layer from a Selection

You can promote both raster and vector selections to layers, but the new layers are always raster layers. Selections cannot be promoted or converted to vector layers. First, make a selection. Then, use one of the following methods to promote a raster or vector selection to a raster layer within an image.

To promote a selection to a layer:

- Promote a selection by choosing Selections > Promote to Layer. The name of the new layer is *Promoted Selection*.

- Promote a floating selection by choosing Selections > Promote to Layer.

- Promote a floating selection by right-clicking its Layer Name button on the Layer palette and then choosing Promote to Layer from the context menu.

- Promote a selection by cutting or copying it and then pressing <Ctrl> + <L> or choosing Edit > Paste > As New Layer.

Renaming a Layer

As you add layers to an image, you may find it convenient to rename the layers so that they are easier to identify on the Layer palette. You can rename all three types of layers.

To rename a layer:

1. Open the Layer Properties dialog box for a layer by right-clicking the Layer Name button and choosing Properties from the context menu, by clicking the button and choosing Layers > Properties from the main Menu bar, or by double-clicking the button.

2. Type a new name in the Name box.

3. Click the OK button to close the dialog box.

The Layer palette displays the new name on the Layer Name button.

NOTE: *Alternatively, you can rename a layer by right-clicking the Layer Name button on the Layer palette. Choose Rename from the context menu, type the new name, and press the <Enter> key.*

Moving and Copying Layers

Moving a Layer within the Image

There are two ways to move a layer—vertically up and down within the stack, and horizontally across the image on the same level.

Moving a Layer Vertically

To move a layer up or down within the stack of layers, click its button on the Layer palette and then do one of the following:

- Choose Layers > Arrange > Move Up or Move Down. Each time you choose the command, the layer moves up or down one level. Choose Layers > Arrange > Bring to Top to place the layer at the top; choose Layers > Arrange > Send to Bottom to place it at the bottom or just above the background layer, if there is one.

- On the Layer palette, drag the Layer Name button up or down to a new position in the stack.

You must promote the Background layer to a "regular" layer before you can move it. To promote it, use the Layer Properties dialog box or the Layer palette context menu as described in "Background vs. Background Layer" on page 195.

⊹ Moving a Layer Horizontally

You can move a layer anywhere in the image window by dragging it with the Mover tool. Even if you move part of a layer off the canvas, Paint Shop Pro does not crop it. You can return it to the canvas in its original state.

The Mover tool finds the uppermost visible layer that contains data and moves that layer. To move the current (active) layer, use the Smart Mover tool, described next.

Using the Smart Mover Tool

You can move a layer anywhere in the image window without cropping it, even off the canvas, by dragging it with the Mover tool.

The Mover tool does not automatically move the current (active) layer—it moves the uppermost visible layer that contains data. When you click an image, if you click a transparent area of the top layer, the Mover tool ignores the layer and searches the other layers. When it reaches a layer containing non-transparent pixels, it selects this layer, makes it the current layer, and moves it.

To limit the Mover tool to the current layer, press and hold the <Shift> key while you click the image and drag the layer.

Copying a Layer to Another Image

Copying a Layer

To copy a layer into another image, do one of the following:

- Click the Layer Name button of layer you want to copy and choose Edit > Copy. Place it into the second image by choosing Edit > Paste as New Layer after making the second image active.

- Drag a Layer Name button from the Layer palette of the first image and drop it into the second image.

- Cut or copy a selection from the first image, make the second image active, and then choose Edit > Paste > As New Layer.

The new layer is placed above the current (active) layer of the second image. Its Layer Name button appears at a corresponding position on the Layer palette.

Using the Browser to Copy All Layers

To copy the layers of one image into another:

1. Open the image file that will receive the new layers.

2. Open the Browser.

3. Navigate to and select the folder containing the file whose layers you want to copy.

4. Drag the thumbnail over the open image.

5. Release the mouse button.

The layers are copied into the open image as a linked group. To unlink the layers so that they can be moved separately, use the Group tab on the Layer palette. For more information about the Group tab, please refer to "Grouping Layers" on page 202.

Viewing and Hiding Layers

Viewing All Layers

To make all the layers in an image visible, do one of the following:

- Click the Visibility buttons (👁👁) on the palette until all the layers are visible. When a layer is invisible, its Visibility button displays a red "X."

- Choose Layers > View > All from the main Menu bar.

- Right-click the Layer Name button on the Layer palette, and choose View > All from the context menu.

Viewing Individual Layers

To view only a specific layer, do one of the following:

- Click the Visibility buttons (🔲) on the palette until only that layer remains visible. You can use this method to make as many layers visible as you want.

- Click a Layer Name button to select a layer, and choose Layers > View > Current Only from the main Menu bar.

- Right-click the Layer Name button on the Layer palette, and choose View > Current Only from the context menu.

NOTE: *Making a layer current (active) automatically makes it visible, but a current layer without data appears transparent.*

Modifying Layers

Modifying the Edges

When you promote or paste a selection to create a layer, some of the pixels surrounding the border are included, especially when it has been antialiased or feathered. Matting cleans up the border by removing these pixels.

Removing Black and White Matte

When you promote a selection that contains white or black at its edges into a layer, the edges of the layer now contain black and white pixels. If the promoted layer is above a colored layer, the white or black needs to be removed.

To remove black or white matte:

- To remove the black matte, choose Layers > Matting > Remove Black Matte.

- To remove the white matte, choose Layers > Matting > Remove White Matte.

NOTE: *The Layer Matting and Defringe commands can only be applied to a greyscale or 24-bit color image.*

Defringing a Layer

Defringing bleeds non-feathered pixels in the layer edges outward and over the "jaggies" in the feathered part of the selection. Use the Defringe command when the background of a layer is a color (not black or white).

To defringe a layer:

1. Choose Layers > Matting > Defringe. The Defringe dialog box opens.

2. Enter the pixel width you want to defringe.

3. Click the OK button to close the dialog box defringe the layer.

Applying Effects

You can apply effects to raster and adjustment layers, but not to vector layers. If an image contains a selection, the effect is applied to the selected area of the current (active) layer. When an image does not contain a selection, the effect is applied to the entire layer.

For more information about effects, please refer to Chapter 17, "Adding Effects."

NOTE: *Before applying a command, be sure the appropriate layer is the current layer.*

Using Masks

NOTE: *For more information about using masks, please refer to Chapter 14, "Working with Masks."*

Adding a Layer Mask

You can add a mask to a raster or vector layer, but not to an adjustment layer, in any 8-bit grey-scale or 24-bit color image. When working with masks, you can use the Layer palette to create the mask, view a thumbnail of it, control its visibility on the layer, and link it to the layer. Use the commands in the Masks menu for other functions.

To create a mask:

1. On the Layer palette, click a Layer Name button to make the layer current (active).

2. Use the Create Mask button (🔲)at the upper left of the palette to do one of the following:

   - Left-click to create a mask in the "Hide All" mode,

   - Press <Shift> while left-clicking to create a mask in the "Show All" mode, or

   - Right-click to open a context menu containing the same commands as the Mask > New submenu.

A mask icon appears to the left of the Visibility button (Layer4) on the Layer palette. To view a thumbnail of the mask, move the cursor over the icon.

Enabling a Layer Mask

The Enable Layer Mask option controls whether a layer is viewed with or without its mask. When it is active, the layer mask determines the appearance of the layer. When the option is not active (🔲), the mask is hidden and has no effect on the layer's appearance.

To control this option, do either of the following:

- Click the Enable Layer Mask button (🔲) on the Masks tab of the Layer palette.

- Select or clear the "Mask is enabled for this layer" check box in the Layer Properties dialog box.

Linking to a Mask

Use the Link Mask option when you want to move a mask and layer together within an image. When this option is active ![icon], the Flip, Rotate, and Mirror commands move the mask and layer as one unit. When the option is not active ![icon], the layer and mask move independently. The Mask options are displayed on the Mask tab of the Layer palette.

To control this option, do either of the following:

- Click the Link Mask button (![icon]) on the Mask Tab of the Layer palette.

- Select or clear the "Mask is locked with layer" check box in the Layer Properties dialog box.

Protecting Transparent Areas

The Lock Transparency option restricts the editing of raster layers to the pixels that already contain data. You can select and edit the data on a protected layer, but you can not cover, deselect, or paste to any transparent area. This option does not apply to vector and adjustment layers, so their buttons are unavailable on the Layer palette.

By default, the Lock Transparency button (![icon]) of a layer on the Layer palette displays a red "X" because this option is not active. Use either the Layer Properties dialog box or the Layer palette Lock Transparency button (![icon]) to control this option on a layer.

To control this option, do either of the following:

- Click the Lock Transparency button (![icon]) on the Appearance tab of the Layer palette.

- Select or clear the "Lock Transparency" check box in the Layer Properties dialog box.

NOTE: *You can lock a layer transparency any time; remember to unlock it before trying to add to the layer.*

Grouping Layers

The Layer Group option lets you place layers into a group so that they move in unison. You can combine all types of layers into a group. When you click the Layer Name button of a layer that is part of a group, the Group tab displays a red dot (![icon]).

To group layers in an image, click each layer's Group button on the Group tab of the Layer palette. The button changes from "None" to a number. All the layers having the same number on their Group buttons belong to a single group. Left-click a Group button to increase the number; right-click the button to decrease the number.

You also create a layer group when you use the Browser to copy a layered image to another image. Dragging a thumbnail from the Browser and releasing it over an image adds the thumbnail's layers to the image as a new group.

Changing Layer Opacity

The Appearance tab of the Layer palette displays the opacity bar for each layer. The overall opacity of a layer and the opacity of its pixels are independent of each other. Changing a layer's opacity changes the appearance of the pixels, but not their opacity values.

At an overall opacity of 100%, the default value, a layer is totally opaque and none of the underlying layer shows through. This is the default value for layers. As you drag the slider to the left to reduce the opacity, the underlying layer begins to appear. At 75% opacity, the image displays 75% of the upper layer and 25% of the underlying layer. At 0% opacity, the layer is transparent, and you see only the underlying layer.

To set the opacity of a layer, do one of the following:

- Drag the Opacity slider on the Layer palette (█ 74   ☒]), or
- Enter a value for the Opacity in the Layer Properties dialog box.

Blending Layers

About Layer Blend Modes

The layer blend modes are methods of combining the pixels of the current (active) layer with the pixels of the underlying layers. You are not combining the layers permanently; you are previewing the way they will appear if combined. To combine layers permanently, you need to merge them.

The current layer whose blend mode you are changing is the Blend layer. The pixels of this layer are blended into the result of the combination of the pixels of all the underlying layers, not merely the layer directly underneath it. The blend mode for each layer is displayed on the Appearance tab of the Layer palette (█ Normal ▶]).

The following table describes the blend modes:

Layer Blend Modes

Blend Mode	Description
Normal	Pixels on the current layer are blended with the underlying layer only by varying the opacity.
Darken	Pixels in the selected layer that are darker than the underlying layers are applied to the image. Pixels lighter than the underlying layers disappear.
Lighten	The lighter of the blend and base colors is displayed.
Hue	Applies the hue of the selected layer to the underlying layers.
Saturation	Applies the saturation of the selected layer to the underlying layers.
Color	Applies the hue and saturation of the selected layer to the image. The luminance of the underlying layers is not affected.
Luminance	Applies the luminance values of the selected layer to the luminance values of the underlying layers. The color is not affected.

Layer Blend Modes

Blend Mode	Description
Multiply	Combines the colors of the selected layer with the underlying layers to produce a darker color. Multiplying any color with black produces black; multiplying any color with white leaves the color unchanged.
Screen	Lightens the underlying color by multiplying the inverse of the blend and base colors. The result is a color that is the same or a lightened version of the base color.
Hard Light	Combines two previous blend modes. If the selected layer's color channel value is less then 128 (half of the maximum value), the Multiply blend mode is used. If the selected layer's color channel value is greater than or equal to 128, the Screen blend mode is used. This mode is generally used to add highlights or shadows.
Dissolve	Randomly replaces the colors of some pixels on the selected layer with those of the layer underneath to create a speckled effect. The number of pixels replaced is determined by the layer's opacity, with more pixels being replaced as the opacity decreases.
Overlay	Combines two previous blend modes. If the underlying layers' color channel value is less than half the maximum value, the Multiply blend mode is used. If the color channel value is greater than or equal to half, the Screen blend mode is used. This shows patterns or colors of the upper layer while preserving the shadows and highlights of the lower layers.
Difference	Subtracts the selected layer's color from the color of the underlying layers, depending on which is lighter.
Dodge	The lightness values of the colors in the Blend layer lighten the colors of the underlying layers, lightening the image. Light colors produce the most lightening; black has no effect.
Burn	The lightness values of the colors of the Blend layer reduce the lightness of the underlying layers, darkening the image.
Soft Light	Combines two previous blend modes. If the selected layer's color channel value is less than half the maximum value, the Burn blend mode is used. If the color channel value is greater than or equal to half, the Dodge blend mode is used. This mode is generally used to add soft highlights or shadows.
Exclusion	Creates an effect similar to but softer than the Difference mode.

NOTE: The Multiply, Screen, Difference, and Exclusion modes will produce the same results no matter which layer is on top. The Hue, Saturation, Color, and Luminance modes are available only with 24-bit images.

About Layer Blend Ranges

When you select a blend mode from the Layer Properties dialog box or Layer palette, Paint Shop Pro applies the blend to all the pixels in the layers. Use the controls on the Blend Ranges tab of the Layer Properties dialog box to limit the pixels that the blend mode affects. By setting opacity based on brightness or channel value, you can drop colors out of the current layer and make other colors show through. When you have applied a blend range setting to a layer, its Layer palette button displays the Blend Range icon 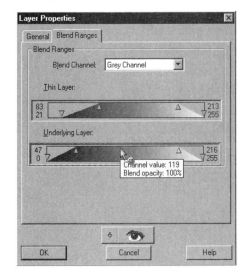.

To use the Blend Range controls:

1. Select a layer and set its Blend mode.

2. Open the Layer Properties dialog box for the layer.

NOTE: *Alternatively, you can open the dialog box first and change the Blend Mode in the dialog box instead of on the Layer palette.*

3. Click the Blend Ranges tab to bring it to the front.

4. In the Blend Channel drop-down box, select a channel for Paint Shop Pro to use for comparing the layers. Your choices are Grey, Red, Green, and Blue. When the Grey channel is selected, the lightness values of the layers determine opacity.

5. Set the opacity ramp for the channel. The upper arrows indicate the values at which the opacity will be 100%. The lower arrows indicate the values at which the opacity will be 0%. The values on the left side indicate the ramp up values, while the values on the right side indicate the ramp down values. For example, in the screen capture, the blend layer's opacity (in the "This Layer" panel) is 100% between lightness values of 83 and 213, and falls off at the darkest and lightest area. The blend opacity for the underlying layer (in the "Underlying Layer" panel) is 100% between lightness values of 47 and 216, blends fully in the range of 47 to 216, and tapers to no blend at the extremes.

6. Click the Proof button to view the image with the new settings before applying them.

NOTE: *If you click the Auto Proof button, the image updates as you change the settings.*

7. Click the OK button. Paint Shop Pro applies the blend only to the pixels that fall within the range.

Using Layer Options

Merging Layers

Merging layers combines multiple layers into one, which decreases the memory requirements of an image. However, because they have been converted into a single layer, they can no longer be edited separately. The merged layer contains all the data from the source layers and bases its appearance on their blend modes. All vector data in the source layers is converted to raster data. When you flatten an image (merge all the layers), the transparent areas of the image are replaced with white. You can merge all the layers in an image or merge only the visible layers.

* Merge all the layers to produce a flat image by choosing Layers > Merge > Merge All (Flatten) or right-clicking a layer in the Layer palette and choosing Merge > Merge All (Flatten) from the context menu.

* Merge only the visible layers by choosing Layers > Merge > Merge Visible or right-clicking a layer in the Layer palette and choosing Merge > Merge Visible from the context menu. The hidden layers are not affected.

Saving a Layered Image

You can save images that contain raster and adjustment layers in either the .psp format or the PhotoShop .psd format. Both formats retain all the layer information for these two types of layers. However, images containing vector layers must be saved in the .psp format to retain the vector information. When you save an image with vector layers in the .psd format, the vector layers are converted to raster layers.

Deleting a Layer

To delete a layer, make the layer active and then choose Layers > Delete from the main Menu bar, or do one of the following on the Layer palette:

* Right-click the Layer Name button and choose Delete from the context menu.

* Click the Layer Name button, and then click the Delete Layer Name button (🗑) at the upper left of the palette. A message appears asking you to confirm this action. Click the Yes button.

* Drag the Layer Name button to the Delete Layer Name button and release the mouse. A message appears asking you to confirm this action. Click the Yes button.

The deleted layer's button disappears from the Layer palette and from the layer list at the bottom of the Layers menu.

Using the
Vector Tools

Paint Shop Pro contains several painting and drawing tools on its Tools palette. These range from standard paint brushes to photo retouching tools to the Text tool. The Paint Brush, Clone Brush, Color Replacer, Retouch, Eraser, Picture Tube, Airbrush, and Flood Fill tools have options to let you use them on raster layers. The Text, Drawing, and Preset Shapes tools have options to let you use them on both raster and vector layers. This chapter discusses the combination tools you can use on both raster and vector layers. For information about the painting tools you can use on raster layers, please refer to Chapter 8, "Using the Painting Tools."

Overview of Vector Layers and Objects

In Paint Shop Pro, you can work on three types of layers: raster, adjustment (which is raster), and vector. A raster layer is pixel oriented, while a vector layer is object oriented. Raster images (and layers) display objects by combining units of colored light, called pixels. If you zoom in, you can see each pixel as a small square. When you move an object in a raster image (or layer), you move the pixels, which affects the entire image.

A vector layer does not use pixels for storing image information. Instead, it stores a vector object as a set of properties that describe its attributes, dimensions, and position in the image. Each time an image is opened, these properties are used as instructions for drawing the objects. Because the objects are independent elements, you can move them without affecting the rest of the image.

You can add vector layers to images of color depths that are too low to support raster layers. While only greyscale and 24-bit color images can contain multiple raster layers, images of any color depth can contain multiple vector layers. When you reduce the color depth of an image, Paint Shop Pro merges both raster and vector layers. You can then create new vector layers in this image, even if it does not support raster layers.

The Layer palette displays the vector icon to the left of a vector layer button. When the layer contains vector objects, a plus sign appears next to the icon. Click it to display the buttons of all the vector objects on the layer.

You cannot place vector objects on raster layers or raster objects on vector layers. If you try to create a vector object on a raster layer, Paint Shop Pro automatically creates a vector layer for you. If you are working on a vector layer, Paint Shop Pro merely adds the new object to the layer.

When a vector layer is selected, the raster painting tools are unavailable, and their buttons are greyed-out. Because many of these tools operate or have the desired effect only on greyscale or 24-bit images, you may need to increase the color (bit) depth of your image before using them. For help with this, please refer to Chapter 5, "Working with Color."

The Drawing, Preset Shapes, and Text tools can create both vector and raster objects. Use the tools as vector tools on vector layers and raster tools on raster layers. There is also a tool for editing vector objects called the Vector Object Selection tool. It cannot be activated unless a vector layer is current (active).

Using the Drawing Tool

Use the Drawing tool to draw single lines, freehand lines, Bezier curves, and Point to Point lines as raster objects on raster layers or as vector objects on vector layers. When you use the Drawing tool in the vector mode, the objects can be moved, deformed, and edited after they are created without affecting the rest of the image.

There are four general steps to creating a line: activate the tool, set the options on the Tool Options palette, set the styles and textures on the Color palette, and draw the line. In addition, you can create and save your own customized line styles and use them again later.

Activating the Drawing Tool

To activate the tool:

*   Click its button (🖉) on the Tool palette, or
*   Click the Tool Options palette Tool Selection (🖉) button and choose the Drawing tool from the drop-down menu.

Setting the Drawing Tool Options

Use the Tool Options palette to set the options for the drawing tool. All of the options are available for 24-bit images. If you are working with a greyscale image or an image of less than 24-bit, some of the options are not available.

To set the tool options:

1. If necessary, make the Tool Options palette visible. To do this, click its toolbar icon (▥) or press <O> on your keyboard.

2. Set the options on the first tab of the Tool Options palette:

    TYPE The Drawing tool creates four types of lines:

    *   Single lines, which are straight lines,
    *   Bezier curves, which are smooth curves with anchor points and controls for creating the curve,
    *   Freehand lines, which are lines of any shape, and
    *   Point to Point lines, which are lines and shapes composed of nodes and line segments.

    WIDTH Use the Width box to set the line to between 1 and 255 pixels wide.

    LINE STYLE Click the down arrow and select a line style. Alternatively, click the Custom button and create your own line style. For specific steps, please refer to "Creating and Saving Customized Line Styles" on page 214.

ANTIALIAS Select or clear the "Antialias" check box. Antialiasing smooths the edges of slanted lines, curves, and corners by partially filling in pixels. This effect is available only with greyscale and 24-bit color images.

CREATE AS VECTOR Select the check box to create the line as a vector object. Paint Shop Pro creates a new vector layer if the current (active) layer is a raster layer. Clear the check box to create a raster line. If the current (active) layer is a vector layer, Paint Shop Pro creates a new raster layer.

This check box is unavailable when you are working on a vector layer in a paletted image. To create a raster line, place it on the background. It is also unavailable when you use the Line tool to edit a mask; masks cannot contain vector information.

CLOSE PATH Select the "Close Path" check box to have Paint Shop Pro automatically add a straight line to connect the endpoint with the starting point (origin of the line). This line is considered part of the original line and appears as part of the path. This check box is not available when creating Point to Point lines.

3. Click the second tab to bring it to the front. The settings on the second tab control the shapes of corners and end points and the size of Freehand line segments of both raster and vector lines. Set the options on the tab:

JOIN Click the down arrow and select a shape for corners you draw. Choose from three styles:

- Miter, which produces mitered (pointed) corners when the width of the corner is within the Miter Limit value and beveled corners when it exceeds it,

- Round, which produces round corners, or

- Bevel, which produces flattened corners.

MITER LIMIT This option is available only when you have selected the Miter Join option. The Miter Limit value, determines whether the outer corner of the join is pointed or beveled (flat). The Miter limit is the maximum allowed ratio of miter length to the width of the intersecting lines. Miter length is the length of the intersecting edge of two line segments, or the depth of the intersection from the inside to outside corner. (See the illustration above.) If a Miter join exceeds the limit, the join is beveled at the limit point. Set a value from 1 to 30.

Corner Join Styles

Miter Join   Round Join   Bevel Join

Miter Limit

CURVE TRACKING This option, which is available only for Freehand lines, controls the distance between the points of the line segments. Use the numeric edit control to enter a value from 1 to 100.

Setting the Styles and Textures

With Paint Shop Pro Version 7, you can use patterns, textures, and gradients with the vector tools. For the drawing tool, you can set stroke and fill (foreground and background) styles as solid color, gradient, pattern, or none; and you can set foreground and background textures.

To set the styles and textures:

Use the Styles and Textures panels of the Color palette to set the styles and textures. For details about the Color palette, please refer to Chapter 9, "Using the Color Palette."

Drawing Lines

After you have set the tool options, styles, and textures, you draw the line. The steps for each line type vary as described in this section.

NOTE: *Edit a raster line as you would any other raster selection. While creating a vector line, use the Drawing tool to rotate, move, and deform the object. After creating a vector line, edit it using the Vector Properties dialog box and the Vector Object Selection tool ( ) as described in Chapter 13, "Editing Vector Objects and Text."*

Drawing a Single Line

To draw a Single line:

1. Position the cursor where you want the line to start. To draw the line at fixed angles in increments of 45°, press and hold the <Shift> key.

2. Press and hold the left mouse button to begin drawing.

3. Drag the cursor to where you want to end the line. An outline showing the width of the line appears as you drag.

4. To end the line, release the mouse button. Paint Shop Pro creates the line using the foreground style and texture (if set) from the Color palette.

Drawing a Multi-Segmented Line

To draw a line composed of angled line segments:

1. Position the cursor where you want the line to start.

2. Press the <Alt> key, and then click the image.

3. Move the cursor to where you want the line segment to end.

4. Click the image (while still pressing the <Alt> key).

5. While still pressing the <Alt> key, move the cursor to the point where you want the next line segment to end, and click the point.

6. Continue pressing the <Alt> key while clicking points.

7. To end the line, release the <Alt> key before clicking for the final time.

NOTE: *If you have set a background style or texture, the area between the line segments automatically fills with the style and / or texture.*

Connecting a New to a Previous Line

You can change the drawing Type and then continue the previous line by pressing the <Alt> key and then clicking the image where you want the new line segment to end.

Drawing a Bezier Curve

To draw a Bezier curve:

1. Position the cursor on the image where you want the curve to begin.

2. Press and hold the left mouse button to begin drawing.

3. Drag the cursor to where you want to end the line, and release the mouse. An outline showing the width of the curve's line appears as you drag.

4. Create the curve by clicking the mouse away from the line two times and dragging to shape the curve. A node handle appears each time you click. The first click sets the angle and target point from the starting node, the second click sets the angle and target point from the ending node.

   - To create a semi-circular curve, click the mouse where you want to position the top of the curve, and then click again to bring the curve from the endpoint up to it.

   - To create an "S" shaped curve, click and drag once on one side of the line and once on the other.

5. Release the mouse after editing the ending node.

NOTE: *If you have set a background style or texture, the area between the line segments automatically fills with the style and / or texture.*

Drawing a Freehand Line

To draw a Freehand line:

1. Be sure to enter a Curve Tracking value on the second tab of the Tool Options palette. The number controls the distance between nodes line segments. Use smaller numbers if you are drawing tighter curves.

2. Position the cursor on the image where you want the line to begin.

3. Press and hold the left mouse button to begin drawing.

4. Drag the cursor on the path you want the line to take. Paint Shop Pro draws an outline to show the width of the line.

5. Release the mouse button. Paint Shop Pro draws the line based on the selected options.

NOTE: *If you have set a background style or texture, the area between the line automatically fills with the style and / or texture.*

Creating a Point to Point Line

The Point to Point line type operates differently from the other line types. When you create a raster or vector point to point line, the Node Edit feature automatically activates for you to edit the nodes while you create the line. After you finish creating the line and quit Node Edit, edit a raster point to point line as you would any other raster selection, and edit a vector point to point line using the Node Edit features. For more information about using the Node Edit features, please refer to Chapter 13, "Editing Vector Objects and Text."

To create a Point to Point line or shape:

1. Position the cursor on the image where you want to begin.

2. Press and hold the left mouse button to begin drawing.

3. Do one of the following:

   • Click and release the left mouse button to create a straight segment node. The node appears as a square.

   • Click and drag with the left mouse button to create a curved segment node. Handles extend from both sides of the node.

4. Move the cursor to where you want to create the second node.

5. Left-click and release the mouse button or drag it to create a straight or curved node. A line connecting the nodes appears.

6. If you are creating straight segments, continue left-clicking to draw the line.

   NOTE: *If you are creating curves, you can shape them while you are drawing the line or after you have finished. To do this, use the Node Edit features. For more information about using the Node Edit features, please refer to Chapter 13, "Editing Vector Objects and Text."*

7. You can continue creating nodes or shape the curved segment.

8. To end the line or shape:

   • Press <Ctrl> + <Q>,

   • Click outside the image,

   • Right-click anywhere in the image and choose Edit Mode from the context menu, or

   • Right-click anywhere in the image and choose Quit Node Editing from the context menu.

9. Paint Shop Pro creates the line using the foreground style and texture (if set) from the Color palette.

NOTE: *If you have set a background style or texture, the area between the line segments automatically fills with the style and / or texture.*

Creating and Saving Customized Line Styles

You can design and save your own line styles and use them again at any time. After you save them, they appear in the Line Styles list on the Tool Options palette for the Drawing, Preset Shapes, and Text tools.

To create and save a customized line style:

1. Activate either the Drawing tool (⬚), the Preset Shapes tool (⬚), or the Text tool (**A**). To do this:

   - Click its button on the Tool palette, or

   - Click the Tool Option palette Tool Selection button (⬚) and choose the tool from the drop-down menu.

2. If necessary, make the Tool Options palette visible. To do this, click its toolbar icon (⬚) or press <O> on your keyboard.

3. On the first tab of the Tool Options palette, click the Custom button. This displays the Styled Lines dialog box. Use this dialog box to design one repeating section of your line. For example, if you want a line that has a repetition of dash, dash, dot, dot, you don't need to design a long line repeating this many times. You only need to design one repetition of the dash, dash, dot, and dot.

   NOTE: *If you want to copy an existing line style to create a new style, or if you want to edit or delete an existing line style, first select that style in the Line Style box and then click the Custom button. When you open the Styled Line dialog box, you might want to click the Reset button (⬚) to set all the options to the defaults, which are the values for a straight line.*

4. In the "Caps" panel design how you want the beginning and end caps of the line segments to look. Set the following options:

   FIRST CAP Click the down arrow and select the cap style you want to use at the beginning of the first segment in the line. Then click the Size button to display the Cap Size dialog box. In the Cap Size dialog box, use the numeric edit controls to set the Height and Width for the cap. To set and adjust both sizes equally, select the "Link axes" check box.

   LAST CAP Click the down arrow and select the cap style you want to use at the end of the last segment in the line. Then click the Size button and adjust the cap size the same way you did for the First Cap.

   DIFFERENT SEGMENT CAPS Select the check box to design separate end caps for all the middle segments in the line. Clear the check box to use the same end caps on the middle segment as the ones used for the first and last segments.

SEGMENT START If you selected the "Different Segment Caps check box, select the end cap style you want to use for the beginning of every middle line segment. Click the Size button and adjust the cap size.

SEGMENT END If you selected the "Different Segment Caps" check box, select the end cap style you want to use for the ending of every middle line segment. Click the Size button to adjust the cap size.

5. In the "Style" panel, design the line segments (dashes) and the gaps between the segments. The name of the numeric edit control changes between Add Dash, Dash and Add Gap, Gap. Do the following to design one repetition for your styled line:

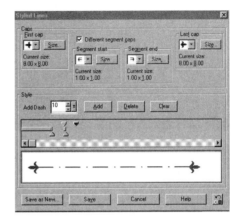

-   Click the Add button and then set the size of the first Dash with the numeric edit controls.

-   Click the Add button again and then set the size of the first gap with the numeric edit controls.

-   Continue adding the dashes and gaps, clicking the Add button before each one.

Alternatively, you can position the cursor over the edit area (below the buttons) and then click to place the dashes and gaps. Then use the triangle sliders to adjust the dashes and gaps. Use the bottom, green, sliders to adjust the dashes and the top, red, sliders to adjust the gaps. To delete the dashes and gaps in reverse order, one at a time, click the Delete button. To delete all the dashes and gaps, click the Clear button.

NOTE: *You can also move the sliders using keyboard commands. For details, click the Help button.*

6. Use the preview area as a visual aid in designing your line repetition. When you are finished, do one of the following to save the line:

-   If you are creating a new line, click the Save As New button. This displays the Styled Line Name box. Type a unique name for the line and click the OK button.

-   If you are editing an existing line, click the Save button.

7. The line appears in the Line Style list on the Tool Options palette.

Using the Preset Shapes Tool

Use the Preset Shape tool to draw rectangles, ellipses, and other shapes as raster objects on raster layers or vector objects on vector layers.

NOTE: *Edit a raster shape as you would any other raster selection. While creating a vector shape use the Preset Shapes tool to rotate, move, and deform the object. After creating a vector shape, edit it using the Vector Properties dialog box and the Vector Object Selection tool (□) as described in Chapter 13, "Editing Vector Objects and Text." A vector shape can be moved, deformed, and edited after it is created without affecting the rest of the image.*

There are four general steps to creating a preset shape: activate the tool, set the options on the Tool Options palette, set the styles and textures on the Color palette, and draw the shape. As an additional fifth step, you can export a customized preset shape and use it again later.

Activating the Preset Shapes Tool

To activate the tool:

- Click its button (□) on the Tool palette, or
- Click the Tool Options palette Tool Selection button (□) and choose the Preset Shapes tool from the drop-down menu.

Setting the Preset Shapes Tool Options

Use the Tool Options palette to set the options for the Preset Shapes tool. All of the options are available for 24-bit images. If you are working with a greyscale image or an image of less than 24-bit, some of the options are not available.

To set the tool options:

1. If necessary, make the Tool Options palette visible. To do this, click its toolbar icon (□) or press <O> on your keyboard.

2. Set the options on the first tab of the Tool Options palette:

    TYPE Click the down arrow and then click the preset shape you want to draw.

    RETAIN STYLE If the selected shape has a style (color, gradient, or pattern), select or clear to the check box. Select the check box to retain the shapes's style. Clear the check box to use the styles you have set in the Color palette.

    ANTIALIAS Select or clear the Antialias check box. Antialiasing smooths the edges of slanted lines, curves, and corners in the shape by partially filling in pixels. This effect is available only with greyscale and 24-bit color images.

CREATE AS VECTOR Select the check box to create the shape as a vector object. Paint Shop Pro creates a new vector layer if the current (active) layer is a raster layer. Clear the check box to create a raster shape. A new raster layer is created if the current (active) layer is a vector layer.

This check box is unavailable when you are working on a vector layer in a paletted image. To create a raster shape, place it on the background. It is also unavailable when you use the Shape tool to edit a mask; masks can contain only raster information.

WIDTH The Line Width value determines the pixel width of the colored outline. The outline of the shape can be between 1 and 255 pixels wide.

LINE STYLE Click the down arrow and select a line style. Alternatively, click the Custom button and create your own line style. For specific steps, please refer to "Creating and Saving Customized Line Styles" on page 214.

3. If you are creating a shape that has corners, click the second tab to bring it to the front. The settings on the second tab control the shapes of corners. These settings apply to both raster and vector shapes. If you are creating a circle or ellipse, these tab options do not apply, and you are ready to draw the shape.

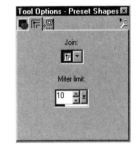

JOIN Click the down arrow and select a shape for corners you draw. Choose from three styles:

- Miter, which produces mitered (pointed) corners when the width of the corner is within the Miter Limit value and beveled corners when it exceeds it,

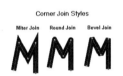

- Round, which produces round corners, or

- Bevel, which produces flattened corners.

MITER LIMIT This option is available only when you have selected the Miter Join option. The Miter Limit value, determines whether the outer corner of the join is pointed or beveled (flat). The Miter limit is the maximum allowed ratio of miter length to the width of the intersecting lines. Miter length is the length of the intersecting edge of two line segments, or the depth of the intersection from the inside to outside corner. If a Miter join exceeds the limit, the join is beveled at the limit point. Set a value from 1 to 30.

Setting the Styles and Textures

With Paint Shop Pro, Version 7, you can use patterns, textures, and gradients with the vector tools. For the shapes tool, you can set the stroke and fill (foreground and background) styles as solid color, gradient, pattern, or none; and you can set foreground and background textures.

When you use the raster tools, you set the foreground and background styles in the Styles panel on the Color palette. When you use the vector tools, you set the fill and stroke styles in the Styles panel. They work the same way, but just have different names. For vector objects, stroke is the outline and fill is what fills the outline.

Also, if the selected shape has its own style (color, gradient, or pattern), the Retain Style check box on the Tool Options palette determines if the shape draws with its style or your style settings on the Color palette. Selecting the check box retains the shape's style. Clearing the check box uses your style settings.

NOTE: *The styles and textures are not related to the mouse buttons like they were in previous versions of Paint Shop Pro. The mouse buttons are now used to set the starting position for the shape, and the Color palette determines the stroke and fill.*

To set the styles and textures:

Use the Styles and Textures panels of the Color palette to set the styles and textures. For details about the Color palette, please refer to Chapter 9, "Using the Color Palette."

Drawing a Preset Shape

After you have set the tool options, styles, and textures, you draw the shape. While creating a vector shape, use the Preset Shape tool to rotate, move, and deform the object.

To draw a shape:

1. Position the cursor in the image where you want the shape to originate.

2. Click and drag the cursor to draw the shape as follows.

> **NOTE:** *To constrain the shape proportionally, press and hold the <Shift> key while drawing.*

- Use the left mouse button to draw from side to side.

- Use the right mouse button to draw from the center out.

An outline showing the width of the edges appears as you drag.

3. Release the mouse button when the shape is the size you want. Paint Shop Pro draws the shape, and a button appears for the shape on the Layer palette.

Exporting a Preset Shape or Other Vector Object

You can save vector objects so that they appear in the shapes Type list of the Tool Options palette when you use the Preset Shape tool. To do this, you save any vector shape, line, or text object by exporting it to a specific folder. By default, this is the Shapes folder in the Paint Shop Pro 7 directory. To use other folders, choose File > Preferences > File Locations and click the Shapes tab.

To export an object:

1. Open the image that contains the object(s) to export. The image should have one or more vector objects.

2. Give each object a unique name:

   - Activate the Vector Object Selection tool (![icon]) and left-click an object to select it. Then right-click the object and select Properties from the context menu. In the Name box, type the new name and then click the OK button, or

3. Select the objects you want to export:

   - To export one object, activate the Vector Object Selection tool and left-click the object to select it.

   - To export several objects, press and hold the <Shift> key while using the Vector Object Selection tool to select the objects.

   - To export all the objects in the image, make sure no objects are selected.

4. Choose File > Export > Shape, or right-click the image and select Export Shape from the context menu.

5. In the Export Shape Library dialog box, type a name for the library file that will contain the objects and click the OK button.

6. The library file saves to your default objects location with the name you gave it and a .jsl file extension. The object(s) appear in the shapes Type list on the Tool Options palette.

   NOTE: *You can choose File > Preferences >File Locations to change the default location. For more information, please refer to Chapter 20, "Setting Preferences." To edit or deleteany of these objects, open the .jsl file. To delete an entire library of shapes, delete the .jsl file.*

▦ Using the Vector Object Selection Tool

Use the Vector Object Selection tool (▦) to move, resize, skew, stretch, and rotate vector objects, to edit vector object nodes, and to apply Edit menu commands to Vector objects.

You can select one or more vector objects from any layer using the Vector Object Selection tool. The objects selected are enclosed in a rectangle that contains handles used to move, rotate, and deform the objects. Right-clicking the selected shape or group displays a context menu containing editing commands. You also use the Vector Object Selection tool to edit nodes and their segments, contours, and paths. Vector node editing is available only when a single object is selected.

To activate the Vector Object Selection tool (▦), click its button on the Tool palette or choose it from the Tool Options palette Tool Selection (🖉) menu. For more information about editing vector objects, please refer to Chapter 13, "Editing Vector Objects and Text."

A Using the Text Tool

Use the Text tool to create raster and vector text and to edit vector text. Vector text can only be placed on vector layers. If you create vector text while working on a raster layer, Paint Shop Pro places it on a new vector layer. You can create text in one of three modes: as a selection on the current layer, as a floating selection above the current layer, or as a vector object on a vector layer. These are described on page 223.

There are three general steps to creating text: activate the tool, set the options on the Tool Options palette, and add the text. When you add the text, you type the text and define its characteristics using the Text Entry dialog box.

Activating the Text Tool

To activate the tool:

- Click its button (**A**) on the Tool palette, or

- Click the Tool Options palette Tool Selection (🖉) button and choose the Drawing tool from the drop-down menu.

Setting the Text Tool Options

Use the Tool Options palette to set the options for the text tool.

To set the tool options:

1. If necessary, make the Tool Options palette visible. To do this, click its toolbar icon (▥) or press <O> on your keyboard.

2. Set the options on the first tab of the Tool Options palette:

WIDTH Use the Width box to set the width of the text outline to between 1 and 255 pixels wide.

LINE STYLE Click the down arrow and select a line style. Alternatively, click the Custom button and create your own line style. For specific steps, please refer to "Creating and Saving Customized Line Styles" on page 214.

3. Click the second tab to bring it to the front. The settings on the second tab control the shapes of corners in both raster and vector text. Set the options on the tab:

JOIN Click the down arrow and select a shape for corners you draw. Choose from three styles:

- Miter, which produces mitered (pointed) corners when the width of the corner is within the Miter Limit value and beveled corners when it exceeds it,

- Round, which produces round corners, or

- Bevel, which produces flattened corners.

MITER LIMIT This option is available only when you have selected the Miter Join option. The Miter Limit value, determines whether the outer corner of the join is pointed or beveled (flat). The Miter limit is the maximum allowed ratio of miter length to the width of the intersecting lines. Miter length is the length of the intersecting edge of two line segments, or the depth of the intersection from the inside to outside corner. If a Miter join exceeds the limit, the join is beveled at the limit point. Set a value from 1 to 30.

Setting the Styles and Textures

With Paint Shop Pro Version 7, you can use patterns, textures, and gradients with the vector tools. For the text tool, you can set stroke and fill (foreground and background) styles as solid color, gradient, pattern, or none; and you can set foreground and background textures.

To set the styles and textures:

You can use the Styles and Textures panels of the Color palette to set the styles and textures, or you can use the same panels located on the Text Entry dialog box, described in the next section.

Adding the Text

To add the text you first select the location for the text in the image and then set the options in the Text Entry dialog box.

Selecting the Location for the Text

To select the location for the text:

Click the image where you want to place the text. Click away from a vector object to create horizontal text. Click a vector object to place text on the object's path. The Text Entry dialog box opens.

NOTE: *If you are creating the text as a selection or floating selection, hold the <Shift> key when clicking to add the text to any existing selection.*

Using the Text Entry Dialog Box

The Text Entry dialog box contains the options for setting the content, font attributes, alignment, styles, textures, mode, leading, and kerning of the text.

NOTE: *All of the options in this dialog box are available for 24-bit images. If you are working with a greyscale image or an image of less than 24-bit, some of the options are not available.*

To use the Text Entry dialog box:

1. In the "Enter Text Here" panel, type the text you want to add to the image. Optionally, click and drag the cursor over any letters or words and then click an attribute button **B** / **U** **A** to change the attributes of the selected text. The buttons are (from left to right): Bold, Italic, Underline, and Strikeout.

2. Click an Alignment button ▤ ▥ ▦ to choose left, center, or right alignment. Alignment determines how the ends of multiple lines of text line up with each other. The alignment setting affects the entire text and cannot be changed for individual lines.

3. In the Name, Size, and Script boxes, click the down-arrows and select the font and size for the text. You can leave the Script box set to Western for most cases.

4. In the Kerning and Leading boxes, set specific leading and kerning by clearing the Auto Kern check box and typing values in the Kerning and Leading boxes. Kerning adjusts the spacing between characters and leading adjusts the spacing between lines.

NOTE: *If you are adding text to a path, you can position the text above or below the path by setting the Leading value. To do this, select the text and use the Leading numeric edit controls to enter a value. Positive numbers position the text below the path; negative numbers position the text above the path.*

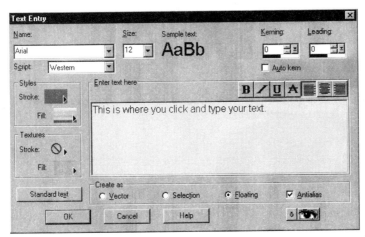

5. In the "Styles" and "Textures" panels, set the stroke and fill styles and textures. These panels are identical to the panels on the Color palette. Changing the settings in this dialog box also changes the settings on the Color palette. For information about using the panels, please refer to Chapter 9, "Using the Color Palette."

6. Optionally, you can click the Standard Text button to reset the styles to no stroke and to a fill using the color selected as the current solid background/fill color, and to reset the textures to none.

7. In the "Create As" panel, choose one of the modes for the text:

    VECTOR Use this option to create vector text on a vector layer. If necessary, Paint Shop Pro creates a new vector layer. The vector text is placed as a vector object that can be edited, deformed, and moved. Text is placed horizontally unless you have created it on a path. When created on a path, the text follows the path.

    SELECTION Use this option to create a selection that is shaped like text. Text created as a selection appears on the current (active) layer as an empty, transparent selection. You can then promote the selection to a layer, color it using a painting tool, or edit it as you would any other selection. For more information, please refer to Chapter 10, "Working with Selections."

    FLOATING Use this option to create text as a floating selection above the current (active) layer. You can then defloat the selection as raster text on a raster layer. Although you cannot defloat a floating selection to a vector layer, you can use this option on a vector layer to create text along the path of a vector object. When you defloat the text, it merges into the raster layer below the vector layer. You can then delete the vector layer.

8. Select or clear the Antialias check box. Antialiasing, which softens jagged edges that can appear on bitmap text by partially filling in pixels, is available only with greyscale and 24-bit color images.

9. Click the OK button. The dialog box closes, and the text appears in the image.

Creating Text on a Path

To create curved text, place vector text on the path of vector lines and shapes. The text follows the shape (path) of the vector object. You can create the text on an existing object or combine existing text with an existing object. When text is combined with an object, the paths of the two are linked and must be on the same layer. If you move one to a different layer, the linked text or path moves with it.

About Paths

A path is the outline that defines the shape of a vector object. It can be composed of one or more contours. Each contour has a start point node, an end point node, and a direction. An object's path is visible while you create and edit an object. At other times, you see only the object.

Creating Text on an Object Path

To create text on the path of an existing object:

1. Activate the Text tool (**A**) by clicking its button on the Tool palette.

2. Move the cursor to the vector object. It changes to the Curved Text cursor().

3. Click the vector object. The Text Entry dialog box appears.

4. Select the text settings. Be sure to choose the Vector option in the "Create As" panel.

5. Click the OK button. The text appears on the path.

Aligning Text

The alignment of the text depends on the alignment setting in the Text Entry dialog box (Left, Center, or Right) and whether the path is open or closed.

Aligning Text on an Open Path

An open path has specific starting and ending points, as in a curved or straight line. Left-justified text is aligned with the starting point of the path. Right-justified text is aligned with the ending point of the path. Center-justified text is placed equidistant between the starting and ending points. If the text is longer than the path, the extra text hangs from the end. The angle of the last segment determines the direction it hangs.

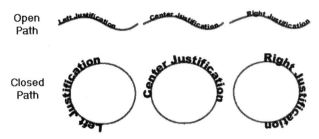

Aligning Text on a Closed Path (Shape)

A closed path has starting and ending points that meet to form a continuous shape, as in a circle. Its edges are used to justify the text. Left-justified text is centered on the midpoint of the left or left side of the shape. Right-justified text is centered on the midpoint of the right or right side of the shape. Center-justified text is centered about the midpoint of the top or upper side of the shape. If the text is longer than an existing closed path, the extra text wraps around itself.

Fitting Existing Text to and Object Path

You can combine vector text with an object so that the text follows its shape.

To combine vector text with an object:

1. Activate the Vector Object Selection tool (▣) by clicking its button on the Tool palette.

2. Press the <Shift> key while clicking the vector object and the text to group them.

3. Right-click the Vector object group and choose Fit Text to Path from the context menu.

The text moves into alignment along the path of the shape.

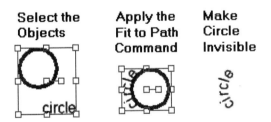

Making the Object Invisible

To make the Object invisible:

• Open the Vector Properties dialog box and clear the "Visible" check box, or

• On the Layer palette, click the Visibility button of the object so it appears crossed out.

Editing Vector Objects and Text

After creating vector objects with the Drawing, Preset Shapes, and Text tools, you can select the objects and edit them without affecting the rest of the image. This chapter contains information about editing vector objects and text. For information about creating vector objects, please refer to Chapter 12, "Using the Vector Tools."

Selecting Vector Objects

In order to edit a vector object, you must first use the Vector Object Selection tool to select the object and make it active.

Using the Vector Object Selection Tool

Use the Vector Object Selection tool (⬚) to move, resize, skew, stretch, and rotate vector objects, to edit vector object nodes, and to apply Edit menu commands to Vector objects.

You can select one or more vector objects from any layer using the Vector Object Selection tool. The objects selected are enclosed in a rectangle that contains handles used to move, rotate, and deform the objects. Right-clicking the selected shape or group displays a context menu containing editing commands. You also use the Vector Object Selection tool to edit nodes and their segments, contours, and paths. Vector node editing is available only when a single object is selected. For information about node editing, please refer to "About Vector Node Editing" on page 240.

To activate the tool:

• Click its button (⬚) on the Tool palette, or

• Click the Tool Options palette Tool Selection button (⬚) and choose the Vector Object Selection tool from the drop-down menu.

To select one object:

• Click the object, or

• Drag the cursor to create a rectangle around the object. The rectangle must enclose the object completely to select it.

To select several objects:

• Press and hold the <Shift> key and click each object,

• Drag the cursor to create a rectangle around the objects. The rectangle must enclose all the objects completely to select them, or

• On the Layer palette, press and hold the <Shift> key and click the Layer Name button of each object.

To select all objects on all visible layers:

IMPORTANT: To prevent vector objects from being selected, make their layers invisible.

• With a vector layer active, right-click the layer and choose Select All from the context menu, or

• Right-click an Object Name button on the Layer palette and choose Select All from the context menu. (This option works when any vector tool is active.)

NOTE: *To undo the Select All command, choose Select None from the context menu.*

Editing Vector Objects

Drawing lines and shapes as vector objects gives you the flexibility of editing them after they are created. The Objects menu has several commands for working with vector objects. Many of these commands also appear as buttons on the second tab of the Vector Object Selection tool's Tool Options palette. In addition, there are two context (context) menus you can use to edit vector objects and text. One appears when right-click on a selected vector object; the other appears when you are using the Node Edit feature on a selected vector object. This section describes the buttons on the Tool Options palette, the Vector Properties Dialog box, and the commands on the context menu that appears when you right-click a selected vector object. For information about the Node Edit context menu, please refer to "About Vector Node Editing" on page 240.

Using the Vector Object Selection Tool Options Palette

NOTE: *If necessary, make the Tool Options palette visible. To do this, click its toolbar icon ( ) or press <O> on your keyboard.*

The first tab of the Tool Options palette contains buttons for selecting the edit mode. The second tab contains buttons for performing commands.

The buttons on the first tab are:

NODE EDIT This button is available only you have selected a vector object selected- a line, a shape, or text that has been converted to curves. Click the button to activate the Node Edit mode. For more information about node editing, please refer to "Creating and Editing Nodes" on page 240.

PROPERTIES This button is available when you have selected any vector object that is not text. Click the button to display the Vector Properties dialog box. This dialog box is described in the next section.

EDIT TEXT This button is available only when you have selected vector text. Click the button to display the Text Entry dialog box. For information about editing text, please refer to "Editing Text" on page 250.

The buttons on the second tab are:

NOTE: *The availability of the buttons depends on the type of object you have selected. Each button corresponds to a command in the Objects menu. This section only lists the commands. Later sections describe the commands.*

ALIGN OBJECT These buttons correspond to the first six Objects > Align menu commands. From left to right they are: Top, Bottom, Left, Right, Vertical Center, and Horizontal Center.

DISTRIBUTE OBJECT These buttons correspond to the first six Objects > Distribute menu commands. From left to right they are: Vertical Top, Vertical Center, Vertical Bottom, Horizontal Left, Horizontal Center, and Horizontal Right.

ON CANVAS These buttons correspond to the last two Objects > Align menu commands and the last two Objects > Distribute menu commands. From left to right they are: Align > Center on Canvas, Align > Horizontal Center on Canvas, Align > Vertical Center on Canvas, Distribute > Space Evenly Horizontally, and Distribute > Space Evenly Vertically.

MAKE SAME SIZE These buttons correspond to the Objects > Make Same Size menu commands. From left to right they are: Horizontal, Vertical, and Both.

GROUP These buttons correspond, from left to right, to the Objects > Group menu command and the Objects > Ungroup menu command.

Using the Vector Properties Dialog Box

You can use the Vector Properties dialog box to edit one vector object or a group of selected objects. When you edit a group of objects, the dialog box displays the properties of the uppermost object in the group, and options that need to be edited individually are unavailable. Use the Vector Properties dialog box to edit the name, color, width, visibility, and other properties of the vector objects.

Opening the Vector Properties Dialog Box

Refer to the "Selecting Vector Objects" on page 228 and select the object(s). Then open the Vector Properties dialog box.

Use one of the following methods:

- Double-click a vector object or group of objects in the image.

- Right-click a vector object or group of objects in the image and choose Properties from the context menu.

Alternatively, on the Layer palette, click the plus sign next to the layer button to display the buttons of the vector objects. Double-click a Vector Object button or right-click it and choose Properties from the context menu.

Changing the Settings in the Vector Properties Dialog Box

Some dialog box options may be unavailable if you have selected a group of objects. Edit the objects individually to change all the settings.

To use the Vector Properties dialog box:

1. If you are editing one object, type a name in the Name box. This box is unavailable if you are editing a group of objects.

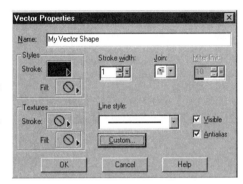

2. In the "Styles" and "Textures" panels, change the stroke and fill styles and textures. These panels are identical to the panels on the Color palette. For information about using the panels, please refer to Chapter 9, "Using the Color Palette."

3. Use the Stroke Width numeric edit controls to change the width of the stroke (outline) on the selected object(s).

4. If the object is a square, rectangle or multi-angle line, click the Join box down arrow and choose a shape for the corners and angles where the segments connect. The choices are Miter (pointed), Round, and Bevel (flat).

5. If you chose a Miter join, use the Miter Limit numeric edit controls to set a miter limit of 1 to 30. The Miter Limit controls the length of Miter joins. The Miter length is the width of the two line segments along the edges where they intersect. As the angle of intersection narrows, the width lines at their intersection increases. The Miter limit is the maximum allowed ratio of length of the intersecting edges to the width of the lines. If a Miter join exceeds the limit, the join is beveled at the limit point.

6. In the "Line Style" panel, click the down arrow to choose a new line style for the stroke (outline). Alternatively, click the Custom button to create a new line style. For more information about custom line styles, please refer to Chapter 12, "Using the Vector Tools."

7. Clear the "Visible" check box to create an invisible object as a path for text.

8. Select the "Antialias" check box to smooth the edges of the object.

9. Click the OK button to close the dialog box and apply the new settings.

Grouping and Ungrouping Vector Objects

You can combine two or more vector objects into a group, which you can then manipulate, save, and load. An object can belong to more than one group, and you can group together several groups of vector objects. You can group up to 100 levels of groups. If an object belongs to a group, you can still select that object individually. If you group objects from several layers, Paint Shop Pro automatically moves them to one vector layer, which is the layer of the first object you selected. On the Layer palette, each group has a Layer Name button and all the objects are shown as components of that layer. After grouping objects, you can ungroup them.

NOTE: *Before using these features, select one or more vector objects. Please refer to "Selecting Vector Objects" on page 228.*

To group selected vector objects:

- Choose Objects > Group from the menu,

- Click the Group button on the second tab of the Tool Options palette. Please refer to "Using the Vector Object Selection Tool Options Palette" on page 229, or

- Right-click the selected object(s) and select Group from the menu.

Alternatively, you can use the Layer palette to group objects. To do this, press and hold the <Shift> key while clicking the Object Name buttons for each object you want to group. Then right-click the selection and choose Group from the menu.

NOTE: *To save (export) and reuse groups of vector objects, please refer to "Exporting a Customized Preset Shape" in Chapter 12, "Using the Vector Tools."*

To ungroup a selected group of objects:

- Choose Objects > Ungroup from the menu,

- Click the Ungroup button on the second tab of the Tool Options palette. Please refer to "Using the Vector Object Selection Tool Options Palette" on page 229,

- Right-click the selected object(s) and select Ungroup from the menu, or

- On the Layer palette, right-click the Layer Name button for the group and select Ungroup from the menu.

To remove a single object from its group:

- Make sure the group is not selected. Press <Ctrl> + <Shift> and click the center of the object to select it. Then drag it outside the group boundary, or

- On the Layer palette, drag the object's button from the group. You can move it into another group or place it on another vector layer.

Deforming Vector Objects

NOTE: *Before using the features described in this section, select one or more vector objects. Please refer to "Selecting Vector Objects" on page 228.*

To deform an object or group of objects:

1. Place your cursor over a handle on the object boundary to display an icon for the type of deformation.

2. Drag the deformation handles to deform the object or group. To keep the original proportions (width to height), use the right mouse button. Deform the object or group using the following methods:

- Resize the object or group by dragging the corner deformation handles. Change the width or height by dragging a handle in the middle of an edge.

- Rotate the object or group by dragging the center bar.

- Change the perspective of the object or group by pressing the <Ctrl> key while dragging the corner deformation handles.

- Skew or shear the object or group by pressing the <Shift> key while dragging the deformation handles in the middle of each edge.

- Distort the object or group by pressing the <Ctrl> and <Shift> keys while dragging the corner handles.

If an object has text mapped to its path and is deformed, the text will be reapplied to the new path after the deformation.

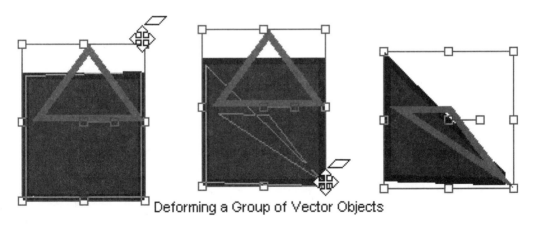

Deforming a Group of Vector Objects

Moving Vector Objects

NOTE: *Before using this feature, select one or more vector objects. Please refer to "Selecting Vector Objects" on page 228.*

1. Place your cursor over the middle handle of the boundary box to display the Mover icon.

2. Drag the object or group of objects to a new location.

Cutting and Copying Vector Objects

NOTE: *Before using this feature, select one or more vector objects. Please refer to "Selecting Vector Objects" on page 228.*

To use the clipboard with vector objects:

- Right-click the object or group of objects and choose Cut or Copy from the context menu,

- Choose Edit > Cut or Edit > Copy, or

   NOTE: *If both raster and vector objects are selected, the Edit menu uses the raster selection.*

- On the Layer palette, right-click the Layer Name button for the object or group and select Cut or Copy from the menu.

Pasting Vector Objects

When you copy one or more vector objects to the clipboard, you can paste the objects as a new image, new layer, or a new vector selection as long as the vector layer is current (active). If you make a raster layer current, you can also paste the objects as a selection or transparent selection.

When the vector layer is current (active), Paint Shop Pro pastes a vector object in the following ways:

- If you paste a vector object as a new image, Paint Shop Pro pastes the object on a vector layer above a transparent background.

- If you paste a vector object as a new layer, Paint Shop Pro creates a new vector layer containing the object.

- If you paste a vector object as a new vector selection, Paint Shop Pro places it on the current (active) vector layer. If a raster layer is current, Paint Shop Pro creates a new vector layer above the current raster layer.

When you make a raster layer current (active), Paint Shop Pro does the following:

- If you paste a vector object as a new selection, Paint Shop Pro pastes the object as a floating raster selection above the raster layer.

- If you paste a vector object as a transparent selection, Paint Shop Pro pastes the object as a floating raster selection above the raster layer. If the object contains the current background color, that color becomes transparent.

Note that if you selected the vector objects using the Vector Object Selection tool, it is de-selected when you click the raster layer; the Arrow tool becomes active. If you selected objects using Drawing or Preset Shape tool, the tool remains active. If you continue drawing, Paint Shop Pro creates a new vector layer and places the object on it. The pasted item continues to be an active floating raster selection until you defloat it.

To paste a vector object from the clipboard:

- Choose Edit > Paste from the menu and choose the appropriate command,

- Right-click a vector layer in the image and choose Paste New Vector Selection from the context menu, or

- On the Layer palette, right-click the Layer Name button for an object on the layer and choose Paste New Vector Selection from the menu.

Deleting Vector Objects

You can delete a vector object or a group of vector objects.

NOTE: *Before using this feature, select one or more vector objects. Please refer to "Selecting Vector Objects" on page 228.*

To delete vector objects:

- Press the <Delete> key while the object is selected,

- Right-click the selected object(s) and select Clear from the menu, or

- On the Layer palette, right-click the Layer Name button for the object or group and select Clear from the menu.

Paint Shop Pro deletes the selected object or group.

Renaming Vector Objects

You can change the name of vector objects and vector object groups.

To rename a vector object or group of objects:

*   On the Layer palette, right-click the Layer Name button for the object or group and select Rename from the menu. Type the new name and press the <Enter> key, or

*   Open the Vector Properties Dialog box and change the Name option. For more information, please refer to "Using the Vector Properties Dialog Box" on page 230.

Aligning Vector Objects

With the Align commands, you can select several vector objects and align them all with the first object you select. You can align their top edges, bottom edges, left edges, right edges, vertical centers or horizontal centers. These Align commands are available when you select two or more vector objects. The Horizontal Center in Canvas and Vertical Center in Canvas commands let you center one or more object(s) on the canvas.

To align vector objects:

1. Use the Vector Object Selection tool (⬚) to select the first object. All the other objects will align with this object. Please refer to "Selecting Vector Objects" on page 228.

2. Press and hold the <Shift> key while clicking each object you want to align with the first object.

3. Do one of the following:

    *   Choose Objects > Align > and the appropriate command,

    *   Click the appropriate "Align Object" or "On Canvas" button on the second tab of the Tool Options palette. Please refer to "Using the Vector Object Selection Tool Options Palette" on page 229, or

    *   Right-click the selected objects and choose Align and the appropriate command from the menu.

Alternatively, you can use the Layer palette to align objects. To do this, press and hold the <Shift> key while clicking the Object Name buttons for each object you want to align. All the objects align with the first object you select. Right-click the selection and choose Align and the appropriate command from the menu.

NOTE: *When you align text on a path, the text is aligned, and the path is aligned relative to the text.*

Distributing Vector Objects

With the Distribute commands, you can evenly space one or more vector objects between two other vector objects. These commands are available when you select three or more vector objects. You can distribute the objects horizontally, where the objects are spaced evenly from left to right; and vertically, where the objects are spaced evenly from top to bottom. You can also distribute the objects horizontally on the canvas, where the objects are spaced evenly from left to right on the canvas; and vertically in the canvas, where the objects are spaced evenly from top to bottom on the canvas. You can use these commands to center an object on the canvas.

Distributing Objects Horizontally

To distribute vector objects horizontally, select one or more objects and then select the appropriate command. The objects move based on the position of the two objects closest to left and right boundaries of the selection.

There are four types of horizontal distribution:

- Horizontal Left, where objects are evenly spaced between the left edges of the left and right objects,

- Horizontal Center, where objects are evenly spaced between the centers of the left and right objects,

- Horizontal Right, where objects are evenly spaced between the right edges of the left and right objects, and

- Space Evenly Horizontally, where objects are evenly spaced between the right and left sides of the image canvas. By selecting only one object, you can use this command to center an object on the canvas.

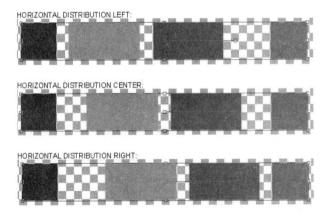

HORIZONTAL DISTRIBUTION LEFT:

HORIZONTAL DISTRIBUTION CENTER:

HORIZONTAL DISTRIBUTION RIGHT:

Distributing Objects Vertically

To distribute vector objects vertically, select one or more objects and then select the appropriate command. The objects move based on the position of the two objects closest to top and bottom boundaries of the selection.

There are four types of vertical distribution:

- Vertical Top, where objects are evenly spaced between the top edges of the top and bottom objects,

- Vertical Center, where objects are evenly spaced between the centers of the top and bottom objects,

- Vertical Bottom, where objects are evenly spaced between the bottom edges of the top and bottom objects, and

- Space Evenly Vertically, where objects are evenly spaced between the top and bottom sides of the image canvas. By selecting only one object, you can use this command to center an object on the canvas.

To distribute vector objects:

1. Use the Vector Object Selection tool () to select the vector objects. Please refer to "Selecting Vector Objects" on page 228.

VERTICAL DISTRIBUTION, TOP, CENTER, BOTTOM

2. Press and hold the <Shift> key while clicking each object you want to include in the distribution.

3. Do one of the following:

- Choose Objects > Distribute > and the appropriate command,

- Click the appropriate "Distribute Object" or "On Canvas" button on the second tab of the Tool Options palette. Please refer to "Using the Vector Object Selection Tool Options Palette" on page 229, or

- Right-click the selected objects and choose Distribute and the appropriate command from the menu.

Alternatively, you can use the Layer palette to distribute objects. To do this, press and hold the <Shift> key while clicking the Object Name buttons for each object you want to include in the distribution. Then right-click the selection and choose Distribute and the appropriate command from the menu.

Equally Sizing Vector Objects

With the Make Same Size command, you can select several vector objects and resize them to the same width and/or height as the first object you select. The Horizontal command changes the width of the selected object(s) to the width of the first selected object; the Vertical command changes the height; and the Both command changes both the width and height. These commands are available when you select two or more vector objects.

To equally size vector objects:

1. Use the Vector Object Selection tool (⬚) to select the first object. All the other objects will resize to this object's size. Please refer to "Selecting Vector Objects" on page 228.

2. Press and hold the <Shift> key while clicking each object you want to resize to the first object's size.

3. Do one of the following:

   • Choose Objects > Make Same Size > and the appropriate command,

   • Click the appropriate "Make Same Size" button on the second tab of the Tool Options palette. Please refer to "Using the Vector Object Selection Tool Options Palette" on page 229, or

   • Right-click the selected objects and choose Make Same Size and the appropriate command from the menu.

Alternatively, you can use the Layer palette to resize objects. To do this, press and hold the <Shift> key while clicking the Object Name buttons for each object you want to align. All the objects resize to the first object you select. Right-click the selection and choose Make Objects Same Size and the appropriate command from the menu.

Arranging Vector Objects

When you have several overlapping vector objects on a layer, you can use the Arrange commands to rearrange the order of the objects on the layer. The Bring to Top command moves a selected object to the top of all the objects on the layer. The Move Up command moves the object above the object that is currently above it. The Move Down command moves the object below the object that is currently below it. The Send to Bottom command moves the object to the bottom of all the objects on the layer.

To arrange a vector object:

1. Use the Vector Object Selection tool (⬚) to select the object to move. Please refer to "Selecting Vector Objects" on page 228.

2. Do one of the following:

   • Choose Objects > Arrange > and the appropriate command, or

   • Right-click the object and choose Arrange and the appropriate command from the menu.

Creating and Editing Nodes

About Vector Node Editing

Every vector object contains a path, which is composed of at least one contour. The path of a circle or other simple object usually has one contour; the path of a complex object may have several. A contour contains at least two nodes, or control points, and the segments that connect them. Each contour has a specific direction. It begins at its start point node and finishes at its end point node. You can view the direction of a contour by pausing the cursor over either end node, which displays the word "Start" or "End." The segments that connect the nodes can be straight or curved.

To edit the nodes of a contour, you activate the Node Edit function to display an object's path. You can edit the nodes of only one path at a time. If you have more than one object selected, Node Edit is unavailable. Vector node editing consists of adding and removing nodes and segments, changing node types, altering the shape of segments, and combining or separating one contour from another.

Object in Node Edit

Object not in Node Edit

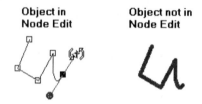

The Node Edit function has two modes: the Drawing mode and the Edit mode. Add nodes while in the Drawing mode; move nodes and segments and change their type while in the Edit mode. The commands you can choose are displayed in a menu that you open by right-clicking the image area. This menu contains two sub-menus. The Node Type menu displays the commands for changing node types and for converting curves into lines and lines into curves. The type of node or segment determines which commands are available. The Edit menu displays the other commands.

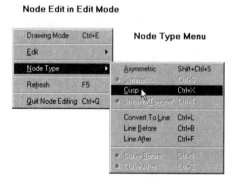

Accessing Node Edit

Use one of the following methods to enter the Node Edit function:

- Activate the Drawing tool, and then select Point to Point from the Type drop-down box on the first tab of the Tool Options palette,

- Activate the Vector Object Selection tool (![icon]), and then right-click a Vector object other than text and choose Node Edit from the context menu, or

- Activate the Vector Object Selection tool (![icon]), click a vector object other than text, and then click the Node Edit button on the Tool Options palette.

Exiting Node Edit

Use one of the following methods to exit the Node Edit function:

- Press the <ESC> key. Paint Shop Pro exits the mode without applying any changes,

- Right-click a node and choose Quit Node Editing from the context menu. Paint Shop Pro applies the changes and exits the Node Editing mode,

- Press <Ctrl> + <Q>. Paint Shop Pro applies the changes and exits Node Edit, or

- Click outside the image.

When you exit the Node Editing mode, Paint Shop Pro applies color to the path and deletes single nodes not connected by segments. You can return to Node Edit using any method described above.

Overview of Nodes

A node and its control arms, or handles, determine the shape segments entering and exiting it. For example, to make smooth curves, use a node with symmetrical control arms.

All drawing points (nodes) have two handles extending from them. These handles determine the shape of a contour. A handle can have a length of 0. Two opposing handles from sequential nodes having zero length form a straight line segment. A curve is formed if one or both opposing handles of sequential nodes have length.

There are three types of nodes:

- Tangent,

- Corner or Cusp, and

- Curve, symmetrical or asymmetrical.

Tangent points have handles that are tangent to a segment in the opposite direction. A tangent node allows a curve to blend seamlessly with a line.

The handles of a corner node move independently.

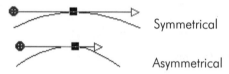

The control arms of curve nodes teeter-totter about producing very smooth curves. There are two types of smooth curves, symmetrical and asymmetrical. The control arms of a symmetrical curve are both the same length and remain so as you drag them around whereas the asymmetrical curves can be different lengths.

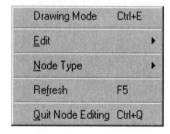

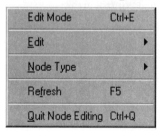

Symmetrical

Asymmetrical

Adding Nodes

To extend a contour by adding nodes, you must be in the Drawing Mode of Node Edit. You can extend the contour from either its Start point or End point node. You can enter the Drawing mode using either the Drawing tool or the Vector Object Selection tool.

Node Edit in Drawing Mode

Edit Mode	Ctrl+E
Edit	▶
Node Type	▶
Refresh	F5
Quit Node Editing	Ctrl+Q

Node Edit in Edit Mode

Drawing Mode	Ctrl+E
Edit	▶
Node Type	▶
Refresh	F5
Quit Node Editing	Ctrl+Q

Entering the Drawing Mode

When you click the Drawing tool button and select the Point to Point line type on the Tool Options palette, you automatically enter the Drawing Mode.

To enter the Drawing mode using the Vector Object Selection tool (), click the object you want to edit, and then do either of the following:

- Click the Node Edit button on the Tool options palette. The object's path appears. Press <Ctrl>+ <E> or right-click the image and choose Drawing Mode from the context menu, or

- Right-click the image and choose Node Edit from the context menu. The object's path appears. Press <Ctrl>+ <E> or right-click the image and choose Drawing Mode from the context menu.

When Node Edit is active, pressing <Ctrl> + <E> alternates between Editing and Drawing mode. Remember that when you are in Drawing Mode, the context menu displays the Edit Mode command, and when you are in Edit Mode, it displays the Drawing Mode command.

Adding a Node as a New Start Point or End Point Node

To extend a contour by adding nodes to either end:

1. Activate Node Edit and enter the Drawing mode.

2. Click the Start Point or End Point node to select it.

3. Move the mouse to where you want to place the new node.

4. Click or click and drag the mouse to shape the segment.

Creating a New Contour

To add a node as the start point node for a new contour, enter the Drawing mode and then left-click the image away from a segment. You add nodes in the same way as you do when creating a Point to Point line:

- To create straight segments, click and release the mouse button.

- To create curved segments, click and drag the mouse.

Control handles extending from both sides of the node appear. The arrow tip indicates the clockwise/counterclockwise winding of the contour.

Inserting a Node into an Existing Contour

You can insert a node along a contour in either the Edit mode or Drawing mode.

To add a node along a contour:

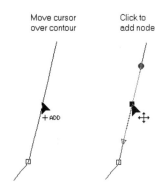

Move cursor over contour   Click to add node

1. Activate the Drawing or Edit mode of Node Edit mode.

2. Press <Ctrl> and move the cursor over a segment on the contour where you want to add the node.

3. When the cursor changes to display with word "Add," click.

The new node appears. It contains handles appropriate to the shape of its segments.

Selecting Nodes

To select one or more nodes:

- To select all the nodes of a path, right-click the image and choose Edit > Select All from the context menu or type <Ctrl> + <A>. To undo the command, right-click and choose Edit > Undo or type <Ctrl> + <Z>. To deselect all the nodes, right-click the image and choose Edit > Select None from the context menu or type <Ctrl> + <D>.

- To select a single node, move the cursor over the node you want to select, click the node to select it.

- To add or remove a node from a selection, press the <Shift> key, move the cursor over a node, click the node. If the node is already selected the node will be deselected and removed from the selection.

- To select a contour, move the cursor over a node on the contour, double-click the node to select the entire contour. Pressing the <Shift> key will add the contour to the current selection.

- To select nodes with a rubber binder, make sure you are in Edit Mode, move the cursor to a position on the image, click and drag the rubber binder around the nodes you want to select, release the cursor to select. Pressing the <Shift> key will add the nodes to the current selection.

- To select the next or previous node, make sure only one node is selected, press and hold the <Shift> key while using the Arrow keys.

Editing Nodes

The Drawing mode of Node Edit allows you to extend the contour; Edit Mode does not. In Edit Mode, you can select nodes by dragging the mouse to create a selection rectangle around the objects. You can enter Node Editing using either the Drawing tool or the Vector Object Selection tool. Using the Point-to-Point Drawing tool automatically opens Node Edit in the Drawing mode. Activating Node Edit with the Vector Object Selection tool opens it in the Editing mode.

Remember that when you are in the Edit mode, the context menu displays the Drawing Mode command; when you are in the Drawing mode, it displays the Edit Mode command.

When working with nodes:

- In Drawing mode, left-click to add nodes anywhere on the layer.

- In both Drawing and Edit Modes, press the <Ctrl> key while left-clicking to add nodes along the contour.

- In both Drawing and Edit modes, use the left mouse button to move the nodes or reshape the curves.

- In both Drawing and Edit mode, right-click to choose context menu commands.

Moving Nodes

Select a node or several nodes, and then drag the contour by one of the selected nodes. If you drag by a segment, you move the entire contour.

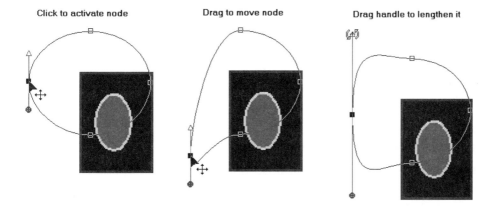

Click to activate node   Drag to move node   Drag handle to lengthen it

Moving the Control Arm Handles

1. Select any node.

2. Move the cursor over a node handle.

3. When the cursor shape changes, click and drag it. The contour redraws as the handle is moved.

Hold the <Shift> key to constrain the control arms to fixed angles in increments of 45°.

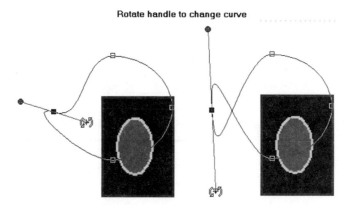

Rotate handle to change curve

Using Undo and Redo

To Undo or Redo any Node Editing command, you can use the standard Windows <Ctrl> + <Z> to undo and <Ctrl> + <Alt> + <Z> to redo, or right-click and choose the commands from the context menu.

Changing Node Types

When editing nodes, you can change the type of a node. This affects the segment ends entering and exiting that node. You can change one or both handles of a node, which will influence its respective segment. The node handles update to display the appropriate controls.

- To change a node's type, right-click the node so that it becomes black, and choose Node Type > "a type" from the context menu.

- To change a node handle, right-click the node to select it, and choose Line Before (<Ctrl> + <B>), Line After (<Ctrl> + <F>), Curve Before (<Ctrl> + <1>), Curve After (<Ctrl> + <2>) or Convert to Line (<Ctrl> + <L>) from the context menu.

You can also change several nodes at once by selecting the nodes first. This applies when you change the node types to Line Before, Line After, Curve Before, Curve After, Line, Symmetrical, Asymmetrical, or Cusp.

> **NOTE:** There are several keyboard commands for contracting and expanding nodes using the <F8> and <F9> keys along with the <Shift> and <Ctrl> keys. For details, click the Help button.

Merging a Node

Merging a node removes it from the path and merges the two segments on either side of it into one continuous segment. If the segment is curved, Paint Shop Pro attempts to retain the curve. You can merge one or more nodes along a contour. Note that a contour contain at least two nodes. If you merge all nodes, you delete the contour.

To merge a node:

- Right-click a node or press <Shift> while clicking more than one node, and then right-click and choose Edit > Merge,

- Click one or mode nodes and press <Ctrl> + <M>, or

- Move the mouse over a singularly selected node and hold the <Ctrl> key down. When the merge cursor appears, click the node.

Deleting Nodes

Deleting a node removes it along with its two segments and converts the contour into two separate contours or opens a closed contour.

- To delete a node, right-click it and choose Edit > Delete, or select it and press <Del>.

- To delete multiple nodes, select the nodes and press <Del> or right-click and choose Edit > Delete.

Editing Contours and Paths

In addition to editing individual nodes and segments, you can edit the entire a contour or path. This is useful when you want to create combinations of filled and empty spaces or to move text to the opposite side of a segment. For example, when you place text on a circle, it appears along the outside edge. If you then activate Node Edit and choose Edit > Reverse Path, Paint Shop Pro moves the text to its inside edge.

NOTE: *If you edit a path containing more than one contour and have not selected a specific node, you can choose only the Edit commands that apply to the entire path. None of the Node Type commands are available.*

Editing Contours

If a path contains several contours, you may not want to edit all of them, but only specific ones. Do this by activating at least one node along the contour to select it.

When editing a contour, you can do the following:

- Move a contour by double-clicking a node to select the contour and dragging any segment or node.

- Drag individual nodes to alter the shape of the contour.

- Traverse from one node to the next along a contour by selecting a node and then pressing <Shift> while using the Arrow keys.

Reversing a Contour

Reverse the or direction of a contour by right-clicking a node and choosing Reverse Contour from the context menu. You can also select one of its nodes and press <Ctrl> + <R>. This reverses the start point and end point nodes and the direction of the node handles. Reversing a contour is used to alter the filling characteristics of a multi contour drawing.

To hollow the center of a closed contour, draw another contour inside, close it, make sure the direction of the outside contour is clockwise and the inside contour is counter-clockwise. To detect the winding direction of a contour, select a node on it. If that node has visible control arms, the arrow points in the direction the contour is drawn. If the node does not has control arms then press the <Shift> key and traverse the nodes with the Arrow keys. Use the Up <↑> and Right <→> Arrows to move clockwise, and the left <←> and down <↓> Arrows to move counter-clockwise.

Closing a Contour

To close a contour:

- Selecting any node on a path and then right-clicking and choosing Edit > Close from the context menu or pressing <Ctrl> + <Shift> + <C>, or

- Selecting the starting point and ending point nodes and then right-clicking and choosing Edit > Join Select or pressing <Ctrl> + <J>.

A segment appears between the two nodes.

Joining Contours

You can join the start point or end point node of one contour with the start or end point node of another to form one contour.

- To join the nodes, press <Ctrl> while dragging one node over the other. When the two overlap, the word "Join" appears. Release the mouse button.

- To join two starting or ending nodes, select two starting or ending nodes and type <Ctrl> + <J> or right-click it and choose Edit > Join Select.

Breaking a Contour in Two

Breaking a contour in two breaks a contour at a selected node and converts the contour into two separate contours.

To break a contour, right-click it and choose Edit > Break or press <Ctrl> + <K>. Drag the nodes to separate them.

Copying and Pasting Contours

To copy a contour, select the nodes and press <Ctrl> + <C>, or right-click and choose Edit > Copy from the menu. Only entire contours are copied.

To paste the contour from the clipboard, press <Ctrl> + <V>, or right-click and choose Edit > Paste from the menu. Each time you paste, the nodes are placed into your current drawing with an accumulative X Y offset from the original nodes. Each time Copy is used, the X Y offset is reset for the next Paste command.

Editing the Entire Path

When editing a path, you can do the following:

- Move a path by dragging it by any line segment. If the path contains more than one con-tour, they all move. To move a contour, drag its nodes.

- Reverse the direction of a path by right-clicking a node and choosing Reverse Path from the context menu. You can also by press <Shift> + <Ctrl> + <R> when no nodes are selected. This reverses the start point and end point nodes of all contours. The path retains its shape, but node handles point in the opposite direction.

- Close every contour (create a segment between the endpoint and starting point of each) of the path by selecting the entire path and then right-clicking and choosing Edit > Close.

- Copy or delete the path by selecting all of it and then right-clicking and choosing Edit > Copy or Edit > Delete.

Reversing the Entire Drawing

To reverse the entire drawing, type <Ctrl> + <Shift> + <R> or use the context menu Edit> Reverse All command from the context menu. You can use this command to place text on the opposite side of a contour.

Editing Text

Vector text can be edited by opening the Text Entry dialog box and changing the settings. Because vector text cannot be converted into a raster selection, the Selection and Floating Selection options are not available. Vector text can also be converted into a vector object so that you can edit its path.

Editing Vector Text

To edit the properties of vector text:

- Activate the Text tool (**A**) and click the text. The Text Entry dialog box opens with the current settings for the text. Select a new color, font, size, or other attribute, and click the OK button. For a description of the Text Entry dialog box, please refer to Chapter 12, "Using the Vector Tools."

- On the Layer palette, expand the vector layer by clicking the plus sign to the left of the layer button. Double-click a text object button. The Text Entry dialog box opens with the current settings for the text. Select new settings and click the OK button.

Converting Vector Text

If you want to manipulate the text, you can convert it into a true vector object. You can convert each letter into its own object or convert the entire text into one object.

To convert text:

1. Use the Vector Object Selection tool (⊞) to select the text.

2. Right-click the selection and choose one of the following:

   - Choose Convert Text to Curves > As Single Shape to convert the entire string of text into one object. This produces one path containing a contour for each letter. This lets you edit the nodes of the entire text string, or

   - Choose Convert Text to Curves > As Character Shape to convert each letter of the text string into its own path. You can select the entire text string as an object, but you must edit the nodes of the letters individually.

Editing Raster Text

Edit raster text as you would any other selection. You can:

- Color the text using a painting tool,
- Copy it to fill the letters with the areas of the image within them,
- Cut or delete it to remove the areas of the letters from the image, and
- Promote it to a layer to edit it without affecting the rest of the image.

Please refer to Chapter 10, "Working with Selections," for more information.

Working with Masks

What is a Mask?

A mask is a greyscale image that you apply to a layer. You can use it to hide and display parts of the layer, to fade between layers, and to create special effects with precision. A mask can be created from a selection, from an alpha channel, or an existing image. It can cover a layer completely or with varying levels of opacity. The grey value of the mask determines how much it covers. Where it is black, it completely masks the layer; where it is white, it leaves the layer unmasked; where it is grey, it produces a semi-visible effect.

All masks are created and edited in a raster, greyscale mode. Therefore, all tools and image processing features that work on greyscale images work on masks. The tools that can be used in either vector or raster mode (Drawing, Preset Shapes, and Text) work only in their raster modes when editing masks.

A mask works the same way with a vector layer as it does with a raster layer. It can be linked to a layer, which moves it with the layer. If a mask is not linked to the layer, moving the layer's content will not affect the position of the mask.

Because a mask is greyscale, you can save it with the image in an alpha channel or as a separate image on a hard disk. You can also load a selection from an alpha channel as a mask and a mask as a selection.

Creating a Mask

Creating a Mask from an Image

Paint Shop Pro creates a mask from an image by converting the image into a greyscale bitmap and using the bitmap as the mask. The original, or source, image is not altered.

NOTE: *To create a mask in an image that is not 8-bit greyscale or 24-bit color, first increase the color depth and then create the mask.*

To create a mask from an image:

1. Select the layer to which you are adding the mask.

2. Choose Masks > New > From Image or right-click the Create Mask button () on the Layer palette and choose From Image. The Add Mask From Image dialog box opens.

3. Select the Source window from the drop-down list. The source window is the image from which you create the mask. It can be any image window open in the workspace.

4. In the "Create mask from" panel, select the value for Paint Shop Pro to use to create the mask:

   - With Source luminance, the luminance value of the pixel color determines the degree of masking. The lighter colors produce less masking.

   - With Any non-zero value, there is no gradation to the masking. Pixels with color are completely masked; pixels without color have no masking.

   - With Source opacity, the opacity of the layer determines the degree of masking.

5. To invert the mask, select the "Invert mask data" check box. Inverting a mask reverses its transparency: black becomes white, white becomes black, and greys are assigned their mirror value.

6. Click the OK button to close the dialog box and create the mask.

On the Layer palette, a mask appears next to the masked layer's button to indicate that the layer has a mask.

NOTE: *After you add a mask, you will not necessarily see a change in the image. To view the mask using the red overlay, choose* Masks > View Mask.

Create Mask Button — Layer Palette - Shadow — Mask Tab — Link Mask to Layer Button — Masked Layer Button — View Mask Button

Creating a Mask from a Selection

When you create a mask from a selection, the area remains selected. To deselect it, chose the Select None command.

To create a mask from a selection:

1. Create a selection.

2. Do one of the following:

   • To mask the selection, choose Masks > New > Hide Selection, or right-click the Create Mask button (📧) on the Layer palette and choose Hide Selection.

   • To mask everything except the selection, choose Masks > New > Show Selection, or right-click the Create Mask button (📧) on the Layer palette and choose Show Selection.

Creating a Mask from a Channel

When you split an image into its RGB, HSL, or CMYK channels, each channel becomes a grey-scale image. You can then create a mask using one of these images.

To create a mask using a channel:

1. Split the image into channels using one of the three Channel Splitting commands in the Colors menu. Leave these new images open or minimized in the workspace.

2. Make the original image active.

3. Choose Masks > New > From Image, or right-click the Create Mask button (📧) on the Layer palette and choose From Image. The Add Mask From Image dialog box opens.

4. In the Source window drop-down list, select which channel image you want Paint Shop Pro to use for creating the mask.

5. Click the Source Opacity option in the "Create mask from" panel.

6. To invert the mask, select the "Invert mask data" check box.

7. Click the OK button to close the dialog box and create the mask.

Masking the Entire Layer

You can apply a mask to an entire single-layered image or to a layer within a multi-layered image. You can then edit the mask to alter areas.

To mask the entire image:

- Choose Masks > New > Hide All, left-click the Create Mask button (▣) on the Layer palette, or right-click the Create Mask button (▣) on the Layer palette and choose Hide All. You can then edit the mask to remove any area you want uncovered (unmasked).

- Choose Masks > New > Show All or right-click the Create Mask button (▣) on the Layer palette and choose Show All to create a mask where the entire area is the non-masked part of it. You can then edit the mask to add any area you want covered (masked).

Viewing a Mask

When you create a mask, you do not automatically see it.

- To view the mask, choose Masks > View Mask or click the View Mask button on the Mask tab of the Layer palette. The image displays the mask as a red-colored overlay. On the Layer palette, the View Mask button (▣) is not crossed out.

- To return to normal viewing, choose Masks > View Mask or click the View Mask button on the Layer palette. The image returns to normal. On the Layer palette, the View Mask button (▣) appears crossed out.

You can also view the mask from the Layer palette. Place your cursor over the mask button (▣) to the right of the layer button. A thumbnail of the mask appears. Note that if you choose the Hide All or Show All command to create the mask, the thumbnail is totally black or white until you edit it.

Editing a Mask

IMPORTANT: You must choose Masks > Edit before painting so that you edit the mask, not the image.

When you work in the Edit Mask mode, the colors available to you become those of a greyscale image. When you click a color box, the greyscale palette appears. When you leave the Edit Mask mode, the color boxes return to their previous colors.

When you edit a mask you change either the areas or the level of masking. For example, painting over an object to mask it changes the area, while making a Gradient Fill edits the degree of masking. Remember that a mask is a greyscale image with 256 levels of grey. The levels of grey correspond to levels of masking. Select black and white as the active colors to mask and erase the mask at 100%.

NOTE: *Any painting tool or effect that can be applied to a greyscale image can be applied to a mask.*

To edit a mask:

1. Choose Masks > View Mask to see the mask. Paint Shop Pro displays the mask as a red-colored overlay.

2. Choose Masks > Edit.

3. Use the painting tools to alter the masked area:

   • Paint with white to remove masking.

   • Paint with black to add masking.

   • Paint with lighter and darker greys to add various levels of masking.

4. After you have finished editing the mask, choose Masks > Edit. Paint Shop Pro exits the Edit mode.

Inverting a Mask

Inverting a mask reverses its transparency: what is black becomes white, and what is white becomes black. Greys are assigned their mirror transparency.

• To invert a mask, choose Masks > Invert.

Linking to a Layer

By default, a mask is linked to its layer and moves with it when you drag the layer. To unlink the mask, click the Link to Mask button (⊗) on the Mask tab of the Layer Palette. It appears crossed out (⊗) to show the mask and layer are not linked. You can also unlink a mask from the layer by deselecting the "Mask is locked with layer" option on the General tab of the Layer Properties dialog box.

Creating a Gradient or Textured Mask

To make a gradient or textured mask:

1. Create a mask using any method described above.

2. If the mask is not visible, choose Masks > View Mask.

3. Choose Masks > Edit.

4. Set the styles and textures on the Color palette. For specific steps, please refer to Chapter 9, "Using the Color Palette."

5. Click the Flood Fill tool (◆) on the Tool palette.

6. Left-click the mask to apply the foreground gradient and/or texture; right-click to apply the background gradient and/or texture.

7. To apply the mask permanently, choose Masks > Delete, and when prompted, merge it into the current layer.

Saving a Mask

Paint Shop Pro lets you save a mask in two ways:

- As a file on your hard drive with the .msk extension, and
- As an alpha channel within the image.

When you save a mask to your hard disk, you save it as a separate file that Paint Shop Pro can later load as an image. When you save a mask as an alpha channel, you save it as a greyscale bitmap within the image.

Saving a Mask to the Hard Drive

When you save a mask to your hard disk, the mask is saved in its own .msk file format. You can then load this mask to other images without opening the original image.

To save a mask to the hard disk:

1. Choose Masks > Save To Disk. The Save Mask Channel dialog box opens.

2. Navigate to the folder in which you want to save your mask.

3. In the "File name" box, type a name for the mask. The "Save as type" drop-down box automatically displays the .msk format.

4. Click the OK button to close the dialog box and save the mask.

Saving a Mask to an Alpha Channel

Both masks and selections can be saved to alpha channels, and each can be loaded as the other. An advantage of the .psp format is that its files store alpha channels within the images. (.tiff, .tga, and .png files can store one alpha channel; the others will not store any.) For more information about alpha channels, please refer to Chapter 10, "Working with Selections."

To save a mask to an alpha channel:

1. Choose Masks > Save To Alpha Channel. The Save To Alpha dialog box opens. The file name of the image containing the mask appears in "Available Documents," and the Preview box displays its thumbnail.

2. In the Available Alpha list, double-click New Channel, or highlight New Channel and click the OK button. The New Channel dialog box opens.

3. Type a name for the new mask.

4. Click the OK button. The mask is saved to the alpha channel and both dialog boxes close.

After you have saved the mask, it still appears in the image. To remove it, choose Delete from the Masks menu and, when prompted, <u>do not</u> merge it into the layer. Although the mask no longer affects the image, it is still in the image's alpha channel.

Loading a Mask

Loading a Mask from the Hard Drive

To load a mask you have saved to your hard disk:

1. Click the layer button of the layer on which you want to place the mask.

2. Choose Masks > Load From Disk. The Load Mask Channel dialog box opens.

3. Navigate to the folder containing the mask you want to load. Masks are saved in the .msk format, which Paint Shop Pro automatically displays in the "Files of type" drop-down box.

4. Click the file to highlight it. Its name appears in the "File name" box.

5. Click the OK button to close the dialog box and load the mask.

Loading a Mask from an Alpha Channel

Selections and masks are both saved to alpha channels, so you can load a mask as a selection. You can load a selection or mask from the alpha channel of the current active image or any other image open in the workspace.

To load a mask from the alpha channel:

1. Click the layer button of the layer on which you want to place the mask.

2. Choose Masks > Load From Alpha Channel. The Load From Alpha dialog box opens.

3. To load a mask from the active image, leave its name in the Available Documents box. To load a mask from another image, highlight its filename.

4. In the Available Alpha list, click the mask or selection that you want to load. The Preview box displays your selected mask. You can view any selection or mask by clicking its name. You can open any selection or mask by double-clicking its name.

5. After you have chosen a mask, click the OK button. The dialog box closes, and the mask loads into the image.

Loading a Mask from the Browser

As an alternative to the Load from Disk command, you can use the drag-and-drop method to load a mask from the Browser window. Any mask that you have saved to a disk can be loaded to an image. The mask must be an 8-bit greyscale bitmap image with the .msk extension. By using the Browser to load a mask, you can see what the mask looks like before applying it.

To drag a mask to an image:

1. Make active (current) the layer of the image to which you want to add the mask

2. Open the Browser.

3. Navigate to and select the folder containing the mask.

4. While pressing either the left mouse button, drag the mask thumbnail from the Browser to the image.

5. When the cursor is over the image, release the mouse button. Paint Shop Pro applies the mask to the active layer.

Deleting a Mask

Deleting a Mask from an Alpha Channel

Deleting a mask from the layer and deleting it from the alpha channel are two separate, independent functions. Deleting a mask from a layer does not delete it from the alpha channel, and deleting it from the alpha channel does not delete it from the layer.

If you delete a mask from the alpha channel and then save the image, the mask will be saved. To delete the mask from the image, delete it from the layer. When you delete it from the layer, you can choose to merge it with the layer; it becomes permanent part of the image.

Deleting a Mask from an Alpha Channel

Use either the Save To Alpha or the Load From Alpha dialog box to delete a mask from the alpha channel. To open one of the dialog boxes, choose either Masks > Save To Alpha or Masks > Load From Alpha.

To delete a mask from an alpha channel:

1. From the Available Documents list, select the image with the mask you want to delete.

2. In the Available Alpha list, highlight the mask. The preview displays the selected mask.

3. Click the Delete button.

4. At the prompt message, click the Yes button. Paint Shop Pro deletes the mask.

5. Click the OK button to close the dialog box.

Deleting a Mask from a Layer

NOTE: *Deleting a mask from a layer does not delete it from the alpha channel.*

When you delete a mask from the layer, you can remove it from or merge it into the layer. Merging it makes it a permanent part of the image.

To delete a mask from a layer:

1. Choose Masks > Delete. Paint Shop Pro displays a message asking whether to merge the mask with the layer.

2. Click the No button to remove the mask from the layer. Click the Yes button to make the mask a part of it.

Editing Images

There are many ways you can edit the information contained in an image and the image itself. This chapter describes how to use the Deformation tool, the Crop tool, the Edit menu commands, and many of the Image menu commands. For information about creating a new image, please refer to Chapter 2, "Creating and Opening Images."

▦ Using the Deformation Tool

NOTE: *To use the Deformation tool, the image must contain a layer. You may need to promote the background to a layer.*
You can apply deformations to greyscale and 24-bit images. If necessary, increase the color depth of your image to make the commands available.
To deform a selection using the Deformation tool, create the selection before choosing the tool.

Use the Deformation tool to rotate, resize, skew, and distort layers, floating selections, and images.

To use the Deformation tool:

1. If necessary, make the Tool Options palette visible. To do this, click its toolbar icon (▦) or press <O> on your keyboard.

2. Click the Deformation tool button(▦) on the Tool palette. The Deformation handles and guides appear on the image.

3. Move the cursor to the area to be deformed. The cursor will change shape whenever it is over a handle.

4. Deform the image by doing one or more of the following:

   • Resize vertically by dragging the center top and bottom handles.

   • Resize horizontally by dragging the center left and right handles.

   • Resize horizontally and vertically at the same time by dragging the corner handles. To constrain the deformation to the current proportions, use the right mouse button while dragging a corner handle.

   • Rotate by dragging the center bar.

   • Change perspective by pressing <Ctrl> while dragging any of the four corner handles.

   • Apply a skew/shear effect by pressing <Shift> while dragging any of the four center handles.

   • Distort (move the corner) by pressing <Ctrl> + <Shift> while dragging any of the four corner handles.

   As the cursor moves over a handle, a rectangle shaped like the distortion appears.

5. To apply the deformation, either click the Apply button on the Tool Options palette or double-click the image.

6. To cancel the deformation, click the Cancel button on the Tool Options palette.

Using the Deformation Settings Dialog Box

NOTE: *To use the Deformation Settings dialog box, the image must contain a layer. You may need to promote the background to a layer.*
You can apply deformations to greyscale and 24-bit color images. If necessary, increase the color depth of your image to make the commands available.
To deform a selection using the Deformation Settings dialog box, create the selection before opening the dialog box.

To use the Deformation Settings dialog box:

1. Open the Deformation Settings dialog box by double-clicking the Deformation tool button (⊞) on the Tool palette.

2. The boxes in the X column control the horizontal distortion; the boxes in the Y column control the vertical distortion:

   - Position determines the X and Y coordinates of the top left corner point.

   - Scale controls the horizontal and vertical resizing.

   - Shear controls the offset of a side. Enter positive values to shear to the right or downward, and negative values to shear to the left or upward. At .5, a side shears 50% of its length.

   - Perspective controls the length of a side to its opposite. Enter a positive number to shorten a side; enter a negative number to lengthen a side. At .5, one side is half the length of the opposing side.

   - Angle is the rotation around the center point. Set the angle to between 0 and 259 to rotate clockwise; for counter-clockwise rotation, set it from 360 to 0.

3. After entering the values, click the OK button to close the dialog box.

4. To apply the Deformation, either click the Apply button on the Tool Options palette or double-click the image.

🔲 Cropping an Image

Cropping eliminates areas of an image. It has the same effect as using the Change Canvas Size dialog box to reduce the dimensions of an image. If a scanned image contains unwanted areas, cropping it should be your first step. You reduce the memory needed to edit the image and, by eliminating extraneous areas of color, you will make better color corrections. After you have cropped the image, you can rotate it to correct any alignment problems.

Paint Shop Pro provides three ways to crop an image:

- The Crop tool,
- The Crop Area dialog box, and
- The Crop *or* Crop to Selection command on the Image menu.

NOTE: *When you crop a multi-layered image, you crop all layers of the image. You cannot apply the Crop or Crop to Selection command to a floating selection.*

Using the Crop Tool

When you use the Crop tool, you select the area of the image you want to keep. The area outside the rectangle is deleted.

To use the Crop tool:

1. Click the Crop tool button (🔲) on the toolbar.
2. Place the cursor over the image at a corner of the area you want to keep.
3. Press the left mouse button and drag. A rectangle appears. The area inside the rectangle will be saved; the area outside the rectangle will be cropped.
4. When the rectangle encloses the area you want to keep, release the mouse button.
5. To change the area the rectangle encloses, do any of the following:
    - Click one of the rectangle's sides and drag to move it,
    - Click inside the rectangle and drag to enclose a different area, or
    - Right-click to remove the rectangle and start over.
6. To crop the image, either:
    - Double-click inside the rectangle,
    - Click the Crop Image button on the Tool Options palette, or
    - Select Image > Crop.

Using the Crop or Crop to Selection Command

The Crop command on the Edit menu becomes available whenever an image contains a crop rectangle as defined in the preceding section. This command changes to the Crop to Selection command whenever an image contains a non-floating selection. Use the Crop to Selection command with irregularly shaped selections. It deletes everything except the selection and reduces the image size to the length and width of the selection.

To apply the command, choose Image > Crop to Selection or press <Shift> + <R>.

Using the Crop Area Dialog Box

If you know the coordinates of the image area you want to crop to or if you want to crop the area of the image that does not contain any data, use the Crop Area dialog box.

NOTE: *To crop around a selection, create the selection before opening the Crop Area dialog box. If the image does not contain a selection, the Surround current selection option is unavailable.*

The options in the dialog box provide four ways to crop:

- Crop an area by entering its coordinates,
- Crop around a current selection,
- Crop a rectangular area using the coordinates of an irregularly shaped selection, and
- Crop the opaque area of a layer or image.

To use the Crop Area dialog box:

1. Open the dialog box by double-clicking the Crop tool button on the toolbar or by clicking the Crop Settings button on the Tool Options palette.

2. At the bottom of the dialog box, choose one of the four crop or selection options:

   - Custom size and position, where you select the area.
   - Surround current selection, where the selected area is used. This option is available only if the image contains a selection. If the image contains an irregularly-shaped selection, Paint Shop Pro creates a rectangle from the coordinates.
   - Select opaque area – current layer, where the areas of the layer that contain data are selected or preserved.
   - Select opaque area – merged, where all areas of the image that contain data are selected or preserved.

3. If you have chosen the Custom size and position option, enter the coordinates in the boxes at the top of the dialog box.

4. Click the OK button to close the dialog box. One of the following occurs:

- If you are using the Select Area dialog box, a marquee appears around the selected area.

- If you are using the Crop Area dialog box, a rectangle appears around the area to be cropped to.

5. To change the area to be cropped:

- Place the cursor inside the rectangle and drag to move it,

- Place the cursor on an edge of the rectangle and drag to increase or decrease it, or

- Place the cursor on a corner of the rectangle and drag to increase or decrease it.

6. To crop the image, double-click inside the rectangle or click the Crop Image button on the Tool Options palette.

Using the Undo, Redo, and Repeat Commands

Undo Command

The Undo command reverses the last edit or command made to the active image. It can remove painting or drawing operations, color alterations, effects, etc. It cannot undo any modification that has been saved or any changes to the filename or file format.

Using Undo returns the file to its state prior to the most recent operation. The number of operations you can undo depends on the settings in the Undo/Redo tab in the General Program Preferences dialog box. It is limited only by your computer's disk space.

- To undo an action, choose Edit > Undo, press <Ctrl> + <Z>, or click the Undo button on the toolbar immediately after performing the action.

Command History Dialog Box

The Command History dialog box contains a list of the recent actions and commands you have made to an image, starting with the most recent. It displays the tool or action that was used and time that has passed since the event occurred. Use it to undo several actions at once. The actions you have applied are preceded by "Undo," and the actions you have undone are preceded by "Redo."

When you have applied but not undone any actions, the list displays "Undo" before every action to indicate that you can choose to undo them. When you have undone some of the actions, the dialog box lists them first and displays "Redo" before them to indicate that they can be re-applied. If you have undone all your actions, your only choice is to re-apply them, so they all are preceded by "Redo." For example, if you apply 10 brush strokes to an image and undo the last three, you can open the Command History dialog box to undo the first seven strokes or re-apply the final three.

To use the Undo History dialog box:

1. Open the dialog box by choosing Edit > Command History or by pressing <Shift> + <Ctrl> + <Z>.

2. In the list of actions, select the ones to undo or to redo. You cannot undo and redo actions simultaneously. If you select actions to undo, the button at the lower left displays "Undo." If you choose action to redo, the button displays "Redo."

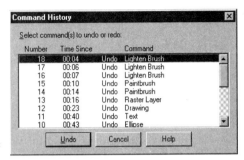

3. Click the Undo/Redo button to close the dialog box and apply the changes to the image.

You can allocate storage space for saving the Command History data, compress the information to save space, select the number of steps to save, and update the Command History with each brush stroke. Select these options using the Undo/Redo tab of the General Program Preferences dialog box.

Emptying the Command History

Use this command to empty the contents of the Command History list, thereby freeing disk space. You can allocate storage space for the Undo list and compress the information using the Undo/Redo tab of the General Program Preferences dialog box.

* To empty the buffers, choose Edit > Empty > Command History.

Revert Command

Use the Revert command to remove all changes made to an image since it was last saved.

* To apply the command, choose File > Revert.

Redo Command

The Redo command re-applies the actions or commands on which you have used the Undo command. Paint Shop Pro supports Multiple Redo, which is particularly useful if you have removed more edits and commands than you had intended. If this occurs, and you want to re-apply them, either choose the Redo command as many times as is necessary or use the Command History dialog box.

* To apply the Redo command, choose Edit > Redo, press <Ctrl> + <Alt> + <Z>, or click the Redo button on the toolbar.

Multiple Redo

To re-apply more than one Undo, you may find it most convenient to use the Command History dialog box, which is described above.

Repeat Command

The Repeat command allows you to repeat many commands. After executing a command, the command name appears with the Repeat command on the Edit menu. This command is particularly useful when you want to apply the same effect to several images without opening the dialog box each time.

To re-apply the last command to your image or apply the same command to another image, choose Edit > Repeat or press <Ctrl> + <Y>.

Using the Cut, Copy, and Paste Commands

Cutting Part of an Image

The Cut command removes part of an image and stores the cut data on the Windows clipboard. The data remains on the clipboard until you replace it by using either the Cut or Copy commands or you empty the clipboard. Note that when working with vector objects, they are converted into raster objects when you paste them to a raster layer. Using the Cut, Copy, and Paste commands with vector objects is described in Chapter 13, "Editing Vector Objects and Text."

If the image contains an active selection, the command affects only the selection. If the image does not contain an active selection, the command applies to the current layer. The cut area is replaced by the background color.

NOTE: *Use the <Delete> key to remove a selection or layer data without storing it on the clipboard.*

- To use the Cut command choose Edit > Cut, press <Ctrl> + <X>, or click the Cut toolbar button.

Copying Part of an Image

When you use the Copy and Copy Merged commands, the Windows clipboard stores the copied data. This data remains on the clipboard until you empty the clipboard or you next use either the Copy or Cut commands.

Copy

If the layer contains an active selection, the Copy command copies the data inside the selection. It places a copy of it on the clipboard while leaving the original image unaffected. If a layer does not contain a selection, using the command copies either the image (if the image contains one layer) or the current layer (if the image contains more than one layer).

- To use the Copy command choose Edit > Copy, press <Ctrl> + <C>, or click the Copy button on the toolbar.

Copy Merged

The Copy Merged command copies data from all the layers rather than just the current layer. It then merges the information into a single layer. When copying a selection, it copies and merges the selection area from all the layers. This command is available only with multi-layered images.

- To use the command, choose Edit > Copy Merged or press <Shift> + <Ctrl> + <C>.

Using the Paste Commands

There are several commands for pasting the contents of the clipboard. When pasting, if the data is in a metafile format and the WMF/Import option is not set to use the file header information, Paint Shop Pro opens the Meta Picture Import dialog box.

Pasting as a New Image

When you choose this command, Paint Shop Pro creates a new image from the contents of the clipboard.

- To use the command, choose Edit > Paste > As New Image, press <Ctrl> + <V>, or click the Paste as New Image button on the toolbar.

Pasting as a New Layer

You can paste the clipboard contents as a new layer into any image that supports layers. Paint Shop Pro uses the data to create a new layer above the current layer.

- To use the command, choose Edit > Paste > As New Layer or press <Ctrl> + <L>.

Pasting as a New Selection

When you paste the clipboard contents as a new selection, Paint Shop Pro adds it as a floating selection above the current layer. If the image already contains a floating selection, it is defloated before the new floating selection is pasted.

To paste data as a new selection:

1. Open or select the image into which you want to paste the clipboard contents.

2. Choose Edit > Paste > As New Selection or press <Ctrl> + <E>.

3. Use the mouse to position the selection.

4. After you have positioned the selection, click once to release it.

Pasting as a Transparent Selection

When you paste the clipboard contents as a transparent selection, Paint Shop Pro changes the current background color of the image to transparent before pasting the selection.

To paste data as a transparent selection:

1. Open image into which you want to paste the clipboard contents.

2. Choose Edit > Paste > As Transparent Selection or press <Shift> + <Ctrl> + <E>.

   Paint Shop Pro pastes the data as a floating selection above the current (active) layer.

3. Use the mouse to position the selection.

4. After you have positioned the selection, click once to release it.

Pasting into the Selection

You can paste the clipboard data into a floating or non-floating selection. Paint Shop Pro replaces the contents of the selection with the clipboard data.

To paste data into a selection:

1. Create the selection into which you want to paste the clipboard contents.

2. Choose Edit > Paste > Into Selection, or press <Shift> + <Ctrl> + <L>.

3. The pasted contents appear in the image. If the selection into which the contents are pasted is a different size than the item being pasted, the clipboard contents are resized to fit the current selection.

Pasting from Animation Shop

Using Paint Shop Pro as an editing program for animation frames is described on the next page in the "Interoperability with Animation Shop" section.

Emptying Contents of the Clipboard

When you use the Cut and Copy functions, the data you have cut or copied is placed on the Windows clipboard, an area of your computer's memory used for temporary storage. You can then paste data from the clipboard to another layer, to another image, or as a new image. If the amount of data on the clipboard is very large, it can consume a considerable amount of memory and slow down your computer.

- To empty (erase) the data from the clipboard choose Edit > Empty > Clipboard.

NOTE: *This removes the clipboard contents, making the data unavailable for pasting.*

When you exit Paint Shop Pro with data still on the clipboard, you can choose to be prompted to remove it. Set this option in the Miscellaneous tab of the General Program Preferences dialog box.

Interoperability with Animation Shop

Importing from Animation Shop

If you are working in Animation Shop, you can export an animation into Paint Shop Pro, edit the frames, and then update them back to Animation Shop. When the frames are exported to Paint Shop Pro, they remain linked to the original animation. For more information about using Paint Shop Pro with Animation Shop, please refer to Chapter 30, "Interacting with Paint Shop Pro" in the Animation Shop section of this manual.

To import frames into Paint Shop Pro:

1. In Animation Shop, select individual frames or choose Edit > Select All to select the entire animation.

2. Choose File > Export Frames > To Paint Shop Pro. Paint Shop Pro opens, and each frame is pasted into the program as an individual image with a transparent background and one layer.

As mentioned above, the new images are linked to their original frames. This makes it easy to apply any changes you make back to the original frames. Choose Edit > Update Back to Animation Shop, and the original animation is updated automatically.

You can also use the clipboard to paste one or more Animation Shop frames as Paint Shop Pro images. However, if you use this method, the images <u>are not linked</u> to their original frames. To apply changes to the original animation, you need to cut or copy each image and paste it back into its original frame.

• To use the clipboard, select one or more animation frames and choose Edit > Copy. Open Paint Shop Pro, if necessary, and choose Edit> Paste > AS Animation as Multiple Frames.

Updating Back to Animation Shop

When you export frames to Paint Shop Pro using Animation Shop's File > Export Frames to Paint Shop Pro command, each frame becomes a new image. These images are linked to their original frames. This gives you the convenience of updating changes back to the animation without having to cut and paste between programs.

NOTE: *When animations are linked to the Paint Shop Pro images, you cannot close Animation Shop until after all the images you have exported to Paint Shop Pro have been closed.*

To update changes back to the original frame:

1. In Paint Shop Pro, click the image you want to update to make it active.

2. Choose Edit > Update Back to Animation Shop.

Changes you have made to the image are applied to the original animation frame. The image remains in the Paint Shop Pro workspace so that you can continue to edit it.

Changing the Size of the Image

When you want to resize an image but not crop it or add new canvas around it, use the Resize command. If you are creating a Web page and have an image that is too large to fit, you can resize it. You can also reduce the number of pixels in an image to make it download more quickly.

NOTE: *To change the dimensions of the image by adding or removing pixels from the edges, use the Canvas Size command.*

To Resize an image:

1. Open the Resize dialog box by choosing Image > Resize.

2. Select a method for resizing the image. You have three options:

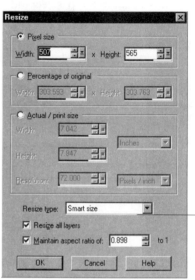

- Pixel Size, where you select a new size by choosing a new measurement in pixels,

- Percentage of Original, where you select a new size based on a percentage increase or decrease from the original, and

- Actual/Print Size, where you select a new size by changing the resolution or the dimensions.

3. Enter new measurements in the Width and Height boxes of the selected panel. In the "Actual/Print Size" panel, you can also change the resolution.

4. In the Resize Type box, select the type of resizing for Paint Shop Pro to apply. There are four choices:

- Smart size, where Paint Shop Pro chooses the best algorithm based on the current image characteristics.

- Bicubic resample, which uses a process called interpolation to minimize the raggedness normally associated with expanding an image. As applied here, interpolation smoothes out rough spots by estimating how the "missing" pixels should appear, and then filling them with the appropriate color. It produces better results than the Pixel resize method with photo-realistic images and with images that are irregular or complex. Use Bicubic resample when enlarging an image.

- Bilinear resample, which reduces the size of an image by applying a similar method as Bicubic resample. Use it when reducing photo-realistic images and images that are irregular or complex.

- Pixel Resize, where Paint Shop Pro duplicates or removes pixels as necessary to achieve the selected width and height of an image. It produces better results than the resampling methods when used with hard-edged images.

5. In an image with more than one layer, select the "Resize all Layers" check box to resize the entire image. Leave the box unchecked to resize only the active layer.

6. To change the proportions of the image, select the "Maintain aspect ratio of" check box and type a new ratio for the image width. Aspect ratio is the relationship of the image's width to height. By default, the Aspect ratio box displays the image's current aspect ratio.

7. Click the OK button to close the dialog box and apply the changes.

NOTE: *After resizing, many images can be improved by using the Sharpen filter.*

Bilinear and Bicubic resampling are available only for greyscale images and 24-bit images. To resample an image with a lower color depth, do the following:

1. Increase the image's color depth.

2. Resize the image.

3. Reduce the image's color depth to the original depth.

⬧ Changing the Size of the Image Canvas

Changing the canvas size changes the dimensions of the image by adding pixels to or removing them from the edges of the image. You can increase or decrease the canvas on a specific side or around the entire image. Use the Change Canvas Size dialog box to select the number of pixels to add or remove. When you are increasing the canvas size, Paint Shop Pro adds pixels using the current background color. Decreasing the canvas size produces the same result as cropping the image.

NOTE: *To change the image resolution, use the Resize command, not the Canvas Size command. When you use the Resize command, you force the entire image into a larger or smaller area.*

When increasing the canvas size:

- On the background layer, Paint Shop Pro uses the active background color for the new pixels. Select a background color before opening the dialog box.

- On other layers, Paint Shop Pro makes the new pixels transparent.

To change the size of the image canvas:

1. Open the Change Canvas Size dialog box choosing Image > Canvas Size.

2. In the "Dimensions" panel, enter a new size (in pixels) for the image in the New Width and New Height boxes. You can type a number or use the spin controls. The current width and height are displayed for your reference.

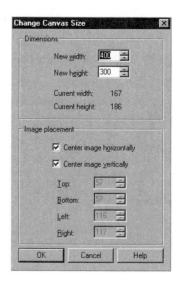

3. Select the placement of the image in the new canvas.

   - To center the image in the new canvas, select both the "Center Image Horizontally" and the "Center Image Vertically" check boxes. The boxes below them become unavailable and Paint Shop Pro adds or removes pixels evenly around the image.

   - To center the image horizontally, select the "Center Image Horizontally" check box. The Left and Right boxes become unavailable and Paint Shop Pro adds or removes pixels evenly to the left and right sides of the image.

   - To center the image vertically, select the "Center Image Vertically" check box. The Top and Bottom boxes become unavailable and Paint Shop Pro adds or removes pixels evenly to the top and bottom sides of the image.

   - To position the image off-center, clear the check boxes.

4. If you have not selected both check boxes, use the Image Placement boxes to position the image. The Top and Bottom boxes control the vertical placement; the Left and Right control the horizontal placement. Each pair of boxes works in unison—as you increase the numbers in one box, the numbers in the other box decrease.

5. After positioning the image, click the OK button to close the dialog box and apply the changes.

Changing the Image Orientation

Flipping and Mirroring

The Flip and Mirror commands change the image orientation. The Flip command reverses an image along its vertical axis, and the Mirror command reverses the image along its horizontal axis. You can flip and mirror an image, layer, or selection of any color depth. When you use these commands on a selection, the area that is flipped or mirrored becomes a floating selection, leaving the original image unchanged.

Flip Command Flipping a selection, layer, or image reverses it vertically. What was the top becomes the bottom, and vice-versa.

• To use the command, choose Image > Flip or press <Ctrl> + <I>.

Mirror Command Mirroring a selection, layer, or image reverses it horizontally. What was the left side becomes the right side, and what was the right side becomes the left.

• To use the command, choose Image > Mirror or press <Ctrl> + <M>.

Rotating an Image

Rotating an image moves it around its center point. You can rotate a selection, layer, or image of any color depth using the Rotate dialog box. It is a convenient command for re-aligning scanned images that are crooked. To rotate an image, layer, or selection:

1. Open the Rotate dialog box by choosing Image > Rotate or by pressing <Ctrl> + <R>.

2. Select the direction of rotation by clicking the Direction's option button or its text. Right is clockwise; left is counter-clockwise.

3. Set the degrees of rotation:

   • To rotate in quarter-circle increments, click the 90, 180, or 270-degree option.

   • To rotate by any other amount, type the value in the Free box.

4. To rotate every layer in a multi-layer image, select the "All layers" check box. Clear the check box to rotate only the current layer. When this check box is selected or when the image consists of a single background layer, the canvas size changes to accommodate the rotated image.

5. Click the OK button to close the dialog box and rotate the image.

Adding Borders to an Image

Adding borders surrounds an image with a color, increasing the dimensions of the image by the width of the borders. Paint Shop Pro uses the background color for the border.

Before opening the Add Borders dialog box:

- Select the border color by selecting a new background color.

- Flatten the image if it contains more than one layer. If you try to open the dialog box before you flatten the image, Paint Shop Pro displays a message stating that it must flatten the image.

To add borders to an image:

1. Open the Add Borders dialog box by choosing Image > Add Borders.

2. To add borders equally on all sides, select the "Symmetric" check box. To add borders of unequal width, leave the check box unchecked.

3. Enter the border size in pixels in the four boxes. If you have selected the Symmetric option, the boxes are linked—changing the width in one box automatically changes the width in the others.

4. Click the OK button to close the dialog box and add the borders to the image.

Using
Adjustment Layers

As you work with your images in Paint Shop Pro, you may want to make manual corrections or adjustments to the colors. Paint Shop Pro has many features that can help you do this. You can adjust your images by adding adjustment layers, or by making the adjustments directly to your images. In addition, Paint Shop Pro has features that let you add special effects to your images or automatically enhance photographs.

This chapter describes the adjustment layer features. If you want to add color adjustments directly to your images, please refer to Chapter 7, "Making Color Adjustments." If you want to add artistic effects to your images, please refer to Chapter 17, "Adding Effects." To enhance your photographs and other images, please refer to Chapter 6, "Improving Photographs." In addition, reading Chapter 5, "Working with Color" should help you understand the color components you will be adjusting.

Understanding Adjustment Layers

Adjustment layers are an advanced feature of Paint Shop Pro that let you make color corrections to an image without actually changing the original image or other layers within the image. This is particularly useful if an image is multi-layered.

You can add Adjustment layers to test various color corrections on an image, or to see how different color corrections look combined. If you don't like the corrections on a layer, you can hide or delete the layers and try different combinations. An adjustment layer, which is a form of a raster layer, contains the color correction information. The pixels in the underlying layers are not affected. You can edit an adjustment layer as many times as you like without permanently altering the pixel values. You can add more than one adjustment layer to an image. An adjustment layer changes the appearance of the layers below it, not the ones above. By creating adjustment layers at various levels in the layer stack, you can apply multiple effects. To make adjustments permanent, you can merge all the layers to flatten the image.

For working with layers, Paint Shop Pro provides the Layer palette, the Layer Properties dialog box, and various commands in the Layers menu. This chapter describes these features as they apply to the Adjustment layers. For general information about layers, please refer to Chapter 11, "Working with Layers."

NOTE: *An image must be a greyscale or 24-bit color image to contain an adjustment layer. To add Adjustment layers, you may need to increase an image's color depth.*

Using the Layer Palette

The Layer palette provides quick access to many of the commands and options in the Layers menu and Layer Properties dialog box. The Layer palette below shows a Raster (bitmap) and Vector layer at the top and a Background layer at the bottom. All the other layers show the available types of Adjustment layers. Notice the icon on the left side of each layer name is different for each type of Adjustment layer.

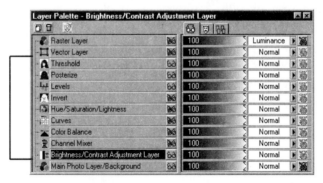

NOTE: *For a complete description of the Layer palette, please refer to Chapter 11, "Working with Layers."*

Creating Adjustment Layers

This section describes the four general steps for creating an adjustment layer: choosing the type of adjustment, setting the options on the General tab of the Layer Properties dialog box, setting the options on the Adjustment tab of the Layer Properties dialog box, and editing the layer.

Choosing the Adjustment Type

You choose the type of adjustment when you create an adjustment layer. If a selection is active when you create a layer, the adjustment only affects the selection.

Use one of the following methods to choose an adjustment type:

- Click the Layer palette button of the layer above which you want to create the adjustment layer and from the menu bar choose Layers > New Adjustment Layer, and then choose one of the adjustments.

- Click the Layer palette button of the layer above which you want to create the adjustment layer, right-click the Layer palette Create Layer button (□), choose Layers > New Adjustment Layer, and then choose one of the adjustments from the context menu.

- Right-click the Layer palette button of the layer above which you want to create the adjustment layer, choose Layers > New Adjustment Layer, and then choose one of the adjustments from the context menu.

NOTE: *An image must be a greyscale or 24-bit color image to contain an adjustment layer or more than one raster layer. To add these layers, increase your image's color depth.*

Setting the General Layer Properties

After choosing the adjustment type from the context menu, the Layer Properties dialog box appears. For an adjustment layer, this dialog box contains two tabs, General and Adjustment. Click the General tab to bring it to the front. The General tab displays the same information as Layer Properties dialog boxes for raster and vector layers. The type of adjustment layer appears in the Name box. In the Layer Name box, leave the default or type a unique name for the layer. You can also change the other options on the tab. For descriptions of these options, please refer to Chapter 11, "Working with Layers.

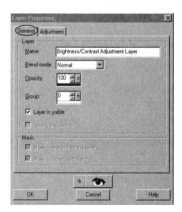

Setting the Adjustment Layer Properties

Click the Adjustment tab to bring it to the front. The Adjustment tab is different for each type of adjustment. Use the options on the tab to create your adjustment. For specific descriptions of the tabs for each adjustment type, please refer to the "Setting Adjustment Properties" section below.

NOTE: *As you configure an adjustment layer, click the Auto Proof button (⬇️)to see the changes on your image as you make them. If you don't click the Auto Proof button, click the Proof button (👁️), to view the changes before applying them. Click the Reset button (🔁)to return the image to its original values.*

Editing the Adjustment Layer

After creating an adjustment layer, you can edit it in several ways. You can duplicate, rename, move, copy, hide or show, modify the edges, group, or merge the layers. For details about editing a layer, please refer to "Editing an Adjustment Layer" on page 284.

Setting Adjustment Properties

To create a new adjustment layer, refer to "Creating Adjustment Layers" on page 277. Use the general steps provided in that section. When you get to the steps in "Setting the Adjustment Layer Properties," refer to this section for the description of the adjustment layer's properties.

🔳 Adding a Brightness/Contrast Adjustment Layer

Use a Brightness/Contrast adjustment layer to lighten or darken the underlying layers and change the amount of shading, or contrast, between areas. The tab displays two controls: one for adjusting the brightness and one for adjusting the contrast.

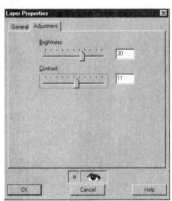

BRIGHTNESS A value of 0 displays the image at its original Brightness level. Drag the slider to the right or type a positive number to lighten the image. Drag it to the left or type a negative number to darken it.

CONTRAST A value of 0 displays the image at its original Contrast level. Drag the slider to the right or type a positive number to increase the contrast and make the image sharper. Drag it to the left or type a negative number to decrease it and make the image more blurry.

Adding a Channel Mixer Adjustment Layer

Use this adjustment layer to increase or decrease a color channel by a percentage of itself and the other two channels.

OUTPUT CHANNEL Select a color channel to edit.

MONOCHROME Select to create a greyscale image. This automatically sets the Output channel to black. You can then use the sliders to set the percentage of each channel to use for the greyscale value of the final image.

SOURCE CHANNELS PANEL These options define the current channel you are editing. For example, if you select the Red channel in the Output channel drop-down box and then set the Red slider to 50, you reduce the amount of red in the image to 50% of its original amount.

CONSTANT NUMERIC BOX AND SLIDER Use to brighten or darken the image across each channel. The default of 0 is the original setting.

Adding a Color Balance Adjustment Layer

Use a Color Balance adjustment layer to alter the underlying layers by shifting the balance of a color and its opposite on the color wheel. There are three pairs: cyan and red, magenta and green, and yellow and blue. Increasing the amount of one decreases the amount of its opposite. You can adjust the balance in each of the three tonal ranges.

TONAL BALANCE PANEL Select which lightness level, or tonal range, of colors to adjust. While you can adjust all three, you adjust each one individually.

- The Shadows option controls the colors at the dark end of the lightness scale,

- The Midtones option controls the colors in the middle range, and

- The Highlight option controls the colors at the bright end of the scale.

Select or clear the "Preserve luminosity" check box to retain or change the luminosity.

COLOR BALANCE PANEL The "Color balance" panel contains the pairs of colors whose balance you shift. The box on the left displays the Cyan/Red balance. The middle box displays the Magenta/Green balance. The box at the right displays the Yellow/Blue balance. The original color balance of the image is represented by values of 0 in the boxes and the slider at the middle of the bar. Drag the sliders or type values in the boxes to set the color balance. Increasing the proportion of one color decreases the proportion of its opposite.

![] Adding a Curves Adjustment Layer

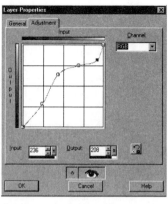

The Curves adjustment layer is similar to the Levels adjustment in that you use it to adjust brightness values. However, the Curves adjustment gives you more flexibility. You can change any brightness value on the 0-255 scale.

CHANNEL Select the channel to edit. You can edit the three RGB channels together or individually. If you change channels, the values on the graph update and display the new settings.

THE GRAPH Charts the relationship between the input and output levels. At the lower left of the graph, both values are 0 (black). At the upper right, both values are 255 (white).

To add a point to the graph, move the cursor over line. When the cursor changes to an arrowhead and displays "+add," click the line. You can then drag this point or enter values in the number box to move it. The input value displays the original setting for the point. As you drag the point, the output value changes. You can add up to 16 points to the curve. You can also slide a point along the line to substitute values.

To remove a point, drag it off the top or bottom edge of the graph.

![] Adding a Hue/Saturation/Lightness Adjustment Layer

NOTE: *For more information about hues, saturation, and lightness, please refer to Chapter 5, "Working with Color."*

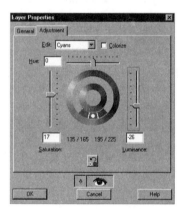

Use this adjustment layer to change the hue, saturation, and lightness (luminance) values for any color or range of colors in the underlying layers, or to colorize greyscale layers.

SLIDER BOXES When the 3 sliders and boxes are set to 0, the image displays its original values. You can return the image to these values at any time by clicking the Reset button.

HUE RINGS The tab contains three concentric hue rings:

- The outer ring, which never changes, displays a color wheel. It represents the original hues. When the tab opens, this ring and the inner ring are displayed fully saturated. Increased saturation levels are not visible.

- The inner ring displays the cumulative effects of all the adjustments. It rotates and changes as you adjust the settings, but does not reflect increases you make to the saturation level.

- The middle ring is the control ring you use to change the settings. When the tab opens, this ring is half saturated. It reflects all adjustments you make, including those to the saturation level. If you edit all the colors in the image by choosing Master in the Edit drop-down box, the entire ring appears. It shows all the colors at their current values. If you restrict the editing to a color range, only the segment of the ring at that color range appears. Drag the controls in the color segment to set where the adjustment starts, where it is at full effect, where it begins to taper off, and where it ends.

NOTE: *While the color ranges must be edited individually, you can edit as many as you want. There is a cumulative effect when you edit multiple color ranges.*

To use the Hue/Saturation/Lightness Adjustment tab:

1. From the Edit drop-down box, select which color range to adjust. Choose Master to edit all the colors simultaneously. Choose a specific color range to limit the adjustment. Your choice determines the appearance of the control ring.

2. If you are adding color to a greyscale image, select the "Colorize" check box below the color rings. The Edit box becomes unavailable.

3. To adjust the saturation and luminance, move the sliders or type numbers in the boxes. Negative numbers decrease the saturation and luminance levels; positive numbers increase them.

4. If you are in the Master Edit mode, move the Hue slider or type a number in the box to shift every color. Negative numbers rotate the wheel to the left; positive numbers rotate it to the right. You can go half the way around the wheel by moving the slider all the way left or right. The control ring displays the new hue for each color. For example, when the slider is at 180, blue becomes yellow and green becomes magenta.

5. If you are restricting the adjustment to a color range, drag the two outer pointers on the control ring to set the range width. They mark the beginning and end of the adjustment area. You can drag them to edit as wide a range as you like. You can also drag the two inner bars. The segment between each outer pointer and inner bar shows where the adjustment is building to its full effect. The area between the two inner bars shows where the adjustment is in full effect. To move control ring, drag the white circle.

6. To choose new colors for the color range, type a number in the Hue box or drag the Hue slider. You can move from –180 to +180.

7. To change the saturation of the color range, type a number from –100 to +100 in the Saturation box or drag the Saturation slider. At –100, the colors are desaturated, or grey; at +100, they are fully saturated.

8. To change the luminance of the color range, type a number from –100 to +100 in the Luminance box or drag the Luminance slider. At –100, the colors become black; at +100, they turn white.

9. Click the OK button to close the dialog box and apply the settings.

Adding an Invert Adjustment Layer

When you choose the Invert adjustment layer command, Paint Shop Pro reads the value for each pixel and subtracts it from 255 on the color value scale. The result is a negative of the image. There are no settings on the Adjustment tab.

Adding a Levels Adjustment Layer

Use a Levels adjustment layer to reset the darkest and lightest values in the image to black and white to increase the tonal range. The corresponding pixels in the other channels are also adjusted to keep the original color balance.

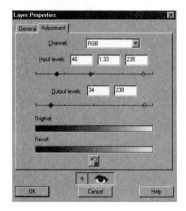

CHANNEL Select the channel to edit. You can edit the three RGB channels together or individually. If you change channels, the values on the graph update and display the new settings.

INPUT LEVELS The Input levels map the image to brightness levels. They modify it by darkening the darkest values and lightening the lightest values. This increases the contrast. Gamma value resets the lightness of medium grey.

The diamond-shaped sliders are visual representations of the values in the boxes. The value in the left box represents where 0 begins. All values below this value become 0 (black). For example, if you enter 50 in the box, all value below 50 become 0. The box on the right represents where 255 begins. All values above it are set to 255 (white). The middle box controls the gamma curve. The range for this curve is 0 to 7.99, with 1 being in the middle. For more information about image gamma, please refer to Chapter 7, "Making Color Adjustments."

OUTPUT LEVELS The output levels lighten the darkest pixels and darken the lightest pixels. You can invert these values so that the upper value is 25 and the lower value is 200 to create a negative image effect.

You can move the sliders (diamonds) by dragging them or using the keyboard. For details about using the keyboard to move the sliders, click the Help button.

🏔 Adding a Posterize Adjustment Layer

Add a Posterize adjustment layer to reduce the number of bits per color channel in the underlying layers. Reducing the bits per color channel decreases the number of colors and levels of lightness the layers can display. This produces a flatter-looking image with bands of color rather than smooth gradients.

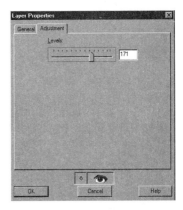

LEVELS Use the slider to reduce the number of red, green, and blue levels. At 255, all the levels are available. As you decrease the number, Paint Shop Pro divides the image into fewer levels, and the result is a flatter-looking image.

🐾 Adding a Threshold Adjustment Layer

Add a Threshold adjustment layer to create a black-and-white image from the underlying layers. The Histogram values are used to determine whether a pixel becomes white or black. For more information about the Histogram, please see to Chapter 6, "Improving Photographs."

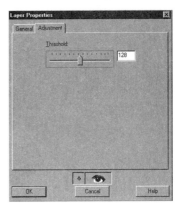

THRESHOLD The tab displays a Threshold slider with levels from 1 to 255, which correspond to those in the Histogram. All pixels with brightness values below the Threshold level you set become black. All pixels with brightness values at or above the level become white.

To set a Threshold level, drag the slider or type a number in the box to its right.

Editing an Adjustment Layer

You can edit an adjustment layer by changing the settings on the Adjustment tab or by painting the layer to alter the adjustment effect. You can edit an adjustment layer as many times as you like without permanently altering the pixel values of the underlying layers until you flatten the image.

NOTE: *For additional information about editing layers, please refer to Chapter 11, "Working with Layers."*

Editing the Adjustment Settings

Edit the settings by opening the Properties dialog box and changing the settings on the Adjustment tab.

Open the Adjustment tab of the Properties dialog box in one of the following ways:

• Choose Layers > Properties,

• Double-click the Layer button of the Layer palette, or

• Right-click the Layer button of the Layer palette, and choose Properties from the menu.

The Properties dialog box opens with the Adjustment tab at the front. It displays the current settings. After you have changed the settings, click the OK button to close the dialog box and apply the adjustments.

Editing the Layer

An adjustment layer is similar to a masked raster layer. You can edit it with the painting tools in the same way you edit a mask. When you select an adjustment layer, the active colors on the Color palette change to greyscale values. Paint with black to remove the adjustment effect; paint with white to add it; paint with greys to vary the strength of its effect.

You can also vary the opacity level and blend mode to edit the layer. Please refer to Chapter 11, "Working with Layers," for information about using these features.

Deleting an Adjustment Layer

You delete an adjustment layer in the same way as you delete the other types of layers.

You can choose Layers > Delete, or use one of the following methods on the Layer palette:

• Right-click the Layer button and choose Delete from the context menu.

• Click the Layer button, and then click the Delete Layer button at the upper left of the palette. A message appears asking you to confirm this action. Click the Yes button.

• Drag the Layer button to the Delete Layer button and release the mouse. A message appears asking you to confirm this action. Click the Yes button.

Adding Effects

Paint Shop Pro has many special effects you can apply to your images, including 3D effects, Artistic effects, Geometric effects, Illumination effects, Reflection effects, and Texture effects. You can also use the Blur, Sharpen, Edge, and Noise commands to add special effects to your images. All of these features are located on the Effects menu.

This chapter briefly describes and illustrates the special effects. For details about using the special effects commands, please use the Help file.

Using the Blur Commands

The Blur commands smooth transitions and decrease contrast by averaging the pixels next to hard edges of defined lines and areas where there are significant color transitions. These commands can be used for photo retouching and for adding effects. This section describes the Motion Blur special effect. For more information about the other Blur commands, refer to Chapter 6, "Improving Photographs."

NOTE: *You can apply these commands to greyscale and 24-bit images. If necessary, increase the color depth of your image to make the commands available. For more information, please refer to Chapter 5, "Working with Color."*

NOTE: *To limit a command to a specific area, create a selection before using the command.*

Using the Motion Blur Command

The Motion Blur command makes the image appear to be moving by adding a blur in a specific direction for a specific distance. Set the distance and direction of the blur to simulate the direction and speed you want the object to appear to be moving.

To use Motion Blur:

1. Choose Effects > Blur > Motion Blur. This displays the Motion Blur dialog box.

2. To set the direction of the blur, drag the needle around the circle or type the degree (from 0 to 359) in the box.

3. Drag the slider to select the intensity. As the intensity increases, The image blurs by an increasing number of pixels in the selected direction.

4. Click the OK button to close the dialog box and apply the effect.

Using the Sharpen, Edge, and Noise Commands

The Sharpen, Edge, and Noise commands can be used for photo retouching and for adding special effects. The Sharpen commands heighten the contrast in an image; they lighten the light pixels and darken the dark pixels. The Edge commands accentuate contrast areas and object edges in an image. The Noise commands remove the random patterns of pixels that give an image a grainy or textured appearance. This section describes the Add Noise command. For more information about the other commands, please refer to Chapter 6, "Improving Photographs."

NOTE: *You can apply these commands to greyscale and 24-bit images. If necessary, increase the color depth of your image to make the commands available. For more information, please refer to Chapter 5, "Working with Color."*

NOTE: *To limit a command to a specific area, create a selection before using the command.*

Using Add Noise

Use this command to reduce the detail in an image and add a grainy texture. By adding a small percentage of noise to an image, you can reduce the appearance of small imperfections and scratches.

To use the Add Noise command:

1. Choose Effects > Noise > Add to open the Add Noise dialog box.

1. Drag the % Noise slider or type a number in the box to select the number of pixels covered with noise. As you increase the percentage, the more of the image is affected.

2. Select whether the Noise is displayed in a Random or Uniform pattern over the image. When you select Uniform, the Noise color more closely resembles the original pixels.

3. Click the OK button to close the dialog box and apply the correction.

Using the Effect Browser

The Effect Browser lets you preview all the available effects. Use the Effect Browser to try out effects before applying them to your image. When you select an effect from the list and click the OK button, that effect's dialog box opens for you to configure its settings.

To use the Effect Browser:

1. Choose Effects > Effect Browser. The Effects Browser opens.

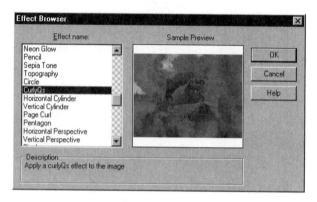

2. Select an effect from the Effect name list. The "Description" panel displays a description of the effect and the "Sample Preview" pane displays the result of the effect.

3. To apply the effect, click the OK button.

4. If the effect has options you can configure, the effect's dialog box opens.

Using the Dialog Boxes

Each of the effects has a dialog box that opens when you select the command. As you use the dialog boxes, you'll notice that the sliders remain in the final position when you close the boxes. This lets you apply an effect to multiple images without having to adjust the settings each time. You'll also notice each dialog box has two preview windows and zoom buttons, a Proof button ( ), an Auto Proof button ( ), and a Reset button ( ). For information about these features, please refer to the *Getting Started Guide*.

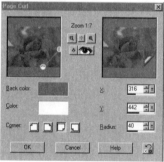

NOTE: *Because the dialog boxes retain their last settings, you might want to click the Reset ( ) button to set all the options to their default values before you begin an adjustment.*

Adding 3D Effects

The 3D effects include Buttonize, Chisel, Cutout, Drop Shadow, Inner Bevel, and Outer Bevel. Use these effects to create images or selections that appear to be dimensional. These effects are particularly useful for creating images for Web pages.

NOTE: *Please notice the following about these commands:*

- *These commands work on 24-bit and greyscale images. If necessary, increase the color depth of your image to use the commands. For more information, please refer to Chapter 5, "Working with Color."*

- *To use the Chisel, Cutout, Drop Shadow, Inner Bevel, or Outer Bevel effects, you must first create a selection in the image.*

- *When you select the command for a special effect, a dialog box appears. For a complete description of the options on a dialog box, click the Help button on that dialog box.*

- *All the examples in this section were made with a rectangle of blue color, as shown here.*

BUTTONIZE applies a three dimensional border that makes an image or selection appear raised. You can create a button from a selection, layer, or flattened image.

CHISEL adds a three-dimensional border around a selection or layer to make it appear as though it were cut out of stone. The chiseled area can either be transparent or be created from the background color.

CUTOUT creates the illusion that part of the image has been removed, allowing you to see through the image to a lower level.

DROP SHADOW adds a shadow behind the current selection. It is most often used to give text a three-dimensional appearance.

INNER BEVEL creates a three-dimensional appearance by curving the inner edges of a selection or an object surrounded by a transparency. It does so without increasing the size of the object.

OUTER BEVEL applies a bevel outside the selection to create raised edges and give the selection a three-dimensional look. You cannot open the dialog box until your image contains a selection.

Adding Artistic Effects

The Artistic effects include Aged Newspaper, Black Pencil, Brush Strokes, Charcoal, Chrome, Colored Chalk, Colored Edges, Colored Foil, Colored Pencil, Contours, Enamel, Glowing Edges, Hot Wax Coating, Neon Glow, Pencil, Sepia, and Topography.

NOTE: *Please notice the following about these commands:*

- *These commands work on 24-bit and greyscale images. If necessary, increase the color depth of your image to use the commands. For more information, please refer to Chapter 5, "Working with Color."*

- *To limit an effect to a specific area, create a selection before choosing a command.*

- *When you select the command for a special effect, a dialog box appears. For a complete description of the options on a dialog box, click the Help button on that dialog box.*

AGED NEWSPAPER gives an image the appearance of old newspaper. It applies a warm brown tone and blurs the image so that it appears the ink has run. This replicates the look of a newspaper that has been left out in the sun for too long.

BLACK PENCIL creates a black and white image that looks like it has been drawn using a black pencil. It is similar to the Charcoal effect, but uses thinner strokes and produces a more detailed image.

BRUSH STROKES makes an image look like an oil painting or watercolor.

CHARCOAL creates a black-and-white image that looks like it has been drawn in charcoal. It is similar to the Black Pencil effect, but the thicker strokes produce an image containing less detail.

CHROME gives an image a metallic look. It works best with images that have distinct areas of contrast.

COLORED CHALK makes an image appear drawn in chalk using the colors in the image. It uses wider strokes than the Colored Pencil.

COLORED EDGES enhances and colors the edges in an image.

COLORED FOIL adds a sculpted look to the edges and applies multiple colors to an image.

COLORED PENCIL makes an image appear drawn in pencil using the colors in the image. Because it uses narrower strokes than the Colored Chalk, the image shows more details.

CONTOURS turns an image into a topographical map.

ENAMEL creates the effect of a shiny, molded coating on an image.

GLOWING EDGES makes an image appear to be created from neon tubes. The program finds and colors the edges in the image. Other areas of the image become black.

HOT WAX COATING creates the appearance of coating an image in a layer of hot wax using the foreground color.

NEON GLOW gives an image a three-dimensional appearance by applying neon effect and heightening the contrast of the edges.

PENCIL enhances and colors the edges in an image to make it look like a pencil drawing.

SEPIA makes an image appear similar to the photographs of the mid- to late 19th century. The effect applies a warm brown tone to an image. You can also create a 1940s style colorized appearance by applying the effect directly to a 24-bit color image.

TOPOGRAPHY turns an image into a system of terraces.

Original Image

Aged Newspaper

Black Pencil

Brush Strokes

Charcoal

Chrome

Colored Chalk

Colored Edges

Colored Foil

Colored Pencil

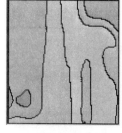

Contours

Enamel

Glowing Edges

Hot Wax Coating

Neon Glow

Pencil

Sepia

Topography

Adding Geometric Effects

The Geometric effects include Circle, Curly Q's, Horizontal and Vertical Cylinder, Page Curl, Pentagon, Horizontal and Vertical Perspective, Pinch, Pixelate, Punch, Ripple, Skew, Spiky Halo, Twirl, Warp, Wave, and Wind.

NOTE: *Please notice the following about these commands:*

- *These commands work on 24-bit and greyscale images. If necessary, increase the color depth of your image to use the commands. For more information, please refer to Chapter 5, "Working with Color."*

- *To limit an effect to a specific area, create a selection before choosing the command.*

- *When you select the command for a special effect, a dialog box appears. For a complete description of the options on a dialog box, click the Help button on that dialog box.*

CIRCLE turns an image or selection into a sphere.

CURLY Qs divides an image into a series of rows and columns composed of curls.

CYLINDERS, HORIZONTAL AND VERTICAL stretch an image. The Horizontal Cylinder effect stretches an image by pulling from the top and bottom to wrap it around the horizontal axis. The Vertical Cylinder pulls an image from the left and right to wrap it vertically.

PAGE CURL makes it appear as though a corner of an image has been rolled up, exposing a colored background.

PENTAGON transforms an image or selection into a pentagon.

PERSPECTIVES, HORIZONTAL AND VERTICAL creates a perspective along the edge of an image. The Horizontal Perspective effect creates a perspective along the horizontal axis by narrowing the left or right side of an image or selection. The Vertical Perspective effect creates a perspective along the vertical axis by narrowing the top or bottom of an image or selection.

PINCH compresses an image by pushing everything in toward the center of the image.

PIXELATE divides an image into rectangles or squares of a size you specify.

NOTE: *To users of Paint Shop Pro 6: This effect was called the Mosaic filter in earlier versions of the program.*

PUNCH stretches an image by pushing everything out toward the edges.

RIPPLE applies concentric waves around a central point in an image. The effect is similar to the rings produced by a pebble dropped in water. To create ripples in a radial pattern, use the Spiky Halo effect.

SKEW tilts an image or selection along its horizontal or vertical up to 45° in either direction.

SPIKY HALO creates a corona of waves in a radial pattern. To create concentric waves, use the Ripple effect.

TWIRL distorts an image by twisting or whirling it around its center. You can twirl an image in either direction by up to two rotations.

WARP makes a circular area of an image appear be at a higher or lower Zoom level than the rest of the image. The area is distorted as if viewed through a convex or concave lens.

WAVE creates a series of undulating vertical and horizontal lines in an image.

WIND blurs an image to make it look as though it has been blown by wind coming from either the left or the right.

Original Image

Circle

Curly Qs

Cylinder - Horizontal

Cylinder - Vertical

Page Curl

Pentagon

Perspective - Horizontal

Perspective - Vertical

Pinch

Pixelate

Punch

Ripple

Skew

Spiky Halo

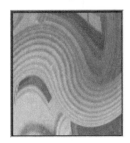

Twirl

Warp

Wave

Wind

Adding Illumination Effects

The Illumination effects include Sunburst and Lights.

NOTE: *Please notice the following about these commands:*

- *These commands work on 24-bit and greyscale images. If necessary, increase the color depth of your image to use the commands. For more information, please refer to Chapter 5, "Working with Color."*

- *To limit an effect to a specific area, create a selection before choosing the command.*

- *When you select the command for a special effect, a dialog box appears. For a complete description of the options on a dialog box, click the Help button on that dialog box.*

SUNBURST creates the effect of an image and its light source viewed through a camera lens. You can adjust the light origin, amount of radiating light, and brightness of the glare spots.

LIGHTS makes an image appear to be lit by up to five spotlights. You can set the intensity, direction, color and origin of the light source.

Original Image

Sunburst

Lights

Adding Reflection Effects

The Reflection effects include Feedback, Kaleidoscope, Pattern, and Rotating Mirror.

NOTE: *Please notice the following about these commands:*

- *These commands work on 24-bit and greyscale images. If necessary, increase the color depth of your image to use the commands. For more information, please refer to Chapter 5, "Working with Color."*
- *To limit an effect to a specific area, create a selection before choosing the command.*
- *When you select the command for a special effect, a dialog box appears. For a complete description of the options on a dialog box, click the Help button on that dialog box.*

FEEDBACK makes an image appear reflected in a series of concentric squared or circular mirrors.

KALEIDOSCOPE turns a pie-shaped area of an image or selection into a circular pattern. The result is similar to the pattern seen when looking through a kaleidoscope.

PATTERN turns any image or selection into an intricate geometric pattern. These patterns can be used to create seamless tiles for the background of a Web page.

ROTATING MIRROR reflects an image or selection along a radial angle. You can rotate the line of reflection around the center of an image to create a reflection at any angle.

Original Image   **Feedback**

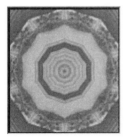

Kaleidoscope   **Pattern**   **Rotating Mirror**

Adding Texture Effects

The Texture effects include Blinds, Emboss, Fine Leather, Fur, Antique Mosaic, Glass Mosaic, Polished Stone, Rough Leather, Sandstone, Sculpture, Soft Plastic, Straw-wall, Texture, Tiles, and Weave.

NOTE: *Please notice the following about these commands:*

- *These commands work on 24-bit and greyscale images. If necessary, increase the color depth of your image to use the commands. For more information, please refer to Chapter 5, "Working with Color."*
- *To limit an effect to a specific area, create a selection before choosing the command.*
- *When you select the command for a special effect, a dialog box appears. For a complete description of the options on a dialog box, click the Help button on that dialog box.*

BLINDS makes an image appear to be drawn on vertical or horizontal window blinds.

EMBOSS converts an image into a bas-relief. It highlights the areas of contrast with black or white pixels and colors the low contrast areas a medium grey. Colors will appear when there is a large difference in the contrast. You can also apply the Emboss effect using the Retouch tool.

FINE LEATHER makes an image look as though you had created it on leather that has a fine grain.

FUR makes an image appear as if it is covered in fur or bristles.

MOSAIC - ANTIQUE makes an image appear to be created from mosaic tiles.

MOSAIC - GLASS makes an image appear to be composed of glass tiles.

POLISHED STONE makes an image look as if it were carved on a hard, shiny surface.

ROUGH LEATHER makes an image look like it has been embossed on leather that has a coarse grain.

SANDSTONE makes an image appear carved in sandstone.

SCULPTURE accentuates the edges of an image so they appear embossed or sculpted. It then overlays the result with a semi-transparent colored pattern. The patterns are 24-bit RGB images stored in the Patterns folder.

SOFT PLASTIC makes an image look as if it were molded from plastic.

STRAW-WALL makes an image look like it has been covered with straws that are oriented along the image contours.

TEXTURE gives an image a three-dimensional appearance as though the image were created on a textured surface.

TILES makes an image appear to be created from tiles. The tiles can be of varying shape, depth, and shininess.

WEAVE makes an image appear to be created with a weave pattern. You can make the strands loosely or tightly woven and fill the gaps between strands with any color.

Original Image

Blinds

Emboss

Fine Leather

Fur

Mosaic - Antique

Mosaic - Glass

Polished Stone

Rough Leather

Sandstone

Sculpture

Soft Plastic

Straw-wall

Texture

Tiles

Weave

Applying User Defined Filters

In addition to using the effects supplied with Paint Shop Pro, you can create and edit your own filters using the User Defined command on the Effects menu. For details about using this feature, select the menu command and then click the Help button on the User Defined Features dialog box.

Combining Two Images

Paint Shop Pro can combine two images to produce a third one that is the product of the color data of the two source images. To do this, open the two images you want to combine, choose Image > Arithmetic from the menu, and then click the Help button on the Image Arithmetic dialog box.

Adding a Picture Frame

Paint Shop Pro lets you add a picture frame to an image as a separate layer. After you have added a frame, you can change its color by adjusting the hue in the Hue/Saturation/Lightness dialog box.

NOTE: *Because you are working with layers, your image must be greyscale or 24-bit color to add a picture frame.*

To add a picture frame:

1. Choose Image > Picture Frame. The Picture Frame Wizard dialog box opens.

2. Select a frame from the drop-down list. A thumbnail of the selected frame appears as you make your selection. The type of frame chosen determines what you do next:

   • If the frame extends to the edges of the image, click the Next button to proceed to the frame placement options page.

   • If the frame does not extend to the edge of the image, you need to choose a background color to fill the area. Select the desired color for the area of the image that appears outside the frame from the drop-down list, and click the Next button to proceed to the frame placement options page.

3. Select the desired frame placement option. You can choose whether to place the frame inside or outside the borders of the image.

4. If you select "Frame inside of the image," Paint Shop Pro resizes the frame to fit within the edges of the image. Part of the image is covered by the picture frame, and the dimensions of the image are not altered.

5. If you select "Frame outside of the image," Paint Shop Pro increases the canvas size to accommodate the frame. The original image is not covered, and the dimensions of the image are increased by the size of the frame. The new canvas uses the current background color.

6. Click the Finish button. Paint Shop Pro closes the Wizard, resizes the frame so that it fits the image, and, if necessary, fills the area between the frame and the image edge with the selected color. The frame appears in the image as a new layer named "Picture Frame."

> **NOTE:** *If the width and height differ by a considerable amount, the frame appears thicker along the shorter sides.*

Using the
Web Features

Saving an Image for the Web

The majority of Web images are saved as GIF or JPEG files because most browsers support these two formats. The more recent PNG format, which newer versions of Web browsers recognize, is becoming increasingly popular.

When deciding on which format to choose for your Web graphic, consider its color depth, file size, and color distribution. None of the Web browsers can display layered images, so you will need to make a copy of the image and flatten it before saving it to the final format. Choose Layers > Merge > Merge All (Flatten).

Color Depth

Some computers are only capable of displaying up to 256 colors. If an image on a Web page contains more colors, the Web browser uses its own dithering method to display the image. This can produce color distortion. If you reduce the color depth of the image to 256 colors before placing it on your Web page, its appearance is more consistent.

File Size

File size affects most users accessing a Web page. As the size of an image file increases, it takes more time to download; viewers have a longer wait. Use a file format that reduces the image size most efficiently while keeping the quality as high as possible.

Web File Formats

GIF Use this format to compress line art and images with areas of similar colors. It supports 8-bit (256) color. There are two versions of GIF: 87a and 89a, which can save transparency and animation information. Both are recognized by most browsers and use lossless compression.

JPEG Use this format to compress photographic images. It supports 24-bit (16.7 million) color, uses lossy compression, and is recognized by most browsers.

PNG This format compresses most images efficiently. It supports up to 24-bit (16.7 million) color and uses lossless compression, but it is not recognized by as many browsers.

Optimizing a GIF File

Paint Shop Pro provides a GIF Optimizer feature to assist you in creating GIF files with or without transparency for you to place on your Web pages. To use this feature, choose File > Export > GIF Optimizer. The GIF Optimizer dialog box opens. It displays "before" and "after" previews so you can view the image as you select the transparency, color reduction, and other format options. You can configure the settings using the tabs below the preview boxes or click the Use Wizard button at the lower left of the dialog box and let Paint Shop Pro guide you through the process.

Using the GIF Optimizer Dialog Box

The GIF Optimizer dialog box contains four tabs where you configure the transparency, color, and format options of the file. The fifth tab displays estimated download times of the image at various modem speeds. For information on using the preview boxes, numeric edit controls, and other dialog box features, please read Chapter 3 of the *Getting Started Guide*.

To create a transparency from a selection in the image, make the selection before opening the dialog box. You can also save your image as a GIF file without a transparency. Choose the None option in the Transparency tab and ignore the Partial Transparency tab.

GIF Optimizer Transparency Tab

The option you choose in this tab determines which area of the image becomes transparent.

There are five choices:

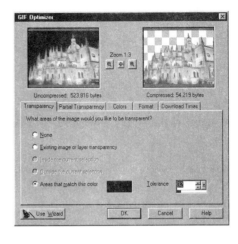

- None, which produces a GIF file that does not contain a transparency,

- Existing image or layer transparency, which uses the current transparency information,

- Inside the current selection, which is only available for images that contain a selection,

- Outside the current selection, which is only available for images that contain a selection, and

- Areas that match the color in the box. You can select any color. To choose a color from the image, move the cursor over the image and click the color. You can also click inside the color box to open the Color dialog box (24-bit images) or Image palette (8-bit images), or right-click it to open the Recent Colors dialog box. Set a tolerance factor for the color. The tolerance factor indicates how closely colors must match the color in the box before they become transparent.

GIF Optimizer Partial Transparency Tab

A GIF file cannot contain partially transparent pixels. All pixels must be either transparent or opaque (visible). However, the original image may contain partially transparent pixels if you have reduced the opacity of a layer, added a mask, feathered a selection, or used a brush or the eraser at a reduced opacity setting. Use the options in this tab to determine whether the partially transparent pixels become transparent or opaque, and whether they are blended with another color. If you have chosen the "None" option in the Transparency tab, the options in this tab are unavailable.

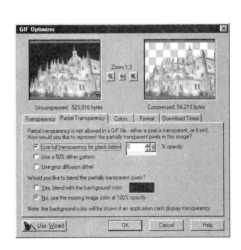

REPRESENTING PARTIALLY TRANSPARENT PIXELS

Paint Shop Pro can make partially transparent pixels transparent or use a dithering method to make them opaque:

- Choose the Use full transparency for pixels below x% opacity option and enter a value in its box to determine which partially transparent pixels become transparent. As you lower the value, you reduce the number of transparent pixels.

- Choose the Use a 50% dither pattern option to apply this method of dithering after the partially transparent pixels have been made opaque using either the color chosen for blending or the image color. The blending option determines which color is used.

- Choose the Use error diffusion dither option to apply this method of dithering after the partially transparent pixels have been made opaque using either the color chosen for blending or the image color. The blending option determines which color is used.

BLENDING PARTIALLY TRANSPARENT PIXELS

The second set of options determine whether partially transparent pixels are blended with another color or converted to total opacity using each pixel's color.

Choose one of the following options:

- Choose Yes to blend each partially transparent pixel with the color in the color box. To choose a new color, click in the color box to open the Image palette or Color dialog box. Right-click to open the Recent Colors dialog box. Partially transparent pixels below the value you enter are blended with this color.

- Choose No to increase each partially transparent pixel to 100% opacity using its color.

GIF Optimizer Colors Tab

GIF images have an 8-bit color depth, which means they can display up to 256 colors. Because these colors are stored in a palette, an image containing 256 or fewer colors is called a paletted image. Use the options in this tab to select the colors and type of palette used.

NUMBER OF COLORS You need to reduce your image to 256 or fewer colors. As you remove colors, the size of the file decreases, but so does the quality of the image. Use the preview boxes to help you determine the best balance between file size and image quality.

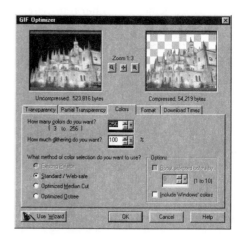

AMOUNT OF DITHERING Dithering refers to the way the program arranges pixels in an image to compensate for missing colors in the adjacent pixels. Use the preview boxes to help you determine the best setting.

TYPE OF PALETTE Choose one of the following palettes to use with the image:

- Choose the Existing Palette option if your image is already paletted and you want to use its palette.

- Choose the Standard/Web-safe option if your image will be used on the Web and you want it to display consistently on the viewers' monitors.

- Choose the Optimized Median Cut option if you need to reduce the image to only a few colors.

- Choose the Optimized Octree option if your original image contains only a few colors, and you want to keep those exact colors.

Depending on your needs, you may want to try both "Optimized" options and choose the one that gives you the best looking result or the smallest file size.

OPTIONS PANEL Boosting selected colors gives them more weight by a factor of the value you enter. The selected colors stand out from the rest of the image. To boost colors, make a selection of an area that contains these colors and then select this option. Select the "Include Windows' colors" check box to include the 16 standard Windows colors in the palette. If the image will be used on the Web, leave this check box selected.

GIF Optimizer Format Tab

Use this tab to choose the interlacing and version options.

INTERLACE OPTION The Interlace options determine how an image appears as it is downloaded. There are two choices:

- Non-interlaced, where the image downloads one line at a time, starting from the top, and

- Interlaced, where the image is displayed incrementally in several passes, and detail is added each time. Use this option with larger images so that the viewer can get an idea of how the image looks while waiting for it to download.

VERSION OPTION You must choose the 89a Version option to save transparency information. It is selected automatically if the image contains transparent pixels. Version 87a is available only if the image does not contain a transparency.

GIF Optimizer Download Times Tab

This tab displays the size of the compressed file and an estimate of the download time at four modem speeds. If the file size is too large, decrease it by clicking the Colors tab and reducing the number of colors.

Saving the File

After you have selected the options, click the OK button to open the Save As dialog box. Navigate to the folder in which you want to save the new image and type a name for the file. When you click Save, Paint Shop Pro saves a copy of the image as a GIF file and leaves the original image unchanged.

Using the GIF Wizard

The first page of the GIF Wizard opens when you click the Use Wizard button at the bottom left corner of the dialog box. It displays five pages that correspond to the dialog box tabs.

GIF Wizard Page 1

On the first page of the Wizard, choose the color that you want to make transparent. When the page opens, the color box displays the current background color. If the Wizard does not detect transparent information in the image, the page displays the following two options:

- No transparency, which you choose to create a GIF file that does not contain a transparency, and

- Convert matching colors to transparent, which you choose to create a GIF file containing a transparency.

To choose a color from the image, move the cursor over the image and click a color. You can
also click inside the color box to open the Color dialog box (24-bit images) or Image palette (8-bit images), or right-click it to open the Recent Colors dialog box.

If the Wizard detects a transparency in the image, it displays a third option. This option, which is for retaining the existing transparency in the final image, is chosen by default. To use a different transparent color, choose the second option and select the new color. Click the Next button to proceed to page 2.

GIF Wizard Page 2

On this page, you enter the background color of the Web page on which you will be using the image. When the page opens, the color box displays the current background color. Choose a new color from the image by moving the cursor over the image and clicking a color. You can also click inside the color box to open the Color dialog box (24-bit images) or Image palette (8-bit images), or right-click it to open the Recent Colors dialog box.

A GIF image cannot contain partially transparent pixels. If the image contains them, the Wizard blends them with the color you choose. Reducing layer opacity, adding a mask, feathering a selection, and using a brush set at reduced opacity are some of the actions that can produce partially transparent pixels. Click the Next button to proceed to page 3.

GIF Wizard Page 3

This page contains two Image palette options. Use the default Web-safe palette option to create an image that looks the best with most browsers. If you choose to use the other palette, some image colors may not display correctly when downloaded. Click the Next button to proceed to page 4.

GIF Wizard Page 4

Use the slider on this page to set the file size. As you drag the slider up, you increase the size by adding colors, which creates a better-looking image. As you drag the slider down, you remove colors, decrease the file size, and lower the image quality. Click the Next button to proceed to page 5, where you can view the image.

GIF Wizard Page 5

The final page displays the result of your settings. To change a setting, click the Back button to return to the previous pages. Click the Finish button to close the Wizard and open the Save As dialog box, where you type a name and select a location for saving the GIF file. The original image is not altered.

Optimizing a JPEG File

Paint Shop Pro provides a JPEG Optimizer feature to assist you in creating JPEG files. To use this feature, choose File > Export > JPEG Optimizer. The JPEG Optimizer dialog box opens. It displays "before" and "after" preview boxes so you can view the image as you select the settings. You can configure the settings using the tabs underneath the previews or click the Use Wizard button at the bottom left corner of the dialog box and let Paint Shop Pro guide you through the process.

Using the JPEG Optimizer Dialog Box

The JPEG Optimizer dialog box contains two tabs where you configure the settings and a third that displays estimated download times of the image at various modem speeds. Because JPEG uses lossy compression, which discards data, be sure to save the file as the final step and to save it only one time.

For information on using preview boxes, numeric edit controls, and other dialog box features, please read Chapter 3 of the "Getting Started" guide.

JPEG Optimizer Quality Tab

Use this tab to set a compression value for the file. JPEG uses lossy compression, which reduces the file size by deleting image information. This means that as you increase the compression, you lower the quality of the image. Use the image preview boxes to help you find the best balance between the two.

JPEG Optimizer Format Tab

The options on this tab determine how an image
appears as it is being loaded. There are two choices:

- Standard, where the image downloads one line
  a time, starting from the top, and

- Progressive, where the image is displayed incrementally in several passes, and detail is added
  each time. Use this option with larger images so
  that the viewer can get an idea of how the
  image looks while waiting for it to download.

JPEG Optimizer Download Times Tab

This tab displays the size of the compressed file
and an estimate of the download time at four
modem speeds. To change the file size, click the
Quality tab and increase or reduce the compression value.

Saving the File

After you have selected the options, click OK to
open the Save As dialog box. Navigate to the folder
in which you want to save the new image, and type
a name for the file. When you click Save, Paint
Shop Pro saves a copy of the image and leaves the
original image unchanged.

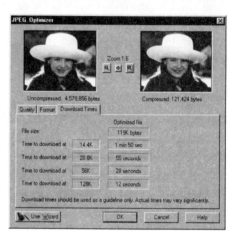

Using the JPEG Wizard

The first page of the JPEG Wizard opens when
you click the Use Wizard button at the bottom left corner of the dialog box. It displays two
pages that correspond to the tabs of the dialog box.

JPEG Wizard Page 1

Drag the slider on the first page of the Wizard to set the compression value. As the saved
file size decreases, so does the image quality. Click the Next button to proceed to page 2,
which displays the compressed image and its file size.

JPEG Wizard Page 2

The second page displays the compressed image and its file size. To change the compression
value, click the Back button to return to the previous page. Click the Finish button to close
the Wizard and open the Save As dialog box, where you type a name and select a location
for saving the JPEG file. The original image is not altered.

Optimizing a PNG File

Paint Shop Pro provides a PNG Optimizer feature to assist you in creating PNG files. To use this feature, choose File > Export > PNG Optimizer. The PNG Optimizer dialog box opens. It displays "before" and "after" preview boxes so you can view the image as you select the settings. You can configure the settings using the tabs underneath the previews or click the Use Wizard button at the bottom left corner of the dialog box and let Paint Shop Pro guide you through the process.

Using the PNG Optimizer Dialog Box

The PNG Optimizer dialog box contains three tabs where you configure the color, transparency, and format options of the file. The fourth page displays estimated download times of the image at various modem speeds. For information on using the preview boxes, numeric edit controls, and other dialog box features, please read Chapter 3 of the "Getting Started" guide.

PNG Optimizer Colors Tab

Use this tab to select a color depth for your PNG image. Remember that a 24-bit image is larger than an 8-bit image. While it can display more colors, it also takes more time to download. If you want to use the Alpha Transparency option (on the Transparency tab) with your image, you must choose either the Greyscale or 24-bit color option.

Images with an 8-bit color depth can display up to 256 colors. These colors are stored in the image palette. When you choose to create a Palette-Based image, the other options on this tab become available. Use them to select the colors and type of palette used.

NUMBER OF COLORS As mentioned, a paletted image contains 256 or fewer colors. As you remove colors, the size of the file decreases, but so does the quality of the image. Use the preview boxes to help you determine how small you can make the image without compromising quality.

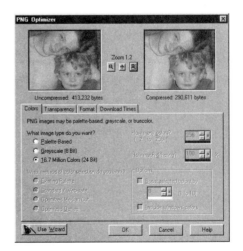

AMOUNT OF DITHERING Dithering refers to the way the program arranges pixels to compensate for missing colors in the adjacent pixels. Use the preview boxes to help you determine the best setting.

TYPE OF PALETTE Choose one of the following palettes to use with the image:

- Choose the Existing Palette option if your image is paletted and you want to use its palette.

- Choose the Standard/Web-safe option if your image will be used on the Web and you want it to display consistently on the viewers' monitors.

- Choose the Optimized Median Cut option if you need to reduce the image to only a few colors.

- Choose the Optimized Octree option if your original image contains only a few colors, and you want to keep those exact colors.

Depending on your needs, you may want to try both "Optimized" options and choose the one that gives you the best looking result or the smallest file size.

OPTIONS PANEL Boosting selected colors gives them more weight by a factor of the value you enter. The selected colors stand out from the rest of the image. To boost colors, make a selection of an area that contains these colors, and then select this option. Select the "Include Windows' colors" check box to include the 16 standard Windows colors in the palette. If the image will be used on the Web, leave this check box selected.

PNG Optimizer Transparency Tab

To save your image without a transparency, select the No transparency option. To create a transparency from a selection, make the selection before opening the dialog box.

To have one color become transparent, select the Single Color Transparency option. You can then select the "Existing image or layer transparency" if your image contains transparency, or you can select the "Areas that match this color" option if it doesn't. If the image contains a selection, the Inside and Outside the current selection options are also available.

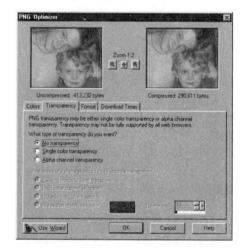

If you selected the Greyscale or 24-bit color depth option on the Colors tab, the Alpha Channel Transparency option is available.

The Single Color Transparency option usually creates a smaller file than the Alpha Channel Transparency option, but selecting it causes the image to lose existing alpha channel transparency.

After you have determined the type of transparency for the image, select one of the "What areas of the image would you like to be transparent?" choices.

There are four options:

- Existing image or layer transparency, which is available if the image contains transparency information,

- Inside the current selection, which is available for images that contain a selection,

- Outside the current selection, which is available for images that contain a selection, and

- Areas that match the color in the box. You can select any color. To choose a color from the image, move the cursor over the image and click a color. You can also click inside the color box to open the Color dialog box (24-bit images) or Image palette (8-bit images), or right-click it to open the Recent Colors dialog box. Set a tolerance factor for the color. The tolerance factor indicates how closely colors must match the color in the box before they become transparent.

PNG Optimizer Format Tab

Use this tab to determine how an image appears as it is downloaded. It is similar to the GIF Optimizer Format tab on page 307.

There are two choices:

- Non-interlaced, where the image downloads one line at a time, starting from the top, and

- Interlaced, where the image is displayed incrementally in several passes, and detail is added each time. Use this option with larger images so that the viewer can get an idea of how the image looks while waiting for it to download.

PNG Optimizer Download Times Tab

This tab displays the size of the compressed file and an estimate of the download time at four modem speeds. If the file size is too large, decrease it by clicking the Colors tab and reducing the number of colors.

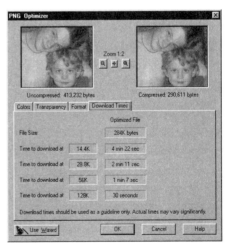

Saving the File

After you have selected the options, click OK to open the Save As dialog box. Navigate to the folder in which you want to save the new image, and type a name for the file. When you click Save, Paint Shop Pro saves a copy of the image and leaves the original image unchanged.

Using the PNG Wizard

The first page of the PNG Wizard opens when you click the Use Wizard button at the bottom left corner of the dialog box. For information on using this feature, please refer to the Help file within Paint Shop Pro.

🎬 Previewing an Image in a Web Browser

If you have a Web browser installed on your computer, you can use the Paint Shop Pro or Animation Shop Preview in Web Browser feature to see how your active image or animation will look on the Web. Preview Bitmap, GIF, JPEG, and PNG files in Paint Shop Pro; preview Animated Gif and AVI files in Animation Shop. To use this feature, open the Preview in Web Browser dialog box by choosing View > Preview in Web Browser in either program.

NOTE: *You must have at least one Web browser installed on your computer before you can preview an image.*

Before viewing your active image, select the options on file formats, browsers, Web page background color, and image dimensions to be used when displaying it.

Using the Preview in Web Browser Dialog Box

To use the Preview in Web Browser Dialog Box:

1. The Formats box lists the image formats in which you can view your image. Click to select as many as you want to use. The browser will display an HTML page containing a separate image for each format.

2. The Web browsers box displays the browsers you have selected on the Web Browsers tab of the File Locations dialog box. Click to select the browsers to use for viewing the image. If the list is empty, click the Edit Web Browser button to open the Web Browsers tab. Locate up to three browsers you want to be able to use for displaying your image, and click OK. For more information on using the File Locations dialog box, please refer to Chapter 20, "Setting Preferences."

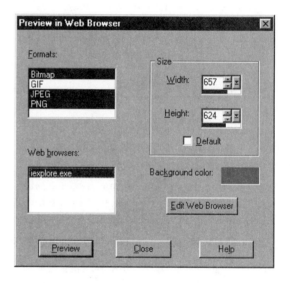

3. Use the Size panel to select a new pixel width and height for the image. To keep the original dimensions of the image, select the Default check box. Note that the resizing is done using HTML rather than Paint Shop Pro or Animation Shop.

4. To select a background color for the Web Page on which the image will be displayed, left-click the Background color box to open the Jasc Color dialog box or right-click it to open the Recent Color dialog box.

5. Click the Preview button. If you selected the Bitmap format from the Formats box (see Step 1), Paint Shop Pro launches the Web Browser and displays the image. If you have chosen any other format, the program opens the appropriate Optimization dialog box. Select your choices for optimizing the image and click OK.

6. The Web browser or browsers display your image or animation in the selected formats. For each format, the browser displays the file size, color depth, and approximate download times at different modem speeds.

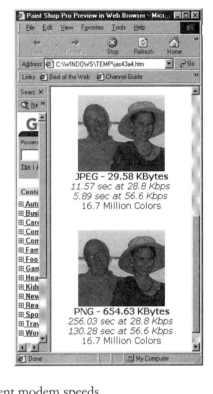

Image Mapping

You can use the Paint Shop Pro Image Mapper dialog box to create image maps for your Web pages. An image map is a graphic that contains a hotspot, or map area, that usually is a link to a URL. The hotspot can be a circle, rectangle, or irregular shape. When a user moves the mouse over this area, the cursor changes to display a hand. When he or she clicks the hotspot, the browser jumps to the assigned destination, usually a new Web page.

To open the dialog box, choose File > Export > Image Mapper.

Using the Image Mapper Dialog Box

NOTE: *The Image Mapper affects the active image. Before opening the dialog box, select the image you want to map.*

The preview area of the dialog box displays the active image. Use the Zoom In, Zoom Out, and Navigation buttons underneath it to change your view of the image. Use the Proof button to view your image in your Web browser.

To map an image, you create the map area, assign the URL and other properties to it, and save the map files. When you save the files, Paint Shop Pro generates the HTML code that you paste into the code for your web page. The settings for the map areas can be saved so that they can be loaded into the same or other images. Also, you can choose to create rollovers for the areas. Rollovers are graphics that the hotspot displays when the user makes a specified mouse action. For example, you can have a new image appear in the hotspot when the user clicks it.

Using the Tools to Create and Edit Map Areas

The Tools panel contains the tools you use to create and edit the image map areas. To activate a tool, click its button. The button of the active tool appears pressed in. As you create and edit map areas, you may want to magnify the image. When the image is too large to fit within the preview box, drag it with the Pan tool to bring other parts of it into view.

To create a map area:

1. Click the Rectangle tool ☐, Circle tool ◯, or Polygon tool ⌐⌐ to activate it.

2. To create a rectangle or circle, click the image in the preview box (not the original image) and drag the cursor until the area you want to make into the hotspot is enclosed.

   • The Rectangle tool starts the square or rectangle at one of the corners.

   • The Circle tool begins at the center of the circle.

3. The Polygon encloses an area using straight line segments. To create a polygon, click the image in the preview box to set the starting point, move the cursor to where you want the line to change directions, and click the image. Continue moving the cursor and clicking the image to change the direction of the line.

   To complete the polygon, return to and click the starting point or right-click the image. When you right-click the image, Paint Shop Pro creates a line back to the starting point.

To change the shape of a map area, use the Arrow tool ⬉ or Mover tool ✛.

   • Click and drag the upper left or lower right corner of a rectangle.

   • Click and drag a circle by the dot at its upper left or lower right.

   • Click and drag any of the point along a polygon.

To move the entire outline of the map area within the image, use the Mover tool. Click inside the area and drag the shape.

To remove a map area from the image, click it with the Delete tool ⬤. To delete all the map areas and return the image to its original state, click the Clear button.

Map Preferences Dialog Box

The Map Preferences dialog box opens when you click the Preferences button of the Image Mapper dialog box. Use it to select new colors for the grid and lines and for the border of the active cell and to control how many entries the URL and Alt text drop-down boxes display.

Assigning Map Area Properties

After you have created the map areas, use the drop-down boxes in the Object Properties panel to assign URLs, alternate text, and targets to them.

To assign object properties:

1. Make a map area active by clicking inside it with the Arrow or Eraser tool. The positions of its boundaries are displayed in the lower portion of the Object Properties panel.

NOTE: *In the URL drop-down box, type the address of the Web page to which you want to link the area. Click the box to display and select addresses already used in the image.*

NOTE: *In the Alt text box, type alternate text that the browser can display* 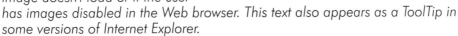 *image doesn't load or if the user* 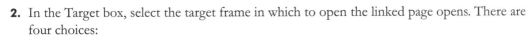 *has images disabled in the Web browser. This text also appears as a ToolTip in some versions of Internet Explorer.*

2. In the Target box, select the target frame in which to open the linked page opens. There are four choices:

   • _blank loads the linked page in a new browser window.

   • _parent loads the linked page in the parent window or frameset of the link. If the link is not in a nested frame, the image loads in the full browser window.

   • _self loads the linked page in the same window or frame as the link.

   • _top loads the linked page in the full browser window and removes all frames.

3. To assign a rollover to a map area, click the Rollover Creator button. Please refer to page 318 for information on creating rollovers.

Choosing Format and Optimization Settings

Optimizing an image reduces its file size so that it loads more quickly. Use the Format panel to save and optimize the image in the following way:

1. Click the drop-down box and select a file format in which to save the image. Your choices are GIF, JPEG, and PNG.

2. To optimize the image, click the Optimize Image button. The appropriate Optimize dialog box for the selected format opens.

Saving and Loading the Map Settings

When you save the Map settings, you save the map area arrangement and the information from the Object Properties, Rollovers, and Format panels. You can then re-load them into the same or use the settings with a different image.

To save the map settings:

1. Click the Save Settings button. The Save Map Settings dialog box opens.

2. Navigate to the folder in which you want to save the settings file. The file is saved in the JMD format.

3. Type a name for the file and click Save.

To load the map settings:

1. Click the Load Settings button. The Load Map Settings dialog box opens.

2. Navigate to and select the JMD file you want to load.

3. Click Open.

Previewing the Image in a Web Browser

You can preview your map areas and rollovers in a Web browser at any time by clicking the Proof button underneath the image preview. The Web browser opens and displays your image. You must have at least one Web browser installed on your computer to preview the image. For more information on using the Preview in Web Browser feature, please refer to page 314.

Image Rollover Creation

A rollover is an image or section of an image that changes appearance when the user activates it. It can also be linked to a URL. Web designers frequently create rollovers for the buttons of a navigation bar. When a user clicks a button, the browser displays the linked Web page (or file), and the rollover area displays a different button.

You can assign a rollover to an image slice (cell) or hot spot (map area) by choosing a file for the slice or area to display when the user performs a specific mouse action. Use the Rollover Creator dialog box to choose the mouse action and the rollover.

To open the Rollover Creator dialog box, click the Rollover Creator button in either the Image Slicer or Image Mapper dialog box.

Rollover Creator Dialog Box

You can assign rollovers to individual image slices (cells) and map areas using the Rollover Creator dialog box.

To select the file for the active rollover area and the mouse action that activates it:

1. Make a cell or area active by clicking it with the Arrow tool. or Eraser tool. For a map area, use the Arrow or Mover tool.

2. Click the Rollover Creator button in the Rollovers panel. The Rollover Creator dialog box opens.

3. Select the check box of the action you want used to activate the rollover.

4. In the Rollovers panel, click the Open icon to the right of the File box. The Select Rollover dialog box opens.

5. Navigate to and select the graphics file you want to use.

6. Click Open. The File box displays the file path.

7. For each action you want associated with a rollover, select the check box and associate a rollover file.

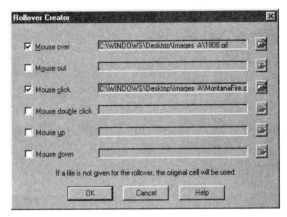

8. Click Close to close the dialog box and return to the Image Mapper or Slicer dialog box.

Image Slicing

When you slice an image, you divide it into several smaller sections that you can save in different formats or at different levels of optimization. Because these optimized sections take less time to download than one large image, your Web pages will load more quickly.

Slicing an image also can reduce the number of graphics you need to save. If your Web site displays the same logo or other graphic in more than one image, you only need to save that section once if you slice the images; you reload the same logo or graphic section into all the images.

The Paint Shop Pro Slicer works by creating a table from the image, saving the location of each sliced section as a cell in the table, and generating the HTML code for the table and cells. You copy this code to your source files so that the image can be reassembled when the user downloads the Web page.

The Image Slicer can also create rollovers, which are areas that display secondary images when the user clicks or moves a mouse over them.

To open the Image Slicer dialog box, choose File > Export > Image Slicer.

NOTE: *The Image Slicer affects the active image. Select the image you want to slice before opening the dialog box.*

Using the Image Slicer Dialog Box

Use the Image Slicer dialog box to slice an image by dividing it into rectangles, called cells, based on grids and lines. The cells can be save in different formats or at different levels of optimization.

You can also create rollovers, which are cells that display secondary images when the user clicks or moves a mouse over them.

The preview area of the dialog box displays the active image. Use the Zoom In, Zoom Out, and Navigation buttons underneath it to change your view of the image. Click the Proof button to view the image in your Web browser.

Using the Tools to Create and Edit Cells

The Tools panel contains the tools you use to divide the image into cells and to edit the cell boundaries. To activate a tool, click its button. The button of the active tool appears pressed in. As you work with the cells, you may want to magnify the image. When the image is too large to fit within the preview window, drag it with the Pan tool to bring other parts of it into view.

To create the cells:

1. Click either the Grid ⊞ or Line tool ✎ to activate it.

- Use the Grid tool to create evenly spaced and sized cells.

- Use the Line tool to isolate a specific area, such as a logo, that you want to save.

2. Click the image. The two tools differ in the way they work:

- Clicking with the Grid tool opens the Grid Size dialog box, where you set the number of rows and columns. To create a grid within an existing cell, click inside the cell.

- Clicking with the Line tool creates a vertical or horizontal line across any cell into which you drag the cursor. To create a vertical line, click and drag vertically; to create a horizontal line, click and drag horizontally.

To move a line or grid border:

1. Click the Arrow ↖ or Line tool ✎ .

2. Move the cursor over a line.

3. When the cursor changes to the double-sided arrow, click and drag the line to a new position. To move only the segment within the current cell, press the <Shift> key before clicking the line.

Note that you can move lines up to, but not across, adjacent parallel lines. Also, you can move individual lines and lines that are part of a grid. As you drag a line, Paint Shop Pro moves the longest segment that can be repositioned without creating a non-rectangular cell.

To delete a line or grid border:

1. Click the Eraser tool ✐ and move the cursor over the line.

2. When the cursor changes to the Eraser, click to delete the line. If deleting the line would create an invalid area, Paint Shop Pro displays an icon ⊗ to indicate that you cannot erase the line.

Slice Preferences Dialog Box

Click the Preferences button of the Image Slicer dialog box to open the Slice Preferences dialog box. Select new colors for the grid and lines and for the border of the active cell, select the number of URL and Alt text entries for the drop-down boxes to display, and choose whether to be prompted for file location and name when you save the slices and the HTML code.

Assigning Cell Properties

Assign a URL, alternate text, and target to the cell in the Cell Properties panel. You also set whether the cell should appear in the downloaded image. By omitting cells, you can add cells from other images (such as logos or text) and create images in non-rectangular shapes.

To assign cell properties:

1. Make a cell active by clicking inside it with the Arrow tool or Eraser tool. The positions of the cell boundary lines are displayed in the lower portion of the Cell Properties panel.

2. In the URL drop-down box, type the address of the Web page where you want the cell to appear. Click the arrow in the box to display and select addresses already used in the image.

3. In the Alt text box, type alternate text that the browser can display while the cell is downloading, if the cell doesn't download, or if the user has images disabled in the Web browser. This text also appears as a ToolTip in some versions of Internet Explorer.

4. In the Target box, select the target frame or window in which you want the image to open. There are four choices:

   • _blank loads the image in a new browser window.

   • _parent loads the image in the parent window or frameset of the link. If the link is not in a nested frame, the image loads into the full browser window.

   • _self loads the image in the same window or frame as the link.

- _top loads the image in the full browser window and removes all frames.

5. By default, the "Include cell in table" check box is selected, and the cell appears in the image. To omit the cell from the downloaded image, clear the check box.

6. To assign a rollover to a map area, click the Rollover Creator button. Please refer to page 318 for information on creating rollovers.

Applying a Format and Optimization Setting

Optimizing an image reduces its file size so that it loads more quickly. Use the Format panel to save and optimize the cell in the following way:

1. Make the slice active by clicking inside it with the Arrow or Eraser tool.

2. Click the drop-down box and select a file format in which to save the slice. Your choices are GIF, JPEG, and PNG.

3. To optimize the cell file, click the Optimize Cell button. The appropriate Optimize dialog box for the selected format opens.

4. To save all cells in the same format with the same optimization settings, select the "Apply optimization to whole image" check box.

Saving and Loading the Settings

When you save the settings, you save the cell arrangement and the information from the Cell Properties, Rollovers, and Format panels. You can then re-load them into the same image or use them with a different image.

To save the slice settings:

1. Click the Save Settings button. The Save Slice Settings dialog box opens.

2. Navigate to the folder in which you want to save the settings file. The file is saved in the JSD format.

3. Type a name for the file and click Save.

To load the slice settings:

1. Click the Load Settings button. The Load Slice Settings dialog box opens.

2. Select the JSD file you want to load and click Open.

If you are loading a grid to a different image, Paint Shop Pro automatically adjusts the grid size if the dimensions of the image are not the same.

Previewing the Image in a Web Browser

You can preview your cells and rollovers in a Web browser at any time by clicking the Proof button. The Web browser opens and displays your image. You must have at least one Web browser installed on your computer to preview the image. For more information on using the Preview in Web Browser feature, please refer to page 314.

Saving the Slice Files and Generating the HTML Code

When the Image Slicer generates the HTML code for the positions of the cell slices, it also saves each slice to a file. This information is used for reassembling the image on a Web page.

To save the HTML file and files of individual slices:

1. Click the Save or Save As button the first time you save the settings for the image. The HTML Save As dialog box opens. If you continue editing the image, click Save to update the changes to the original file.

2. Choose a folder and title for the HTML file.

3. Click the OK button.

4. If you have previously selected the "Prompt for image folder on Save or Save As" check box in the Slicer Preferences dialog box, the Image Slice Save As dialog box opens. You can choose to save the individual slice files in a new folder and to rename them. The name of each file automatically includes its row and column number.

Click the Save to Clipboard button to open the HTML Destination Browse box. Use this dialog box to navigate to the folder where you want to save the HTML code.

Exporting Images to StudioAvenue.com

The StudioAvenue.com Web site is a place for users of Jasc Software products to display their images. Your free StudioAvenue.com membership gives you 50MB of space to store as many pictures and albums as you want. Friends and family members can then visit the site and view your pictures.

To place your pictures on the site, choose File > Export StudioAvenue.com to open the Studio Avenue Upload dialog box. You can choose this command from the File > Export menu of both the Browser and main window. In the Browser, you can also right-click any selected thumbnail and choose Send To StudioAvenue.com from the pop-up menu. Before choosing the command from the Browser, select the thumbnails of pictures you want to copy to the site.

Registering with StudioAvenue.com

Before you send images to the Web site, you need to register. Registration is free and gives you space at StudioAvenue.com for displaying your images.

You can register in one of two ways:

- By navigating to the StudioAvenue.com site and completing the registration form, or

- By entering the information in the StudioAvenue.com New User dialog box.

To register using the StudioAvenue.com New User dialog box:

1. Click the New User button in the Login panel. The Studio-Avenue.com New User dialog box opens.

2. Type the appropriate information in each box. You must enter information in all the boxes.

3. To read the Terms & Conditions, click the View Site button to open StudioAvenue.com in your browser. Close the browser after you have read the information.

4. To complete the registration, click the I Accept button. The dialog box closes, and your user name and password appear in the Send to StudioAvenue.com dialog box.

You are now registered and can upload images.

To register at the StudioAvenue.com Web site:

1. Click the View Site button at the lower right of the dialog box. Your browser navigates to Jasc StudioAvenue.com.

2. Click the Start Here button at the upper left of the StudioAvenue.com page. The Registration page opens.

3. Type the requested information and choose a password.

4. Click the Submit button.

If you need more help or have questions about this site, please refer to the Help files at the StudioAvenue.com site. You are now registered and can upload images.

Uploading Images to StudioAvenue.com

To upload images to an album on StudioAvenue.com:

1. If your User name and Password are not displayed in the Login panel, type them. Select the Save password check box to have your password automatically entered each time you open the dialog box.

2. Create an album by typing a name in the Album name text box. If you are adding images to an existing album, type in that album's name. Because all images are stored in an album, you must type a name before you can upload the images.

3. If you have opened the dialog box from the main window, the selected image appears in the Images list. You can upload any image that is open or minimized in the workspace. To add images, click the Add button. When the Select Images list box opens, select the check boxes of the images you want to add and clear those you want to remove. Note that if you have opened the dialog box

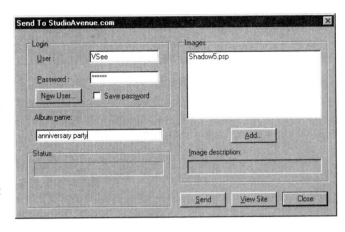

from the Paint Shop Pro Browser, the names of the selected thumbnails appear in the Images list. To select other thumbnails to upload, close the dialog box, select new thumbnails, and re-open the dialog box.

4. To include a description of an image, highlight it in the list and type up to 150 characters in the Image description box. The description appears below the image when a viewer selects it from the album.

5. To upload the images, click Send. As the images are sent to StudioAvenue.com, the Status panel displays messages on the progress of the upload.

When images are uploaded, they are converted to JPEG files. If an image is paletted, its color depth is increased to 24 bits.

Sending an Image Using E-mail

You can use Paint Shop Pro to e-mail any image open or minimized in the workspace. Paint Shop Pro opens a new e-mail message containing the image. The image is in its current file format whenever possible.

- To send the image, choose File > Send or click the Send Mail button on the toolbar.

Using Digital Watermarks

A digital watermark is a permanent proof of authenticity for an image. While a computer can detect it, it is imperceptible to the viewer. A water-mark contains information about the creator, the

Watermark Symbol on Image Title Bar

copyright, and the image. When a viewer chooses to see this information, the program opens a dialog box that also contains a link to the Digimarc Web page, which displays contact information for the artist.

NOTE: *An image can contain only one watermark. You cannot embed a new watermark in an image that already contains one.*

Embedding a Digital Watermark

A digital watermark can only be embedded in an image once. Because its quality may be degraded by further changes to the image, you should apply it to a flattened copy of the finished image. If you try to embed a watermark in a layered image, Paint Shop Pro displays a message recommending that you flatten the image before proceeding. To embed a watermark, choose Image > Watermarking > Embed Watermark to open the Embed Watermark dialog box.

Using the Embed Watermark Dialog Box

Use this dialog box to choose the information you want a watermark to contain. You can select the following options: creator ID, image copyright dates, image attributes and restrictions on use, and watermark durability. You can change the copyright date, image attributes, and durability each time you embed a watermark. You only need to configure the Creator ID the first time you use this dialog box.

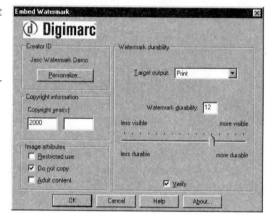

CREATING A PERSONAL IDENTIFICATION

Initially, Creator ID is set to "Jasc Watermark Demo." To receive your own Creator ID, you need to register with Digimarc. To do this, click the Personalize button to open the Personalize Creator ID dialog box.

ENTERING THE COPYRIGHT DATES

You can type either one or two years in the copyright boxes. Digimarc accepts years from 1922 to the present. If you try to enter a year before 1922, a message appears asking you to choose a year from 1922 to the present.

CHOOSING THE IMAGE ATTRIBUTES

The Image Attributes are the restrictions shown when the program displays the watermark information. Select the check boxes of the attributes you want to apply to the image.

SELECTING THE WATERMARK DURABILITY

The durability you choose depends on how the image will be displayed. When the image will be printed, stronger watermarks are recommended. When the image will be displayed on a monitor, weaker watermarks are better because they are not as visible. While stronger watermarks are easier to detect, harder to remove, and longer lasting, they are also more visible in the image. You can make two copies of the image and apply a stronger watermark to the copy you are printing and a weaker one to the copy you are displaying electronically.

To set the watermark durability:

1. Select Monitor or Print from the Target Output drop-down box after determining how you will display the image. If you select the Print option for an image with a resolution under 300 dpi, Paint Shop Pro displays a message recommending that you increase the image resolution before embedding the watermark.

2. To set the watermark strength, type a number from 1 to 16 in the Watermark Durability box, drag the slider below it, or use the default values. The default for the Monitor option is 8; for the print option, it is 12.

To verify that the watermark information is embedded correctly, select the "Verify" check mark. The program checks that the watermark has been applied and displays its attributes and durability.

Personalizing the Creator ID

Initially, Paint Shop Pro's watermark Creator ID is set to "Jasc Watermark Demo." Customizing the watermark with your own identification number is a two-step process:

* First, you register with Digimarc to obtain your own ID number. (This service is free.)

* Second, you enter the information in the Personalize Creator ID dialog box.

REGISTERING WITH DIGIMARC

If your computer has Web access, do the following to obtain a personal identification number:

1. Click Register. Your Web browser opens and navigates to the Digimarc Web page.

2. Follow the on-screen instructions to receive a Creator ID number, a PIN number, and a password. You may want to write them down for later use.

3. Close the browser to return to the Personalize Creator ID dialog box.

If your computer does not have Web access, you can phone Digimarc using the toll-free number displayed below the URL to register and receive your Creator ID number, a PIN number, and a password.

ENTERING YOUR INFORMATION

To personalize the watermark:

1. Type the PIN and Creator ID numbers in the appropriate boxes.

2. Click OK to close this dialog box.

3. Click OK to close the Embed Watermark dialog box. If the "Verify" check box is selected, the Embed Watermark: Verify dialog box opens.

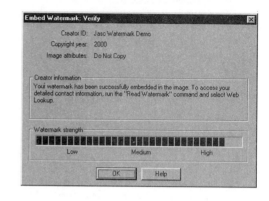

Verifying an Embedded Watermark

If you have selected the "Verify" check box in the Embed Watermark dialog box, the Embed Watermark: Verify dialog box appears. It lets you know that the watermark has been embedded and displays the creator, copyright, image attribute, and durability information from the Embed Watermark dialog box.

Reading a Watermark

Whenever Paint Shop Pro opens an image, it automatically checks for a digital watermark. If one is detected, the program displays a copyright symbol in front of the filename on the title bar. You can view the watermark information by choosing Image >Image Information, and then clicking the Watermark Information tab.

While most watermarks are detected, some may be too weak to read. To do a more thorough search, use the Read Watermark command by choosing Image > Watermarking > Read Watermark. If Paint Shop Pro does not detect a watermark, it displays a message stating that no watermark was found. If it detects a watermark, it opens the Watermark Information dialog box.

If your computer is connected to the Web, click the Web Lookup button to open your browser and view the Digimarc database page that displays information about the creator.

Printing Images and Thumbnails

With Paint Shop Pro, you can print one image on a page, several images on a page, or use the Browser to print thumbnails of the images in a specific folder.

Factors to Consider When Printing

Image Resolution Laser and ink-jet printers work by applying dots of black or colored ink to the paper. While the image resolution is measured in pixels per inch (ppi), the printer resolution is measured in dots per inch (dpi). To determine the printed image size in inches, the printer divides the image size in pixels by the pixels per inch. An image with a high resolution appears smaller when printed at its original size than an image with a low resolution.

You can change the size of the printed image by changing the Scale value in the Page Setup dialog box. However, this can lower the quality of the print, as it enlarges each pixel. You will get better results if you create the image using a resolution that is appropriate for the printer. Use the following guidelines to determine the image size for printing:

- For a printer that prints 300 dpi use an image set at 72 to 120 ppi.

- For a printer that prints 600 dpi, use an image set at 125 to 170 ppi.

- For a printer that prints 1200 dpi, use an image set at 150 to 200 ppi.

Image Color and Lightness Computer monitors display color by combining red (R), green (G) and blue (B) color light on the screen. Color printers, however, use a combination of cyan (C), magenta (M), yellow (Y), and black (K) ink. The difference in these two color modes can cause images to appear darker on paper than on the screen. As you become familiar with how your printer handles color, you will be able to adjust your images to compensate. If the printed image appears too dark, you can use the Brightness/Contrast command to adjust it.

Paper Quality The texture and color of the paper affects the quality of the image printed on it. Porous paper can cause colors to bleed into each other; colored paper can alter the image colors; off-white paper can reduce the contrast and vibrancy of colors. For the best results, you should use "bright white, coated" paper.

Saving an Image for Printing

If you are printing your image on a personal printer, save it in the .psp format. This gives you the most flexibility. Paint Shop Pro prints all the layers in an image, so you don't need to flatten it. If you are using a black-and-white printer, choose the Greyscale option in the Page Setup dialog box.

If you are sending the image to a printing service, you should flatten the image before saving it. Ask the printer about the requirements for file format, resolution, and color depth. If CMYK color separations are needed, you can print them by choosing that option in the Page Setup dialog box.

Printing a Single Image

Choosing the Page Setup Options

Paint Shop Pro can print CMYK separations and negative images can place a background color around the image. Select these options, as well as the page orientation, margin width, image size, and type of output, in the Page Setup dialog box before printing your image.

To use the Page Setup dialog box:

1. Open the dialog box in one of the following ways:

   • Choosing File > Page Setup, or

   • Clicking the Setup button in the Image Print Preview window.

2. In the "Paper" panel, select the paper size and its source.

3. Select one of the following page orientations:

   • Portrait orientation places the top of the image against one of the page's narrow sides.

   • Landscape orientation places the top of the image against one of the page's wide sides.

4. In the "Position" panel, select from the following image placement options:

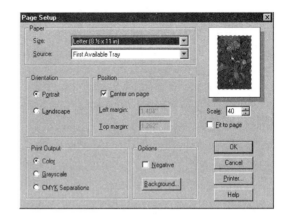

- Select the "Center on page" check mark to place the image in the middle of the page. The margin boxes are unavailable when you select this check box.

- To place the image elsewhere on the page, enter the appropriate values in the margin boxes. The left and top margins indicate the position on the page of the image's left and top edges.

5. Choose from the following size options:

- Select the "Fit to page" check box to enlarge or reduce the image size to cover as much of the page as possible. Selecting this check box makes the "Position" panel options unavailable.

- To print the image at a different size, enter a percent of the original size in the Scale box.

6. Select one of the following Print Output options:

- Select the Color option to print the image in color. You must have a color printer to print in color.

- Select the Greyscale option to convert an image to greyscale. Paint Shop Pro will replace the colors in the image with greys of equal luminance. The effect is similar to a black-and-white photograph.

- Select the CMYK Separations option to enable CMYK color separations. Paint Shop Pro will generate 4 separate greyscale prints, each representing one CMYK color.

7. To print a negative of the image, select the "Negative" check box in the "Options" panel. This replaces each color with its opposite.

8. To print a color on the page around the image, click the Background button to open the Color dialog box, where you can choose a color.

9. Click the Printer button to select a different printer.

10. Click the OK button to close the dialog box and save the settings.

Previewing the Printed Image
Using the Print Preview Window

Use the Print Preview window to see how the image will look when printed. To activate this view, choose File > Print Preview or click the Print Preview toolbar button. The Print Preview window opens. It displays the image within an outline of the page. There are five buttons across the top of the window: Print, Setup, Zoom In, Zoom Out, and Close.

PRINT BUTTON Click it to close the Print Preview window and open the Print dialog box.

SETUP BUTTON Click it to close the Print Preview window and open the Page Setup dialog box, where you can resize the image and make other changes. Click the OK button to close the dialog box and return to the Print Preview window.

ZOOM IN AND ZOOM OUT BUTTONS Click them to change the magnification level. You can also zoom in and out by clicking the image.

CLOSE BUTTON Click it to close the Print Preview window and return to the Paint Shop Pro workspace. You can also close the window by clicking the Close button on the title bar.

Using the Full Screen Preview

The Full Screen Preview mode displays the image against a black background that covers the screen.

*   To see an image in the Full Screen Preview mode, choose View > Full Screen Preview, press <Shift> + <Ctrl> + <A>, or click the Full Screen Preview button on the toolbar.

*   To close the Full Screen Preview mode, either left-click the mouse or press any key on the keyboard.

Printing the Image

After you select the Page Setup dialog box options and preview the image, you are ready to print it. Use the Print dialog box to print one image at a time. If you want to print more than one image on a page, choose the Print Multiple Images command. To print thumbnails, open the Browser and print from it.

To print a single image:

1. Open the Print dialog box by choosing File > Print, pressing <Ctrl> + <P>, clicking the Print button in the Print Preview window, or clicking the Print button on the toolbar.

2. Select a printer in the Name box.

3. To print registration or crop marks, select their check boxes in the "Print Options" panel. If you typed a title in the Creator Information tab of the Current Image Information dialog box, you can select to print it. If there is no Creator Information, the filename is used.

4. To print the image to a file rather than to paper, select the "Print to file" check box. Clicking the Print button opens the Print to File dialog box, where you can choose a location and name for the new file.

5. Set the number of copies you want to print.

6. Click the OK button. Paint Shop Pro sends the file to the printer or opens the Print to File dialog box.

Printing Multiple Images on a Page

Use the Print Multiple Images feature when you want to print more than one image on a single sheet of paper. The command opens a WYSIWYG (What You See Is What You Get) window that displays a blank page and thumbnails of the images. You can arrange and resize the images to fit as many as you want on the paper. If you prefer to let the program place them, use the Auto Arrange feature.

• To open the Multiple Image Printing window, choose File > Print Multiple Images.

About the Multiple Image Printing Window

When you open this window, it displays a blank page in the workspace. Any images open or minimized in Paint Shop Pro appear as thumbnails along the left side.

To open an image, you can either drag the thumbnail to the page or workspace, or double-click its thumbnail. The image appears in the upper left corner of the page. You can then arrange, rotate, and resize the images by choosing the menu commands, clicking the desired toolbar button, or dragging with the mouse. If you need to print your images more than once, you can save the layout and use it again.

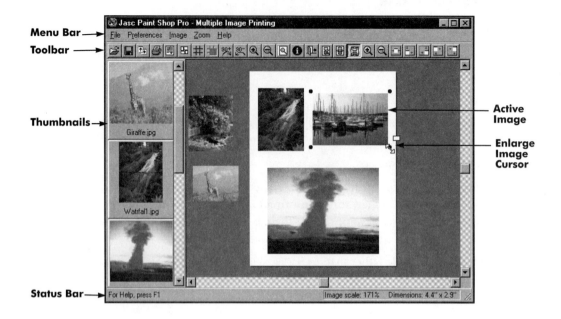

Using the Multiple Image Printing Toolbar

The Multiple Image Printing toolbar appears only when the Multiple Image Printing window is open. The toolbar contains buttons for accessing frequently used menu commands in the window. To see the name of a button, place the cursor over it without clicking. This toolbar cannot be customized, moved, or hidden.

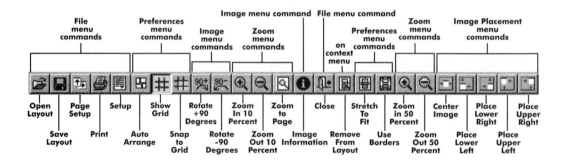

Using the Context Menus

You can access the most frequently used commands by right-clicking the image, the page, or the workspace. Right-clicking the image displays the image context menu; right-clicking the page or the workspace displays the window context menu.

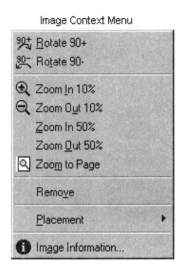

Image Context Menu

Window Context Menu

Viewing Image Information

You can open the Current Image Information dialog box to view information about an image that is open.

- Click the image to make it active, and then click the Image Information toolbar button, choose Image > Image Information, or right-click the image and choose Image Information from the context menu.

Using the Zoom Commands

As you arrange images, you may want to change the magnification level (size) of the page. It changes automatically when you resize the window automatically. When you want to adjust the page magnification without altering the window size, use the Zoom commands.

To access the commands, you can choose a command from the Zoom menu, click one of the Zoom toolbar buttons, or right-click the paper, an image, or the workspace and choose a command from the context menu.

ZOOM IN 10% AND ZOOM OUT 10% COMMANDS Choose these commands or click the toolbar buttons to change the page size/magnification in smaller increments. Each time you click the toolbar button or choose one of the commands from the menu, the page either increases or decreases by 10% of its current size.

ZOOM IN 50% AND ZOOM OUT 50% COMMANDS Choose these commands or click the toolbar buttons to change the page size/magnification quickly. Each time you choose one of the commands, the page either increases or decreases by 50% of its current size.

ZOOM TO PAGE COMMAND Choose this command or click the toolbar button to resize the page so that it fits in the window. If you inadvertently scroll the window or drag the page and can't see it, use this command to center the page in the window.

Using the Print Multiple Images Grid

Use the grid to help you align images evenly on the page. You can change the grid color, display it using lines or dots, and configure its spacing in inches or centimeters. Select these preferences in the Print Preview Setup dialog box of the window.

DISPLAYING AND HIDING THE GRID

- To display the grid, choose Preferences > Show Grid, click the Show Grid button on the toolbar, or right-click the page or workspace and choose Show Grid from the menu.

- When the grid is visible, its buttons on the menus and toolbar appear pressed in. Choose the command or click the button again to make the grid invisible.

USING THE SNAP TO GRID FEATURE

The Snap to Grid function automatically places the images along the grid. When you release an image, Paint Shop Pro moves it until the edges are aligned with the nearest grid lines. Choosing the Snap to Grid command does not affect images already placed on the page. You need to move an image again to align it.

NOTE: *You must choose the Show Grid command before you can activate this feature.*

- To use the feature, choose Preferences > Snap to Grid, click the Snap to Grid toolbar button, or right-click the page or workspace and choose Snap to Grid from the menu.

- When the Snap to Grid function is active, its buttons on the menus and toolbar appear pressed in. Choose the command or click the button again to turn off the function.

Arranging the Images

To arrange an image, use the menu commands or drag it to position it on the page. The commands in the image menu can only be used on an open image, not on a thumbnail. As you work, you can right-click the image, page, or workspace for easy access to many of the menu commands. If you prefer to have Paint Shop Pro arrange the images, use the Auto Arrange feature.

Positioning and Rotating an Image

You can rotate or position any image that is open on the page or in the workspace, and you can drag images on and off the page. When you place the cursor over an image, it changes to the Image Mover tool to indicate that you can drag the image.

When choosing a Rotate or Placement command, first click the image to select it. The currently selected image displays a handle at each corner. To position an image, drag it, click one of the Placement toolbar buttons, use one of the Image > Placement commands, or right-click the image and choose a command from the context menu. The placement commands position the image in one of the four corners of the page or at its center.

Images can be rotated in increments of 90°. To rotate an image, click to select it and then:

- Click the Rotate left or Rotate Right toolbar button,
- Choose Image > Rotate+90 or Image > Rotate–90, or
- Right-click the image, and then choose +Rotate or –Rotate from the context menu.

Resizing an Image

You can resize any image on the page or in the workspace. Click the image to select it. The currently selected image displays a handle at each corner. Move the cursor over the handle. It changes to a double-ended arrow. Drag a handle to enlarge or reduce the image size.

Locating an Image

If you misplace an open image, click the Auto Arrange toolbar button to place it on the page.

Removing an Image

To remove an image from the page, drag it to the workspace, click the toolbar button, double-click the image, or right-click the image and choose Remove from the context menu. The thumbnail of an image you have closed appears on the left side of the window at the bottom of the thumbnail list.

Using the Auto Arrange Feature

Use the Auto Arrange feature to have Paint Shop Pro automatically arrange your images. It divides the paper into sections of equal size and places an image in each section. Only the images on the paper or in the workspace are used. Because no thumbnails are added, be sure to open all the images you want arranged before choosing the command.

When using Auto Arrange, you can choose to leave a specific amount of space between images (the border) and to enlarge (stretch) the images, if necessary, to fill their sections of the page. Set the width of this border in the Print Preview Setup dialog box. Then, before choosing Auto Arrange, you can decide whether to use the Border and Stretch options.

To activate these options:

Choose Preferences > Use Borders and/or Preferences > Stretch to Fit,

- Click the Use Borders or Stretch to Fit toolbar button,
- Right-click the page or workspace and choose the commands from the context menu, or
- Select their check boxes in the Print Preview Setup dialog box.

After you have selected the options, do one of the following to use the Auto-Arrange feature:

- Choose Preferences > Auto Arrange,
- Click the Auto Arrange button on the toolbar, or
- Right-click the workspace or page and choose Auto Arrange from the context menu.

Using the Print Preview Setup Dialog Box

Use the Print Preview Setup dialog box to access the printer settings, to configure the Auto Arrange function border, and to select the grid preferences. To display the dialog box, click its toolbar button, choose Preferences > Options, or right-click the workspace and choose Options from the context menu.

UNITS BOX From the Units drop-down box, select to use either Inches or Centimeters as the unit of measurement for the borders and grid.

PRINTER SETTINGS BUTTON Click the Printer Settings button to open the dialog box for your printer or the standard Windows print dialog box. Use the Properties or Options buttons to change the paper size, page orientation (portrait or landscape view), number of copies printed, and other print options.

BORDER OPTIONS PANEL The border refers to the minimum space left between images when you choose the Auto Arrange command. To set the border options:

1. Select the "Use Borders on Auto Arrange" check box to separate the images by at least the distance displayed in the Vertical and Horizontal Border Size boxes.

2. Select the "Stretch to Fit on Auto Arrange" check box to enlarge images as much as possible while retaining their aspect ratios.

3. Type the distance or use the spin controls in the Vertical Border and Horizontal Border Size boxes to set the minimum width between images.

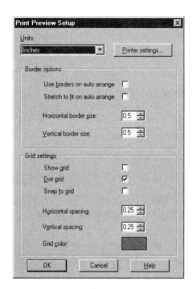

GRID SETTINGS PANEL Set the grid color, style (configuration – lines or dots) and spacing in inches or centimeters. To set the grid options:

1. Select the "Show Grid" check box to display the grid. You can also activate this feature from the toolbar and the Preferences menu.

2. Select the "Dot Grid" check box to view the grid as evenly spaced dots rather than intersecting lines.

3. Select the "Snap to Grid" check box to automatically align images to the grid. You can also activate this feature from the toolbar and Preferences menu.

4. Type the distance or use the spin controls in the Horizontal Spacing and Vertical Spacing boxes to set the measurement between grid lines or dots.

5. To change the grid color, left-click the color box to open the Color dialog box or right-click to open the Recent Colors dialog box.

Saving and Loading Layouts

A layout is a specific arrangement of images on the page. You can save any layout you create and load it again later. If you need to print certain images more than once, you may want to arrange them together on a page and save the layout. The layout contains information on the names and locations of the image files and how the images are positioned on the page. It does not contain the images.

Saving a Layout

To save a layout:

1. Open the Save As dialog box by choosing File > Save Layout, clicking the Save Layout button on the toolbar, or right-clicking the page or workspace and choosing Save Layout from the context menu.

2. Use the Save In drop-down box and Windows buttons to navigate to the folder in which you want to store the layout. If necessary, use the Up One Level button to help navigate or the Create New Folder button to create a new folder.

3. Type a name for the layout in the File Name box. The correct file format automatically appears in the Save as type box.

4. Click the Save button. If the layout contains an image that has not been saved, the file Save As dialog box opens. Chose a name, file format, and location for the image. When you click the Save button, the program saves the image and then the layout.

Loading a Layout

Use the Open dialog box to load any layout you have saved. Loading a layout removes the thumbnails and any images not contained in the layout from the window.

To load a layout:

1. Open the Open dialog box by choosing File > Open Layout, clicking the Open Layout button on the toolbar, or right-clicking the page or workspace and choosing Open Layout from the context menu.

2. Use the Look In drop-down box and Windows buttons to navigate to the folder in which you saved the layout. If necessary, use the Up One Level button to help navigate.

3. In the contents list box, either double-click the layout or click it and then click the Open button. The dialog box closes.

If you move an image after saving the layout, Paint Shop Pro may be unable to locate it. If this happens, a message appears showing which image could not be found and asking if you want to continue. Click Yes to load the layout; click No to cancel the operation.

Printing the Page

After you have arranged the images, print the page by choosing File > Print, clicking the Print button on the toolbar, or right-clicking the page or workspace and choosing Print from the context menu. The page is sent directly to the printer. No Print dialog box opens because any changes could affect the arrangement of the images.

Closing the Multiple Image Printing Window

To close the Multiple Image Printing window and return to the Paint Shop Pro workspace, you can choose File > Close, click the toolbar button, click the Windows Close button on the title bar, or choose the Close command from the Control menu.

Printing Browser Thumbnails

When the Browser is open, you can print thumbnails of the images in the active folder. Before you print, use the Page Setup dialog box to choose the setup options. You can also use the Print Preview window to see how the thumbnails will look when printed.

Choosing the Page Setup Options

To configure the Browser Page Setup dialog box options:

1. Open the Page Setup dialog box for Browser thumbnails by doing one of the following when the Browser is open:

   - Choosing File > Page Setup, or

   - Clicking the Setup button in the Browser Image Print Preview window.

2. Select the paper size and source from the drop down boxes in the "Paper" panel. The options will vary with printers. (For some printers, the drop down boxes may be unavailable.)

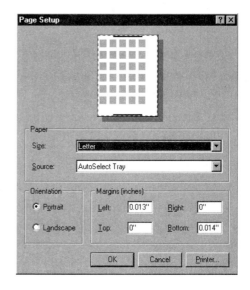

3. Select a page orientation from the "Orientation" panel. There are two page orientations, portrait and landscape. Printing in portrait orientation places the top of the image against one of the page's narrow sides. Printing in landscape orientation places the top of the image against one of the page's wide sides.

4. Set margins for the printed page by typing the measurements (in inches) in the margin boxes.

5. Click Printer if you want to open the Printer Setup dialog box and make changes.

6. Click the OK button to close the Browser Page Setup dialog box and save the new settings.

Previewing Printed Thumbnails

Use the Print Preview to see how the thumbnails will look when printed. To open the Print Preview window, choose File > Print Preview or click the Print Preview button on the toolbar. The window contains several buttons.

PRINT BUTTON Click to close the Browser Print Preview window and open the Print dialog box.

SETUP BUTTON Click to close the Print Preview window
and open the Page Setup dialog box, where you:

- Select the paper size and source in the
  "Paper" panel.

- Select either a landscape or portrait
  orientation in the "Orientation" panel.

- Set the margins in the Margins boxes.

When you close the Page Setup dialog box, Paint Shop
Pro returns to the Browser Print Preview window.

NEXT PAGE AND PREV PAGE BUTTONS These buttons
are accessible if the thumbnails cover more than one
page. Click to move forward and back by one page
respectively.

TWO PAGE / ONE PAGE BUTTON Click to switch the display between two pages and one.

ZOOM IN AND ZOOM OUT BUTTONS Click to change the magnification level. You can also zoom
in and out by clicking the image.

CLOSE BUTTON Click to close the Browser Print Preview window.

Printing Thumbnails

To print the thumbnails:

1. Open the Print dialog box by choosing File > Print, clicking the Print button on the toolbar, or
   clicking the Print button in the Print Preview window.

2. Select a printer in the Name box.

3. To change the selected printer's properties, click the Properties button. Paint Shop Pro opens
   the appropriate Properties dialog box. For help using the dialog box, try pressing <F1>.

4. To print the image to a file rather than to paper, select the "Print to File" check box. When you
   click the Print button, the Print to File dialog box opens. Enter a location and name for the
   new file in this dialog box.

5. Select the Print Range. You can print all the thumbnails, a range of pages, or just the selected
   thumbnails. If you select "Pages," enter the first and last pages to print in the "from:" and
   "to:" boxes.

6. Set the number of copies you want to print. If your printer does not support multiple copies,
   the Number of copies box will be grayed out.

7. Click the OK button. Paint Shop Pro sends the file to the printer or file.

Setting Preferences

You can use the Paint Shop Pro preference settings to customize how various features in the application appear and respond. This chapter describes the preferences, which include:

- General Program Preferences
- CMYK Conversion Preferences
- File Format Preferences
- File Format Associations
- File Locations
- Color Management
- Monitor Gamma
- Autosave Settings

The chapter also describes how to customize the Browser and main program toolbars.

Setting General Program Preferences

The general program preferences determine how Paint Shop Pro displays and uses various features. You can use the default settings or select new ones. The general program preferences include: Undo/Redo, Viewing, Dialogs and Palettes, Browser, Miscellaneous, Rulers and Units, Transparency, and Warnings.

To change any general program preference:

1. Choose File > Preferences > General Program Preferences. The Paint Shop Pro Preferences dialog box opens.

2. Click the tab containing the preference information you want to change.

3. Select the new settings, and then click the OK button to close the dialog box and apply the changes.

Undo/Redo Preferences

Use the options on the Undo preferences tab to enable the Undo and Redo systems and to select how Paint Shop Pro stores the Undo and Redo information.

The numeric edit controls used in this tab provide a variety of ways to change the settings. You can type a number in the box, click the spinner controls, drag the meter bar, or press the pop-out button and drag the slider.

ENABLE THE UNDO SYSTEM Select this check box to use the Undo and Redo commands. If the box is not selected, you cannot undo individual steps. You can, however, still undo all changes by choosing the Revert command from the File menu.

LIMIT UNDO/REDO DISK USAGE PER OPEN IMAGE Select this check box and enter the amount of disk space for Paint Shop Pro to use when storing the Undo and Redo information. The value can be between 5 and 999 MB of storage per open image.

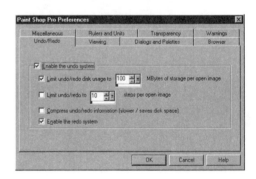

LIMIT UNDO/REDO STEPS PER OPEN IMAGE Select this check box and enter a value to place a limit on the number of steps of Undo information Paint Shop Pro stores per image. The range is from 1 to 99 steps per open image.

COMPRESS UNDO/REDO INFORMATION Select this check box to compress the Undo and Redo information. This conserves disk space, but it slows Undo and Redo operations.

ENABLE THE REDO SYSTEM Select this check box to use the Redo commands, which re-apply actions that you have undone.

Viewing Preferences

The Viewing preferences tab controls whether Paint Shop Pro automatically sizes images and image windows after using the Zoom tool, after creating an image, and after resizing an image window, and how it resizes them.

ZOOMING The Zooming options determine if Paint Shop Pro automatically resizes an image window when you zoom in or zoom out. A window is resized to include as much of the image as will fit.

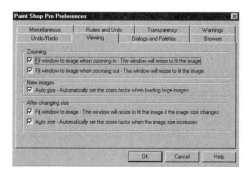

NEW IMAGES When the "Auto size" check box is selected, if you open an image that is too large to fit in its image window, Paint Shop Pro automatically resets the image's magnification so that the entire image is visible.

AFTER CHANGING SIZE When the "Fit window to image" check box is selected, Paint Shop Pro automatically resizes the image window whenever you resize an image. When the "Auto size" check box is selected, if you increase an image's size to more than can fit in its window, Paint Shop Pro reduces the image's magnification accordingly.

Dialogs and Palettes Preferences

Use the Dialogs and Palettes preferences tab to choose a color dialog box, palette style, and default file format for the Save As dialog box, and whether to display command confirmation messages and activate the Automatic Roll-up feature.

DISPLAY OPTIONS When you select the "Display large text and icons on palettes" check box, Paint Shop Pro displays larger icons on each palette tool button. When you select the "Display flat style toolbars" check box, Paint Shop Pro displays flat buttons. If you are working on a laptop, clear the check box; the three-dimensional toolbar buttons are easier to see on a laptop. When you select the "Display menu icons" check box, the program menus display an icon next to each command.

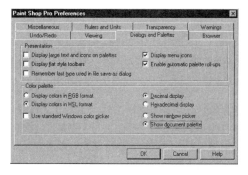

LAST FILE TYPE USED OPTION When you select this check box, the file format previously used to save an image automatically appears in the "File of type" box of the Save As dialog box. This is convenient when you are saving several files in a specific format but don't want to use the Batch Conversion command.

AUTOMATIC ROLL-UP FEATURE Select the "Enable Automatic Roll-ups" check box when you want the Overview window, Histogram window, Tool Options palette, and Layer palette to minimize to their title bars when you move the cursor away from them. They return to the original size when you move the cursor back over them. This feature keeps these items readily accessible while giving you more workspace.

COLOR PALETTE OPTIONS The Color palette options determine how Paint Shop Pro displays color data on the Color palette. You can display color using its Red/Green/Blue (RGB) or its Hue/Saturation/Lightness (HSL) values. You can display the values in decimal or hexadecimal format. Because Web browsers use the hexadecimal format, you may prefer to display it when you are creating art for use on the Web. Paint Shop Pro also displays the hexadecimal value of colors in the Jasc Color dialog box.

WINDOWS COLOR PICKER When you open the Color dialog box, it displays either the default Paint Shop Pro color palette or the standard Windows color palette. Select the "Use standard Windows color picker" check box to use the Windows color palette instead of the Jasc color palette.

DOCUMENT PALETTE COLOR PICKER This option lets you change how the "Available Colors" panel of the Color palette appears for an image with a low color depth. When a 24-bit image is active, the panel displays the Rainbow picker, which is a rainbow of colors. If an image is paletted (8-bit or lower), it does not contain all the colors displayed in the rainbow. Therefore, when you pick a color from the rainbow, Paint Shop Pro chooses the color in the image palette closest to the color you select.

The "Show document palette" check box, which is enabled by default, will cause a paletted image's palette of colors to display in the "Available Colors" panel instead of the rainbow of colors. Selecting this check box replaces the rainbow of colors with rectangles containing the image's available colors. This lets you select exact colors in paletted images. In addition, when working with masks or adjustment layers on 24-bit images, it lets you alternate easily between choosing greyscale colors (for masks and adjustment layers) and 24-bit colors.

NOTE: *The color depth of the image determines the number of rectangles in the "Available Colors" panel. If the image contains fewer colors than it can support, the remaining rectangles are black. For example, a 4-bit image can contain up to 16 colors. If it actually contains only 9 colors, the available colors area displays 9 colored rectangles and 7 black rectangles.*

Browser Preferences

The Browser preferences tab displays the options for the thumbnails and the cache file.

THUMBNAIL SIZE While the default thumbnail size is 80 by 80 pixels, you can choose any other size from 50 to 150 pixels. To keep the width and height of the thumbnails equal, leave the "Symmetric" check box selected. Clear it to enter different values in the Width and Height boxes.

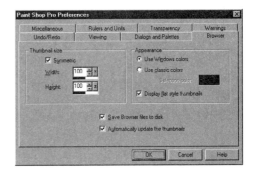

APPEARANCE By default, the Browser uses your Windows default color settings to highlight a selected thumbnail (this is generally blue). To use a different color, select the "Use classic colors" check box. Then click the color box and choose a new color from the Color dialog box, or right-click it and choose a color from the Recent Colors dialog box.

DISPLAY FLAT STYLE THUMBNAILS Clear this check box to display "buttonized" toolbar and palette buttons.

SAVE BROWSER FILES TO DISK As you view a folder using the Browser, Paint Shop Pro saves the folder's image information to a cache file named "pspbrwse.jbf," and it stores that file in the folder. When you next view the folder, the Browser reads and displays the information from the cache file. This is much faster than having the Browser re-scan the folder's images. If you prefer not to have the program create and save a cache file for each folder you browse, clear the "Save Browser files to disk" check box.

AUTOMATICALLY UPDATE THE THUMBNAILS When you view a folder using the Browser, it either reads and displays the saved cache file, or compares the information in the cache file to the images in the folder to check for additions, deletions, and modifications, and updates the thumbnails to reflect the changes. To compare and update the cache file information each time you browse a folder, select the "Automatically update the thumbnails" checkbox.

Miscellaneous Preferences

The numeric edit controls used in the Miscellaneous preferences tab provide several ways to change the settings. You can type a number in the box, click the spinner controls, drag the meter bar, or press the pop-out button and drag the slider.

RECENT FILE LISTING Use the Recent File Listing option to set the maximum number of files that the File menu displays in the Most Recently Used list. Note that:

- You must restart Paint Shop Pro before the new setting will take effect.

- If you increase the setting, you will not reach the new maximum list length until you have opened a sufficient number of new files. For example, if the old list contained four files and you increase the setting to ten, you will have to open six new files before you reach the new maximum length.

TRANSPARENT PASTE COLOR TOLERANCE When you paste data as a transparent selection, Paint Shop Pro adds it to the current image, defines it as a selection, and then deselects all the pixels that match the current background color. The tolerance value you enter determines how closely the background color must match the transparent color for it to become transparent. The Tolerance setting uses a scale of 0% to 200%, with 0 being no tolerance (only pixels with a perfect match are deselected), and 200 being total tolerance (all pixels are deselected).

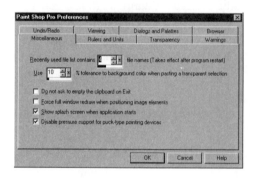

DO NOT ASK TO EMPTY CLIPBOARD ON EXIT When you select this check box, Paint Shop Pro does <u>not</u> prompt you to empty the Windows clipboard when you exit Paint Shop Pro.

FORCE FULL WINDOW REDRAW WHEN POSITIONING IMAGE ELEMENTS When you select this check box, Paint Shop Pro redraws the information in the active window whenever you move objects in the image.

SHOW SPLASH SCREEN WHEN APPLICATION STARTS When you select this check box, the program displays its splash screen each time you start it. The splash screen shows the Jasc Software, Inc. logo and the program version number.

DISABLE PRESSURE SUPPORT FOR PUCK-TYPE POINTING DEVICES A puck-type pointing device is used with a graphics tablet. Some of these devices have the same pressure-sensitive feature as the graphics pens. When you use the pen, you can vary the pressure you apply to the tablet to control opacity, color, or line width. With a puck-type pointing device, you use its buttons to control the pressure applied. Push the button in more to apply greater pressure; ease up on it to reduce the pressure. When you select the "Disable pressure support for puck-type pointing devices" check box, the pressure-sensitive feature is not available.

Rulers and Units Preferences

The Rulers and Units Preferences tab options control how rulers and grids are displayed on the screen and what unit settings (pixels, inches, or centimeters) are used.

RULERS Select whether to display pixels, inches, or centimeters on the ruler. Set the ruler colors either to match the other toolbars or to be black on white.

DEFAULT RESOLUTION Choose a default resolution for new images. You can override this resolution on an image-by-image basis by changing the settings in the New Image dialog box.

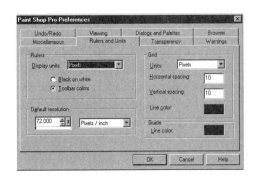

GRID Select the units of measurement (pixels, inches, or centimeters) and the horizontal and vertical grid spacing measured in the units. To change the default color for grid lines, click the color box to open the Color dialog box. Right-click in the color box to open the Recent Colors dialog box. You can also change the grid settings for an individual image by double-clicking the rulers on the image's window.

GUIDE To change the default color of the guide lines, click in the color box to open the Color dialog box. Right-click in the color box to open the Recent Colors dialog box. You can also change the guide settings for an individual image by double-clicking the rulers on the image's window.

NOTE: *Grid and Guide settings applied to individual images will override the default settings defined in Ruler and Unit Preferences.*

Transparency Preferences

The Transparency tab options control how Paint Shop Pro displays the grid representing transparent backgrounds and transparent areas of layers. From the Grid Size drop-down box, choose a grid size. (The default is Medium.) In the "Grid Colors" panel, choose a color scheme. The two Color boxes and the Preview box display the new grid.

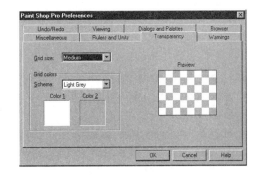

To use custom colors, click inside the Color 1 and Color 2 boxes. When the Color dialog box opens, choose a color, and then click OK. To choose colors from the Recent Colors dialog box, right-click inside the color boxes. The Preview box displays your selection.

Warnings Preferences

The Warnings tab options let you control the behavior of the warning messages that appear when you perform certain operations. By default, the check boxes on the Warnings tab are selected, and Paint Shop Pro displays a warning message whenever you are about to perform an operation that will result in lost information or one that can't be applied to the image in its current state. For each type of message you prefer not to have Paint Shop Pro display, clear its check box. Alternatively, click the Disable All button to clear all the check boxes or click the Enable All check box to select all the check boxes.

You can also prevent a message from appearing in the future by selecting the "Don't warn about this anymore" check box the first time the message appears. If you then change your mind and want to see the message, return to this tab and select the appropriate check box.

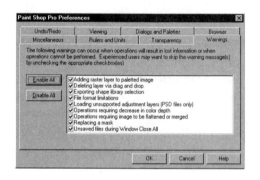

ADDING RASTER LAYER TO PALETTED IMAGE When you clear this check box, Paint Shop Pro will not warn you that a paletted image can contain only one layer.

DELETING LAYER VIA DRAG AND DROP When you clear this check box, Paint Shop Pro will not prompt you to confirm that you want to delete the layer you when you drag a layer to the Delete Layer button on the Layer palette.

DRAWING A SINGLE LINE WITH NO STROKE STYLE DEFINED When you clear this check box, Paint Shop Pro will not warn you if you try to draw a single line when the Foreground/Stroke Style box on the Color palette does not display a solid color, pattern, or gradient. You must define a stroke style before you can draw a single line.

EXPORTING SHAPE LIBRARY SELECTION When you clear this check box, if you have a specific vector shape selected when you choose the File > Export > Shape command, Paint Shop Pro will not warn you that only the selected shape will be saved. To save all the vector shapes, make sure no shape is selected.

FILE FORMAT LIMITATIONS When you clear this check box, Paint Shop Pro will not warn you that you may lose data when you save an image in a format that doesn't support all the data contained in the image.

LOADING UNSUPPORTED ADJUSTMENT LAYERS (PSD FILES ONLY) When you clear this check box, Paint Shop Pro will not warn you when you open a PhotoShop ® image that contains features Paint Shop Pro does not support.

OPERATIONS REQUIRING DECREASE IN COLOR DEPTH When you clear this check box, Paint Shop Pro will not warn you before it automatically decreases the color depth of an image.

OPERATIONS REQUIRING IMAGE TO BE FLATTENED OR MERGED When you clear this check box, Paint Shop Pro will not warn you before it automatically flattens an image.

REPLACING A MASK When you clear this check box, Paint Shop Pro will replace the mask without warning you that it is deleting the current mask.

UNSAVED FILES DURING WINDOW CLOSE ALL When you clear this check box, Paint Shop Pro will not prompt you to save files when you choose Window > Close All. All unsaved changes to all open files will be discarded.

WARN ON USING TOOLS WITH A NULL STYLE When you clear this check box, Paint Shop Pro will not warn you that you must define a style before using the tools requiring stroke or fill styles.

WARN WHEN STYLES NOT SUPPORTED ON PALETTED IMAGES When you clear this check box, Paint Shop Pro will not warn you when you try to apply a style on an image that does not support it.

Setting CMYK Conversion Preferences

In a CMYK (cyan, magenta, yellow, and black) conversion, Paint Shop Pro replaces the RGB (Red, Green, and Blue) colors you see on the monitor with the CMYK colors used in printing. You can then print a separate page for each CMYK color by selecting the CMYK Separations option in the Page Setup dialog box. This is useful if you are using a prepress shop and doing high-end printing.

Before printing the separations, configure the CMYK preferences to determine how Paint Shop Pro handles the conversion from RGB to CMYK. Save these preferences in a file called a profile. Use the CMYK Conversion Preferences dialog box to select the preferences and manage your CMYK profiles.

To open the dialog box, choose File > Preferences > CMYK Conversion Preferences.

- To select a profile, click the Current Profile drop-down box to view the profile choices, and click a profile.

- To create a new profile, click the New button. The New CMYK Profile dialog box opens.

- To modify a new profile, click the Modify button. The CMYK Profile dialog box opens. Use the three tabs in this dialog box to modify the properties for the profile.

- To remove a profile, highlight the profile and click the Remove button.

Creating a Profile

There are two ways to create a CMYK profile:

- You can create a new profile and then modify the settings.

- You can modify the settings of an existing profile and then save it with a new name.

Use the New CMYK Profile dialog box to select the initial settings and name the profile by doing the following:

1. In the New CMYK Profile dialog box, select the initial settings for the profile. You can start with the program's default settings or with the settings currently selected.

2. Type a name for the new profile.

3. Click the OK button to close the dialog box and return to the CMYK Conversion Preferences dialog box.

CMYK Profile Black Generation

Use the Black Generation tab of the CMYK Profile dialog box to set how the black ink component is used. To use the Black Generation tab:

1. Select a black generation method:

   - Undercolor Removal (UCR) replaces some of the cyan, magenta, and yellow components of neutral grey and shadow areas with black. This helps compensate for some of the trapping problems that occur in multicolor printing.

   - Grey Component Replacement (GCR) replaces grey components in colored areas of a reproduction with black. The least prominent color is reduced or removed completely, along with proportional amounts of the other two colors, to define a grey component, which is then replaced with black ink.

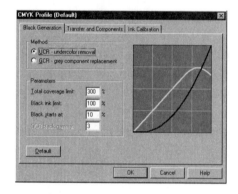

2. Select the black parameters. The black line in the graph represents the black value and updates as you change the settings. The settings are:

   - Total Coverage Limit, which can range from 200 to 400%,

   - Blank Ink Coverage Limit, which can range from 0 to 200%,

   - Black Starts At, which can range from 0 to 100%, and

   - GCR Black Gamma, which can range from 1 to 4.

3. To return to the default settings for the black generation method, click the Default button.

CMYK Profile Transfer and Components

The left panel of the Transfer and Components tab displays a graph of the transfer curves for cyan, magenta, yellow, and black. The right panels display parameters for grey and color components. To use the Transfer and Components tab:

1. Adjust the transfer curves by highlighting the name of a curve in the Transfer Curves drop-down box, and then dragging the points of the curve up or down. Each transfer curve contains five adjustable points that define the curve based on its zero-tone, quarter-tone, mid-tone, three-quarter-tone, and full-tone percentages. The default curve is a straight line from 0 to 100%. A curve that slopes above this 45° line produces darker tones.

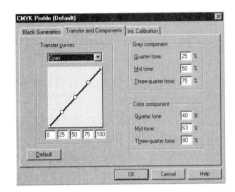

2. Set the Grey and Color Component percentages by typing values into the corresponding text boxes. Values can range from 0 to 100%.

3. To return a curve to its default settings, click the Default button.

CMYK Profile Ink Calibration

The Ink Calibration tab provides text boxes to adjust for color shifts. The Hue and Greyness panel displays six colors, along with the combined CMY color. The Grey Balance panel includes the text boxes for adjusting CMY percentages.

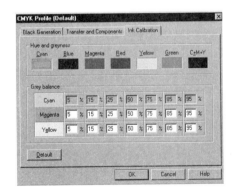

To use the Ink Calibration tab:

1. Select Hue and Greyness colors.

2. Adjust Grey Balance percentages.

3. To return to the default settings for a color box or grey value, click the default button.

Setting File Format Preferences

Setting PCD File Preferences

PCD (the Kodak PhotoCD format) is used by many photo developers for delivering photos on CDs. This format can provide multiple resolutions of an image in one file. It does not support transparency or layers. On this tab, you set a default resolution for PCD images when opening them. There are two choices:

- Choose one of the seven size options to open all PCD files in a specific pixel width and height, or

- Choose the "Ask when loading each file" option to be prompted for a resolution each time that you open a PCD file.

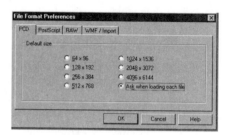

If you choose the "Ask when loading each file" option, Paint Shop Pro displays a dialog box containing the size choices when you open a PCD file.

Setting PostScript File Import Preferences

Paint Shop Pro can read PostScript files through level 2 and convert them into raster information. It can convert up to 100 pages (depending on the memory in your computer), antialias the objects, and retain information on transparency. However, if you open a PostScript file and then save it, the file is not identical to the original because the information has been converted into raster format.

If you select the "Prompt for size and options" check box, Paint Shop Pro displays a dialog box each time you open a Postscript file. The dialog box contains the same options as this tab. If you clear the check box, Paint Shop Pro does not prompt you. It opens a PostScript file using the settings from the "Size and options when not prompting" panel.

To set the options:

1. Choose a resolution for the image or leave the default setting of 72 dpi.

2. Choose a paper size by clicking a selection in the drop-down box. The bounding box, which is available when the EPS file has a recommended size, is usually the best choice.

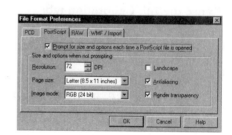

3. Choose a color depth for the image by clicking a selection in the Image Mode drop-down box. The choices are Monochrome (1-bit), Greyscale (8-bit), and RGB (24-bit).

4. By default, the page is set to the Portrait orientation, where it is taller than it is wide. To reverse the orientation, select the "Landscape" check box.

5. The "Antialiasing" check box is selected by default. Antialiasing smoothes the edges of objects. If you prefer not to use this feature, clear the check box.

6. The "Render Transparency" check box is selected by default. Clear this check box to substitute a white background for the transparency.

Setting RAW File Preferences

Use the RAW tab to determine how Paint Shop Pro interprets RAW pixel data. For information about a RAW file's format, refer to the documentation for the application that created the image. If you are familiar with RAW files, the RAW options should be self-explanatory. If you are new to the format, please find and read information about RAW data in general and the file you are trying to open in particular.

Setting WMF / Import File Preferences

WMF (Windows Meta File) is the Microsoft Windows native vector format. It is used for clip art in Microsoft Office as well as other programs. It does not support transparency or layers. Although it is size independent because it is a vector format, some WMF files do provide a header containing a default size.

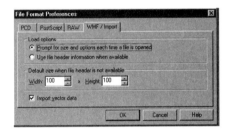

Choose either to be prompted for the size each time or to use the header information and your chosen defaults when no header is available.

The "Import vector data" check box is enabled by default. This option will read vector data from several formats, including WMF and EMF, so it can be edited as vector data in Paint Shop Pro. If this option is disabled, vector data will be converted to raster data. Imported images will usually also open faster if this option is disabled.

Setting File Format Associations

The File Associations Preferences function allows you to select the file formats that will be associated with Paint Shop Pro. Associating a file format with Paint Shop Pro means that your computer will automatically open all files of that format using Paint Shop Pro. These files display the Paint Shop Pro icon. Use the File Format Associations dialog box to associate a file format with Paint Shop Pro. To open the File Format Associations dialog box, choose File > Preferences > File Associations.

Using the File Format Associations Dialog Box

1. The right side of the dialog box provides keys to associate any or all of the unused formats.

   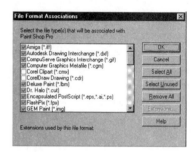

   - To associate all listed formats, click the Select All button.

   - To associate any file formats that are not associated with other applications, click the Select Unused button.

   - To have no file formats associated with Paint Shop Pro, click the Remove All button.

2. To associate a specific file format with Paint Shop Pro, select its check box. The extensions used by the format will appear below the list.

3. To add or remove extensions you want to have automatically associated with the selected format, click the Extensions button to open the Extensions dialog box. Change the extensions, and then click OK to return to the File Format Associations dialog box.

4. After you have selected files to associate with Paint Shop Pro, click the OK button to close the dialog box and apply the associations.

5. To close the dialog box without changing any associations, click the Cancel button.

Using the Extensions Dialog Box

NOTE: *You must restart Paint Shop Pro to apply the changes. Also, you cannot delete the default extension.*

Use the Extensions dialog box to add and delete extensions associated with specific file formats. You can add extension names that contain up to 24 letters and underscore symbols (_). New extensions are added to the formats displayed in the Open, Save, Save As, and Save Copy As dialog boxes. Open the dialog box by clicking the Extensions button.

- To add a file extension, click the Add button to open the Define File Extension dialog box. Type the extension you want associated with the format, and then click the OK button to close the dialog box.

- To delete an extension you have added, highlight it and then click the Delete button.

- To change an extension to the preferred status, highlight it and then click the Preferred button.

- To return the format to its default extension, click the Reset button.

After you have made your changes, click the OK button to close the dialog box.

Setting File Location Preferences

Use the tabs in the File Locations dialog box to set the paths and folders you want Paint Shop Pro to search for tubes, patterns, textures, gradients, brushes, frames, and shapes you have created and saved. You can also enter the path of any Web browsers and third party plug-in filters you want to use with the program. If you want to save the undo and temporary files to a folder other than the default system temporary directory, you can use this dialog box to set the new location.

When you install Paint Shop Pro, the program creates some default folders for the objects included with the program. The first text box of a tab displays this path and folder. If you want to store objects in additional folders, you can add them using the Browse button.

NOTE: *You can also access the Frames, Brushes, Gradient, Patterns, and Texture tabs by clicking the Edit Paths button on the Picture Frame Wizard, Custom Brush, Gradient, Patterns, and Textures dialog boxes. These dialog boxes open when you are adding a picture frame, selecting a custom brush tip, or setting gradients, patterns, and textures on the Color palette.*

To add a new folder to a tab:

1. Create the folder. The folder must exist before you can add it.

2. Click the Browse button to open the Browse for Folder navigation box.

3. Use the scroll bar and the directory tree to locate the new folder.

4. Click the folder to select it.

5. Click the OK button to close the box and display the path in the tab.

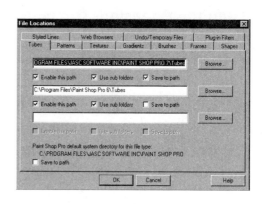

ENABLE THIS PATH Select this check box to make the path active in the application.

USE SUB FOLDERS Select this check box to have Paint Shop Pro search for filters in sub-folders as well as the selected folder.

SAVE TO PATH Select this check box to make the path the default path for saving files. You can select this check box for only one path on each tab.

Setting Color Management Preferences

Color Management is a Windows 98 or later feature that improves color rendition when you display an image or page on your monitor and print it on your printer. It also allows you to preview, within the limitations of the monitor, how the image will look when printed on a specific color printer. Color profiles are installed when a monitor or printer is installed, and the profiles are used whenever colors are displayed or printed. For more information on Color Management, please refer to your Windows documentation.

NOTE: To use Color Management, you must have Windows 98 or later installed on your computer. This feature is not available in Windows 95.

To use the Color Management dialog box:

1. Open the dialog box by choosing File > Preferences > Color Management.

2. Select the Enable Color Management check box.

3. Select Basic Color Management if you want to set how colors will appear on your monitor and printer. Select Proofing if you want to preview how colors would appear on a particular device.

4. Select the applicable device profiles and settings in the drop-down boxes.

5. Click the OK button to apply the settings and close the dialog box.

Setting Monitor Gamma Preferences

Monitors display colors by exciting phosphors to produce red, green, and blue light. Because these phosphors do not excite equally, they can produce distortions in the brightness, contrast, and color balance of images. For example, if a computer reads a lightness value from a photographic image and sends it directly to the monitor, the displayed color will be dimmer than in the original photograph.

To compensate for this non-linearity of phosphor excitation, you can alter the color values sent to your monitor. Use the Monitor Gamma Adjustment to adjust the values.

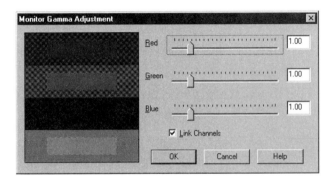

To adjust the Monitor Gamma:

1. Open the Monitor Gamma Adjustment dialog box by choosing File > Preferences > Monitor Gamma.

2. Look at the red, green, blue, and grey rectangles on the left side of the dialog box. Each one contains an inner rectangle. The pixels in this area have a lightness value of 128. The outer area is a dithered pattern of pixels with lightness values of 0 and 255.

3. Drag the red, green, and blue slider controls to adjust the dithered areas until they are of equal brightness.

    • Select the "Link Channels" check box to adjust the levels in unison.

    • Clear the check box to adjust colors individually.

4. Click the OK button to close the dialog box and apply the settings.

Setting Autosave Preferences

Choose this command when you want images you have open to be saved automatically at specific intervals. Paint Shop Pro saves the files to the folder you select in the Undo/Temporary Files tab of the File Locations dialog box. If anything causes the system or program to close unexpectedly, Paint Shop Pro loads these files the next time you start the program.

Use the Autosave Settings dialog box when you want Paint Shop Pro to create a temporary file for each open image. The program creates an .ats file containing the location of the original image and the backup file, and a .tmp file of each open image.

The Autosave feature can prevent you from losing your work if the system or program crashes. If this occurs, after you restart Paint Shop Pro, the program scans your Autosave directory for any ATS files. If it locates one, it reloads the temporary images.

To use the Autosave Settings Dialog box:

1. Select the Enable autosave check box to have Paint Shop Pro create temporary feature. Clear the check box if you do not want to use the feature.

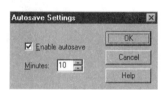

2. Select a number from the Minutes box to determine how frequently Paint Shop Pro creates a temporary file.

NOTE: *Be default, temporary files are stored in the system temporary folder (Windows\Temp in Windows 95/98). If you prefer to save them elsewhere, select a new folder using the Undo/Temporary tab of the File Location dialog box.*

Customizing the Toolbars

As you work in Paint Shop Pro, you will probably find yourself using some commands more often than others. These commands have buttons that you can add, remove, and rearrange on any of the four main window toolbars. The Browser also has a toolbar that you can customize with its commands. By customizing the toolbars, you can access the commands more quickly.

Use the Customize Toolbar dialog box to customize the Browser toolbar or the main program toolbars. To open the dialog box, choose View > Toolbars, click the Standard, Web, Photo, Effects, or Browser toolbar name, and then click the Customize button. You can also open the dialog box by right-clicking a background area on the toolbar and choosing Customize from the menu.

Adding and Removing Buttons

You can add and remove buttons by dragging them between the "Available toolbar buttons" list and the "Current toolbar buttons" list or by using the Add and Remove buttons.

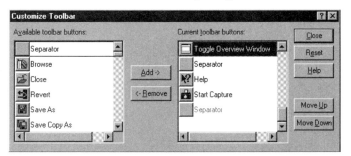

- To add a button, click the name of the button in the "Available toolbar buttons" list. In the "Current toolbar buttons" list, click the name of the button that is directly below where you want to add the new button. Click Add Button to move the button from the "Available toolbar buttons" list to the selected position in the "Current toolbar buttons" list.

- To remove a button, click the name of the button in the "Current toolbar buttons" list. Click the Remove button to move the button from the "Current toolbar buttons" list to the "Available toolbar buttons" list.

Rearranging Buttons

You can move a button by dragging it within the Current toolbar buttons list or by using the Move Up and Move Down buttons. To use these buttons, click the button that you want to move in the Current toolbar buttons list. Then click either Move Up or Move Down to move the button one space.

To return the toolbar to its original settings, click the Reset button. After you have finished customizing the toolbar, click the Close button to close the dialog box and apply the new settings.

Creating a New Animation

Chapter
21

Using the New Command

Use the New command to create a new animation, as described below.

1. Choose File > New, or click the New Animation button □ on the toolbar. The "Create New Animation" dialog box opens.

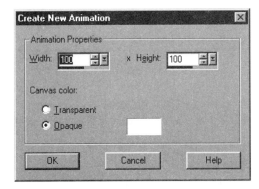

2. Set pixel width and height values in the "Width" and "Height" edit boxes.

3. Set a the canvas color. Either:

- Choose the "Transparent" option to select a transparent canvas for the animation. (The transparent canvas will be denoted by a checkered grid.)

   Or,

- Choose the or the "Opaque" option to select a solid canvas color for the animation. The canvas color is displayed in the color box next to this option. Click inside this box to display the Color dialog box; right-click to display the Recent Colors dialog box. You can then choose your own canvas color.

4. Click the OK button in the Create New Animation dialog box.

The new animation will be created and will contain one frame using the dimensions and canvas color you selected.

NOTE: As an alternative option, double-clicking the File New toolbar button while pressing the <Shift> key will open a new animation without running the settings dialog. Animation Shop will keep the settings you selected on your last animation, and apply them to the new one.

Using the Animation Wizard

The Animation Wizard provides a step by step method of creating a new animation. When you start up the wizard, a series of wizard pages will prompt you for information. After completing one wizard page, you then click the Next button and move on to the next page.

Starting the Animation Wizard

Start the Animation Wizard in one of the following ways:

- Choose File > Animation Wizard,
- Click the Animation Wizard button ▨ on the toolbar, or
- Press <Shift> + <A>.

A series of wizard pages will appear, prompting you through creating an animation. After finishing each page, click the Next button at the bottom of the page to move to the next page. You may move forward or backward by clicking the Back and Next buttons at the bottom of the Wizard pages.

The first page prompts you to set the frame size.

Setting the Frame Size

The first page of the Animation Wizard prompts you to set the dimensions of the animation frames. Use this Wizard page as described below.

- Choose the "Same size as the first image frame" option if you want all frames to match the size of the first frame. (You will then add the first frame in a later Wizard page.)

- Choose the "As defined here" option to activate the Width and Height edit boxes for you to set the exact dimensions of the animation frames. Dimensions are measured in pixels.

- Click Next to move to the next Wizard page.

The second page prompts you to set the canvas color.

Setting the Canvas Color

The second page of the Animation Wizard prompts you to set a transparent or an opaque canvas color. Use this Wizard page as described below.

- Choose the "Transparent" option to allow any images behind your animation to show through in the canvas. A transparent canvas is indicated by the current color settings in the "Transparency" tab of the General Program Preferences.

- Choose the "Opaque" option to select a canvas color for your animation. The current canvas color appears in the color box to the right of this option. Click inside this box to display the Color dialog box; right-click inside this box to display the Recent Colors dialog box. You can then choose your custom color. The canvas will use the dimensions you set in the previous Wizard page.

- Click Next to move to the next Wizard page.

The third wizard page prompts you to set a position for the frames.

Positioning the Frames

The third page of the Animation Wizard prompts how you would like to place your frames in the animation. Use this Wizard page as described below.

If the images you will be adding do not have the same dimensions as the frame size you set in the first Wizard page, you can choose one of the following positioning options:

- Choose the "Upper left corner of the frame" option to align all images having aspect ratios different than the first image in the upper left corner of their respective frames.

- Choose the "Centered in the frame" option to center all images in their frames regardless of each image's aspect ratio.

If an image's dimensions are smaller than the first image, the empty area surrounding the image can be filled in one of two ways:

* Choose the "With the canvas color" option to fill in the smaller-sized image's empty area with the canvas color.

* Choose the "With the preceding frame's contents" option to fill in the smaller-sized image's empty area with the contents of the previous frame. If there is no previous frame, the "With canvas color" option will be used.

If images need to be scaled to fit inside frames:

* Mark the "Scale frames to fit" check box. This will resize the image to fill the frame while maintaining the image's aspect ratio. If you do not mark this check box, parts of images that have larger dimensions than the frame size may not be visible.

* Click Next to move to the next Wizard page.

The fourth wizard page prompts you to set properties for the animation.

Setting the Animation Properties

The fourth page of the Animation Wizard prompts you in setting the looping and delay animation properties. Use this Wizard page as described below.

* Choose the "Yes, repeat the animation indefinitely" option to continuously cycle your animation until you manually stop it (see the Note below).

* Choose the "Play it *n* times" option to play your animation the number of times you set in the edit box.

NOTE: *Not all internet browsers currently support the loop feature.*

* Set the display time for each frame in the display time edit box. All frames in the animation will be set to the same display time. These values can be changed later while editing the animation.

* Click Next to move to the next Wizard page. The fifth wizard page prompts you to add frames to the animation.

Adding Frames to the Animation

The fifth page of the Animation Wizard prompts you in adding images to your animation. You must include at least one image to create an animation. Use this Wizard page as described below.

1. Click the Add Image button. The Open dialog box will appear.

2. From the Open dialog box, choose the file(s) for your animation.

3. To select multiple images at once, hold the <Ctrl> key while clicking on filenames. You can also select consecutive files by holding <Shift> and clicking on the first and last filenames in your selection. If your image files are located in more than one folder, you will need to reenter the Open dialog box for each folder.

4. If you wish to delete an image you have added to the list, do so by clicking on the filename to select it and then clicking the Remove Image button.

5. Verify the order of your images and reorder any of them by selecting one or more image files and clicking on the Move Up and Move Down buttons.

6. When you are done adding images, click the Next button to move to the final Wizard page.

The sixth and final wizard page prompts you to finish the animation.

Finishing the Wizard

The final page of the Animation Wizard prompts you to finalize the Wizard to create the animation. Use this Wizard page as described below.

*   Click the Finish button. The Animation Wizard will generate your animation, close the Animation Wizard pages, and open the animation in a Frames View window.

Viewing the Resulting Animation

To see what your animation looks like when played, choose View > Animation, or click the View Animation button on the toolbar. The Play View window will appear and the animation will play.

Closing the Play View Window

To close the Play View window, use one of the following methods:

*   Click the Close button in the Play View window's upper right corner

*   Double-click the file Control icon in the Play View window's upper left corner, or

*   Choose File > Close. ***Note**: Choosing this menu item will close both the Play View window and the Frames View window for the open animation.

▦ Duplicating an Existing Animation

The Duplicate Animation feature is a quick way to create another animation by copying frames from an existing animation. You can use the Duplicate Animation feature in one of two ways:

- Choose Window > Duplicate Animation, or

- Press <Shift> + <D>.

A copy of the animation will appear in another Frames View window.

NOTE: *The Edit > Duplicate menu item, the Duplicate toolbar button* ▣, *and the Duplicate item in the frame context menu are used to duplicate selected frames, not an entire animation.*

▣ Modifying an Existing Animation

Another method of creating an animation is to simply save an existing animation using a different file name (and/or a different animation file format). To do this, choose File > Save As. The Save As dialog box will appear. Use this dialog box to assign the animation a different file name, and if desired, a different file format and folder location. Refer to the "Saving an Animation" topic in chapter 22 to find more information on using the Save As dialog box.

Managing Animations

Opening Animations

You can open any supported animation file or any supported single image in Animation Shop. Note that when you open a single image file, Animation Shop will create a new animation consisting of just that frame.

Animations or images can be opened using any of the following methods:

- Choose File > Open or click the Open button on the toolbar, and then use the Open dialog box.

- Choose a previously opened file in the Most Recently Used list at the bottom of the File menu.

- Choose File > Browser, navigate to the folder where the file is located and then double-click the thumbnail image of the file you want to open.

Using the Open Dialog Box

Animation Shop 3 uses the same Open dialog box as Paint Shop Pro 7. Please refer to chapter 2 to find more information on how to use this dialog box.

Opening From the Most Recently Used List

The Most Recently Used list, shown below, contains the filenames most recently opened by Animation Shop. This list appears before the Exit item in the File menu. The list will be empty until you have opened a file in Animation Shop. To open a file via the Most Recently Used list, simply click the filename in the list.

Using the Browser

Animation Shop 3 uses the same browser window as Paint Shop Pro 7. Please refer to chapter 3 to find more information on how to use the browser.

NOTE: *If you chose to open a WMF or PCD image file, Animation Shop will display a format-specific dialog box requesting additional information about the file. Click the Help button for information on using the dialog box.*

NOTE: *If you choose to open an AVI, FLC or FLI animation file, an import dialog box specific to that file type will appear, requesting additional information about the file. Click the Help button for information on using the dialog box.*

Large File Warning

If you attempt to open an extremely large animation file, a warning message will appear stating the following:

"This file will exceed available physical memory if opened as proposed, which could impact system performance. Do you wish to continue?"

You can choose to continue or abort the opening of the file. Be aware that if you choose to continue, you may experience a slowdown in your computer's performance.

🖫 Saving an Animation

To save changes to an animation, choose File > Save, or click the Save button 🖫 on the toolbar. If you are saving modifications to a previously saved animation but are not choosing a different animation format, choosing Save will simply save the file to the hard disk.

If you are Saving a new animation or saving an existing animation to another file format by choosing File > Save As, the Save As dialog box will appear. Available animation file formats include GIF, MNG, AVI, ANI, FLC and FLI. Animation Shop 3 uses the same Save As dialog box as Paint Shop Pro 7. Please refer to chapter 4 to find more information on how to use this dialog box.

Saving in the AVI File Format

When you choose to save an animation in the AVI file format, Animation Shop will launch a wizard consisting of a series of pages that let you save your opened frames into a previously existing AVI file, or as a new file. The saving of modifications made to a previously saved file which was opened using only a subset of frames will not result in a loss of any of the unopened frames. To obtain more information on each of the wizard pages, refer to the Help file.

Optimizing the File

Saving an animation in GIF, FLC, FLI, or AVI format starts up Animation Shop's optimization process. Three optimization pages will appear. Follow the prompts on each page to optimize the file.

🖽 Saving Individual Frames

Save an individual animation frame or multiple frames to any of the supported output file formats as described below.

1. Select the frame(s).

2. Choose the Save Frame As command in one of the following ways:

- Choose File > Save Frames As,

- Click the Save Frames As button 🖽 on the toolbar, or

- Place the arrow tool inside the selected frame, right-click to display the Frame context menu, and then choose Save Frames As.

The "Save Frame As" dialog box, shown below, will open:.

NOTE: *If you selected multiple frames, the command will be labeled "Save Frames As."*

3. Use this dialog box to save the frame(s). If you want to save the frame(s) in a folder different from the current folder, choose the new location in the "Save in" drop down box. To create a new folder, click the Create New Folder button next to the "Save in" drop down box.

4. In the "File name" field, enter a name for the file.

5. In the "Save as type" drop down box, choose a file format for the frame. Be aware that some file formats have Save options available. Click the Options button in the Save Frame As dialog box to access these options.

6. Use the "File name formatting options" as follows:

- Choose the "Long file names" option if you want to use more than 8 characters in the root file name. The maximum number of characters is 256.

- Choose the "DOS 8.3 file names" option if you want to use DOS-compliant file names consisting of a maximum of 8 characters in the root and 3 characters in the extension.

- · (*Note: This option is only available when saving a single frame.) Mark the "Save frame number in file name" check box to append the frame number to the file name.

- Mark the "Append leading zeros to frame index" check box to add an appropriate number of zeros (if the animation contains 10 or more frames) to the filename as a way to sort the files in explorer views. For example, if you are saving frames 1, 2 and 3 in a 100-frame animation, the digits "001", "002", and "003" respectively would be added to the file names for frames 1, 2, and 3.

- Mark the "Save total frame count in file name" option to append a hyphen (-) character and the total frame count to the file name. *Note: This option is not available if you chose the "DOS 8.3 file names" option.

- Mark the "Save comment in file name" option to append the only the legal characters of the frame's comments to the file name. (Frame comments are applied by selecting a frame and choosing Animation > Frame Properties (or by choosing Properties in the frame context menu), clicking the Comments tab, and entering comments for the selected frame.) Be aware, however, that this option is not available if you chose the "DOS 8.3 file names" option.

NOTE: *If you have chosen to include leading zeros, the frame count, and frame comments in the file name and the resulting file name exceeds 256 characters, the comments characters will be shortened first, followed by the source animation name, until the name becomes less than or equal to 256 characters. Frame numbers will not be altered.*

NOTE: *When you decide to save more than one frame in the .psp file format the Save Frames As dialog box will offer you the option to create a separate image for each of the selected frames, or a single multilayered image in which each of the selected frames is turned into a layer. Select or unselect the appropriate check box accordingly.*

Closing an Animation

There are a number of ways in which you can close an open animation:

• Choosing File > Close, or

• Clicking the Close button ⊠ , or

• Using the File Control Icon 🖼 , or

• Choosing Window > Close All.

Each method is described below.

Choosing File > Close

Close an open animation by choosing File > Close. If you have modified the animation but have not yet saved the changes, the Save File window, shown below, will appear.

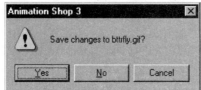

• Click Yes to save the changes and close the animation.

• Click No to close the animation without saving the changes.

• Click Cancel leave the animation open without saving the changes.

Clicking the Close Button

You can also close an animation by clicking the Close button ⊠ in the upper right corner of the animation's title bar. If you have modified the open animation but have not yet saved the changes, the Save File window will appear. Use this window as described on the previous page.

Using the File Control Icon

Another way to close an animation is by using the File Control icon 🖼 , located in the left corner of the animation's title bar. Double-click this icon to close the animation, or click it to display the Control menu, and choose Close. If you have modified the open animation but have not yet saved the changes, the Save File window will appear. Use this window as described on the previous page.

Choosing Window > Close All

To close all open animations, choose Window > Close All. If you have modified any of the open animations but have not yet saved the changes, the Save File window will appear, prompting you to save changed files. *Note that you will only see this prompt if the "Do not ask to save changes on Window Close All" check box is not marked in the "Miscellaneous" preferences dialog box.

Deleting Frames and Animations

Deleting Frames

You can delete selected frames from the animation as described below.

1. Select the frame(s) to delete.

2. Do one of the following:

- Click the Delete button 🔳 on the toolbar,

- Choose Edit > Delete,

- Press <Ctrl> + <X>, or

- Press the <Delete> key (<u>not</u> the <Del> key on the numeric keypad).

NOTE: *The Cut feature will also remove the frame(s) from the animation but will place them on the clipboard.*

Deleting an Animation

To delete an open animation from within Animation Shop, choose File > Delete. The "Confirm File Delete" window, shown below, will appear.

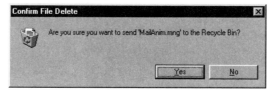

- Click Yes to close the file, delete it from its current folder, and place it in the Recycle Bin.

NOTE: *You will only be prompted to confirm deletion if the "Display delete confirmation dialog box" option is selected in the Recycle Bin properties. To verify the setting of this option, right-click on the Recycle Bin, choose Properties, and make sure this option is selected.*

- Click No to abort the deletion.

NOTE: *The Delete button 🔳 on the toolbar and the Delete item in the Frame context menu do <u>not</u> delete an animation, but only selected frames.*

Previewing a Printed Animation

To preview a page before printing, choose one of the two options available when using the Print Preview item in the File menu:

- Choose File > Print Preview > Animation to preview multiple frames on each page.
- Choose File > Print Preview > Frames to preview each frame on a separate page.

Previewing a Printed Animation

When you choose File > Print Preview > Animation, the animation print preview window, shown on the next page, appears. Use this window as described below.

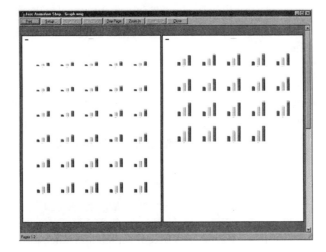

- Click the Print button to close the print preview window and display the Print dialog box.
- Click the Setup button to close the print preview window and display the Page Setup dialog box.
- If your animation spans multiple pages, click the Prev Page and Next Page buttons to navigate between pages.
- The button next to the Next Page button is labeled One Page or Two Page. When your animation spans multiple pages, click this button to toggle between previewing one page at a time or two pages.
- To zoom in and out, click the Zoom In or Zoom Out buttons. You can also click anywhere inside the preview window (the cursor will be shaped like a magnifying glass) to zoom.

Previewing Printed Frames

When you choose File > Print Preview > Frames, the frames print preview window, shown on the next page, appears. Use this window as described below.

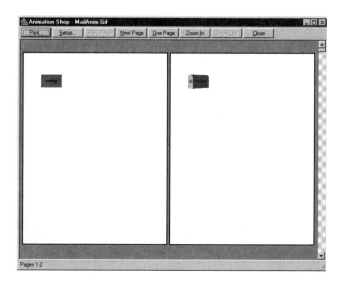

- Click the Print button to close the print preview window and display the Print dialog box.

- Click the Setup button to close the print preview window and display the Page Setup dialog box.

- Click the Prev Page and Next Page buttons to navigate between frames.

- The button next to the Next Page button is labeled One Page or Two Page. Click this button to toggle between previewing one frame at a time or two frames.

- To zoom in and out, click the Zoom In or Zoom Out buttons. You can also click anywhere inside the preview window (the cursor will be shaped like a magnifying glass) to zoom.

Page Setup for Printed Animations

Setting up a page for printing involves determining the paper source and the placement of the image(s) on the printed page. There are two options available when using the Page Setup item in the File menu:

- Choose File > Page Setup > Animation to print multiple frames on each page.

- Choose File > Page Setup > Frames to print individual frames on each page.

Page Setup for an Animation

When you choose File > Page Setup > Animation, the Page Setup dialog box for animations, shown below, appears. Use this dialog box as described below.

In the "Paper" area:

- Choose a paper size in the "Size" drop down box.

- Choose a paper source in the "Source" drop down box.

In the "Orientation" area:

- Choose either "Portrait" or "Landscape" for the orientation. Note that the thumbnail image at the top of the dialog box reflects the current setting.

In the "Margins (inches)" area:

- Click inside the "Left", "Right", "Top", and "Bottom" edit boxes to set the desired values.

NOTE: *To switch from "inches" to metric measurements, go into the Windows Control Panel, select Regional Settings, select the Numbers tab, and set the Measurement System setting to "metric."*

- Click the Printer button to select a printer other than the current default printer.

Page Setup for Frames

When you choose File > Page Setup > Frames, the Page Setup dialog box for frames, shown below, appears. Use this dialog box as described below.

In the "Paper" area:

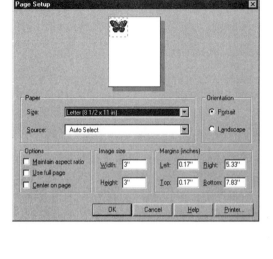

- Choose a paper size in the "Size" drop down box.

- Choose a paper source in the "Source" drop down box.

In the "Orientation" area:

- Choose either "Portrait" or "Landscape" for the orientation. Note that the thumbnail image at the top of the dialog box reflects the current setting.

In the "Options" area:

- Mark the "Maintain aspect ratio" check box to preserve the image's original width to height ratio.

- Mark the "Use full page" check box to fill as much of the printed page with the image.

- Mark the "Center on page" check box to center the image on the printed page.

In the "Image size" area:

- Click inside the "Width" and "Height" boxes to set the desired values.

NOTE: *You can choose any combination of options. Different combinations will produce different results and may override "Image size" and "Margins" settings.*

In the "Margins" area:

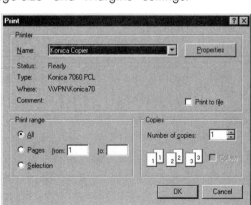

- Click inside the "Left", "Right", "Top", and "Bottom" boxes to set the desired values.

NOTE: *To switch from "inches" to metric measurements, go into the Windows Control Panel, select Regional Settings, select the Numbers tab, and set the Measurement System setting to "metric."*

- Click the Printer button to select a printer other than the current default printer.

Printing an Animation

There are three ways to print an animation or animation frames:

- Click the Print button 🖶 on the toolbar, or
- Choose File > Print > Animation to print animation frames, or
- Choose File > Print > Frames to print individual frames.

Using the Print Button

A quick way to print animation frames is to click the Print button on the toolbar. No dialog box or prompt will appear. The frames will print in the same way as choosing File > Print > Animation and then choosing "All" in the "Print range" area of the Print dialog box.

Printing Animation Frames

When you choose File > Print > Animation, the Print dialog box appears. Use this dialog box as described:

In the "Printer" area:

- Select a printer from the "Name" drop down box.

In the "Print range" area:

- Choose the "All" to print all animation frames, where each printed page contains multiple frames.
- Choose the "Pages" option, and then enter a page range, to print selected pages.
- Choose the "Selection" option to print selected frames. If no frames are selected, this option will be greyed out (unavailable).

In the "Copies" area:

- If you want to print multiple copies, set the "Number of copies" edit box to the desired value.

When you click the Print button, the printed page(s) will use the settings in the Page Setup dialog box accessed by choosing File > Page Setup > Animation.

Printing Individual Frames

When you choose File > Print > Frames, the Print dialog box, shown above, appears. Use this dialog box as described below.

In the "Printer" area:

- Select a printer from the "Name" drop down box.

In the "Print range" area:

- Choose the "All" option to print all animation frames, where each printed page contains a single frame.

- Choose the "Pages" option, and then enter a page range, to print selected pages.

- Choose the "Selection" option to print selected frames. If no frames are selected, this option will be greyed out (unavailable).

In the "Copies" area:

- If you want to print multiple copies, set the "Number of copies" edit box to the desired value.

When you click the Print button, the printed page(s) will use the settings in the Page Setup dialog box accessed by choosing File > Page Setup > Frames.

Manipulating Animations

Setting Animation Properties

Change animation properties by using the Animation Properties dialog box. This dialog box contains three tabs, labeled "Looping", "Comments", and "Canvas Color". To access the Animation Properties dialog box, do one of the following:

• Choose Animation > Animation Properties, or

• Right-click anywhere inside or outside the filmstrip border to display the Animation context menu, and then choose Animation Properties.

Using the Looping Tab

The Looping tab is used to set options for when your animation is used on the output medium (such as a CD-ROM or a website). Use the Looping tab as described below.

NOTE: *This feature applies only to GIF animations.*

* Choose the "Repeat the animation indefinitely" option to continuously cycle the animation until you manually stop it (see the Note below).

* Choose the "Play it *n* times" option, and then enter a value for *n* in the edit box, to play the animation the specified number of times. **Note:** Not all internet browsers currently support the loop feature.

Using the Comments Tab

The Comments tab provides a place for you to enter information such as notes, copyright, and author information. Use the Comments tab as described below.

* Click inside the text entry area, then enter your animation-related comments or notes.

Using the Canvas Color Tab

The Canvas Color tab allows you to select a canvas color for the animation. Use the Canvas Color tab as described below.

* Select the "Transparent" option to have a transparent canvas color.

* Select the "Opaque" option to have a non-transparent canvas color. The current canvas color appears in the color box. Left-click inside this color box to display the Color dialog box; right-click inside this color box to display the Recent Colors dialog box. Select the new canvas color using either of these dialog boxes.

* In the Animation Properties dialog box, click OK to return to your animation.

Setting Frame Properties

Change frame properties by using the Frame Properties dialog box. This dialog box contains two tabs, labeled "Display Time" and "Comments". To access the Frame Properties dialog box, do one of the following:

- Choose Animation > Frame Properties, or

- Right-click anywhere inside the filmstrip border to display the Frame context menu, and then choose Properties.

Using the Display Time Tab

The Display Time tab is used to set the duration of a selected frame. Use this tab as described below.

1. Select the frame(s).

2. Display the Frame Properties dialog box by choosing Animation > Frame Properties, or by right-clicking inside the filmstrip border to display the Frame context menu and choosing Frame Properties.

3. If it is not already selected, select the Display Time tab.

4. In the "Display time" field, set the desired display time and then click OK. Valid values range from 1 to 32,767. Setting the value to 100 will display the frame for one second.

Using the Comments Tab

The Comments tab provides a place for you to enter information such as notes, copyright, and author information. Use the Comments tab as described below.

- Click inside the text entry area, then enter your frame-related comments or notes.

Inserting Frames into an Animation

The menu item Animation > Insert Frames has two options for allowing you to insert frames into an animation. You can insert empty frames, or frames from another animation or image.

Inserting Empty Frames

You can insert empty frames into an animation using any of the following methods:

- Press the <Insert> key to insert an empty frame before the current frame. (not the <Ins> key on the numeric keypad)

- Choose Animation > Insert Frames > Empty

- Right-click inside the filmstrip border to display the Frame context menu, and then choose Insert Frames > Empty

- Drag-and-Drop an empty frame from one animation into another

- Copy an empty frame from one animation and paste it into another

NOTE: *There are two keyboard shortcuts you should be aware of. To insert an empty frame <u>before</u> the current frame, press <Ctrl> + <T>. To insert an empty frame <u>after</u> the current frame, press <Shift> + <Ctrl> + <T>.*

Each method is described below.

Via the <Insert> Key

When inserting blank frames via <Insert> key, they are placed before the selected frame or the most recently selected frame. The empty frames will use the current canvas color as well as the display time of the preceding frame. If there is no preceding frame, the empty frame will use the next frame's display time.

Via the Animation Menu Item

Choose Animation > Insert Frames > Empty. The Insert Empty Frames dialog box appears. Use this dialog box as described below.

- In the "Number of frames" edit box, enter the number of empty frames to insert.

- In the "Insert before frame" edit box, enter the frame number to insert the empty frame(s) before.

- In the "Frame delay time", set the delay time for the empty frame(s).

- In the "Contents of new frames" area, choose the "Blank to canvas color" option to fill the empty frame(s) with the current canvas color. Choose the "Carry forward contents of preceding frame" to copy the preceding frame's contents into the inserted frame(s).

Via the Frame Context Menu Item

Right-click inside the filmstrip border to display the Frame context menu, and then choose Insert Frames > Empty. The Insert Empty Frames dialog box appears. Use this dialog box as described in "Via the Animation Menu Item" above.

Via Drag-and-Drop

If another open animation contains an empty frame, you can use the Drag-and-Drop feature to add the empty frame to another animation as described below.

1. Position both animations so they are visible in the workspace.

2. Select the empty frame in the first animation and continue holding down the left mouse button.

3. Drag the cursor into the second animation and position it between the frame that will be before and the frame that will be after the inserted frame. The cursor shape will appear like the cursor in this example:

4. Release the mouse button to insert the empty frame.

Via Copy and Paste

If another animation contains an empty frame, you can copy the empty frame and then paste it into another animation as follows:

1. Select the empty frame and choose Edit > Copy (or press <Ctrl> + <C>).

2. In the animation you wish to insert the empty frame, select the frame that will be after the empty frame you copied in step 1.

3. Paste the empty frame into the animation by choosing Edit > Paste > As New Frames (or press <Ctrl> + <L>).

Inserting Frames from a File

You can insert frames from another animation or image into an animation using any of the following methods:

- Choose Animation > Insert Frames > From File
- Right-click inside the filmstrip border to display the Frame context menu, and then choose Insert Frames > From File
- Drag-and-Drop an image or a frame from one animation into another
- Copy an image or a frame from one animation and paste it into another

Each method is described below.

Via the Animation Menu Item

Choose Animation > Insert Frames > From File. The Insert Frames from Files dialog box appears.

Use this dialog box as described below.

- Click Add File button. The Open dialog box appears. Use the Open dialog box to choose the frames or image file you wish to add. Click the Open button to return to the Insert Frames from File dialog box. The file(s) you add will appear in the list box. If you added multiple files, you can use the Move Up and Move Down buttons to rearrange the order the files will be added. To remove a file from the list, select the file and then click the Remove File button.

In the "Placement of new frames" area:

- Use the "Insert before" edit box to select the frame that will come before the new frames.
- Use the "Delay time" edit box to set the delay time for the added frames.

In the "Images with different size/aspect ratio than animation" area:

- Set the location for the contents of the added frames by choosing either the "Upper left corner" option or the "Centered" option.

- Choose what to fill the rest of the frame with by choosing either the "Canvas color" option or the "Preceding frame's contents" option.

- Mark the "Scale frames to fit" check box to symmetrically scale the added frames to fit inside animation frame size.

Via the Context Menu Item

Right-click inside the filmstrip border to display the Frame context menu, and then choose Insert Frames> From File. The Insert Frames from Files dialog box appears. Use this dialog box as described in "Via the Animation Menu Item" above.

Via Drag-and-Drop

Use the Drag-and-Drop feature to add frames to another animation as described below.

1. Position both animations so they are visible in the workspace.

2. Select the frame in the first animation and continue holding down the left mouse button.

3. Drag the cursor into the second animation and position it between the frame that will be before and the frame that will be after the inserted frame. The cursor shape will appear like the cursor in this example:

4. Release the mouse button to insert the frame.

Via Copy and Paste

Copy a frame and then paste it into another animation as described below.

1. Select the frame to copy and choose Edit > Copy (or press <Ctrl> + <C>).

2. In the animation you wish to insert the frame, select the frame that will be after the frame you copied in step 1.

3. Paste the frame into the animation by choosing Edit > Paste > As New Frames (or press <Ctrl> + <L>).

Moving Around an Animation

There are a number of ways to move among animation frames, including the following:

- Using the Go To Frame feature
- Using the horizontal scroll bar in the animation's Frames View window
- Using the left and right arrow keys on the keyboard
- Using the <Home> and <End> keys

Also, a vertical scroll bar will appear in each frame if you are sufficiently zoomed in.

▓ Using the Go To Frame Feature

The Go To Frame feature allows you to move directly to a specified frame. Use this feature as described below.

1. Choose the Go To Frame menu item using one of the following methods:

   - Choose Edit > Go To Frame
   - Right-click outside the filmstrip border to display the Animation context menu, and then choose Go to Frame

   The Go To Frame dialog box will appear.

2. In the "Frame number" edit box, enter the frame number you wish to view, and then click OK. Note that the frame you move to does not automatically become the currently selected frame.

Using the Scroll Bar

To move through an animation quickly, place the cursor over the slider button inside the horizontal scroll bar, and then drag the button left or right. This is generally the fastest way to move among a large number of frames. Note that you can also click the left scroll button or the right scroll button to move left or right one frame at a time. The slider button and scroll bar buttons are illustrated below.

Using the Vertical Scroll Bar

If you are sufficiently zoomed in enough such that the height of the frames exceeds the height of the Frame View window, a vertical scroll bar will appear. You can then use this scroll bar to move a frame's view up and down.

Using the Arrow Keys

To move through an animation one frame at a time, press the left or right arrow key on the keyboard. The current frame changes according to the arrow key pressed. For example, if frame 3 is the current frame, pressing the right arrow key will make frame 4 the current frame.

Using the <Home> and <End> Keys

To go to the first animation frame, press the <Home> key. To go to the last animation frame, press the <End> key.

Arranging Frame View Windows

When you have multiple animations open in the workspace, you can arrange their windows by using the following Window menu items:

- Choose Window > Cascade to stack the frame view windows from the upper left corner of the workspace toward the lower right corner.

- Choose Window > Tile to align the frame view windows in rows and/or columns, depending on the number of open animations and the current size of the workspace.

Arranging Animation File Icons

When multiple animation files have been reduced to icons, you can arrange the icons along the bottom of the workspace. To do so, choose Window > Arrange Icons.

Displaying Another Open Animation

Open animations are listed at the bottom of the Window menu. The currently active animation will have a check mark to the left of the file name.

To make an inactive animation the active animation, select its file name from the list in the Window menu.

Viewing an Animation

You can see what your animation will look like when played by doing one of the following:

* Click the View Animation button ▦ on the toolbar

* Choose View > Animation

* Right click anywhere inside or outside the filmstrip border and select "View Animation" from the context menu.

The animation will play in a Play View window.

Stopping the Animation

You can stop the animation in any of the following ways:

* Click the View Animation button again, or

* Choose View > Animation again, or

* Click the Close button ⊠ in the upper right corner of the animation's Play View window.

* Right click anywhere inside or outside the filmstrip border and select "View Animation" from the context menu.

Viewing an Animation's HTML Code

To view the HTML code required to insert a saved animation onto a web page, choose View > HTML Code. The HTML Code dialog box, shown below, will appear. Use this dialog box as described below.

NOTE: *This feature is only available after you have saved the animation.*

* Click the "Copy to Clipboard" button to copy the HTML code to the clipboard. From there, you can use the Paste feature in your HTML editor to place the code onto a web page.

* Click the "Close" button to close the HTML Code dialog box.

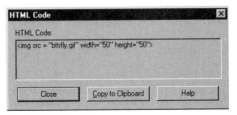

🐾 Previewing an Animation in a Web Browser

1. To preview an image/animation in a single or multiple web browsers, choose View > Preview in Web Browser. The Preview in WWW Browser dialog box will appear. Use this dialog box as follows:

2. The "Formats" field box offers you the different animation formats that your web browser will use to display your image or animation. Select the file format/s in which you want your web browser to display your current image or animation. Any images or animations whose original file format differs from the one/s you choose will be converted to match your file format selection.

3. Select the Browser you wish to use for your preview from the listbox "Web Browser". If this box is empty or if want to add a browser to this list, click the "Edit Web Browser" button to open the File Locations dialog box. Click the Browse button for the entry you wish to add or modify and use the Browse for Web Viewer dialog box to search for the Browser's .EXE file. After selecting the .EXE file, click the OK button to close the dialog box and return to the Browse for Web Viewer.

4. Select the width and the height of the animation from the "Size" panel. You can always go back the original dimensions of your image or animation by selecting the Default check box.

5. 4. Use the "Background color" box to select the HTML page background color. Left-clicking this box opens the Color dialog box from the Color dialog box. Right-clicking it will open the Recent Colors dialog box.

6. Click the "Preview" button and move through the next optimization dialog boxes by clicking the "Next button". When the optimization process is completed, click the Finish button. Animation Shop will start your web browser application to display your animation, according to the settings you selected.

Using the Basic Features

The Workspace

The workspace is the area where animation files and image files appear in Frames View windows, and where the Play View window plays an animation. You can expand the size of the workspace by stretching the top, bottom, left and right boundaries of the Animation Shop window. You can also use the Windows buttons in the upper right corner of the Title bar to maximize, minimize, or restore the size of the Animation Shop window.

Note also that right-clicking in the workspace displays the Paste As New Animation command. Choosing this command will paste any recognized image file on the clipboard into Animation Shop as a new single-frame animation. If the clipboard contents are not recognized by Animation Shop as a valid image file, this command will be greyed out (unavailable).

Saving, Loading and Deleting the Workspace

Animation Shop allows you to save your current workspace arrangement such as the open files and their positions, toolbar states, active tool, and zoom level, so you don't have to restore this environment manually.

To save the current workspace, choose File > Workspace > Save. The emerging Save Workspace dialog box will prompt you to assign a name and location for the workspace.

NOTE: *If your workspace contains any newly created animations that you have not yet saved, Animation Shop will prompt you to save them. If your click the "Yes" button in the query box the Save As dialog box will emerge, where you can assign a name and location for saving the new animations. If you press Cancel, the animation is not saved as part of the workspace*

NOTE: *If an animation cannot be saved in its current format because of the modification, a message appears describing the format limitation. Press OK to modify the animation and save it in its current format. Press Cancel to display the Save As dialog box, where you can change the file format. If you cancel the dialog box rather than saving the altered animation, Animation Shop will save the original, unmodified animation with the workspace.*

After saving your workspace, you can always retrieve its environment by choosing File > Workspace > Load. The emerging Load Workspace dialog box will prompt you to select the location and file name of the workspace you wish to load. Select one of your saved workspaces and click the Open button. Animation Shop will restore all the environment information contained in the selected workspace.

To delete a saved workspace, choose File > Workspace > Delete. The emerging Delete Workspace dialog box will prompt you to select the location and file name of the workspace you wish to delete. Select one of your saved workspaces and click the Delete button.

Whenever you save a workspace, Animation Shop only records the filename and the file-location of any animation currently open in the workspace but not the actual animation file itself. Please note that if you move or delete a file that you have saved, it will not be available when you load the workspace.

Selecting Frames

Select an individual frame by clicking on it with the arrow tool .

To select a consecutive series of frames, click the first frame in the series, hold down the <Shift> key, and then click the last frame in the series— all frame in between will be selected.

To select every frame in the animation, choose Edit > Select All.

To select non-consecutive frames, click the first frame, hold down the <Ctrl> key, and then click the other frames you wish to select.

Deselecting Frames

You can deselect any selected single frame by holding down <Ctrl> and clicking on it with the arrow tool. If multiple frames are selected, clicking on a frame (without holding down <Ctrl>) will deselect the other frames.

To deselect all selected frames, choose Edit > Select None.

Using Undo and Redo

The Undo and Redo features allow you to cancel the execution of an action, or redo what you have just "undone". Use these features as described below.

Using Undo

The Undo feature removes a modification or action you have just performed. Be aware that you cannot undo any modification that has been saved, nor can this feature undo changing the file-name or file format.

After modifying the file and before saving it, undo a modification using these methods:

- Choosing Edit > Undo, or
- Clicking the Undo button on the toolbar, or
- Clicking the down arrow on the toolbar (located directly to the right of the Undo button) and selecting the action you want to undo, from the undo history list

NOTE: *When you Undo an action using the history list you will delete the selected action and all actions that occurred after the selected action.*

- Using the keyboard shortcut <Ctrl> + <Z>, or
- Choosing Undo in the Frame context menu.

Using Undo will return the file to its state prior to the most recent operation. The number of operations you can undo depends on the settings in the "Undo" tab in the General Program Preferences dialog box.

Using Redo

The Redo feature re-applies the modification or action on which you have used the Undo feature.

To redo a modification that has been undone, use one of the following methods:

- Choose Edit > Redo, or
- Click the Redo button [icon] on the toolbar, or
- Clicking the down arrow [icon] on the toolbar (located directly to the right of the Redo button) and selecting the action you want to redo, from the undo history list

NOTE: *When you Redo an action using the history list you will Redo the selected action and all actions that occurred after the selected action.*

- Use the keyboard shortcut <Ctrl> + <Alt> + <Z>, or
- Choose Redo in the Frame context menu.

Reverting to the Previously Saved File

To abandon all modifications to the current file since it was last saved, choose File > Revert. The following prompt will appear:

- Click Yes to abandon all modifications since the file was last saved.

- Click No to cancel the Revert operation.

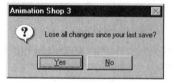

NOTE: *Revert only works on an animation. If you open a single-image file you must save it in an animation file format (GIF, MNG, AVI, FLC, or FLI) before using Revert to abandon modifications.*

Using the Cut, Copy, and Paste Commands

[icon] Using the Cut Command

The Cut command is used to remove frames from an animation and place them on the clipboard. You can then paste the frame into another animation or another application. Use the Cut command as described below.

1. Select the frame or frames you want to cut.

2. Cut the frame(s) from the animation and place them on the clipboard using one of the following methods:

    - Click the Cut button [icon] on the toolbar, or
    - Choose Edit > Cut, or
    - Press the keyboard combination <Ctrl> + <X>, or

- Right-click inside the filmstrip border to display the Frame context menu, and then choose Cut.

The frame(s) will be removed from the animation and placed on the clipboard.

Using the Copy Command

The Copy command is used to copy frames to the clipboard. You can then paste the frame(s) into another animation or another application. Use the Copy command as described below.

1. Select the frame or frames you want to copy.

2. Copy the frame(s) to the clipboard using one of the following methods:

- Click the Copy button 📋 on the toolbar, or

- Choose Edit > Copy, or

- Press the keyboard combination <Ctrl> + <C>, or

- Right-click inside the filmstrip border to display the Frame context menu, and then choose Copy.

The frame(s) will be copied to the clipboard.

Using the Paste Into Selected Frame Command

The Paste Into Selected Frame command is used to merge a frame from the clipboard into another frame either in the same animation or in a different animation. After it is pasted, the source frame (the frame you copied or cut to the clipboard) will use the properties of the target frame. This is useful to know when the source frame and target frame have different dimensions. Use the Paste Into Selected Frame command as described below.

1. Select the frame you want to paste (the source frame).

2. Cut or copy the frame to the clipboard by using the Cut or Copy command.

3. Select the target frame into which you want to paste the frame on the clipboard.

4. Paste the clipboard frame into the target frame using one of the following methods:

- Click the Paste Into Selected Frame button 📋 on the toolbar, or

- Choose Edit > Paste > Into Selected Frame, or

- Press the keyboard combination <Ctrl> + <E>, or

- Right-click inside the target frame to display the Frame context menu, and then choose Paste > Into Selected Frame

The source frame will be affected in the following ways:

- It will use the properties of the target frame.

- If necessary, it will be symmetrically resized to fit inside the target frame, and it will be positioned beginning in the top left corner.

Using the Paste Before 🖹/After 🖺 Current Frame Commands

The Paste Before/After Current Frame commands are used to place a frame or frames from the clipboard into another animation or into the same animation. (The latter usage would be helpful, for example, if you wanted to use the same frame or frames in another part of the same animation.) Use the Paste Before/After Current Frame commands as described below.

1. Select the frame or frames you want to paste.

2. Cut or copy them to the clipboard by using the Cut or Copy command.

3. Select the frame in front of or behind which you want to paste the frames you cut or copied to the clipboard.

4. Paste the clipboard frames using one of the following methods:

   • Choose Edit > Paste > Before/After Current Frame, or

   • Press the keyboard combination <Ctrl> + <L> (for pasting before current frame), or <Ctrl> + <Shift> + <L> (for pasting after current frame).

   • Right-click inside the filmstrip border to display the Frame context menu, and then choose Paste > Before/After Current Frame.

The frames will be pasted into the animation in the order they appeared in their source animation. Note also that the pasted frames will use the frame properties of the animation they are merged into. For both commands, once the pasted frames have been inserted into the animation, the pasted frames will be selected, all other frames will be unselected, the first of the pasted frames will be made current and anchor, and all the pasted frames will be made visible in the Frameview window.

🖼 Using the Paste As New Animation Command

The Paste As New Animation command allows you to create a new animation from a frame or frames cut or copied to the clipboard. For example, you could copy all or part of a Paint Shop Pro image to the clipboard, and then use the Paste As New Animation command to create a new single-frame animation. Or you could copy some text from a Microsoft Word document and create a new single-frame animation consisting of just the text.

Paste the clipboard contents as a new animation using any of the following methods:

• Click the Paste As New Animation button 🖼 on the toolbar, or

• Choose Edit > Paste > As New Animation, or

• Press the keyboard combination <Ctrl> + <V>, or

• Right-click on any empty part of the workspace to display the Paste As New Animation command, and then choose this command. *Note that if the clipboard contents are not recognized by Animation Shop as a valid image file, this command will be greyed out (unavailable).

Using the Propagate Paste Command

The Propagate Paste command allows you to drag-and-drop one or more source frames into target frames all having the same selection state (either the target frames are all selected or all unselected). This feature is actually a "mode," meaning you are in this mode until you turn it off. You can use this feature on the same animation or between multiple animations. Propagate Paste is a very useful feature when you want to copy or move a frame into a number of target frames simultaneously. Use the Propagate Paste command as described below.

1. Click the Propagate Paste button on the toolbar to "turn on" this mode. You will be in Propagate Paste mode until you click the button again to turn it off. (When it is turned on, the Propagate Paste button appears recessed in the toolbar; when it is turned off, the button appears flat on the toolbar.)

2. Select the source frame(s) and use drag-and-drop to place it/them onto the first target frame. Be aware of these factors when using drag-and-drop:

    *   Carefully consider the mouse pointer position when you begin dragging the source frame. This can affect how much of the source frame will appear in the target frames if the source frame is larger than the target frames.

    *   To copy the source frame(s), hold down the <Ctrl> key while dragging.

    *   To move the source frame(s) and snap them to one of nine target points shown in the illustration below, hold down the <Shift> key while dragging.

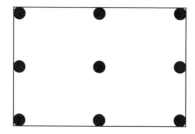

3. Position the source frame(s) as desired in the first target frame and release the mouse button. The source frame(s) will be placed in the same position in each frame that has the same selection state as the first target frame.

Frame Manipulation Commands

Duplicating Frames

You can quickly duplicate a frame or series of frames using the Duplicate command as described below.

1. Select the frame or frames you want to duplicate. Note that if you are selecting multiple frames, they do not have to be adjacent.

2. Choose the Duplicate command using one of these methods:

   • Choose Edit > Duplicate, or

   • Click the Duplicate button on the toolbar, or

   • Right-click inside the filmstrip border to display the Frame context menu, and then choose Duplicate.

3. The duplicated frame(s) will be inserted directly after the last selected frame.

Reversing Frames

You can reverse the order of all frames in the animation or selected frames as described below.

1. Select two or more frames. The frames do not have to be in a series (for example, you could reverse just frames 1 and 5).

2. Choose Animation > Reverse Frames. The order of the selected frames will be reversed.

Flipping Frames

You can flip a selected frame or frames vertically as described below.

1. Select the frame(s) to flip.

2. Choose Animation > Flip Frames. The selected frame(s) will be flipped vertically.

Mirroring Frames

You can mirror a selected frame or frames horizontally as described below.

1. Select the frame(s) to mirror.

2. Choose Animation > Mirror Frames. The selected frame(s) will be mirrored horizontally.

Culling Frames from an Animation

The Cull Animation command provides a useful way to remove frames that you might consider unnecessary or redundant. This can be helpful to reduce the size of your animation when it contains a large number of frames, many of which are very similar and can be removed without dramatically affecting the look of the animation when it is played. Use the Cull Animation command as described below.

1. Select multiple frames from which you can safely remove some of them, or do not select any frames in the animation.

2. Choose Animation > Cull Animation. The Cull Animation dialog box will appear.

3. In the "Remove 1 frame for every *n* frames" edit box, enter a value for *n* to set the number of frames to remove from the candidate frames.

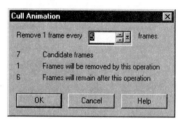

Note that listed below this edit box are the number of candidate frames, along with the number of frames removed and the number of frames remaining after the culling operation. These last two figures are automatically updated as you set the value for *n*.

The frames will be removed from the animation.

Rotating Frames

You can rotate a selected frame or frames as follows:

1. Select the frame(s) to rotate.

2. Choose Animation > Rotate. Animation Shop will open the Rotate dialog box.

3. Select the direction and a degree value for the rotation by choosing the appropriate radio buttons. If the degree value to want to apply is other than the ones included in the "Degrees" panel, type it in the "Free" text box.

4. Select the "Selected frames only" check box if you want to apply the rotation only to the frames you selected in the first step. Keep it empty if you want to rotate all the frames in the animation.

5. Use the "Expand canvas if needed" check box to control whether the canvas for all frames in the animation will be expanded if a rotation of angle other that 180 is specified.

6. Click the OK button. Animation Shop will rotate your animation according to the settings you selected.

Using the Onionskin Preview

The Onionskin Preview feature allows you to modify each selected frame in the active frameview by superimposing images from one or more adjacent or nearby frames on the frame being modified. This feature is especially helpful when painting specific frames with the contents of other frames. On applying the Onionskin Preview, your animation will be temporarily altered, as layers are "borrowed" from all frames participating in an overlay. The borrowed layers are returned to their original frames, as soon as each overlaid frame is painted. Use the Onionskin Preview feature as follows:

1. Adjust the Onionskin Preview settings by choosing View > Onionskin > Settings or double-clicking the Onionskin button on the toolbar. Animation Shop will open the Onionskin Settings dialog box, in which you can select the following options:

   - The **Onionskin Preview** checkbox controls whether the entire feature is enabled or disabled. It is synchronized with the View > Onionskin > Enabled menu item and the Onionskin button on the toolbar. Its default value is unchecked.

   - The **Overlays Per Side** radio-button group controls the number of onionskin overlays which will be placed on top of an image from each side that is contributing overlays. There are buttons for 1, 2, and 3 overlays per side. A shortage of frames for overlay on one side of a frame will not reduce the number of frames which can be overlaid from the other side. If an insufficient number of frames on either side are available and the Wrap checkbox is checked, the missing frames will be made up from the other end of the animation. The default number of overlays per side is 1.

   - The **Direction** group of radio buttons have the following effects:

     - If the "From left" radio button is checked, the specified number of overlays will be taken from the frames to the left of each frame being overlayed. For example, if frame 8 is to be overlayed with 2 overlays per side, it will be overlayed with frames 7 and 6 at reduced opacity.

     - If the "From right" radio button is checked, the specified number of overlays will be taken from the frames to the right of each frame being overlayed. For example, if frame 8 is to be overlayed with 2 overlays per side, it will be overlayed with frames 9 and 10 at reduced opacity.

     - If the "From left and right" checkboxes are checked, the specified number of overlays will be taken from the left and right of each frame being overlayed. For example, if frame 8 is to be overlayed with 1 overlay per side, it will be overlayed with frames 7 and 9 at reduced opacity.

- The **overlay opacity** is controlled by setting the "One frame away", "Two frames away", and "Three frames away" numeric edit controls. The "Two frames away" control is enabled only if the number of overlays per side is 2 or 3. The "Three frames away" control is enabled only if the number of overlays per side is 3. Each of these controls specifies, as a percentage, the opacity multiplier that will be applied to the opacity of each layer in the frames being used for the overlay.

- The **Proof** button will write the current settings to the registry and broadcast a request to all thumbviews to reload the Onionskin settings from the registry and then repaint their visible frames.

- The **Revert** button will write the settings which were read from the registry when the dialog was opened back to the registry, change the controls to reflect these original settings, and broadcast a request to all thumbviews to reload the Onionskin settings from the registry and then repaint their visible frames.

- The **Auto proof** checkbox controls whether any change in the Enabled, Overlays Per Side, Direction, Overlay Opacities, or Wrap controls will result in a "virtual" press of the Proof button, updating each of the thumbviews.

- The **Wrap** checkbox controls whether one end of each animation is thought to wrap around to its other end for the purpose of determining which frames are one, two, or three frames away during overlaying. For example, if an animation having 10 frames is being overlaid with Wrap unchecked, frame 1 of the animation has no frames to its left; if Wrap is checked, the frames to the left of frame 1 are 10, 9, and 8, and the frames to the right of frame 10 are 1, 2, and 3. Its default value is unchecked.

2. Select the **OK** button. Animation Shop will perform a "virtual" press of the Proof button, resulting in the settings being written out to the registry, all thumbviews being updated, and the dialog being closed.

Deleting Frames

You can delete selected frames from the animation as described below.

1. Select the frame(s) to delete.

2. Do one of the following:

   - Click the Delete button on the toolbar, or

   - Choose Edit > Delete, or

   - Press the <Delete> key (not the <Del> key on the numeric keypad).

Note that you can also use the Cut command to remove the frame(s) from the animation, but this will also place the frames on the clipboard.

⬚ Resizing an Animation

Although the dimensions of an animation's frames are set when you initially create the animation, you can resize the frames at any time by using the Resize Animation command. Open the Resize dialog box by choosing Animation > Resize Animation. Animation Shop 3 uses the same Open dialog box as Paint Shop Pro 7. Please refer to chapter 2 to find more information on how to use this dialog box.

Moving a Frame's Contents

You can move a frame's contents around by using the Mover tool. For more information, refer to the "Using the Mover Tool" section in Chapter 25, "Selecting Colors and Using Tools."

⬚ Replacing Colors

You can replace a color or transparent region within a selection of frames or a whole animation, either with another color or with a transparent region as follows:

1. Select the frame(s) on which you want to perform the color replacement.

2. Choose Animation > Replace Color. This will open the Replace Color dialog box.

3. Use the radio buttons in the "Replace color in" panel to specify whether you wish to perform the color replacement on all the animation frames or just on the selected ones.

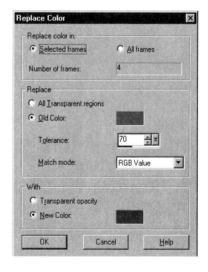

4. Select the color to be replaced.

   • Click on a specific area of a frame. The selected color will automatically appear in the "Replace" panel, or

   • Click the colored rectangle in the "Replace" panel and choosing a color from the Color dialog box, or

   • If instead of replacing a color you want to fill all the transparent regions inside the selected frames, select the appropriate radio button in the same panel. Use the Tolerance and Match Mode boxes to adjust the settings of the color replacement.

5. Select the replacement color by right clicking on a specific area of a frame. The selected color will automatically appear in the "With" panel. As in the previous step, you can also make your selection by clicking the colored rectangle in the "With" panel and choosing a color from the Color dialog box. If instead of using a color for your replacement you wish to use a transparent opacity, select the appropriate radio button in the "With" panel.

6. Click the OK button. Animation Shop will perform the color replacement according to the settings you selected.

Emptying the Clipboard

When you use the Cut and Copy commands, the data you have cut or copied is placed on the Windows clipboard, an area of your computer's memory used for temporary storage. You can then paste data from the clipboard to an animation. If the amount of data on the clipboard is very large, it can consume large amounts of memory and slow down your computer.

To empty (erase) the data in the clipboard, choose Edit > Empty Clipboard. Note, however, that this will remove the clipboard contents, making the data unavailable for pasting.

When you choose to exit Animation Shop with data still on the clipboard, you can choose to be prompted whether you wish to leave the data on the clipboard. Set this option in the "Miscellaneous" preferences dialog box in General Program Preferences as described in Chapter 29.

Minimizing All the Windows

The Minimize All command will minimize all non-minimized windows in the workspace and arrange them across the bottom of the workspace. Although this command is not undoable, you can restore or maximize each minimized window individually. To use the Minimize All command, choose Window > Minimize All in the main menu.

Selecting Colors and Using Tools

About the Color Dialog Box

The Color dialog box, which can be accessed by left-clicking on the foreground or background color box in the Active Colors Panel, contains the selection of available colors, and allows you to select and create colors to use in your animations.

There are actually two Color dialog boxes you can use: the Jasc Color dialog box, and the Standard Windows Color dialog box.

Until you change this setting, the Jasc Color dialog box is used to select and/or modify the foreground or background colors. You can, however, use the Standard Windows Color dialog box.

Choosing a Color Dialog Box

Select which color dialog box to use as described below.

1. Choose File > Preferences > General Program Preferences. The Preferences dialog box, shown below, will appear.

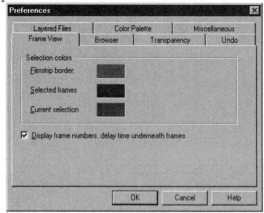

2. Select the "Color Palette" tab.

3. Do one of the following:

   - To use the standard Windows Color dialog box, mark the "Use standard Windows color picker" check box.

   - To use the Jasc Color dialog box, do not mark the "Use standard Windows color picker" check box.

4. Click OK to close the Preferences dialog box.

Using the Jasc Color Dialog Box

Animation Shop 3 uses the same Jasc Color dialog box as Paint Shop Pro 7. Please refer to chapter 9 to find more information on how to use this dialog box.

Using the Standard Windows Color Dialog Box

Animation Shop 3 uses the same Windows Color dialog box as Paint Shop Pro 7. Please refer to chapter 9 to find more information on how to use this dialog box.

Using the Recent Colors Dialog Box

Animation Shop 3 uses the same Windows Color dialog box as Paint Shop Pro 7. Please refer to chapter 9 to find more information on how to use this dialog box.

Using the Tool Palette Tools

Using the Arrow Tool

The Arrow tool is normally just used to select animation frames. The Arrow tool does, however, have additional functionality as described below.

Moving a Frame

To move a frame's contents into another frame, place the arrow inside the frame and drag (press and hold the left mouse button) the contents into the desired frame. The frame whose contents you moved will be removed from the animation, and the remaining animation frames will automatically reposition themselves. *Note that by holding down the <Shift> key while dragging, you can "snap" the frame into one of nine positions. Refer to the illustration in the "Using the Propagate Paste Command" topic in Chapter 7 for more information.

Copying a Frame's Opaque Pixels

You can use the arrow tool to duplicate a frame's contents. To do so, hold down the <Ctrl> key and then drag the frame's contents into another frame.

Creating a New Animation

You can create a new animation by using a frame or frames from the current animation. To do so, select a frame or frames and drag them onto the workspace. If you do not hold down the <Ctrl> key while dragging the frame(s), the frame(s) will be removed from the current animation. If you hold down <Ctrl> while dragging, you are essentially copying the frame(s) to create the new animation.

Accessing the Context Menus

The context menus contain easily accessible commands for modifying and manipulating frames or animations, as well as editing frame and animation properties. There are two context menus: the Frame context menu, and the Animation context menu. The illustration below shows where you need to right-click to display each context menu.

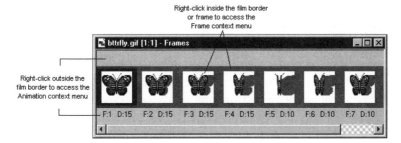

⌕ Using the Zoom Tool

The Zoom tool is used to zoom in or out on an animation. Animation Shop 3 uses the same zoom tool as Paint Shop Pro 7. Please refer to chapter 4 to find more information on how to use this tool.

✛ Using the Registration Mark Tool

The Registration Mark tool is a useful way to mark a specified position on each animation frame as a visual reference aid. You could then use a tool (such as the paintbrush, line, or text tool, for example) to modify each frame in the same location. The registration mark itself does not become part of the animation when it is played or printed, and it can be cleared away at any time.

Use the Registration Mark tool as described below.

1. Select the Registration Mark tool on the toolbar.

2. Use the tool's Style Bar options as follows:

- In the "Mark Style" drop down box, choose Small Cross (10 pixels across from origin to the edge), Medium Cross (20 pixels across from the origin to the edge), or Spanning Cross (spans the width of each frame). The lines ti draw the crosses are 1 pixel thick.

- Mark the "Auto Color" check box to override the foreground and background color settings and draw the cross in a color that contrasts the underlying color. If you do not mark the "Auto Color" check box, the cross will be the foreground color (if you left-click) or the background color (if you right-click).

3. (*You may want to zoom in on the animation for this step). Position the crosshairs cursor at the frame position you wish to mark, and then click to mark each frame.

Removing the Registration Mark

To remove the registration mark from the frames, click the Clear button in the Registration Mark style bar. Note that the Undo feature will not remove the registration mark from the frames.

Aligning Registration Marks

By holding down the <Shift> key and dragging selected frames from one registration-marked animation to another, you can snap the centerpoint of the dragged frames' registration mark to the centerpoint of the target frames' registration mark. This is useful when you want to precisely combine elements from one animation to another.

Using the Crop Tool

The Crop tool can be used to reduce the size of all animation frames, with the added effect of reducing the size of the animation file. Use the Crop tool as described below.

1. Click the Crop tool on the toolbar. The style bar will display the Crop tool buttons.

NOTE: *Because the Crop Tool is a standard Windows rectangle, the pixels in the right edge and the bottom edge of the selected area will not be included in the cropped image.*

2. At this point, you can set the size of the crop area in a number of ways:

- (*You may want to zoom in on the animation for this step.) Position the crop tool cursor at the frame position you want to begin drawing the crop rectangle (for example, the upper left corner of the desired crop area). The crop rectangle will begin drawing from the center of the crop cursor. Using the left mouse button, drag the cursor to create the crop rectangle. The rectangle will appear in each animation frame.

- Click the Crop button in the Style Bar to display the Crop Options dialog box. The Crop Options dialog box, shown below, is used to specify the cropping area.

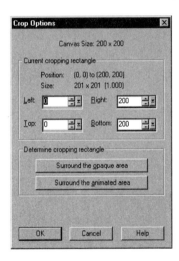

  Specify values for the Left, Right, Top, and Bottom positions. You can also click the "Surround the opaque area" button to automatically crop the frame to the least area which has all the opaque pixels in the animation. Or you can click the "Surround the animated area" button to automatically crop the frame to the least area containing pixels not constant for all frames. Note that clicking either button will update the Left, Right, Top, and Bottom pixel values in the "Current cropping rectangle" area of the dialog box.

- Double-click on the Crop tool button in the toolbar to display the Crop Options dialog box. Use this dialog box as described above.

3. To crop the animation, click the Crop button in the style bar, or double-click inside the crop rectangle. Each animation frame will be cropped.

If you wish to undo the crop operation, use the Undo command.

Clearing the Crop Rectangle

To clear the crop rectangle without cropping the frame, click the Clear button in the Crop style bar.

✛ Using the Mover Tool

The Mover tool ✛ allows you to move the frame contents within the frame itself.

To use the tool, select it from the Tool palette, place the Mover cursor ✛ into the frame, and drag inside the frame to move the contents. When you release the left mouse button, the contents will be essentially clipped to reveal only the parts of the original contents bounding box that have not been moved off the frame. To undo the move, use the Undo command.

Moving the Contents Horizontally or Vertically

To move the contents horizontally, hold down <Ctrl> when moving. To move the contents vertically, hold down <Shift> when moving.

✎ Using the Dropper Tool

The Dropper tool is used to select a foreground or background color. Animation Shop 3 uses the same Dropper tool as Paint Shop Pro 7. Please refer to chapter 9 to find more information on how to use this tool.

Activating the Dropper via Other Tools

You can also activate the Dropper tool by holding down the <Ctrl> key while using any of the following tools:

- Registration Mark
- Eraser
- Text
- Shape
- Paintbrush
- Flood Fill
- Line

✎ Using the Paintbrush Tool

The Paintbrush tool is used to paint on your animation frames. Use the Paintbrush tool as described below.

1. Select the Paintbrush tool ✎ from the tool palette. When you move the cursor over the image, the cursor shape changes to a brush.

2. Set the paintbrush tool's style bar options to the desired settings as described below.

   - Zoom drop down box: Choose a magnification level for working on the frame. The options for zooming in range from 2:1 (two times the normal view) to 32:1 (thirty two times the normal view). The options for zooming out range from 1:2 (one half the normal view) to 1:24 (one twenty-fourth the normal view).

   - Width edit box: Set the width of the paintbrush. Valid values range from 1 to 200. Note that the brush shape is round.

3. Animation Shop 3 uses the same Paintbrush tool as Paint Shop Pro 7. Please refer to chapter 8 to find more information on how to use this tool.

Using the Eraser Tool

The Eraser tool is used to replace pixels in a frame with the canvas color. Animation Shop 3 uses the same Eraser tool as Paint Shop Pro 7. Please refer to chapter 8 to find more information on how to use this tool.

Using the Flood Fill Tool

The Flood Fill tool is used to fill an area on a frame with a color. Use the Flood Fill tool as described below.

1. Select the Flood Fill tool from the tool palette.

2. Set the Style Bar options to the desired settings as described below:

- Match Mode drop down box: Choose the type of image pixels to fill. Choose "RGB value", "Hue", or "Brightness" to fill only the image pixels that match the RGB value, Hue value, or Brightness value of the pixels beneath the crosshair of the Flood Fill cursor. Choose "None" to fill all pixels in the frame with the color.

- Tolerance edit box: Set the desired tolerance value to determine how close a pixel color must be to the pixel you click on in order to be overwritten. Valid values range from 0 (no tolerance – only pixels with a perfect match will be filled) to 200 (full tolerance – all contiguous pixels will be filled).

- To Canvas Color check box: Mark this check box to use the animation's canvas color as the fill color. If the canvas is set to transparent, overwritten pixels will be transparent. If you do not mark this check box, pixels will be filled with the appropriate active color (the foreground or background color).

3. To fill the pixels, position the crosshair of the Flood Fill cursor over the frame area you wish to fill, and then left-click to fill with the foreground color, or right-click to fill with the background color. *Note: If the "To Canvas Color" check box is marked, clicking either mouse button will fill pixels with the canvas color instead of the foreground or background color.

Using the Text Tool

The Text tool is used to add non-animated text to a frame. You can only add text one frame at a time. Unlike other tool palette tools, options for the Text tool are set in a dialog box, not on the Style Bar. Add text to a frame as described below.

1. Select the Text tool from the tool palette. When moved into the frame the cursor's shape will change to this: ⁺ₐ

2. To determine text color, left-click (to use the foreground color) or right-click (to use the background color) on the frame. The Add Text dialog box will appear.

3. Use the Add Text dialog box to enter the text and set text options.

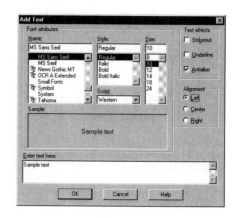

4. Select the desired Font Attributes, Text Effects, and Alignment options:

    *   Font Attributes: Select a font "Name" (typeface), "Style", and "Size" from the list boxes provided.

    *   Text Effects: Select any combination of the Strikeout, Underline, or Antialias effects by marking the check boxes.

    *   Alignment: Select either the Left, Center, or Right alignment options.

5. In the "Enter text here" box, type the text that will appear in the frame. Note that a preview of the text and the selected effects appears in the "Sample" area.

6. Click the OK button. Animation Shop will close the Add Text dialog box and the text will be attached to the mouse cursor and into the target frame. 5. The next click of any mouse button will detach the data from the mouse cursor and merge it into the target frame at the point where the mouse was clicked.

NOTE: *If you wish to change the text position or change the text color, use the Undo command and go back to step 2. You can also use the flood fill tool to change the text color.*

Using the Line Tool

The Line tool is used to draw straight lines as well as Bezier curves. Use the Line tool as described below.

Drawing Straight Lines

Draw straight lines as described below.

1. Select the Line tool ╱ from the tool palette.

2. Set the Style Bar options to the desired settings as described below:

    *   Line Type drop down box: Choose "Normal" to draw standard straight lines. (To draw Bezier curves, refer to the section below.)

    *   Width edit box: Set the pixel width for the line. Valid values range from 1 to 100.

    *   Antialias check box: Mark this check box to make line edges appear smoother.

3. To draw a line, position the crosshair center of the Line tool cursor ✝ where you want to begin the line, and then drag with the mouse button to the where you want to end the line. Release the mouse button. *Note the following points:

   - Drag with the left mouse button to draw with the foreground color.

   - Drag with the right mouse button to draw with the background color.

   - To draw lines in 45 degree increments, hold down <Shift> while dragging the mouse.

Drawing Bezier Curves

Draw a Bezier curve as described below.

1. Select the Line tool on the tool palette.

2. Set the Style Bar options to the desired settings as described below:

   - Line Type drop down box: Choose "Bezier" to draw Bezier curves.

   - Width edit box: Set the pixel width for the curve. Valid values range from 1 to 100.

   - Antialias check box: Mark this check box to make curve edges appear smoother.

3. To draw a Bezier curve, position the crosshair center of the Line tool cursor where you want to begin the curve, and then drag with the mouse button to the where you want to end the curve. Release the mouse button. A line will appear as you drag the mouse. *Note the following points:

   - Drag with the left mouse button to draw with the foreground color.

   - Drag with the right mouse button to draw with the background color.

4. Create the curve by clicking away from the line and dragging the mouse to the simultaneously shape the curve.

   - To create a semi-circular curve, click the mouse where you want to position the top of the curve, and drag the mouse to shape the curve.

   - To create an S-shaped curve, click and drag once on both sides of the line.

5. Click again to set the curve shape. The appropriate color will be applied.

▣ Using the Shape Tool

The Shape tool is used to draw rectangles, squares, ellipses, and circles. Use the Shape tool as described below.

1. Select the Shape tool ▣ from the tool palette.

2. Set the Style Bar options to the desired settings as described below.

- Shape drop down box: Choose the desired shape, either "Rectangle", "Square", "Ellipse", or "Circle."

- Style drop down box: Choose "Outlined" to draw just the outline of the shape. Choose "Filled" to fill the shape with either the foreground or background color.

- Outline Width edit box: Set the pixel width for the shape outline. Valid values range from 1 to 100. This edit box is disabled when the "Filled" shape style is chosen.

- Antialias check box: Mark this check box to make the shape's outline appear smoother.

3. To draw the shape, position the crosshair center of the Shape tool cursor ⌖ where you want to begin drawing. If you are drawing a rectangle or a square, drag from one corner to the opposite corner. If you are drawing an ellipse or a circle, drag from the center outward. An outline of the shape will appear as you drag the mouse. *Note the following points:

- Drag with the left mouse button to draw with the foreground color.

- Drag with the right mouse button to draw with the background color.

4. Release the mouse button when the shape reaches the desired size. If you are drawing a filled shape, the shape will be filled with the appropriate color when you release the mouse button.

Notes About Drawing

Be aware of the following points when drawing shapes:

- If you choose the Rectangle or Ellipse shape, you can draw a square or circle by holding down the <Shift> key before drawing the shape.

- You can draw arcs by choosing either the Ellipse or Circle shape and dragging the cursor outside the frame edges.

Using Transitions and Effects

Transitions and Effects Overview

The five items in the Effects menu provide a variety of transitions and effects you can apply to your animations. (These five menu items are also available in the Frame context menu.) By inserting and applying these transitions and effects, you can quickly, easily, and automatically create a sequence of dynamic animation frames.

Transitions vs. Effects

About Transitions

The transitions create additional frames, inserted between the source frame and the next frame, which serve as a transition between the frames. Transitions are created by choosing Effects > Insert Image Transition, or by choosing Insert Image Transition in the Frame context menu.

About Effects

The effects either create additional frames or modify selected frames by using an effect on the frames. The menu items Effects > Insert Image Effect and Effects > Insert Text Effect will create additional frames; the menu items Effects > Apply Image Effect and Effects > Apply Text Effect will modify existing frames. Note that these menu items can also be chosen in the Frame context menu.

Inserting Effects vs. Applying Effects

The task of inserting an effect or applying an effect are two slightly different tasks. The sections below provide an explanation of what each task does.

Inserting an Effect

When you choose to insert an effect, you select one animation frame as a starting point and, via the Insert Image Effect dialog box, you choose options to modify the starting frame by adding additional frames using the effect you have selected. This function basically copies the source frame a specified number of times and applies the effect to the new frames. You can choose to add the frames either before or after the source frame.

An Example Usage:

A good example use of the Insert Image Effect command would be if you had a frame that depicted a fish tank. If you wished to have the effect of sunlight dappling and water movement, the Underwater effect would be appropriate. In this case, a selected number of frames would be added to the single fish tank frame to create an animation of the fish tank.

Applying an Effect

When you choose to apply an effect, you select one or more animation frames as a starting point and, via the Apply Image Effect dialog box, you choose options to replace the source frame(s) with frames incorporating the effect you have selected. Unlike the Insert Image Transition or Insert Image Effect menu items, no additional frames are added to the animation. You can choose how many frames will be affected as well as how you wish to apply the effect.

An Example Usage: A good example use of the Apply Text Effect command would be if you had an animation of the earth rotating and you wished to add the text "World Wide Web" and have it scroll through the animation while the earth continues to rotate behind it. The Marquee text effect would be appropriate. In this case, no new frames are added to the animation, but the scrolling text would be applied to each frame.

Inserting an Image Transition

Image transitions, as the name implies, move you from one image to another using a visual transformation. Transitions are created by rendering and adding frames to an animation. There are many different effects you can create using the various transitions offered by Animation Shop. Some transitions work best between two dissimilar images, and some work best with similar images. Experiment to find the effect that works best for your animation.

Insert an image transition as described below.

1. Open an animation.

2. Select a frame to which you want to apply the transition. This is the "source" frame.

3. Choose Effects > Insert Image Transition, or right-click on the selected frame and choose Insert Image Transition from the Frame context menu. The Insert Image Transition dialog box will appear. You will define the transition using this dialog box.

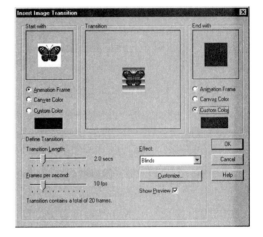

4. Use the options in the "Start with" area as described below.

- The "Start with" area displays the first image of the transition. Choose "Animation Frame" to use a selected frame in the current animation. Choose "Canvas Color" to use the canvas color as the starting image. Choose the "Custom Color" option to use a color of your own choice to start the transition. The current color is displayed in the color box below this option. Left-click inside this box to display the Color dialog box; right-click to display the Recent Colors dialog box. You can then choose your custom color.

5. Use the options in the "End with" area as described below.

- The "End with" area displays the ending image of the transition. Choose "Animation Frame" to use the next frame as the ending frame. Choose "Canvas Color" to use the canvas color as the starting image. Choose the "Custom Color" option to use a color of your own choice to end the transition. The current color is displayed in the color box below this option. Left-click inside this box to display the Color dialog box; right-click to display the Recent Colors dialog box. You can then choose your custom color.

6. Use the options in the "Define Transition" area as described below.

- Set the "Transition Length" slider to the number of seconds it will take to display the transition. Note that as you adjust this value the message below the "Frames per second" will correspondingly display the number of frames the transition will contain.

- Set the "Frames per second" slider to the number of frames to display in each second. Note that as you adjust this value the message below the "Frames per second" will correspondingly display the number of frames the transition will contain.

- From the "Transition" drop down list, choose a transition to use. If the transition can be customized, the Customize button will be active. Refer to the Animation Shop Help file for a description of each transition.

- To set custom parameters for the transition, click the Customize button and then use the transition's customize dialog box. Click the Help button in the transition's customize dialog box for details on using the dialog box.

- To preview what the transition will look like, mark the "Show Preview" check box. The preview will appear in the "Transition" area of the dialog box.

7. When you are finished defining the transition, click OK to insert the transition into the animation.

NOTE: *For a complete listing of Image Transitions, as well as explanations on their use, refer to the Animation Shop Help file.*

Inserting an Image Effect

Inserting an image effect provides a way to create additional frames using a visual transformation. There are many different effects you can create using the various options offered by Animation Shop. Experiment to find the effect that works best for your animation.

Insert an image effect as described below.

1. Open an animation.

2. Select the frame on which the effect will be based. The effect can be inserted either before the frame or after the frame. This is called the "Start with" or "source" frame. If multiple frames are selected, the effect will be inserted relative to the current frame (indicated by the "current selection" border color defined in the "Frames View" tab of the General Program Preferences). If no frames are selected, the most recently selected frame will be the source frame.

3. Choose Effects > Insert Image Effect, or right-click on the selected frame and choose Insert Image Effect from the Frame context menu. The Insert Image Effect dialog box will appear. You will define the effect using this dialog box.

4. Use the options in the "Start with" area as described below.

- The "Start with" area displays the source frame for the effect. Choose the "Animation Frame" option to start the effect with the current frame. Choose the "Canvas Color" option to start the effect with the canvas color (if the canvas color is transparent, the first frame in the effect will be transparent). Choose the "Custom Color" option to use a color of your own choice to start the effect. The current color is displayed in the color box below this option. Left-click inside this box to display the Color dialog box; right-click to display the Recent Colors dialog box. You can then choose your custom color.

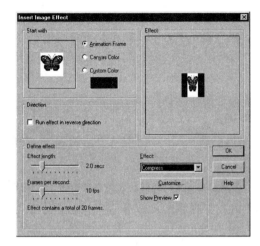

5. The "Effect" area shows what the effect will look like if the "Show Preview" check box, located in the "Define effect" area, is marked.

6. Use the options in the Define Effect area as described below.

- In the "Direction" area, do not mark the "Run effect in reverse order" check box if you wish to insert the frames in their normal order after the "Start with" frame. Mark this check box to insert the frames in reverse order before the "Start with" frame. Note, however, that the "Effect" will not preview the frames in reverse order.

- Set the "Effect length" slider to the number of seconds it will take to display the effect (this does not include the display time of the "Start with" frame). The range is from 0.1 to 10 seconds, and adjustments can be made in 0.1 second intervals. Note that as you adjust this slider, the message below the "Frames per second" slider will correspondingly update the total frames for the effect.

- Set the "Frames per second" slider to the desired display time for the effect frames. The range is from 1 to 50 in increments of 1. Note that as you adjust this slider, the message below the "Frames per second" slider will correspondingly update the total frames for the effect.

- From the "Effect" drop down list, choose an effect to use. If the effect can be customized, the Customize button will be active. Refer to the Animation Shop Help file for a description of each effect.

- To set custom parameters for the effect, click the Customize button and then use the effect's customize dialog box. Click the Help button in the effect's customize dialog box for details on using the dialog box.

- To preview what the effect will look like, mark the "Show Preview" check box. The preview will appear in the "Effect" area of the dialog box.

7. When finished defining the effect, click OK. The new frames will be added to the animation.

NOTE: *For a complete listing of Image Effects, as well as explanations on their use, refer to the Animation Shop Help file.*

Applying an Image Effect

Applying an image effect provides a way to replace selected frames with frames using a visual transformation. There are many different effects you can apply using the various options offered by Animation Shop. Experiment to find the effect that works best for your animation.

Apply an image effect as described below.

1. Open an animation.

2. Select a frame or frames (called the "source" frame(s)) to which you want to apply the effect.

3. Choose Effects > Apply Image Effect, or right-click on a selected frame and choose Apply Image Effect from the Frame context menu. The Apply Image Effect dialog box, shown below, will appear. You will define the effect using this dialog box.

4. The "Source" area of the dialog box displays the frame you have selected. Use the options in the "Apply effect by" area of the dialog box as described below.

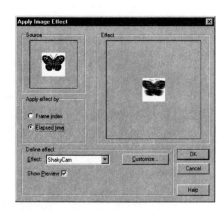

- Choose the "Frame index" option to apply the effect in an increasing intensity relative to the frame's position (its "index" value) in the effect. An illustrated example of this concept is shown on the next page.

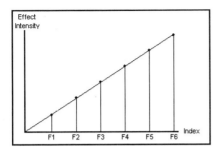

An example: You choose to apply an effect to six frames. In order, the frames have the following frame delays: 10, 10, 50, 10, 10, and 10. Choosing the Frame Index option, the effect would be applied to each frame in equally increasing steps (regardless of each frame's delay time). This is shown in the graph on the left.

- Choose the "Elapsed time" option to apply the effect in an increasing intensity relative to the sum of the delay times of all frames in the effect, including the current frame. An illustrated example of this concept is shown below.

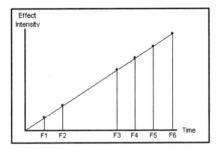

An example: You choose to apply an effect to six frames. In order, the frames have the following frame delays: 10, 10, 50, 10, 10, and 10. Choosing the Elapsed Time option, the effect would be applied to frames 1 and 2 in equally increasing steps, but proportionally more to frame 3 due to its greater frame delay time, and then again to frames 4, 5, and 6 in equally increasing steps. This is shown in the graph on the left.

5. Use the options in the "Define effect" area as described below.

- From the "Effect" drop down list, choose an effect to use. If the effect can be customized, the Customize button will be active. Refer to the Animation Shop Help file for a description of each effect.

- To set custom parameters for the effect, click the Customize button and then use the effect's customize dialog box. Click the Help button in the customize dialog box for details on using the dialog box.

- To preview what the effect will look like, mark the "Show Preview" check box. The preview will appear in the "Effect" area of this dialog box.

6. When finished defining the effect, click OK. The selected frame(s) will be replaced with frames containing the effect you applied.

NOTE: *For a complete listing of Image Effects, as well as explanations on their use, refer to the Animation Shop Help file.*

Inserting a Text Effect

Inserting a text effect provides a way to create additional frames that provide an eye-catching textual transformation. There are a variety of text effects you can use. Experiment to find the effect that works best for your animation.

Insert a text effect as described below.

1. Open an animation.

2. Select a frame to which you want to insert the effect after. This is called the "Start with" or "source" frame. If multiple frames are selected, the effect will be inserted relative to the current frame (indicated by the "current selection" border color defined in the "Frames View" tab of the General Program Preferences). If no frames are selected, the most recently selected frame will be the source frame.

3. Choose Effects > Insert Text Effect, or right-click on the selected frame and choose Insert Text Effect from the Frame context menu. The Insert Text Effect dialog box, shown below, will appear. You will define the effect using this dialog box.

4. The "Start with" area displays the source frame for the effect. Use the options in the "Start with" area as described below.

    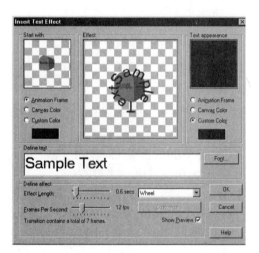

    • Choose the "Animation Frame" option to start the effect with the current frame. Choose the "Canvas Color" option to start the effect with the canvas color. (If the canvas color is transparent, the first frame in the effect will be transparent.) Choose the "Custom Color" option to use a color of your own choice to start the effect. The current color is displayed in the color box below this option. Left-click inside this box to display the Color dialog box; right-click to display the Recent Colors dialog box. You can then choose your custom color.

5. The "Effect" area shows what the effect will look like if the "Show Preview" check box, located in the "Define effect" area, is marked.

6. The "Text Appearance" area displays the image that text will have when incorporated into the effect. Use the options in the "Text appearance" area as described below.

- Choose the "Animation Frame" option to apply the frame that follows the current frame to the text (the text will be a "cutout" of this animation frame). Choose the "Custom Color" option to apply a color of your own choice to the text. The current color is displayed in the color box below this option. Left-click inside this box to display the Color dialog box; right-click to display the Recent Colors dialog box. You can then choose your custom color— the color you select will appear in the "Text Appearance" box.

7. In the "Define Text" area, click the Font button. This will display the Add Text dialog box. Use this dialog box to define the text. The text you enter in the Add Text dialog box will be displayed in the "Define text" area.

8. Use the options in the "Define Effect" area as described below.

- Set the "Effect length" slider to the number of seconds it will take to display the effect (this does not include the display time of the "Start with" frame). The range is from 0.1 to 10 seconds, and adjustments can be made in 0.1 second intervals. Note that as you adjust this slider, the message below the "Frames per second" slider will correspondingly update the total frames for the effect.

- Set the "Frames per second" slider to the desired display time for the effect frames. The range is from 1 to 50 in increments of 1. Note that as you adjust this slider, the message below the "Frames per second" slider will correspondingly update the total frames for the effect.

- From the "Effect" drop down list, choose an effect to use. If the effect can be customized, the Customize button will be active. Refer to the Animation Shop Help file for a description of each effect.

- To set custom parameters for the effect, click the Customize button and then use the effect's customize dialog box. Click the Help button in the effect's customize dialog box for details on using the dialog box.

- To preview what the effect will look like, mark the "Show Preview" check box. The preview will appear in the "Effect" area of the dialog box.

9. When finished defining the effect, click OK. The new frames will be added to the animation.

NOTE: *For a complete listing of Text Effects, as well as explanations on their use, refer to the Animation Shop Help file.*

▐ Applying a Text Effect

Applying a text effect provides a way to replace selected frames with frames that provide an eye-catching textual transformation. There are a variety of effects you can apply using the various options offered by Animation Shop. Experiment to find the effect that works best for your animation.

Apply a text effect as described below.

1. Open an animation.

2. Select a frame or frames (called the "source" frame(s)) to which you want to apply the effect.

3. Choose Effects > Apply Text Effect, or right-click on a selected frame and choose Apply Text Effect from the Frame context menu. The Apply Text Effect dialog box, shown here, will appear. You will define the effect using this dialog box.

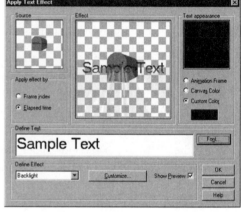

4. The "Source" area of the dialog box displays the frame(s) you have selected. Use the options in the "Apply effect by" area of the dialog box as described below.

• Choose the "Frame index" option to apply the effect in an increasing intensity relative to the frame's position (its "index" value) in the effect. An illustrated example of this concept is shown below.

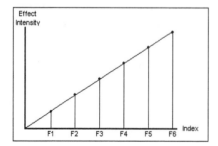

An example: You choose to apply an effect to six frames. In order, the frames have the following frame delays: 10, 10, 50, 10, 10, and 10. Choosing the Frame Index option, the effect would be applied to each frame in equally increasing steps (regardless of each frame's delay time). This is shown in the graph on the left.

- Choose the "Elapsed time" option to apply the effect in an increasing intensity relative to the sum of the delay times of all frames in the effect, including the current frame. An illustrated example of this concept is shown below.

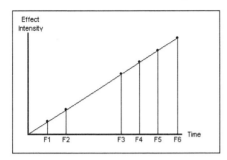

An example: You choose to apply an effect to six frames. In order, the frames have the following frame delays: 10, 10, 50, 10, 10, and 10. Choosing the Elapsed Time option, the effect would be applied to frames 1 and 2 in equally increasing steps, but proportionally more to frame 3 due to its greater frame delay time, and then again to frames 4, 5, and 6 in equally increasing steps. This is shown in the graph on the left.

5. The "Text Appearance" area displays the image that text will have when incorporated into the effect. Use the options in the "Text appearance" area as described below.

- Choose the "Animation Frame" option to apply the frame that follows the current frame to the text (the text will be a "cutout" of this animation frame). Choose the "Custom Color" option to apply a color of your own choice to the text. The current color is displayed in the color box below this option. Left-click inside this box to display the Color dialog box; right-click to display the Recent Colors dialog box. You can then choose your custom color— the color you select will appear in the "Text Appearance" box.

6. In the "Define Text" area, click the Font button. This will display the Add Text dialog box. Use this dialog box to define the text. The text you enter in the Add Text dialog box will be displayed in the "Define text" area.

7. Use the options in the "Define Effect" area as described below.

- From the "Effect" drop down list, choose an effect to use. If the effect can be customized, the Customize button will be active. Refer to the Animation Shop Help file for a description of each effect.

- To set custom parameters for the effect, click the Customize button and then use the effect's customize dialog box. Click the Help button in the effect's customize dialog box for details on using the dialog box.

- To preview what the effect will look like, mark the "Show Preview" check box. The preview will appear in the "Effect" area of the dialog box.

8. When finished defining the effect, click OK. The selected frame(s) will be replaced with frames containing the effect you applied.

NOTE: *For a complete listing of Text Effects, as well as explanations on their use, refer to the Animation Shop Help file.*

Creating an Animated Banner

Banner Wizard Overview

The Banner Wizard provides a quick, automated method of created an animated text banner. When you start up the wizard, you are guided through the process by a series of simple wizard pages on which you choose all the properties you'll need to create an animated text banner.

Starting the Wizard

Start the Banner Wizard in one of the following ways:

* Choose File > Banner Wizard,
* Click the Banner Wizard button ▶ on the toolbar, or
* Press <Shift> + <B>.

A series of wizard pages will appear, prompting you in creating an animated text banner. After finishing each page, click the Next button at the bottom of the page to move to the next page. You may move forward or backward by clicking the Back and Next buttons.

The first page prompts you to set the background.

Setting the Background

The first page of the Banner Wizard prompts you to set the background for the banner. Use this page as described below.

- Choose the "Transparent background" option to have a transparent banner background. A transparent canvas is indicated by the current color settings in the "Transparency" tab of the General Program Preferences.

- Choose the "Opaque background" option to have an opaque banner background. The current background color is displayed below this option. Left-click inside this color box to display the Color dialog box; right-click inside this box to display the Recent Colors dialog box. You can then choose your custom color.

- Choose the "Use a background image" option to have an image for your banner background. The Browse button becomes available. Click this button to choose the background image to use for the banner.

- Click Next to move to the next Wizard page.

The second page prompts you to set the banner size.

Setting the Banner Size

The second page of the Banner Wizard prompts you to define the size of the banner. Use this page as described below.

- Choose the "Use a standard banner size" option to set the banner size to one of the six internet standard choices in the drop down list.

- If you selected the "Use a background image" option in the previous Wizard page, choose the "Same as the background image" option to set the banner to match the background image size. If you did not select the "Use a background image" option in the previous Wizard page, this option will be greyed out.

- Choose the "As defined here" option, and then enter custom banner size values in the "Width" and "Height" edit boxes.

- Click Next to move to the next Wizard page.

The third wizard page prompts you to set the timing.

Setting the Timing

The third page of the Banner Wizard prompts you to define the display time for each frame, the number of frames displayed per second, and whether you want the animation looped indefinitely or a set number of times. Use this page as described below.

- Set the display time for each frame in the display time edit box. All frames in the animation will be set to the same display time. (You can change the display time for individual frames or all frames by using the Frame Properties feature.) The default value is 10. The value you set here (n) is displayed below each frame as "D:n".

- Set the number of animation frames to display per second in the number of frames edit box.

NOTE: *The total number of animation frames is determined by this formula:*

(Display Time / 10) * Frames Per Second

For example, if you set the display time value to 30 and the frames per second value to 15, the total number of animation frames will be 45: $(30/10) * 15 = 45$

- Choose the "Yes, repeat the animation indefinitely" option to continuously cycle your animation until you manually stop it (see the Note below).

- Choose the "Play it *n* times" option to play your animation the number of times you set in the edit box.

NOTE: *Not all internet browsers currently support the loop feature.*

- Click Next to move to the next Wizard page.

The fourth wizard page prompts you to define the banner text.

Defining the Banner Text

The fourth page of the Banner Wizard prompts you to enter and define the text for the banner. Use this page as described below.

- Click inside the text box and enter the text you want to appear in the banner.

- To change any of the font attributes (typeface, style, size, etc.), click the Set Font button and make the desired changes in the Add Text dialog box. Click OK in this dialog box to return to the fourth Wizard page.

- Click Next to move to the next Wizard page.

The fifth wizard page prompts you to set the text color.

Setting the Text Color

The fifth page of the Banner Wizard prompts you to define the color of the banner text, or if you want to use an image cutout for the text color. Use this page as described below.

- Choose the "Opaque text" option to set the text to an opaque color. The current text color is displayed in the color box below this option. Left-click inside this box to display the Color dialog box; right-click to display the Recent Colors dialog box. You can then choose your text color.

- Choose the "Image text" option to define the text color as the cutout of an image. The Browse button becomes available. Click this button to choose the image to use as a cutout for the text.

- Click Next to move to the next Wizard page.

The sixth wizard page prompts you to select a transition to use for the animated banner.

Selecting a Transition

The sixth page of the Banner Wizard prompts you to define the transition to use for the text. Use this dialog box as described below.

- Choose a transition from the "Transition Name" drop down list. Your choices include: Backlight, Bouncing, Drop Shadow, Flag, Highlight, Marquee, and Wheel.

- Click the Customize button to set additional options for the customizable transitions. Note that the Wheel effect is not customizable.

- If there is anything about the banner that you would like to change, click the Back button to go back to the desired Wizard page.

- To complete the Banner Wizard and display the banner in a Frames View window, click the Finish button.

Viewing the Resulting Animation

To see what your animation looks like when played, choose View > Animation, or click the View Animation button ▦ on the toolbar. The Play View window will appear and the animation will play.

Closing the Play View Window

To close the Play View window, use one of the following methods:

- Click the Close button in the Play View window's upper right corner, or

- Double-click the file Control icon in the Play View window's upper left corner, or

- Choose File > Close. *Note: Choosing this menu item will close both the Play View window and the Frames View window for the open animation.

Optimizing an Animation

Optimization Wizard Overview

The Optimization Wizard provides a way for you to determine the image quality of your animation and how that will affect the output size of the file. This process can be initiated whenever you save a new animation to any paletted format, or save an edited animation, or when you simply choose to run the Optimization Wizard feature in the File menu.

The wizard consists of a series of easy-to-use pages containing Back and Next buttons for navigating between pages.

Starting the Wizard

Start the Optimization Wizard by choosing File > Optimization Wizard. A series of wizard pages will appear, prompting you in optimizing the file. If applicable, make selections on the page, then click the Next button at the bottom of the page to move to the next page. You may move forward or backward by clicking the Back and Next buttons.

The first wizard page prompts you to optimize the output.

Optimizing Output

The first page of the Optimization Wizard prompts you to choose a file format and choose whether you wish to replace the file or create a new animation from the optimized animation. Use this page as described below.

In the "Optimize for" section:

• Choose the animation file format option appropriate for the animation.

NOTE: *Autodesk Animation (FLI) file support is not available at this time.*

In the "When finished" section:

• Choose the "Replace the current animation with the optimized version" option to overwrite the current animation with the optimized animation.

• Choose "Create a new animation from the optimized animation" option to create a new animation that you will then need to save.

The second wizard page prompts you to set the quality of the animation in relation to its file size. This page also contains some customization options.

Balancing Quality vs. Size

The second page of the Optimization Wizard prompts you to balance the animation's quality in relation to its file size. Use this second page as described below.

• Adjust the optimization slider on the left side of the wizard page to one of the four levels indicated by the mark on either side of the slider. When optimizing a file, you can choose to preserve image quality and consequently save a larger file, or you can sacrifice some image quality for a smaller file size. Note that the window to the right of the slider will display details specific to the slider setting.

• Mark the "Use these settings when saving unoptimized files" check box to skip the optimization interface and have Animation Shop automatically optimize with the current settings whenever an animation file is saved. Do not mark this check box if you wish to use the optimization interface when saving a file.

• Click the Customize button to access additional optimization settings. These settings are described in the next section.

Customizing Options

When you click the Customize button in the second optimization wizard page, the following customization screens will allow you to do the following:

- customize color settings
- customize optimization settings
- customize partial transparency settings
- customize canvas color settings

NOTE: *When optimizing a file in an animation format that does not support transparency, the third tab in the "Customize Optimization Settings" dialog box will be labeled "Canvas Color". When optimizing a file in a format that does support transparency, the third tab will be labeled "Partial Transparency".*

Customizing Color Settings

Use the Colors tab as described below.

- In the "Number of Colors" drop down box, choose the number of colors you want available in the animation. The current number of colors is displayed to the right of the drop down box.

In the "Create palette by" area:

- Choose "Optimized Octree" to use an 8-bits per channel palette. This palette is not as good at weighting color importance as the Optimized Median Cut palette.

- Choose "Optimized Median Cut" to use a palette that uses occurrence of colors as weighting, and ranks these colors accordingly. It is accurate only to 5-bits per channel.

- Choose "Standard palette" to use a generic palette that contains a balanced number of colors.

- Choose "Browser palette" to a pre-defined, web-safe palette.

- Choose "Custom palette" and then click the Browse button to use a custom palette not listed here.

In the "Reduce colors by" area:

- Choose "Ordered Dithering" to reduce colors by adjusting adjacent pixels of different colors to give the illusion of a third color. It uses set patterns based on a known palette to adjust the pixels. This method can result in distinct patterns of light and dark areas.

- Choose "Error Diffusion" to reduce colors by a method similar to "Nearest color", except that it spreads out the inaccuracy in representing a pixel's color to the surrounding pixels. When it replaces a color, the inaccuracy, or "error," is carried to the next pixel, where the error is added to the color before selecting the nearest color. This process is repeated for every pixel in the image.

- Choose "Nearest Color" to reduce colors by replacing a pixel's original color with the nearest matching color in the newly generated palette.

Customizing Optimization Settings

Use the Optimizations tab as described below.

- Mark the "Remove Non Visible Animation Elements" check box to help control the size of the animation by removing the non-visible elements.

- Mark the "Write Minimal Frames" check box to have Animation Shop automatically compare each frame to the previous frame and, if possible, write a smaller frame containing only the pixels that have changed. By default, this check box is marked for all quality levels.

- Mark the "Collapse Identical Frames" check box to have Animation Shop remove identical frames as another way to reduce the size of the animation. This option allows you to combine sequential frames having identical content into one frame. The display time of the frame will be the combined times of all the identical frames.

- Mark the "Map Identical Pixels To Transparent" check box to use transparent color in compressing a file. For file formats that support transparency, this check box is marked by default.

- Mark the "Enable Browser-Specific Optimizations" check box to enhance the optimization if you know that the audience for your animation will be using just one particular browser (for example, you'll be placing the animation on a website that can only be viewed via Internet Explorer). Note, however, that because not all browsers support this option, the animation may contain image artifacts when viewed with an unsupported browser.

Customizing Partial Transparency Settings

When optimizing a GIF file, use the Partial Transparency tab as described below.

In the "Partial transparency is not allowed …" area:

- Choose the "Convert pixels …" option and set the opacity threshold edit box to the desired level. Valid values range from 0 to 255. The percentage displayed to the right of the edit box will update in relation to the value you set. Pixel values at or above the value you set will be made fully opaque; pixel values below the value you set will be made fully transparent.

- Choose the "Use a 50% dither pattern" to use a halftone dither. Pixels below 25% opacity will be made fully transparent. Pixels above 75% opacity will be made fully opaque. Pixels between 25% and 75% will have the halftone dither applied, meaning the pixels will alternate between fully opaque and fully transparent in both the X and Y directions.

- Choose the "Use error diffusion dither" option to apply a 1-bit per pixel mask and error diffusion dithering.

In the "Would you like to blend …" area:

- Choose the "Yes, blend with this color" option. This will blend partially transparent pixels with the current blend color, displayed in the color box next to this option. To choose a different blend color, left-click inside this color box to display the Color dialog box, or right-click to display the Recent Colors dialog box. You can then choose a different blend color.

- Choose the "No, use the existing image color at 100% opacity" option to leave the color of partially transparent pixels unaffected.

Customizing Canvas Color Settings

When optimizing an AVI, FLC, or FLI file, use the Canvas Color tab as described below.

- Choose a color that will replace transparent canvas pixels. The current replacement color is displayed in the color box. To change this color, click inside the color box. This will display the Color dialog box, which you can use to choose a new replacement color.

Viewing Optimization Progress

The third page of the Optimization Wizard prompts you to view the progress of the optimization process. When the process is finished, click the Next button to move to the fourth page.

Viewing Optimization Preview

This wizard page allows you to preview the optimized animation before completing the Optimization Wizard. When you are done viewing the optimized animation, click the Next button to move to the fifth and final wizard page.

Viewing Optimization Results

The fifth and final page of the Optimization Wizard prompts you to view the results of the optimization process. Use this page as described below.

- This wizard page provides information about your animation's file size and estimated download times at various connection speeds. This can be helpful if you plan to use the animation on a web page. The "Current File" column displays pre-optimization file information. The "Optimized File" column displays file information after optimization.

- Click the Finish button. Your animation will be modified based on your wizard page choices and the Optimization Wizard will close.

Preferences and File Associations

Setting General Program Preferences

The general program preferences are a number of settings and options used by Animation Shop to determine how you display and work with your animations.

You can view or change any setting in the Preferences dialog box as follows:

1. Choose File > Preferences > General Program Preferences. The first tabbed screen in the Preferences will appear.

2. Select the tab containing the preference information you are looking for, and then set the desired options in the tab.

Animation Shop 3 contains seven General Program Preferences tabs. Each tab is described in the sections below.

Setting Browser Preferences

Animation Shop 3 uses the same Browser preferences tab as Paint Shop Pro 7. Please refer to chapter 20 to find more information on how to use this dialog box.

Setting Frame View Preferences

Set preferences in the Frame View tab as described below.

- The "Filmstrip border" color is displayed in the color box next to this option. To change the color, left-click inside this box to display the Color dialog box; right-click to display the Recent Colors dialog box. You can then choose another color.

- The "Selected frames" color is displayed in the color box next to this option. To change the color, left-click inside this box to display the Color dialog box; right-click to display the Recent Colors dialog box. You can then choose another color.

- The "Current selection" color is displayed in the color box next to this option. To change the color, left-click inside this box to display the Color dialog box; right-click to display the Recent Colors dialog box. You can then choose another color.

- The "Display frame numbers, delay time underneath frames" check box determines whether these two items will appear below each animation frame. Mark this check box to have them displayed; unmark this check box if you do not want them displayed.

The illustration below points out filmstrip border, selected frame border, and the current selection border.

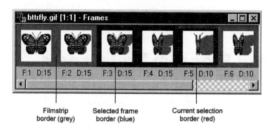

Setting Transparency Preferences

Animation Shop 3 uses the same Transparency preferences tab as Paint Shop Pro 7. Please refer to chapter 20 to find more information on how to use this dialog box.

Setting Undo Preferences

Animation Shop 3 uses the same Undo preferences tab as Paint Shop Pro 7. Please refer to chapter 20 to find more information on how to use this dialog box.

Setting Layered Files Preferences

Set preferences in the Layered Files tab as described below.

1. Select the "Export frames to Paint Shop Pro as layered images" checkbox to have Paint Shop Pro create a single multilayered image in which each of the exported frames is turned into a layer. Deselecting this check box will revert into a separate image per exported frame.

2. Choose one of the following four options:

- Choose the "Keep layers as separate frames" option to open each layer of the multi-layer file into a separate frame. Using the example layer letters above, the first frame will contain layer A, the second frame will contain layer B, the third frame will contain layer C, and the fourth frame will contain layer D. *Note: This is the default setting.

- Choose the "Merge layers into a single frame" option to open the multi-layer file into one frame containing each layer. For example, if you have a 4-layer file (where the layers are A, B, C, and D), selecting this option will open each layer into one frame: A on top of B on top of C on top of D.

- Choose the "Each frame contains all previous layers" option to open each layer of the multi-layer file into frames containing successive layers. Using the example layer letters above, the first frame will contain layer A, the second frame will contain layers A and B, the third frame will contain layers A, B, and C, and the fourth frame will contain layers A, B, C, and D.

- Choose the "Each frame shows first and current layers" option to open each layer of the multi-layer file into frames containing the first and current layer. Using the example layer letters above, the first frame will contain layer A, the second frame will contain layers A and B, the third frame will contain layers A and C, and the fourth frame will contain layers A and D.

3. Set the "Preserve overall layer transparency" check box as follows:

- Mark the check box to retain the transparency level set for each layer.

- Unmark the check box to ignore each transparency level and instead set them all to 100% opaque.

4. Close and re-open Animation Shop to apply the preferences that you selected.

Setting Color Palette Preferences

Set preferences in the Color Palette tab as described below.

1. Set the "Use standard Windows color picker" check box as follows:

- Do not mark this check box if you wish to use the Jasc Color dialog box when selecting or modifying colors.

- Mark this check box if you wish to use the standard Windows Color dialog box when selecting or modifying colors.

2. Choose one of the following two options for displaying color values:

- Choose the "Display colors in Decimal" option to show decimal values in the Current Color panel.

- Choose the "Display colors in Hexadecimal" option to show hexidecimal values in the Current Color panel.

Setting Miscellaneous Preferences

Set preferences in the Miscellaneous tab as described below.

- Do not mark the "Do not ask to save changes on Window Close All" check box if you want to be prompted to save modified animations when you choose Window > Close All. Mark this check box if you do not want to be prompted to save modified animations.

- Do not mark the "Do not ask to empty the clipboard on Exit" check box if you want to be prompted to manage the contents of the clipboard when you exit Animation Shop. Mark this check box if you do not want to be prompted to manage the clipboard contents.

- Do not mark the "Show splash screen when application starts" check box if you do not want to see the Animation Shop splash screen when starting the program. Mark this check box if you want to see the splash screen.

- Do not mark the "Display menu icons" check box if you do not want Animation Shop to display the icons associated with most menu items.

- Do not mark the "Show warning when reading PSD files containing adjustment layers" check box if you do not want to be warned when opening Photoshop files that contain adjustment layers. Mark this check box if you want to be warned when opening these files.

- The "Display frame count in window under animation" check box determines whether the frame number will appear below each animation frame as it runs in a Play View window. Mark this check box to have the frame number appear; unmark this check box if you do not want the frame number to appear.

Setting File Format Preferences

The file formats listed via the menu item File > Preferences > File Format Preferences warrant special user attention for reasons specific to each file format. Most file types can be opened in Animation Shop by using the File > Open menu item. Animation Shop can correctly display these files without special intervention from you. Other file types, however, such as PCD, PostScript, and WMF, warrant special attention because they may not contain all the information Animation Shop needs to display them correctly. Information about setting preferences for these two file types is described below.

Setting PCD File Format Preferences

Set preferences for the PCD file format as described below.

1. Choose File > Preferences > File Format Preferences. The File Format Preferences dialog box will appear.

2. If it is not already displayed, click the "PCD" tab. Use the PCD preferences dialog box as follows:

- Choose one of the seven defined sizes (expressed as pixel width by pixel height) to open a Kodak Photo-CD image in that size.

- Choose the "Ask when loading each file" option to display this dialog box when loading a Kodak Photo-CD image; you would then select one of the available sizes.

Setting PostScript File Format Preferences

Set preferences for the PostScript file format as described below.

1. Choose File > Preferences > File Format Preferences. The File Format Preferences dialog box will appear.

2. Click the "PostScript" tab. Use the PostScript file format preferences dialog box as follows:

- Mark the "Prompt for size and options each time a PostScript file is opened" check box to display the "PostScript Renderer" dialog box (see the Note below) whenever you open a PostScript file in Animation Shop. Be aware that if you are using this option, the settings in the "Size and options when not prompting" panel will be ignored.

- Do <u>not</u> mark the "Prompt for size and options each time a PostScript file is opened" check box if you wish to open PostScript files using the options in the "Size and options when not prompting" panel. These options are described below. (**Note:** These are the same options used in the "PostScript Renderer" dialog box.)

  * In the "Resolution" edit box, set an image resolution. The default setting is 72 dpi. Valid values range from 1 to 32767.
  * In the "Page Size" drop down box, choose a paper size for the image.
  * In the "Image Mode" drop down box, choose a color depth for the image.
  * Mark the "Landscape" check box if you wish to use this orientation. If you do not mark this check box, the portrait orientation will be used.
  * Mark the "Antialiasing" check box to use this edge smoothing technique.
  * If the image has a transparent background you wish to retain, mark the "Render Transparency" check box. If you do not mark this check box, the image will have a white background.

A Note About Opening and Saving PostScript Files in Animation Shop

Animation Shop can read PostScript files through Level 2 and convert them into raster files. It can convert up to 100 pages (depending on your computer's RAM), antialias the objects, and retain information on transparency. Note, however, that if you open a PostScript file and then save it, the file is not identical to the original because it has been converted into raster format.

Setting WMF File Format Preferences

Animation Shop 3 uses the same WMF/Import preferences tab as Paint Shop Pro 7. Please refer to chapter 20 to find more information on how to use this dialog box.

Using the Meta Picture Import Dialog Box

When you choose to open a Windows Metafile image, the Meta Picture Import dialog box will appear if you selected the appropriate option in the WMF file format preferences dialog box. The Meta Picture Import dialog box allows you the option of opening the image using pixel dimensions that differ from the original dimensions. Use this dialog box as follows:

- To use the original pixel dimensions (listed in the "Original size" area), simply click the OK button at the bottom of the dialog box.

- In the "Import size" area, you can use different pixel dimensions by entering them in the "Width in pixels" and the "Height in pixels" edit boxes.

- Mark the "Maintain original aspect ratio" check box to automatically keep the width and height pixel values within the same aspect ratio as the original dimensions. Do not mark this check box if you wish to ignore the original aspect ratio when setting pixel values.

Setting File Associations

File associations allow you to associate (link) specific file types with Animation Shop. By associating a file type, double-clicking the file name in Windows Explorer or My Computer, for example, would automatically open up the file in Animation Shop.

When Animation Shop is started up for the first time, you will be asked to select file types for association. The selected file types may be changed at any time using the File Format Associations dialog box. Access this dialog box by choosing File > Preferences > File Associations.

Using the File Format Associations Dialog Box

Animation Shop 3 uses the same File Format Association dialog box as Paint Shop Pro 7. Please refer to chapter 20 to find more information on how to use this dialog box.

Interacting with Paint Shop Pro

Starting Up Paint Shop Pro from within Animation Shop

To start up Paint Shop Pro 7 from within Animation Shop 3, choose File > Run Paint Shop Pro. Paint Shop Pro 7 will start up, and you can use the two complementary applications as described in this chapter.

Another way to start up start up Paint Shop Pro is by selecting a frame (or frames) and then choosing File > Export Frames to Paint Shop Pro, or to choose Export Frames to Paint Shop Pro from the Frame context menu. This will automatically place the frame(s) into Paint Shop Pro and establish the link between the two applications.

▓ Exporting Animation Frames to Paint Shop Pro

Export selected animation frames into Paint Shop Pro as described below.

1. Select the frame(s) you want to export into Paint Shop Pro.

2. Export the selected frame(s) using any of the following methods:

- Choose File > Export Frames > To Paint Shop Pro, or

- Click the Export Frames to Paint Shop Pro button ▓ on the toolbar, or

- Right-click anywhere inside the animation to display the Frame context menu, and then choose Export Frames to Paint Shop Pro.

If it is not already running, the Paint Shop Pro application will start up and the selected frame(s) will open. You can then modify these frames as you would any other image in Paint Shop Pro.

NOTE: *You cannot modify the animation in Animation Shop until you close the exported frame(s) in Paint Shop Pro. To indicate that exported frames remain open, the Animation Shop cursor shape will change to a wait icon when placed over any frame currently open in Paint Shop Pro.*

▓ Exporting Animation Frames as Paint Shop Pro Tubes

The "Export to Picture Tube" tool allows you to use all or some of the frames in your animation to create Paint Shop Pro picture tubes. Follow the steps below:

1. Select the frames that you want to turn into Paint Shop Pro picture tubes by holding the <Ctrl> key and clicking inside each of the frames.

2. Choose File > Export Frames > To Picture Tube. Animation Shop will open the Export Picture Tube dialog box.

3. Select an option for the three following text panels:

- Export: Select the appropriate radio button according to whether you want to export all the frames in the animation or just the selected ones.

- Placement options:

    1. Select Random or Continuous placement mode to control whether the Picture Tubes appear in the image at random or equal intervals.

    2. Type a step size. As you decrease the step size, the distance between the intervals at which the tubes appear in the image decreases.

3. Paint Shop Pro selects the cells (images) it paints based on the mode you choose from the Selection Mode list:

Random	The Random mode randomly selects images in the tube.
Incremental	The Incremental mode selects the first image in the tube and repeats it only after it has selected all the images.
Angular	The Angular mode selects images based on the direction you drag the cursor as you paint.
Pressure	The Pressure mode uses pressure from a pressure sensitive pad to determine which image to select.
Velocity	The Velocity mode selects images based on the speed you drag the cursor as you paint.

- Save as:

  1. Use the Tube name text box to type a name for your new tube.

  2. Use the File name text box to type the path in which the Paint Shop Pro Tubes folder resides. You can also use the Browse button to navigate to the exact location of the Paint Shop Pro Tubes folder.

4. Click the OK button. Animation Shop will close the Export Picture Tube dialog box and include your newly created tube in the list of available picture tubes of Paint Shop Pro.

Updating the Exported Frames

After modifying exported frames in Paint Shop Pro, you can incorporate the modifications into the associated frames by doing one of the following steps:

- In Paint Shop Pro, choose Edit > Update Back to Animation Shop. This will update the frame to reflect your modifications. *Note that this will not close the file in Paint Shop Pro.

- In Paint Shop Pro, choose File > Exit. When prompted to update the frame before closing the file, choose Yes. The Animation Shop frame will be updated and Paint Shop Pro will close the file.

- In Paint Shop Pro, close the file. You'll be asked to save changes and update the frame in Animation Shop. Choose Yes to update the frames and close the file.

⊞ Breaking the Link with Exported Frames

When a frame (or frames) has been exported to Paint Shop Pro, a link is established between Animation Shop and Paint Shop Pro. This link prevents you from working on the animation until you break the link. You can break the link using one of the following methods:

- In Animation Shop, choose File > Break Link With Exported Frames, or right-click inside the filmstrip border to display the Frame context menu, and choose Break Link With Exported Frames. This closes the file in Paint Shop Pro, but does <u>not</u> update the frame with any modifications you may have made.

- In Paint Shop Pro, choose Edit > Update Back to Animation Shop. This will update the frame to reflect your modifications. This will not close the file in Paint Shop Pro.

- In Paint Shop Pro, close the file. You'll be asked to save changes and update the frame in Animation Shop. Choose Yes to update the frames and close the file; choose No to close the file and not update the frames.

- Using the keyboard shortcut <Ctrl> + <PAUSE>.

Undoing Paint Shop Pro Modifications

After modifying a frame in Paint Shop Pro and then updating the frame in Animation Shop, you cannot undo the modifications until you break the link with Paint Shop Pro. (Refer to the section Breaking the Link with Exported Frames above for information.) Once you have broken the link with Paint Shop Pro, you can use Animation Shop's Undo command as described below.

- Click the Undo button ⟲ on the Animation Shop toolbar, or

- Use the keyboard shortcut <Ctrl> + <Z>, or

- Choose Edit > Undo, or

- Right-click inside the filmstrip border to display the Frame context menu, and then choose Undo Update from PSP.

Drag-and-Drop Between Animation Shop and Paint Shop Pro

Animation Shop 3 and Paint Shop Pro 7 allow you to drag-and-drop files between the two applications. Use this feature as described below.

Dragging from Animation Shop into Paint Shop Pro

The easiest way to do this is to have both application windows visible on your screen.

1. Select a frame (or frames).

2. Hold down the <Ctrl> key, place the cursor inside the frame, and then drag the selected frame(s) into the Paint Shop Pro workspace.

3. Release the mouse button. The frame(s) will open in Paint Shop Pro as an individual image (or images).

NOTE: *Using drag-and-drop means that the frames are not linked to their associated animation in Animation Shop. Thus, any modifications you make in Paint Shop Pro will not be reflected in Animation Shop.*

Dragging from Paint Shop Pro into Animation Shop

The easiest way to do this is to have both application windows visible on your screen.

1. Select an image (or images).

2. Place the cursor inside the image, and then drag the selected frame(s) into the Animation Shop.

3. Drop the images under the following conditions:

   • Drop an image onto an empty part of the Animation Shop workspace to create a new animation. If the image has multiple layers, depending on the setting of the "Layered Files" tab in the General Program Preferences, the new animation could consist of one or more frames.

   • Drop an image onto an animation frame to overlay that frame.

   • Drop an image between animation frames to insert it as a new frame.

Using Cut, Copy, and Paste

You can cut or copy a selected animation frame (or frames) and paste into Paint Shop Pro using that program's available Paste command options. Likewise, you can cut or copy a Paint Shop Pro image (or images) and paste into Animation Shop using this program's available Paste command options. Please, refer to chapter 24 for more information on how to use these commands in Animation Shop 3.

Dragging from the Paint Shop Pro Layer Palette

The redesigned Layer Palette in Paint Shop Pro 7 allows you to drag a layer into Animation Shop under the following conditions:

- Drop an image onto an empty part of the Animation Shop workspace to create a new animation. If the image has multiple layers, depending on the setting of the "Layered Files" tab in the General Program Preferences, the new animation could consist of one or more frames.

- Drop an image onto an animation frame to overlay that frame.

- Drop an image between animation frames to insert it as a new frame.

Refer to the Help file for more information on using the Layer Palette.

File Formats

Paint Shop Pro and Animation Shop directly support a wide selection of file formats, including 34 raster image formats and 13 meta and vector image formats. In addition, Animation Shop supports several video and animation formats as described later in this Appendix.

Supported Raster Formats

A raster format breaks an image into a grid of equally-sized pieces, called pixels, and records color information for each pixel. The number of colors the file contains is determined by the bits-per-pixel: the more information recorded for each pixel, the more shades and hues the file can contain.

Most raster formats support multiple bits-per-pixel levels, and therefore more than one level of color. The table below lists all the bits-per-pixel ratios in the raster formats that Paint Shop Pro supports, and shows the corresponding maximum number of colors.

Bits-Per-Pixel and Color Depth

Bits-Per-Pixel	Maximum Number of Colors
1	2
4	16
8	256
16	32,768 or 65,536 (depends on format)
24	16,777,216
32	16,777,216

Most raster formats record color information on a pixel-by-pixel basis, but some formats use color planes. Each color plane contains all the pixel information for a single color. Color planes are also called color channels. Formats that use color planes/channels are called planar formats.

The bits-per-pixel are determined by multiplying the bits-per-plane by the number of planes. If the resulting number is not a power of two (expressible as 2x, where x is an integer), then the bits-per-pixel are "promoted" to the next highest power of two. For example, if there are two bits-per-plane and three planes, the bits-per-pixel are promoted to eight:

$2 \times 3 = 6$, and $2^2 < 6 < 2^3$

Raster Image Formats

The table below shows the file formats Paint Shop Pro can open and save:

Format	Sub-Format and Description	Bits-Per-Pixel and Color Type 🗁 Open	Bits-Per-Pixel and Color Type 🖫 Save
BMP	RGB encoded (OS/2)	1-bit, 4-bit, 8-bit color, 24-bit	1-bit, 4-bit, 8-bit color, 24-bit
	RGB encoded (Windows)	1-bit, 4-bit, 8-bit color, 24-bit	1-bit, 4-bit, 8-bit color, 24-bit
	RLE encoded (Windows)	4-bit, 8-bit color	4-bit, 8-bit color
CLP	Clipboard bitmap (Windows)	1-bit, 4-bit, 8-bit color, 24-bit	
	Device-independent clipboard bitmap	1-bit, 4-bit, 8-bit color, 24-bit	1-bit, 4-bit, 8-bit color, 24-bit
CT	Continuous Tone CMYK (SciTex)	24-bit	24-bit
	Continuous Tone CMY (SciTex)	24-bit	24-bit
CUT	Dr. Halo	8-bit color	8-bit color
DCX	Multipage Paintbrush (Zsoft)	1-bit	
DIB	RGB encoded (OS/2)	1-bit, 4-bit, 8-bit color, 24-bit	1-bit, 4-bit, 8-bit color, 24-bit
	RGB encoded (Windows)	1-bit, 4-bit, 8-bit color, 24-bit	1-bit, 4-bit, 8-bit color, 24-bit
	RLE encoded (Windows)	4-bit, 8-bit color	4-bit, 8-bit color
EPS	Image only (Adobe)	1-bit, 4-bit, 8-bit color, 24-bit	1-bit, 4-bit, 8-bit color, 24-bit
FPX	Compressed (Kodak)	8-bit grey, 24-bit	8-bit grey, 24-bit
	Uncompressed (Kodak)	8-bit grey, 24-bit	8-bit grey, 24-bit

Format	Sub-Format and Description	Bits-Per-Pixel and Color Type 📂 Open	Bits-Per-Pixel and Color Type 💾 Save
GIF	v. 87a Interlaced (Compuserve)	1-bit, 4-bit, 8-bit color	1-bit, 4-bit, 8-bit color
	v. 87a Non-interlaced (Compuserve)	1-bit, 4-bit, 8-bit color	1-bit, 4-bit, 8-bit color
	v. 89a Interlaced (Compuserve)	1-bit, 4-bit, 8-bit color	1-bit, 4-bit, 8-bit color
	v. 89a Non-interlaced (Compuserve)	1-bit, 4-bit, 8-bit color	1-bit, 4-bit, 8-bit color
IFF	Compressed (Electronic Arts)	1-bit, 4-bit, 8-bit color, 24-bit	1-bit, 4-bit, 8-bit color, 24-bit
	Uncompressed (Electronic Arts)	1-bit, 4-bit, 8-bit color, 24-bit	1-bit, 4-bit, 8-bit color, 24-bit
IMG	Old style (GEM Paint)	1-bit, 4-bit, 8-bit color	1-bit, 8-bit color
	New style (GEM Paint)	1-bit, 4-bit, 8-bit color	
JIF	Huffman compressed	8-bit grey, 24-bit	8-bit grey, 24-bit
JPG	Huffman compressed	8-bit grey, 24-bit	8-bit grey, 24-bit
	Progressive	8 bit grey, 24-bit	8-bit grey, 24-bit
KDC	Kodak digital camera	24-bit	
LBM	Compressed (Deluxe Paint)	1-bit, 4-bit, 8-bit color	1-bit, 4-bit, 8-bit color
	Uncompressed (Deluxe Paint)	1-bit, 4-bit, 8-bit color	1-bit, 4-bit, 8-bit color
MAC	With header (MacPaint)	1-bit	1-bit
	Without header (MacPaint)	1-bit	1-bit
MSP	New version (MS Paint)	1-bit	1-bit
	Old version (MS Paint)	1-bit	
PBM	Portable bitmap (UNIX)	1-bit	1-bit
PCD	Photo-CD (Kodak)	24-bit	
PCT	PICT (Apple)	1-bit, 4-bit, 8-bit color, 16-bit, 24-bit, 32-bit	1-bit, 4-bit, 8-bit color, 24-bit
PCX	v. 0 (Zsoft Paintbrush)	1-bit	1-bit
	v. 2 with palette info (Zsoft)	1-bit, 4-bit	1-bit, 4-bit
	v. 3 without palette info (Zsoft)	1-bit, 4-bit	
	v. 5 (Zsoft)	1-bit, 4-bit, 8-bit color, 24-bit	1-bit, 4-bit, 8-bit color, 24-bit

Format	Sub-Format and Description	Bits-Per-Pixel and Color Type 🗁 Open	Bits-Per-Pixel and Color Type 🖫 Save
PGM	Portable Graymap ASCII (UNIX)	8-bit grey	8-bit grey
	Portable Graymap Binary (UNIX)	8-bit grey	8-bit grey
PIC	Pictor/PC Paint	1-bit, 4-bit, 8-bit color	1-bit, 4-bit, 8-bit color
PNG	Interlaced Portable Network Graphics	1-bit, 4-bit, 8-bit color, 16-bit, 24-bit, 32-bit	1-bit, 4-bit, 8-bit color, 24-bit, 32-bit
	Non-interlaced Portable Network Graphics	1-bit, 4-bit, 8-bit color, 8-bit grey, 16-bit, 24-bit, 32-bit	1-bit, 4-bit, 8-bit color, 24-bit, 32-bit
PPM	Portable Pixelmap (UNIX)	24-bit	24-bit
PSD	Photoshop (RGB or Indexed)	1-bit, 8-bit color, 24-bit	1-bit, 8-bit color, 24-bit
PSP	RLE encoded (Paint Shop Pro)	1-bit, 4-bit, 8-bit color,8-bit grey, 24-bit	1-bit, 4-bit, 8-bit color, 24-bit
	LZ77 compressed (Paint Shop Pro)	1-bit, 4-bit, 8-bit color, 8-bit grey, 24-bit	1-bit, 4-bit, 8-bit color, 24-bit
	Uncompressed (Paint Shop Pro)	1-bit, 4-bit, 8-bit color, 8-bit grey, 24-bit	1-bit, 4-bit, 8-bit color, 24-bit
RAS	Type 1 Modern (Sun)	1-bit, 8-bit color, 24-bit, 32-bit	1-bit, 8-bit color, 24-bit
RAW	Unencoded pixel data	8-bit grey, 24-bit	8-bit grey, 24-bit
RLE	Compuserve	1-bit	1-bit
	Windows	4-bit, 8-bit color,	4-bit, 8-bit color,
SCT	Continuous Tone CMYK	24-bit	24-bit
	Continuous Tone CMY	24-bit	24-bit
SGI	Uncompressed	8-bit grey, 24-bit	8-bit grey, 24-bit
	RLE Compressed	8-bit grey, 24-bit	8-bit grey, 24-bit
TGA	Uncompressed (Truevision)	8-bit grey, 8-bit color, 16-bit, 24-bit, 32-bit	8-bit grey, 8-bit color, 24-bit, 32-bit
	Compressed (Truevision)	8-bit color, 16-bit, 24-bit, 32-bit	8-bit color, 24-bit, 32-bit

Format	Sub-Format and Description	Bits-Per-Pixel and Color Type 🗁 Open	Bits-Per-Pixel and Color Type 🖫 Save
TIF	Huffman compressed	1-bit	1-bit
	Uncompressed	1-bit, 4-bit, 8-bit grey, 8-bit color, 24-bit	1-bit, 4-bit, 8-bit grey, 8-bit color, 24-bit
	Uncompressed CMYK	24-bit	24-bit
	Pack bits compressed	1-bit, 4-bit, 8-bit grey, 8-bit color, 24-bit	1-bit, 4-bit, 8-bit grey, 8-bit color, 24-bit
	Pack bits compressed CMYK	24-bit	24-bit
	LZW compressed	1-bit, 4-bit, 8-bit grey, 8-bit color, 24-bit	1-bit, 4-bit, 8-bit grey, 8-bit color, 24-bit
	LZW compressed CMYK	24-bit	24-bit
	Fax Group 3 compressed	1-bit	1-bit
	Fax Group 4 compressed	1-bit	
WPG	v. 5.0 (WordPerfect)	1-bit, 4-bit, 8-bit grey, 8-bit color	1-bit, 4-bit, 8-bit grey, 8-bit color
	v. 5.1 (WordPerfect)	1-bit, 4-bit, 8-bit grey, 8-bit color	1-bit, 4-bit, 8-bit grey, 8-bit color
	v. 6.0 (WordPerfect)	1-bit, 4-bit, 8-bit grey, 8-bit color, 24-bit	1-bit, 4-bit, 8-bit grey, 8-bit color, 24-bit

Supported Meta and Vector Formats

Meta and vector image formats can both contain vector information. Vector data is a collection of instructions about the location and characteristics of shapes that combine to make an image, recorded as mathematical formulas. Vector data cannot reproduce photo-realistic images, but for other types of images it has two advantages over raster data:

- It is scaleable without distortion (the "jaggies" that come with re-sizing a bitmap), and

- It produces smaller files.

In the strictest definition, a vector format can only contain vector information. In common practice, many formats that are considered to be vector allow the user to include non-vector data, such as raster images or text.

Meta formats explicitly allow more than just vector data. For example, a typical Windows metafile might contain a bitmap, vector information, and text, with the bitmap constituting the majority of the image, and the vector and text data providing annotation.

Meta and Vector Image Formats

The following table lists the meta and vector formats. Paint Shop Pro can open and save.

Format	Source/Standard	Open 📂 (Read)	Save 💾 (Write)
CDR	CorelDRAW!	Y	
CGM	Computer Graphics Metafile	Y	
CMX	Corel Clipart	Y	
DRW	Micrografx Draw	Y	
DXF	Autodesk	Y	
EMF	Windows Enhanced Metafile	Y	Y
EPS	Encapsulated PostScript	Y	Y*
GEM	Ventura / GEM	Y	
HGL	Hewlett-Packard Graphics Language	Y	
PCT	Apple	Y	Y*
PIC	Lotus Development Corp.	Y	
WMF	Microsoft Windows Metafile	Y	Y
WPG	WordPerfect	Y	Y*

* When you save data in these formats, the file contains raster data only.

Supported Video and Animation Formats

The table below shows the video and animation formats Animation Shop can open and save.

Format	Source/Standard	Bits-Per-Pixel and Color Type 🗁 Open	Bits-Per-Pixel and Color Type 🖫 Save
AVI	Microsoft	1-bit, 4-bit, 8-bit color, 24-bit	24-bit
FLC	Autodesk	1-bit, 4-bit, 8-bit color	1-bit, 4-bit, 8-bit color
FLI	Autodesk	1-bit, 4-bit, 8-bit color	1-bit, 4-bit, 8-bit color
GIF	Compuserve	1-bit, 4-bit, 8-bit color	1-bit, 4-bit, 8-bit color
MNG	Jasc	24-bit	24-bit
MPEG	Moving Picture Experts Group	24-bit	
ANI	Microsoft	1,4,8,16,24,32-bit	24-bit

NOTE: *On opening an AVI, FLI, FLC, or MPEG file, Animation Shop will open the Import Options dialog box asking for imported frame range, imported frame interval, and whether to combine adjacent identical frames. The defaults will be to import all frames, and to combine redundant frames.*

Other Formats

Using the Meta Picture Import Dialog Box

When you choose to open a Windows Metafile image or paste it from the clipboard, the Meta Picture Import dialog box appears. You can enter new values to open the image using pixel dimensions that differ from the original image dimensions.

To open a MetaFile image:

1. Read the dimensions of the original image in the "Original Size" panel.

2. To use the original dimensions, click the OK button at the bottom of the dialog box.

3. To use different pixel dimensions, enter them in the Width in Pixels and the Height in Pixels boxes in the "Import size" panel.

4. Select the "Maintain original aspect ratio" check box to keep the width and height pixel values within the same aspect ratio as the original dimensions. Clear this check box to ignore the original aspect ratio when setting pixel values.

5. Click the OK button to close the dialog box and open the image.

Using the Raw Options Dialog Box

You use the RAW Options dialog box to tell Paint Shop Pro how to interpret RAW pixel data. For information about a RAW file format, please refer to the documentation for the program that created the image. If you are familiar with RAW files, the dialog box should be self-explanatory. If you are unfamiliar with the format, please find and read information about the format in general and the particular image you are trying to open. A discussion of RAW pixel data is beyond the scope of this manual.

Using the PostScript Renderer Dialog Box

If you selected the "Prompt for size and options each time a PostScript file is opened" option in the File Format Preferences dialog box, Paint Shop Pro displays the PostScript Renderer dialog box whenever you open a Postscript file. To use this dialog box:

1. In the Resolution box, choose a new resolution for the image or leave the default setting of 72 dpi.

2. By default, the page is set to the Portrait orientation, where it is taller than it is wide. To reverse the orientation, select the "Landscape" check box.

3. In the Page Size drop-down box, choose a selection. The bounding box, which is available when the EPS file has a recommended size, is usually the best choice.

4. In the Image Type drop-down box, choose a color depth for the image. The choices are Monochrome (1-bit), Greyscale (8-bit), and RGB (24-bit).

5. The "Enable Antialiasing" check box is selected by default. Antialiasing smoothes the edges of objects. If you prefer not to use this feature, clear the check box.

6. The "Enable Transparency" check box is selected by default. Clear this check box to substitute a white background for the transparency.

Glossary

Additive Colors   Emitted color light. The color used on computer monitors. When the primary additive colors (red, green, and blue) are combined, they produce white. The opposite of additive color is subtractive color.

Adjustment Layer   A layer used to apply color corrections to the layers below it.

Alpha Channel   A greyscale channel for storing selections and masks that can be reloaded into an image.

Antialias   The blending of the pixel colors along the edges to eliminate the stair-stepping look (called "jaggies") of curved and slanted lines. This feature is commonly used with text.

Aspect Ratio   The ratio of width to height. When an image is displayed on different screens, the aspect ratio must be kept the same to avoid "stretching" in either the vertical or horizontal direction.

Asymmetrical Curve   A vector curve that can have direction handles of differing lengths. This results in a curve that is shaped differently on each side of the node.

AVI   Stands for Audio Video Interlaced. The file format for Microsoft Windows digital video and audio. This format is cross platform compatible, allowing AVI video files to be played on other computer platforms.

Background   The "canvas" on which you create an image in an image window.

Background Color   The "canvas" color on which you create an image. Also used as a secondary color for the painting and drawing tools. See also Foreground Color.

Background Layer   The bottom layer in any non-transparent image. It can be promoted to a standard layer.

Batch Conversion   A process that converts multiple image files to a single file format.

Bevel	A three-dimensional edge on an object.
Bezier Control Points	Points on a vector object that determine the shape of Bezier curves.
Bezier Curve	A smooth curve with anchor points and direction handles at both ends. The Bezier curve can be reshaped by moving the direction handles.
Bit Depth	See color depth.
Bitmapped Image	An image composed of an array of small squares, called pixels, arranged in rows and columns. Each pixel has a specific color value and location.
Blend	To combine two layers or areas of an image together.
Blend Modes	Methods of combining the pixels from the current layer with the layers under it. The layers are not permanently combined, but this allows you to preview the way they will appear if combined.
Blur	Reduces areas of high contrast and softens the appearance of an image.
BMP	Stands for Bitmap. A standard Microsoft Windows image format. Supports paletted, 24-bit RGB color, and greyscale images. This format does not support alpha channels, layers or vector data.
Brightness	The amount of light in a hue—how light or dark it is. See also Luminance.
Browser	Windows Explorer-like interface that lets you quickly locate files and preview images.
Burn	A blend mode option which darkens an image. The lightness values of the Blend layer's colors reduce the lightness of the underlying layers. The opposite of Dodge.
Canvas	The area on which an image or animation frame is displayed.
Canvas Size	The size of the area within an image window that can be edited.
Cap	A shape added to the end points of a line.
Channel	Contains all of the pixel information for a single color. A greyscale image has one channel, an RGB image has three channels, and a CMYK image has four channels.
Clone	To duplicate a portion of an image.
CMYK	Stands for Cyan/Magenta/Yellow/Black. The four standard ink colors used in printing. Because of impurities in inks, cyan, magenta, and yellow produce a muddy brown when combined. Black (K) is often added. See also Subtractive Colors.
CODEC	Stands for Compression/Decompression. CODECs are algorithms used in multimedia.

Color Bleeding	An effect by which the colors of an image run and become mixed like dyes on wet cloth, causing an image loss at the edges. Error diffusion dithering causes colors to bleed from left to right.
Color Channel	See Channel.
Color Depth	The number of bits of color information available for each pixel. An 8-bit image can display 256 colors, a 16-bit image can display 65,536 colors, and a 24-bit image can display over 16.7 million colors.
Color Palette	Contains the selection of available colors and displays the active foreground and background colors. It appears on the right side of the window when you first start Paint Shop Pro or Animation Shop.
Color Wheel	The circular color spectrum on the Jasc color palette in the Colors dialog box, from which you can pick and create custom colors.
Colorize	Converts an image or selection to a uniform hue and saturation while retaining its lightness. You can use it to create sepia tones (the brown seen in old photographs) and other single-color effects.
Compression	The process by which some of an image's data is either stored in patterns or eliminated in order to reduce file size.
Contour	Two or more nodes connected by line and / or curve segments.
Contract Command	Shrinks a selection by a specific number of pixels while retaining its original shape.
Contrast	The difference between the light and dark areas of an image.
Control Palette	Contains the options for modifying the image-editing tools, as well as the controls for configuring brushes and access to custom brushes.
Crop	To remove part of an image outside a specified boundary.
Cusp	A corner on a vector object. The node defines the bend point and angles of the segments on either side.
Data Rate	The number of bytes per second a device is capable of transferring. For CD-ROMs this is represented in multiples of 100 bytes per second. 1X equals 100 bytes per second, 2X equals 200 bytes per second, etc.
Decompression	To reverse the compression software algorithm to return data to its original size and condition. For files compressed with lossy compression, some data will not be restored.
Defloat	To merge a floating selection into a layer. After a selection is defloated, editing commands affect the entire image or layer.
Deformation	To change an image's appearance by moving data from one area to another. The result is a deformed version of the original image.

Defringe	To clean the edges of a selection by removing pixels of the background color.
Delta Frame	An animation frame that contains only the pixels different from the preceding Key Frame. Delta Frames reduce the overall size of the video clip to be stored on the output medium.
DIB	Stands for Device Independent Bitmap. This is a portable data format that is designed not to be limited to a specific type of display hardware.
Difference Frame	See Delta Frame.
Diffuse	To randomly scatter colors to create an impressionistic effect.
Digital Camera	A camera that takes pictures with a CCD (charge-coupled device) and stores them in a memory module or on removable media. The pictures can usually be transmitted to a computer.
Dithering	A process to display colors not available on an output device by intermixing monochrome pixels with color pixels to produce shading and highlighting that appear to the eye as different colors.
Dodge	A retouch mode setting that lightens and brings out the details in shadowed areas. The opposite of Burn.
DPI	Stands for Dots Per Inch. A unit used to measure the resolution of a printer. The more dots per inch, the sharper an image appears.
8-bit Image	An image containing a maximum of 256 colors.
Effect	A graphic function that, when applied to an image or selection, creates a modified version of the image or selection. The differences between the source and the output images vary according to the type of effect being used.
Em	A unit of typographical measure equal to the width of the letter "M" in a given typeface.
Emboss	An effect that causes the foreground to appear raised from the background by suppressing color and tracing the edges in black.
Error Diffusion	A method of color reduction that spreads out the inaccuracies in representing a pixel's color to the surrounding pixels.
Expand a Selection	Increases the size of a selection by a specific number of pixels while retaining its original shape.
15-bit Image	An image containing a maximum of 32,768 colors.
4-bit Image	An image containing a maximum of 16 colors.

Feather	Fades an area on both sides of a selection marquee over a specified number of pixels.
Filter	A tool that applies special effects to an image.
Flip Command	Reverses the selection, layer, or image vertically. What was the top becomes the bottom, and vice-versa.
Float Command	Temporarily separates a selection from an image or layer.
Foreground Color	The primary color used by the painting and drawing tools. This is displayed in the "Solid Colors" and "Active Styles" panels of the Color palette.
FPS	Stands for Frames Per Second. This is the rate at which animations are displayed.
Frame	A single, complete image in a connected series of images such as an Animation Shop animation, a video recording, or a film recording. A border around an image.
Full Screen Preview	Displays the selected image at the center of a black background that occupies the whole screen area.
Gamma	The range of color values a monitor, scanner, or printer can display.
Gamma Correction	Corrects the brightness levels in an image. On a computer monitor, a small change in brightness at a low brightness level is not equal to the same change at a high level. Gamma correction compensates for that.
GIF	Stands for Graphic Interchange Format. This is a file format commonly used on the Internet. It uses lossless compression and creates images in 8-bit color. GIF89a supports single-color transparency and animation, but it does not support layers or alpha channels.
Gradient Fill	A fill created by a gradual blending of colors together.
Greyscale Image	An image that uses up to 256 shades of grey to represent brightness.
Grid	An equally spaced series of vertical and horizontal lines to help you align your artwork and arrange image elements symmetrically. The grid spacing can be set at any size.
Grow Command	Adds color pixels adjacent to an active selection.
Halftone	A collection of black and white dots arranged to simulate the brightness values of greyscale images.
Handles	Control points attached to vector nodes that control the shape of line segments on either side of a vector node.
Hexidecimal Color System	Describes color code values by means of different combinations of sixteen numbers and letters (0-9 and A-F) as part of the color palette.

Highlight	The lightest part of an image.
Histogram	A graph of an image's brightness levels. It records the number of pixels at each brightness level.
Histogram Equalizing	Adjusts the Histogram by distributing the lightness values of the pixels evenly across the spectrum.
Histogram Stretching	Adjusts the Histogram by pulling the Histogram graph from both ends so that it covers more of the spectrum.
HSL (Hue/Saturation/Lightness)	A method for defining colors in an image.
Hue	The shade or tint of a color. Also, one of the three components of the HSL color definition method.
Hue Mapping	Replacing all the pixels of one hue with another hue.
Image Arithmetic Function	Combines the color data from two images on a pixel by pixel basis according to an arithmetic function.
Image Resolution	The number of pixels per unit of area. A display with a finer grid contains more pixels and thus has a higher resolution, capable of reproducing more detail in an image.
Image Palette	A collection of available colors in images with 8 bits of color or less. You can change a color in the palette, but not increase the number of colors.
Image Window	Active image area in which Paint Shop Pro places an image file when you open it.
INDEO	Intel's compression/decompression algorithm for scalable software playback video. Intel licenses Indeo technology to companies such as Microsoft who integrate it into products like Microsoft's Video for Windows. Indeo technology can record 8, 16, or 24-bit sequences and stores the sequence as 24-bit for scalability on high-end PCs.
Interlacing	A method of displaying images that lets the viewer see a rough, blurry copy of the image as it downloads. The file gradually sharpens as the image loads.
Interpolated Resolution	Most commonly associated with image scanners, this is enhanced resolution that adds to the data provided by the optical resolution. It analyzes image data such as color and brightness and makes up additional pixels based on that information to reach the selected resolution.
Join	Points where lines meet at angles other than 0 degrees or 180 degrees.

JPEG	Stands for Joint Photographics Experts Group. A compression technique that supports 24-bit images and can reduce a file's size by as much as 96%. It removes some color information, while retaining the brightness data. At higher compressions it can result in a visible loss of quality. It is best for photographs and for images that contain a variety of tonal values. JPG has been adapted to video, but it provides no frame compression.
JPG File Format	An image format commonly used on the web. It uses JPEG lossy compression and creates images up to 24-bit color. It does not support layers, transparency, or alpha channels.
Kerning	The distance between characters of text. Measured in units of 1/300th of an em.
Key Frame	A baseline frame against which other frames are compared for differences. If the clip has a large amount of motion, better playback will occur with every frame being a Key Frame. If there is very little motion, such as a narrator, a higher number of Delta Frames (intervening frames that are compressed based on differences from the key frames) will give satisfactory playback. In general making every 3rd frame a Key frame is a good choice with the current Indeo algorithm.
Layer	A discrete level of an image that can be edited independently from the rest of the image.
Leading	The distance between lines of text measured in 1/1000ths of a point. Positive values add leading, while negative values reduce leading.
Lightness	One of the components of HSL.
Line Art	An image composed entirely of lines of one color (no greyscale component).
Lossless Compression	A compression method that retains all of the original image data and reduces the file size by storing patterns of pixels in the image.
Lossy Compression	A compression method that eliminates data to reduce the file size.
Luminance	The brightness of a color. A color with a luminance of 100% is white; a color with a luminance of 0% is black.
Marquee	The animated, black and white border that surrounds a selection and defines its edges. This is also the name of a text effect in Animation Shop.
Mask	A device used to protect and isolate an area of a layer from changes applied to the rest of the layer.

Matting	To clean an image border by removing excess pixels included in a selection. When a layer is created by removing it from an image, some of the pixels surrounding the border are included, especially when it has been antialiased or feathered.
Metafile Formats	File formats that included several types of data. For example, a typical Windows metafile might contain a bitmap, vector information, and text, with the bitmap constituting the majority of the image, and the vector and text data providing annotation.
Midtones	The shades midway between the highlights and shadows.
Mirroring	Used to reverse the selection, layer, or image horizontally. What was the left side becomes the right side, and vice-versa.
Miter Limit	The miter limit is the maximum allowed ratio of the miter length to the line width. The miter length is the distance from the inside of the corner to the outside corner point. If a Miter join exceeds the limit, the corner is flattened at the limit point.
Monitor Gamma	Manages the amounts of red, blue, and green in an image to ensure that the on-screen and printed image match as closely as possible and that the colors are consistent from image to image.
Negative Image	An image created by reversing the colors of the original. Each color is replaced by the one directly opposite it on the color wheel. The effect is the same as a photograph negative.
Node	A control point on a vector object. The type of each node dictates the shape of the line segment on either side of it.
Noise	A grainy pattern created by the random re-coloring of pixels.
1-bit Image	An image containing a maximum of 2 colors.
Octree Palette	One of the palette generation choices for decreasing an image color depth. It is accurate to 8-bits per channel, but it is not as good at weighting color importance as the optimized median cut palette.
OLE	Stands for Object Linking and Embedding. A Windows feature that enables two or more programs to work together and share files. A link is a pointer from a file in one application to a file that may be from a different program. Linking saves space on your hard drive. Embedding allows information from one program to be contained in a file from another program. Embedding lets you keep all parts of a document in a single file even if the parts come from several programs.

Opacity	The density of a color or layer. A color or layer with an opacity of 0 is transparent; a color or layer with an opacity of 100 is completely opaque (solid).
Optical Resolution (scanner)	The actual physical number of pixels per inch at which a scanner is capable of capturing an image.
Optimized Median Cut Palette	One of the palette generation choices for decreasing an image color depth. The palette uses occurrence of colors as weighting, and ranks accordingly. It is accurate only to 5-bits per channel.
Palette	As in a painter's palette, the different palettes included in Paint Shop Pro offer you the ability to select and mix colors, organize the different layers of paint on the canvas and pick a customized brush for a specific task.
Palette Transparency	Specific color in the palette that is assigned a transparent value. This is useful when working with some file formats, such as GIF and PNG.
Paletted Image	An image with 256 or fewer colors.
Paper Texture	A variety of simulated surfaces to make it look as though you are painting on paper having that texture.
Path	The guiding line for a vector object. It traces from a starting point to either an ending point or a closing point.
Photo-CD File Format	File format used by Kodak in digital cameras and Photo-CDs. When you open an image with a PCD file format, Paint Shop Pro may open a dialog box requesting additional information.
Pixel	A picture element. One of the individual squares that make up a raster image and the smallest element that can be assigned a color.
Pixel Depth	See Color Depth.
Planar Format	Formats that use color planes to determine an image's color. Most raster formats record color information on a pixel-by-pixel basis, but planar formats use color planes, which are sometimes called color channels. Each color plane contains all of the pixel information for a single color.
PNG	Stands for Portable Network Graphics. A file format designed for web graphics. It supports 24-bit color with lossless compression, one alpha channel, and alpha transparency.
Posterize	To reduce an image's colors or shades of grey to the lightest shade, darkest shade, and a few shades in between.
PPI	Stands for Pixels Per Inch. A unit used to measure the resolution of a computer monitor and scanner. The more pixels per inch, the sharper an image appears.

Preserve Transparency	A layer option that restricts the editing of a layer to the pixels that already contain data. You can edit this data, but you can not cover any transparent areas.
Primary Additive Colors	Red, green, and blue. When these three colors are combined, they produce white.
Primary Subtractive Colors	Cyan, magenta, and yellow. When these three colors are combined, they produce black.
Push	A retouch mode setting that spreads color from the starting point. The effect is similar to smearing paint.
QuickTime	Apple Computer's video environment. QuickTime video files must be converted to AVI format to run under Microsoft's Video for Windows, however Apple provides a QuickTime viewer for Windows. INDEO video is supported under Apple's Macintosh operating system.
Raster Image	See Bitmapped Image.
RAW File Format	A file format that describes the colors in each pixel by means of an 8-bit system in which 255 equals white, and 0 equals black. The format's great flexibility allows you to transfer images between applications, recognizing its channels, CMYK, and RGB values.
Replace Color Command	Allows you to select a specific color and replace it with any new color of your choice.
Resample	To change the resolution of an image. To resample down is to decrease the resolution. To resample up is to increase the resolution.
Resize	To change the width and height of an image or layer.
Resolution	The level of detail of an image, monitor, or printer. See Image Resolution.
RGB (Red/Green/Blue)	See Primary Additive Colors.
RLE (Run Length Encoding)	Microsoft's video compression algorithm for low-end multimedia PCs. It discards continuous regions of duplicate color, and compresses 8-bit sequences only. Playback is also 8-bit and isn't scalable for high-end PCs.
Rotate	To spin a selection, layer, or image in either direction around its center point.
16-bit Image	An image containing a maximum of 65,536 colors.
Saturation	The purity of a hue. A hue with a saturation of 100% is vivid; a hue with a saturation of 0% is grey. One of the three components of the HSL mode.

Screen Capture	A picture of elements on the screen. These pictures can be of an area you draw, of the entire screen, of an active window, of the contents of an active window, or of the controls of a program, such as a toolbar. Screen captures are often used extensively in user documentation as a way to describe a feature, command, or process.
Seamless Pattern	A converted selection which, when tiled over an area, does not show a seam. When Paint Shop Pro converts a selection to a seamless pattern, it uses the area surrounding the selection to eliminate the appearance of seams. If the selection is too close to the edge of the image, a message indicating this appears. When you use this command, a new window is created with the seamless pattern and the original image is not affected.
Segment	The line between two vector nodes.
Selection	An area or object that has been isolated from the rest of the image and can be edited separately.
Shadow	The darkest area of an image.
Sharpen	To bring an image into better focus and increase the detail by increasing the contrast of adjacent pixels.
Shear	A deformation that controls the offset of a side.
Skew	A deformation that tilts an image or selection along its horizontal or vertical axis up to 45% in either direction.
Smudge	A retouch mode setting that spreads color from the starting point and picks up new color as it moves. The effect is similar to smearing paint.
Solarize	A function which inverts all the colors above a certain luminance value.
Source Window	The image from which you can create a mask. It can be any image window open in the workspace.
Stroke	An outline placed on text.
Sub-path	Several segments of a vector path.
Subtractive Color	Absorbs color light. The color used in printing. When the primary subtractive colors (cyan, magenta, and yellow) are combined, they produce black. The opposite of subtractive color is additive color.
Symmetrical Curve	A vector curve that has handles of identical lengths on either side of the node.
24-bit Image	An image containing a maximum of 16,777,216 colors.
Tangent	A vector node that blends a curve and a line.

Threshold level

The lightness value above which colors are inverted in adjustment layers, the Glowing Edges effect, and the Solarize command. All colors with lightness values above the set level are turned into their inverse (on the 255 scale). At a Threshold level of 1, all colors except black change. As the Threshold level increases, colors must be increasingly lighter to invert themselves.

Thumbnail

A small representation of a larger image. Paint Shop Pro and Animation shop provide thumbnails in the browser so that you can preview images without opening the file.

TIFF

Stands for Tagged Image File Format. A file format used for scanning, storing, and interchanging color and greyscale images. It does not support layers or animation.

Title Bar

Located at the top of every window, this displays the program's name, as well as the control icon, the name of the open file, and the minimize, maximize, restore, and close buttons.

Toggle

To switch an item back and forth from one state to another, such as hiding and displaying a palette.

Tone Balance

Balances the Highlight, Midtone, and Shadow levels.

Tool Palette

Part of the Animation Shop and Paint Shop Pro interface that provides the image-editing tools. When you click a tool button, the Control palette (in Paint Shop Pro) or the Style Bar (in Animation Shop) displays its usage options.

Toolbar

Part of the Animation Shop and Paint Shop Pro interface that provides buttons having the same functionality as some of the frequently used menu commands. If a command is unavailable, its button appears greyed-out.

Transparency

The degree of visibility assigned to a specific color or selection.

Transparent Color

An image palette color which is designated to allow the background to show through. Usually used when working with web formats like GIF and PNG. While working in Paint Shop Pro, the transparent color will remain visible until you choose the View Palette Transparency command.

Transparent Selection

A pasted selection which Paint Shop Pro adds to the current image as a selection after deselecting pixels that match the color and tolerance settings in the Transparent Color Select dialog box. Any deselected pixels are transparent.

True Color

The common name for 24-bit color. "True" is used because the human eye can distinguish among approximately six million different colors, which is fewer than the number of colors available in a 24-bit color system. 24-bit images use 8 bits for each RGB channel. With 32-bit color depth, another 8 bits are used for an Alpha Channel.

TWAIN An industry-wide compatibility standard for devices such as scanners and digital cameras to communicate with applications like Paint Shop Pro, allowing you to import an image into Paint Shop Pro without leaving the program.

Undo Buffer Storage area for undo information.

Unsharp Mask A filter that sharpens an image by subtracting a blurred copy image from the original.

Vector Graphic An image composed of a set of instructions for drawing objects such as shapes, lines, and text.

Watermark Embedded information in an image. A watermark can include such items as copyright and author information. In most implementations, watermarks are imperceptible to humans, but readable by computers.

Workspace In Paint Shop Pro and Animation Shop, this is the area of the main window where you work with images and the Browser.

Zoom To increase or decrease the magnification of an object or image.

Troubleshooting

This section contains answers to common technical support questions. Refer to the README.DOC file in your Paint Shop Pro folder for additional important information.

NOTE: *We recommend configuring your system display for the highest color depth it supports at a screen resolution of 800x600 or higher. To determine your current display resolution, choose About Paint Shop Pro from the Help menu, and then click the System Info button at the bottom of the screen. In the System Information list, scroll to the Video Driver Information section. Look at the line marked "Number of Colors." It shows the number of colors that your display supports. For help changing your video driver, consult the documentation that came with your video card.*

Nothing happens when I put the Paint Shop Pro disk in my CD drive.

If the Auto insert notification (also called "Auto Run") feature of Windows is disabled, you can start the Paint Shop Pro autorun program by opening the Paint Shop Pro CD-ROM using My Computer and double-clicking on AUTORUN.EXE. If the autorun program still does not start, double-click on SETUP.EXE file in the \PSP directory on the Paint Shop Pro 7 disk to start the Paint Shop Pro 7 setup program.

The colors in the image are wrong or Wallpaper is flickering as different images are displayed.

When Windows is running a 256 color display driver, it reserves 20 colors for its own use. This lowers an image's palette to 236 colors (256 - 20 = 236) plus the 20 fixed Windows colors. Paint Shop Pro attempts to optimize the remaining 236 colors for the image that it is currently working with. This can cause your Wallpaper, or other Windows to flicker. Also, If the color in the image is not in the palette Paint Shop Pro creates, it is replaced by the nearest color that is.

Editing, creating, scanning an image causes memory error messages.

Depending on its size and color depth, an image may require a substantial amount of memory to be displayed and even more memory to be edited. The following example shows how the memory requirements of a single layer image escalate as its color depth increases.

Height	Width	Bits/Pixel (color depth)	Display (KB)	Max Edit (KB)
800	600	1	59	176
800	600	8	469	1,406
800	600	24	1,406	4,219

Adding layers also increases the image's memory requirements. Here's what happens when layers are added to the 24-bit image:

Layers	Display	Max. Edit
2 Layers	3.2 MB	9.6 MB
3 Layers	5 MB	15 MB

Remember that editing an image may require up to three times the memory required to display it.

There is an outlined box around the vector object I've just created.

The box indicates a vector selection. Press the <ESC> key while your mouse is positioned over the image to remove the vector selection marquee.

There are moving lines in my image or around text I have just created. How do I remove them?

These lines indicate that a selection marquee is present. To remove the selection, choose Selections > Select None.

I cannot find all of my fonts in the Text Entry dialog box.

Paint Shop Pro does not support bitmap (or raster) fonts, such as MS Sans Serif. Use a similar True Type or Type 1 font or create the text in an Animation Shop frame and copy or export the text to Paint Shop Pro.

Some painting tools or menu commands are unavailable (like the Flood Fill tool).

Some tools and commands are not available when working with vector objects. A vector layer can be converted to a raster data layer by right clicking on the layer in the Layer palette and choosing the Convert to Raster command. This step typically enables the desired commands and tools. Vector data that has been converted to raster data is no longer editable as a vector object. If you wish to preserve the original vector layer, you can use the Duplicate command in the Layer palette and convert the duplicated vector layer.

The Vector Object Selection tool or the "Create as vector" option in the Tool Options Palette is unavailable.

Vector tools are not supported when editing masks, and the Vector Object Selection tool is only available when the active layer is a vector layer. Exit the Mask Edit mode and/or change the layer you want to edit to a vector layer in order to make these options available.

Paint Shop Pro 5 or 6 cannot read PSP format files created in Paint Shop Pro 7.

Whenever additional file features (such as styled lines) are added to a new version of Paint Shop Pro, we update the PSP file format to store the new type of image data. Since previous versions in which such features were not available cannot read this data, it must be converted into a supported form. To save a PSP format file for use in version 5 or 6, click the Options button in the Save or Save As dialog box, and select the desired version compatibility before saving the file.

How can I use Picture Tubes created in an earlier version of Paint Shop Pro with version?.

Picture Tubes created with Paint Shop Pro 6 can be used with Paint Shop Pro 7. However, we recommend converting them into Paint Shop Pro 7 Tubes for best results. Picture Tubes created in Paint Shop Pro 5 must be converted to use them with Paint Shop Pro 7, and you must have a TUBES.CTL file in the same directory as the Paint Shop Pro 5 tubes. Picture Tubes from both previous programs can be converted by using the Picture Tube converter, which can be run by selecting Start > Programs > Jasc Software > Utilities > Picture Tube Converter.

Some functions (effects, deformations) are unavailable.

Certain effects require different conditions in order to work. Some require a selection, others require that the image is 24bit (16.7 million colors) or greyscale, while others yet cannot be used on certain types of layers (e.g. Vector or Adjustment layers). The last condition that you may find is if you are editing a mask. If you find that an effects is not available, you may want to consult the help to find out how this effect works, and what conditions you should be concerned with.

I cannot use my scanner because the Acquire and Select Source commands are unavailable.

If the Acquire and Select Source commands are disabled, Paint Shop Pro could not find the file TWAIN_32.DLL on your system. Reinstall the software bundled with your scanner or digital camera to properly install this file.

Painting or drawing tools produce no apparent results.

If a tool produces no apparent output, try the following steps:

- Choose the Selections > Select None command to remove any existing selections.

- Click on a different layer in the Layer palette.

- Disable the Layer mask toggle on the Layer palette.

- Activate the Dropper tool, left-click and right-click anywhere on the Available Color Panel in the Color palette, and try using the affected tool again

- Increase the brush size or line width in the Tool Options palette

- If you are using a pressure-sensitive tablet, check its settings in the Windows Control Panel to ensure it is working properly. Consult the user's manual for your tablet for more information.

Certain file types launch Paint Shop Pro, while others do not.

If a file's extension is associated with Paint Shop Pro, you can open the file by double-clicking the filename in Windows Explorer. If Paint Shop Pro is not running, double-clicking the filename will also start or launch the program. Associated file types use the Paint Shop Pro image file icon. To select file types to be associated with Paint Shop Pro, set the File Associations Preferences, as discussed in the "Setting Preferences" chapter. If you are not sure which file types to associate with Paint Shop Pro, you can use the default settings of the File Associations dialog box (Select Unused and .psp).

How do I make a transparent GIF?

Select File > Export > Gif Optimizer, then select the desired transparency setting from the resulting dialog box.

When I select Effects > Reflection Effects > Pattern, there aren't any options for choosing which pattern I want to use.

The Effects > Reflection Effects > Pattern command can only create a pattern from the image or selection itself. Therefore, to obtain a different Pattern, you will need to open and possibly select the area that you want for your pattern.

How can I re-size a vector shape I've just drawn without changing the shape?

Right-click one of the corner nodes and drag the shape. The left mouse button will allow you to change the aspect ratio (thereby changing the shape), while the right mouse button will maintain the aspect ratio allowing you to resize your shape without distorting, or elongating it.

When I attempt to install the program, I receive a message that "An I/O error has occurred".

Typically this is caused by residue from previous installers inside your Windows Temporary folder. To remedy this issue, you will need to delete its contents. If you are using Windows 98 or 2000, this can be done quite easily by choosing Start > Programs > Accessories > System tools > Disk cleanup. There, select the Temporary Files (not Temporary Internet Files) and click the OK button. You should now be able to install the program. Please note, as with deleting any files or folders from your system, be sure that there are no files that you wish to keep before deleting the folder.

Every time I go to save a file, it goes back to the Paint Shop Pro format. How to I set it to a different format by default?

This can be done by choosing File > Preferences > General Program Preferences. In the window that appears, click the Dialogs and Palettes tab. You will then want to select the "Remember last type used in Save As dialog" check box.

After I resize an image, it appears to get larger. How is this possible?

Paint Shop Pro has a feature called Auto Size. This will cause Paint Shop Pro to zoom out on an image that is too big to be displayed at 1:1. After resizing, if a different zoom level will fill the window without causing the image to scroll, then it will zoom to that level. If you wish not to have this feature enabled, choose File > Preferences > General Program Preferences. Click the Viewing tab, and clear the Auto Size check box (there is an option for both when it opens or creates the image, and for resizing).

I scanned two images in from my scanner, and when I copy one into the other, it is too big even though both pictures are the same size.

This happens if either image was scanned in at a different resolution (pixels per inch, or per centimeter). Due to the nature of computers, images are stored by pixels. This means that your scanner must convert the physical size of the image to pixels. This will cause the image to be larger or smaller depending on the resolution that you scan in at.

I have scanned an image in at 150 pixels per inch. After I changed the resolution to 300, it prints at half the size.

The resolution of your image is used to convert the number of pixels in your image to a size in inches (or centimeters) that a device such as your printer can print it at. So if you increase your resolution, you are condensing the pixels and making your printed image smaller. In the same regard, if you decrease your image's resolution, you will increase the size of your printed image.

The Color Management Preference menu choice is unavailable.

This command is disabled if you are using Windows 95 or Windows NT 4.0. Windows Color Management is not supported by Microsoft in either of these operating systems.

When I choose to enable Color Management either the monitor or printer profile is listed as <none>.

These settings are retrieved from Windows and must be configured through their respective properties dialog boxes inside your Control Panel. For your monitor, go into Display, and select the Settings Tab. There, click the advanced button and you will find the Color Management Tab. For your printer, choose Printers and right click the Printer. Now choose Properties and then the Color Management tab. (Please note, black and white printers may not have a Color Management tab.) If you are unable to configure or find a profile that you wish to use for your printer or monitor, contact the respective manufacturer for more information.

I have a utility that gives me the ability to type in an Asian language on an English version of Windows, but I cannot get the characters into Paint Shop Pro.

Currently, Paint Shop Pro strictly adheres to the Operating System's language. Because the English version of Windows does not support double byte languages, such as Japanese or Chinese, Paint Shop Pro is unable to support them. If you are using a double byte version of Windows, such as a Chinese version of Windows98, you should find that you will be able to type in that language in Paint Shop Pro.

When I try to capture an area, I see the numbers for the size inside my captured image.

This can occur if your display is set below true color. To perform area captures, you need to be in a true color display mode (either 24bit or 32bit). You can change this by going to Start > Settings > Control Panel > Display > Settings and increase the number of colors there.

I have a digital camera, but I can't seem to find it in your list of cameras. Can I still use it with Paint Shop Pro?

Quite possibly yes. Many digital cameras have support for TWAIN, use a floppy disk, or use a card reader. When using these cameras, you need to install their software. With TWAIN enabled cameras, you can choose File > Import > TWAIN > Select Source to choose your camera and File > Import > TWAIN > Acquire to retrieve your image from within Paint Shop Pro. For cameras that use floppy disks and card readers, you can choose File > Open or File > Browse to open your images.

How do I use plug-in filters with Paint Shop Pro?

To load third-party plug-in filters, select File > Preferences > File Locations, then click on the "Plug-in Filters" tab and select the appropriate folders.

How do I change settings when I perform screen captures?

Select File > Import > Screen Capture > Setup to configure the screen capture utility. If you would like to make it easier to access this command, you can right-click on the Toolbar, choose the Customize command, and add this function to the toolbar.

Trademark Acknowledgements

Animation Shop	Trademark of Jasc Software, Inc.
Autodesk	Trademark of Autodesk
CorelDRAW	Trademark of Corel Corporation
CT	Registered Trademark of Scitex Corporation
Deluxe Paint	Trademark of Electronic Arts
Dr. Halo	Trademark of Media Cybernetics
GEM	Trademark of Digital Research Inc.
GEM Paint	Trademark of Digital Research Inc.
GIF	Service mark property of CompuServe Inc.[a]
Graphic Interchange Format	Copyright property of CompuServe Inc.
ImageCommander	Trademark of Jasc Software, Inc.
Jasc	Registered Trademark of Jasc Software, Inc.
Jasc Media Center	Trademark of Jasc Software, Inc.
Kodak Photo CD	Trademark of Eastman Kodak Company
Lotus 1-2-3	Trademark of Lotus Development Corporation
Macintosh	Trademark of Apple Computer, Inc.
MacPaint	Product and trademark of Claris Corporation
Micrografx Draw	Trademark of Micrografx, Inc.
Microsoft Paint	Trademark of Microsoft Corporation
Microsoft Windows	Trademark of Microsoft Corporation

Microsoft Word	Trademark of Microsoft Corporation
OS/2	Trademark of International Business Machines Corporation
Paint Shop Pro	Trademark of Jasc Software, Inc.
Photoshop	Trademark of Adobe Systems Incorporated
PostScript	Trademark of Adobe Systems Incorporated[b]
Ventura Publisher	Trademark of Corel Corporation
Video For Windows	Trademark of Microsoft Corporation
WordPerfect	Trademark of the WordPerfect Corporation
ZSoft Paintbrush	Trademark of ZSoft Corporation

a. For further information, please contact:
Compuserve Incorporated
Graphics Technology Department
500 Arlington Center Boulevard
Columbus, Ohio 43220 U.S.A.

b. The PostScript language is copyrighted by Adobe Systems Incorporated.

All other trademarks or registered trademarks are the property of their respective owners.

Software License and Limited Warranty

This is a legally binding agreement between you and Jasc Software, Inc. ("Jasc"). By installing and/ or using this software, you are agreeing to become bound by the terms of this agreement.

IF YOU DO NOT AGREE TO THE TERMS OF THIS AGREEMENT, DO NOT USE THIS SOFTWARE. PROMPTLY RETURN THE ENTIRE PACKAGE TO THE PLACE WHERE YOU OBTAINED IT FOR A FULL REFUND.

GRANT OF LICENSE. Jasc grants to you a non-exclusive right to use this software program (hereinafter the "Software") in accordance with the terms contained in this Agreement. You may use the Software on a single computer. If you have purchased a site license, you may use the Software on the number of computers defined by and in accordance with the site license.

UPGRADES. If you acquired this Software as an upgrade of a previous version, this Agreement replaces and supercedes any prior Agreements. You may continue to use the previous version of the Software, provided that both the previous version and the upgrade are installed on the same computer at all times. You may not have a previous version and the related upgrade version installed on separate computers at any time.

OWNERSHIP OF SOFTWARE. Jasc and its suppliers retain the copyright, title and ownership of the Software and the written materials.

COPIES. You may make one (1) copy of the Software solely for backup purposes. You must reproduce and include the copyright notice on the backup copy. No other copying is permitted. You may not distribute copies of the Software or accompanying written materials to others.

TRANSFERS. You may transfer the Software to another person provided that you notify Jasc of the transfer and the person to whom you transfer the Software agrees to be bound by this Agreement. You may also transfer the Software from one of your computers to another. Upon a transfer, you must remove all copies of the Software from the computer from which it was transferred. Upon a transfer to a third party you must destroy all backups. You may not transfer the Software in exchange for consideration. In no event may you transfer, assign, rent, lease, sell or otherwise dispose of the Software on a temporary basis.

TERMINATION. This Agreement is effective until terminated. This Agreement will terminate automatically without notice from Jasc if you fail to comply with any provision of this Agreement. Upon termination you shall destroy the written materials and all copies of the Software, including modified copies, if any.

LIMITED WARRANTY. Jasc warrants the media on which the Software is furnished to be free of defects in material and workmanship, under normal use, for a period of ninety (90) days following the date of delivery to you. In the event of defects, Jasc's sole liability shall be to (a) replace the defective media or (b) refund the purchase price, at Jasc's option. You must return the Software to Jasc or an authorized dealer with your dated invoice during the 90-day warranty period in order to receive a refund or replacement.

DISCLAIMER OF WARRANTIES. JASC DISCLAIMS ALL OTHER WARRANTIES, EXPRESS OR IMPLIED, INCLUDING, BUT NOT LIMITED TO, ANY IMPLIED WARRANTIES OF MERCHANTABILITY, FITNESS FOR A PARTICULAR PURPOSE AND NONINFRINGEMENT.

OTHER WARRANTIES EXCLUDED. JASC SHALL NOT BE LIABLE FOR ANY DIRECT, INDIRECT, CONSEQUENTIAL, EXEMPLARY, PUNITIVE OR INCIDENTAL DAMAGES ARISING FROM ANY CAUSE EVEN IF JASC HAS BEEN ADVISED OF THE POSSIBILITY OF SUCH DAMAGES. CERTAIN JURISDICTIONS DO NOT PERMIT THE LIMITATION OR EXCLUSION OF INCIDENTAL DAMAGES, SO THIS LIMITATION MAY NOT APPLY TO YOU.

IN NO EVENT WILL JASC BE LIABLE FOR ANY AMOUNT GREATER THAN WHAT YOU ACTUALLY PAID FOR THE SOFTWARE. Should any other warranties be found to exist, such warranties shall be limited in duration to ninety (90) days following the date you receive the Software.

EXPORT LAWS. You agree that you will not export the Software or documentation except in compliance with the laws and regulations of the United States.

US GOVERNMENT RESTRICTED RIGHTS. The Software and any accompanying materials are provided with Restricted Rights. Use, duplication or disclosure by the Government is subject to restrictions as set forth in subparagraph (c)(1)(ii) of The Rights in Technical Data and Computer Software clause at DFARS 252.227-7013, or subparagraphs (c)(1) and (2) of the Commercial Computer Software - Restricted Rights at 48 CFR 52.227-19, as applicable. Contractor/manufacturer is Jasc Software, Inc., PO Box 44997, Eden Prairie MN 55344.

GENERAL. This Agreement shall be governed by and construed in accordance with the laws of the State of Minnesota and the Federal Arbitration Act and shall benefit Jasc, its successors and assigns. Any claim or dispute between you and Jasc or against any agent, employee, successor or assign of Jasc related to this Agreement or the Software shall be resolved by binding arbitration in Minneapolis, MN by and under the rules of the American Arbitration Association. Any award of the arbitrator(s) may be entered as a judgment in any court of competent jurisdiction. The United Nations Convention on Contracts for the International Sale of Goods shall not apply to this Agreement.

A

496   **Index**

498   Index